ENVIRONMENTAL GOVERNANCE
Approaches, Imperatives and Methods

ENVIRONMENTAL GOVERNANCE
Approaches, Imperatives and Methods

Editors

Jayanta Bandyopadhyay
Kanchan Chopra
Nilanjan Ghosh

Published for

INSEE
THE INDIAN SOCIETY FOR ECOLOGICAL ECONOMICS

BLOOMSBURY
LONDON • NEW DELHI • NEW YORK • SYDNEY

First published, 2013
First reprint, 2013

BLOOMSBURY PUBLISHING INDIA PVT. LTD.
London New Delhi New York Sydney

ISBN: 978-81-924302-5-6

Published by Bloomsbury Publishing India Pvt. Ltd.
VISHRUT Building, DDA Complex, Building No. 3, Pocket C-6 & 7
Vasant Kunj, New Delhi 110070

Laser Typeset by DEEPA JUYAL
C2/01, Sector 17, Rohini, New Delhi 110089

Printed at Anvi Composers
1 DDA Market, Block A-1B, Pachim Vihar, New Delhi 110063

To
Our Parents
and Grandparents

Acknowledgements

This book would not have seen the light of the day without the support and cooperation of many colleagues subscribing to the cause of strengthening the interface of ecology and economics, in the context of environmental governance. We choose to move almost randomly in acknowledging their contributions.

At the outset, it needs to be declared that this volume consists, in the main, of papers selected from those prepared for (invited and contributed) the Fifth Biennial Conference of the Indian Society for Ecological Economics (INSEE), titled "Environmental Governance". We thank the members of the Scientific Committee of the Conference, for their commitment of valuable time and expertise in designing of the conference sessions, in screening of the abstracts, and in assessing the papers submitted. We also acknowledge the reviewers who helped in reviewing the various papers for selection in the volume.

Gujarat Vidyapith, where the INSEE Conference was held, provided an appropriate cultural environment for an event themed "Environmental Governance". Our special thanks go to Prof. Sudarshan Iyengar, Vice-Chancellor of Gujarat Vidyapith, and erstwhile President of INSEE, for his strong support and many contributions towards the success of the Conference. We are also thankful to all the members of the Local Organizing Committee for their very useful contributions. The large number of participants, invited speakers and guests, who came from all parts of India and several other countries, made the Conference an exciting and rewarding event. Thanks to all of them!

Several organizations extended financial support for holding the Conference and for travel of invited speakers and participants. These are: Sir Ratan Tata Trust, Gujarat Vidyapith, Mundra Port and Special Economic Zone Ltd, and Narayan Desai Multipurpose Charitable Trust. We thank them for their valuable support and contribution.

The INSEE office, hosted at the Institute of Economic Growth, Delhi, played a key role in coordination work for the volume in the last two years. In particular, we wish to thank Dr. Sushil Sen, Office-in charge for his enduring inputs during this period of time.

Last but not the least, we thank subsequent Executive Committees of INSEE (for years 2010-12 and 2012-14), who helped in taking this initiative forward.

Jayanta Bandyopadhyay
Kanchan Chopra
Nilanjan Ghosh

Contents

1

Environmental Governance: The Crucial Interface of Science, Economics and Policy

Jayanta Bandyopadhyay, Kanchan Chopra and Nilanjan Ghosh

At the Outset ...

Governance of the natural environment in the world of today has emerged as, arguably, one of the most complex challenges ever faced by humanity. The variety of environmental changes generated by human activities, from the local to the global levels, are not new. However, the magnitude of the diverse changes and the resulting impacts on the functioning of the natural eco-systemic processes grew vary rapidly over the past two centuries, and more so in the second half of the last century. Their cumulative environmental impacts expressed themselves in various forms (for example, the depletion of forests in Africa or the widespread acid-rain over Europe) and posed threats not only to human socio-ecosystemic existence, but to life on earth, at a broader scale. Such impacts became the basis of natural resource conflicts in the developing world and environmental movements across the industrialized economies. These movements presented themselves as strong challenges to economic growth driven solely by modern technologies of agriculture and manufacture. The business as usual approach to economic development clearly had to ponder over such challenges.

The Stockholm Conference on Human Environment in 1972 turned out to be a watershed event in the recognition of the challenges in environmental governance by the global community. Since then, environment got increasingly internalized in the governance agenda at all spatial levels of governance. The growing conflict between environment and economic development was not merely confined to intellectual debates on academic platforms. The developing world faced the daunting dilemma of providing basic needs to the people and satisfying their aspirations for a higher quality of life while addressing the environmental challenges. Though governmental policies remained in favour of economic growth, citizens' environmental concerns could not be held back from creating a pressure for a new pattern of environmental governance. This sensitization of the civil society, associated with peoples' movement was indeed driven by experiences and concerns that recognized the critical linkage between stability of the environment and sustainability of human society. The pollution of rivers all over the industrialized world during the 1960s, the acid rain over northern Europe, the crisis in the fishing industry, global loss of biodiversity both in the wild and cultivated areas, the transfer of hazardous wastes to the underdeveloped countries, release of genetically modified organisms, etc., contributed to a complex political process (Peet et al., 2011). The rapid growth of the Green movement in the industrialized countries was the eventual result. With rapid economic growth increasingly characterizing the situation in many parts of the developing world, these countries, meanwhile, were generating another set of complex governance problems. The globally known non-violent movement for local people's access to forest resources in the Indian Himalaya, the *Chipko Andolan* successfully drew the attention of governments and policy makers to the environmental degradation in the rural areas in the Himalaya (Bandyopadhyay, 1999). At the global level the Brundtland Report made it clear that "what is needed now is a new era of economic growth – growth that is forceful and at the same time, socially and environmentally sustainable (Brundtland 1987). How could this kind of growth be brought about? What are the challenges of societal institutions? These questions have dominated the global policy domains over the last three decades.

In the last few decades, environmental governance has rightly become an area of attention of many serious researchers all over the world (for example, see Pretty et al. 2007). With the complexity of environmental changes growing steadily and environmental movements gathering increasing popularity, the demand for a more informed and comprehensive system of governance of the environment increasingly resulted in policy changes. Such policy interventions needed to draw increasingly on interdisciplinary knowledge and new institutions that were guided by multiple objectives. Rethinking of policies informed by interdisciplinary natural sciences, law, methods of amicable sharing of intellectual property rights related to biodiversity, role of functional institutions for natural resource management, recognition of value of ecosystem processes and their services, etc. slowly but steadily became objects of mainstream policy research and formulation. At the international level, as exemplified by the various events related to the UN Framework Convention on Climate Change (UNFCCC), environmental governance has emerged as a sensitive subject in international relations (Haas 2008) that also brought global business as a central player (ICC 1995). Indeed, environmental governance has emerged as an area needing extensive attention of interdisciplinary professionals and leaders in industry. The range of interdisciplinary knowledge spans from, for example, the advances in physical and biological sciences to indigenous cultures and modern international diplomacy. Thus, the topical spread associated with modern environmental governance is very large. This is amply reflected in the collection of papers in this book which aims at articulating that diversity in the approaches, imperatives and methods of environmental governance, at spatial levels from the micro to the global.

What Constitutes Environmental Governance?

Environmental governance therefore requires an integration of behavioural constituents from the social and economic processes related to the natural environment, human understanding of the processes in this natural environment and the changes impinging on natural ecosystems. Knowledge alone is not enough. New and reformed institutions are needed for facilitating a change in human behaviour and to increase local appreciation of shared global concerns. Societal institutions need to be capable of using disciplinary and interdisciplinary knowledge systems to guide and moderate social and economic activities, and ensure conservation of ecosystems and continued availability of ecosystem services.

Governance, in this context, is not merely confined to government, but extends to business and civil society, thereby highlighting the need for a systems approach to several interrelated and intricate complex problems posed at the socio-ecosystemic interface of human endeavour and even beyond. The forces involved here are, no doubt, quite dynamic and changing across time and space. To capture this diverse range of dynamic forces, environmental governance often necessitates founding alternative systems of governing, by way of new institutions, both complementary with and substituting for existing ones. Rather, crafting of new institutions is central to environmental governance. This encompasses the entire gamut, starting from amendments to customary laws to newly crafted international agreements. In this context, Paavola (2007) has made available an important review of literature on institutions for environmental governance. The global exercise of the Millennium Ecosystem Assessment, has also stressed the role of participatory initiations at all levels of decision making (Chopra et al., 2005). While Ostrom (1990 and 2005) and Rothman et al. (2007) have also recognized such an institutional framework, Breton et al. (2009) provide a wider review of salient institutional issues in environmental governance.

It needs to be kept in mind that governance and management of the environment at various scales, from the micro-level to the meso-level and extending to the global levels, need the right type of knowledge of the natural ecosystem. Such knowledge cannot be confined to the boundaries of a single discipline. Ages of disciplinary specialization in scientific inquiry, despite being successful in helping human understanding of certain nuances of the physical world, has failed to create the understanding of the interactive dynamics between the human society and its ambient ecosystem. This poses a critical challenge even today. Again, the overwhelming task of generating an interdisciplinary knowledge based on the diverse and complex earth systems poses another great challenge, more so when that knowledge is to be used in governance. Understanding of the earth systems constitutes today an important agenda in global environmental governance (Boardman, 2010). The other challenge is posed by the void in our understanding in the context of the linkages between the global and the local issues (Bandyopadhyay, 2002).

On the other hand, the Malthusian creed of looking at scarce natural resources has dominated human thought process for long. From a local commons perspective, ever since Hardin (1968) typified human behaviour with common pool resources as one of sheer unaware exploitation, neoclassical environmental economics accepted this as *fait accompli*. At the same time, Meadows et al. (1972) recognized the limits to growth posed by scarce natural resources and environmental degradation that can be caused by unbridled exploitation of natural resources, thereby vindicating the Malthusian thought process. Explanations to social conflicts have also been sought from the perspective of scarcity (Homer-Dixon, 1991 and 1994, Ghosh and Bandyopadhyay, 2009). Both such concerns pose threat to governance of the commons at local levels. However, recent literature on institutions reveals the glimmers of hope to escape from such apparent impasses. Ostrom et al. (1994), Cardenas (2001), and Casari and Plott (2003) have attempted to rationalize why citizens are able to craft institutions to cope successfully with commons in certain settings, though not all. Institutions, again, need effective instruments for functioning (Ghosh, 2008 and 2009). Yet, while important research on the institutions and the instruments have taken place in the developing country context (e.g. Chopra et al., 1990; Chopra and Gulati, 2001), in most research they are delinked from each other, and the interdependence of each other is rarely recognized in literature and in policy making process. This poses another challenge to environmental governance (Bandyopadhyay and Ghosh, 2009). From this point of view, this dependence of environmental governance on the body of interdisciplinary knowledge may probably be considered as merely emerging.

Therefore, the extension of governance from this perspective cannot be limited to the straightjacket of legal perspectives alone, much in contrary to the dominant thought process. For effective governance norms to emerge properly, the concept has to address critical issues of new frameworks of economics, ecological engineering and new policy based on interdisciplinary eco-systemic knowledge. The governance of the earth systems (Boardman, 2010) requires access to the latest developments in the diverse disciplines constituting earth science and appropriate instrumentation. The complexity of arriving at a consensus on such issues, for example, global climate change, has been highlighted by many (see, for example, Hulme, 2009; Lomborg, 2001). However, with the need for a high level of investment for creating sophisticated interdisciplinary knowledge about the natural environment, this information deficit, indeed asymmetrical access has become a concern. Limited access to the tools for identifying environmental changes and segments of modern science in general has encouraged, a compromise on democratic running of societies (Jasanoff, 2005). For example, Liverman (2004) has raised the question of the commodification of nature through environmental governance by asking 'who governs, at what scale and at what price?' Jasanoff and Martello (2004) have made a wider articulation of the risks to environmental democracy at the local levels, as opposed to global governance. Indeed, such issues of environmental governance need very open and serious attention if humanity has to stand up to the great challenges that it faces in addressing the duality of environmental sustainability and economic growth. The resultant emergence of green economic policies has been reviewed by Rao (2010).

Addressing the above mentioned constraints to environmental governance needs informed reorientation of values towards knowledge creation and dissemination, and towards crafting of policy and institutions. Many policy decisions need to be taken even when the natural and social sciences undertake research and progress towards providing us with more and better knowledge of issues on the natural environment and its nature of instabilities. In fact a communion of ecology and economics is the need of the hour. This implies the exercise of 'governance'. In a narrow sense, this process could, somewhat tautologically be referred to as 'what governments do'. A broader approach to the same concept is "the exercise of political authority and the use of institutional resources to manage society's problems and affairs". Whichever way we look at it, the debate on the future of the planet permeates through the domains of physical sciences and the social sciences for finally being taken to the level of policy. It is in this context that one needs to provide for the governance mechanism for the environment and the ecosystems at the critical socio-economic-political interface of human existence.

Following this interpretation, governance can be viewed as having three constituents, typically constituting elements of decision making. These are:

1. agreement on facts and acceptance of common areas of interest among the different stakeholders: this often implies an understanding of the existence of different versions of 'knowledge and interests'
2. drawing up the outlines of policy approaches to be followed
3. outlining steps in implementation and checks and balances in the event of non-implementation

The decision making process described by the above constituents consists of a cycle playing out at different scales and over time. A critical element of the cycle is the feedback from implementation to lessons for integrating new knowledge and new interests into the next decision making cycle. In this sense it is a dynamic process spread over time. Further, decision making and governance can take place at different scales, starting from the global to the national and then the local. Depending on the problem at hand, initiatives for governance may profitably begin at one scale or the other and provide directions and linkages for action at other scales. For a global issue such as climate change, international initiatives have taken the first step towards governance, leading on to action plans by national governments and other agencies. At the other extreme, governance in the context of pollution of water bodies and forest management issues has typically been initiated at local or national levels.

Another challenge, more so in environmental governance is that of integrating new knowledge, typically available in segmented disciplines into decision making in an operational sense. At one end is the need to develop new methods and tools to understand the linkages between nature and society. At the other, often simultaneously, the lessons learnt from such explorations need to be spelt out from the policy perspective, in an arena where stakeholder interests diverge significantly. It is indeed a tall order. Indeed, environmental governance has very many dimensions and gets linked with diverse disciplines. The chapters presented in this volume, accordingly, can address only a few of the large number of issues on the agenda.

About the Volume...

This volume divides the contributions[1] into three sections, called respectively: approaches and challenges, imperatives, methods and tools. Through the sections and the constituent chapters runs a common thread of implications for environmental governance in its different dimensions.

The first section begins with a chapter by Forsyth on the politics of environmental science in which he asks the question: "Do scientific laws exist neutrally without social influence?" He argues as expected that they do not; the social and economic context determines their relevance and application. Further, the chapter argues that historic work on the sociology of scientific knowledge now needs to be matched by a more politicized understanding of environmental cause-and-effect in order to make the findings of political ecology more useable among environmental scientists and policy makers. The chapter uses a case study from Thailand, and different approaches to explaining soil erosion, in order to illustrate this more politically situated environmental science.

Norgaard in his chapter argues how the dominant historical beliefs about the nature of reality, science and management are incomplete and segmented by the nature of science. He maintains that environmental problems are not a separate and

[1] Most chapters are based on invited or contributed papers for the Fifth Biennial conference of the Indian Society for ecological economics held in January 2009 at Ahmedabad.

distinct type of problem. Rather, they are the problems that remain insufficiently addressed due to the divisions created both in science, i.e. the disciplines, and in social institutions, i.e. the charging of particular branches of government with solving particular types of problems. He goes on to describe how the Millennium Ecosystem Assessment (MA) set up a participative, deliberative process by which these beliefs may change and how this may assist in reframing science.

Desai's contribution is a tour-de-force of the thorny issues that governance confronts in the context of climate change. He spells out how ecological, economic and ethical issues are all part of the problem here. Developing modes of taking into account risk and uncertainty and the unusual divergence in time frame of ecologists and economists are other aspects impinging on governance which are dealt with in this chapter. Sundaraman's chapter, in a parallel strain, traces the beginning of global environmental governance to the setting up of the first IPCC and traces some of subsequent processes and findings thereof. This chapter stresses the role of government participation in processes of knowledge generation to enable 'buy-in' into policy at national level, in particular for problems relating to the global commons.

Moving to environmental governance within India, there can be little doubt that judicial processes have played a major part in the recent past. Sahu describes at length the effects of this 'judicialisation' in India, also pointing out at length how it is not able to take fully into account the nuanced property rights to land and forests which exist in different parts of the country. Further, most of the innovative methods introduced by the Court have neither been followed consistently nor been institutionalized to make a long-term impact for the environmental governance process. In such a situation, how long will the Supreme Court monitor the implementation of its decisions? As the opposition to judicial intervention in the affairs of other organs increases, what will happen if the implementing agencies and people disobey Court decision for the protection of environment? The challenge then is to institutionalize and democratize the merits of the Court's intervention and to minimize its negative implications and unwanted effects.

Section 2 of the volume entitled 'Imperatives' brings together chapters which spell out the need for environmental governance to be treated as a compelling need of the time. Martinez-Alier looks at ecological distribution conflicts and economic growth, arguing that the imperative for appropriate governance lies in concerns for distribution. Ecological distribution conflicts are of two kinds, resource extraction conflicts and waste disposal conflicts. In both instances, different languages of valuation are used. Martinez-Alier's focus is on environmental justice while focusing on the language of indigenous territorial rights in a context of pluralism of values.

Policy making is an important component of governance and the next two chapters focus on it. Parikh focuses on the role of ecological economics in policy making, both from the aggregative and the sectoral viewpoints. He argues that natural resource accounting using many ideas and techniques of environmental economics can bring greater awareness of the importance of natural resources and guide national developmental policies. At another level, he maintains that environmental economics has an even greater role in sectoral polices. When environmental economists assess the cost of air pollution in a city or the cost of land degradation on agricultural GDP, the affected citizens get empowered to demand action. His chapter provides estimates to make the point.

Alagh argues that the future of Indian agriculture would depend on policies with regard to land and water and points out some directions. He maintains that agriculture will be demand driven and the agricultural growth rate seen in the recent past raises questions of productivity of investment. The real dangers, apart from anti agricultural policies, are in running into real resource constraints. Again here the strategies for land and water management are known and agricultural research can fill in the gaps. Watershed development, reclamation of saline lands, farmer run lower level irrigation systems, aquifer management in difficult situations like coastal aquifers, have all been reported as success stories and studied. The question is replicability on a larger scale.

The next three chapters (by Ghate et al., Banerjee and Nagar, respectively) examine the processes constituting governance and their impact from the perspective of forests, urban wetlands and biofuel policy. Ghate et al examine Forest Development Agencies (FDA) as federations of Joint Forest Management (JFM) committees. The chapter shows that both JFM and FDA programmes concentrate on plantations alone without any focus on institution building. The new tier does not seem to have made any difference. Banerjee illustrates how the government has failed to conserve the wetlands of Kolkata. Multiplicity of government departments is one of the main causes with some departments propagating and devising conservation strategies, while others tolerate and even promote environment-insensitive urbanization. Nagar locates his analysis of biofuel policy in India within the context of different actors and discourses. The evolution of the policy through the period from 2002 onwards is analysed in terms of the impact of different discourses on it. In each of these three chapters, in-depth sectoral analysis reveals how the final impact of a policy and the manner in which it is implemented or not is determined by the role of power structures overruling and moulding institutional strengths and weaknesses.

In the final section, entitled 'Methods and tools', we have focused on a few chapters where innovative approaches and/or in-depth methodological application results in shedding light on appropriate policy. The first two chapters deal with voluntary methods of ensuring conservation. Kaechle, May and others illustrate the conditions under which consumer demand driven markets resulted in the success of forest certification as a tool for governance. While the existence of a set of formal institutions is necessary for certification to be carried through, the cultural, social and economic requirements are related to consumer maturity in trying to understand the origin of the product, the transparency of the information generated and the willingness to pay a little more, if such is the case, for consuming an ecologically responsible product. Similar though more macro-perspective is provided by Shukla's chapter which dwells on how a Gandhian approach both to consumption and production in the economy would function as a self-imposed instrument for environmental governance.

The last three contributions in this section use modelling techniques of different kinds to derive conclusions with respect to policy instruments for policy and governance. Gupta's chapter illustrates how and under what conditions an emission tax may be preferable to an environmental standard in order to regulate pollution. Sharma et al., use bio-economic modelling to show that the biomass growth in a Himalayan watershed becomes sustainable when there is an increase in emigration rate, use of liquefied petroleum gas (LPG), and substitution of improved livestock. Chattopadhyay-Gupta's analysis reveals that, in the fishery case studied, maximization of profit and biodiversity considerations are ultimately in conflict with each other. She goes on to suggest possible schemes of taxation administered through local bodies in order to protect biodiversity without impacting adversely the livelihoods of the poor.

Final Remarks to Set the Stage

Admittedly, the literature on environmental governance has a long way to go, both in India and at the global level. A part of this is due to the challenges it presents in terms of bringing together knowledge of different disciplines, distilled through interaction across them. There is no harm in reiterating that environmental governance, at all levels, needs an integrated approach in terms of addressing crucial issues, all of which are embedded at the interface of nature, economy and society. The sustainability of the natural environment, whether at the level of a local landscape or the atmosphere of the planet as a whole, has become increasingly and critically dependent on new interdisciplinary knowledge in the domains of physical sciences, life sciences, social sciences and new forms of institutions. In this attempt to address the interactive dynamics of the interrelation and co-evolution of the natural ecosystems and society, their impacts on human economy and polity, as also the impacts of the forces generated by the human political economic endeavours on the ecosystem over time and space, a transdisciplinary field of academic research is already emerging, though it still remains at a nascent stage of evolution. It is imperative to have as much information on the natural environment and the ecosystems, as on the critical socio-economic-political interface of human existence, for effective governance systems to emerge. In the making of new environmental policies and institutions for its governance, this emerging knowledge base serves as the much-needed entry point.

However, mere creation of knowledge is not sufficient by itself. Governance is also about integrating knowledge with practice ensuring acceptance by social norms and power structures. This volume is a small effort in the direction of encasing where we stand in this effort and where we could possibly proceed from here.

References

[1] Bandyopadhyay, Jayanta (1999). 'Chipko Movement: of Floated Myths and Flouted Realities', *Economic and Political Weekly*, 34(15): 880-82, April 10-16, 1999.

[2] Bandyopadhyay, Jayanta (2002). 'Environmentalism in India: Between Local and Global Responsibilities', Seminar, 516.

[3] Bandyopadhyay, Jayanta and Nilanjan Ghosh (2009). 'Holistic Engineering and Hydro-diplomacy in the Ganges-Brahmaputra-Meghna Basin', *Economic and Political Weekly*, 44(45), 50-60.

[4] Boardman, Robert (2010). Governance of Earth Systems: Science and Its Uses (London: Palgrave Macmillan).

[5] Breton, Albert, Georgio Brocio, Silvana Dalmazzone and Giovanna Garrone (2009). Governing the Environment: Salient Institutional Issues (Cheltenham, Edward Elger).

[6] Brundtland, G.H. (1987). Chairman's Foreword to Our Common Future (Oxford, Oxford University Press).

[7] Cárdenas, Juan Camilo (2001). 'How Do Groups Solve Local Commons Dilemmas? Lessons from Experimental Economics in the Field', *Environment, Development and Sustainability*, 2(3–4), 305–322.

[8] Casari, Marco and Plott, Charles R. (2003). 'Decentralized Management of Common Property Resources: Experiments with a Centuries-Old Institution', *Journal of Economic Behaviour and Organization*, 51, 217–47.

[9] Chopra, Kanchan, Gopal K. Kadekodi, and M.N. Murty (1990). *Participatory Development and Common Property Resources* (New Delhi and London: Sage Publications).

[10] Chopra, Kanchan, Rik Leemans, Pushpam Kumar and H. Simmons (2005). *Ecosystems and Human Well-being: Policy Responses*, Volume 3 (Island Press).

[11] Chopra, Kanchan and Subhash C. Gulati (2001). *Migration and Common Property Resources: A Study in the Arid and Semi-arid Regions of India* (New Delhi and London: Sage Publications).

[12] Ghosh, Nilanjan (2008). 'A New Look at Integrated Water Resources Management (IWRM) from the Perspective of Scarcity Value of Water Resources', *Journal of Resources, Energy and Development*, 5(1), 27-48.

[13] Ghosh, Nilanjan (2009). Economics of Hostile Hydropolitics over Transboundary Waters: Scarcity Values and Interstate Water Conflicts in India and US (Saarbrucken, Germany: VDM Verlag).

[14] Ghosh, Nilanjan and Jayanta Bandyopadhyay (2009). 'A Scarcity Value-based Explanation of Transboundary Water Disputes: The Case of Cauvery River Basin in India', *Water Policy*, 11(2), 141-67.

[15] Hardin, G. (1968). 'The Tragedy of the Commons', *Science*, 162, 1243–1248.

[16] Hass, Peter M. (Ed) (2008). International Environmental Governance (Aldershot, Ashgate).

[17] Homer-Dixon, Thomas F. (1991). 'On the Threshold: Environmental Changes as Causes of Acute Conflict', *International Security*, 16(2), 76-116.

[18] Homer-Dixon, Thomas F. (1994). 'Environmental Scarcities and Violent Conflict: Evidence from Cases', *International Security*, 19(1), 5-40.

[19] Hulme, Mike (2009). *Why We Disagree About Climate Change* (Cambridge, Cambridge University Press).

[20] ICC (1995). Statement by the International Chamber of Commerce before COP1, March 29, Berlin.

[21] Jasanoff, Sheila (2005). *Designs on Nature: Science and Democracy in Europe and the United States* (Princeton, Princeton University Press).

[22] Jasanoff, Sheila and Marybeth Long Martello (2004). *Earthly Politics: Local and Global Environmental Governance* (Cambridge, MIT Press).

[23] Lomborg, Bjorn (2001). *The Sceptical Environmentalist: Measuring the Real State of the World* (Cambridge, Cambridge University Press).

[24] Levy, D.L. and P. Newell (2000). 'Oceans apart? Business Responses to the Environment in Europe and North America', *Environment*, 42(9), 8–20.

[25] Liverman, Diana (2004). 'Who Governs, at What Scale and at What Price: Geography, Environmental Governance and the Commodification of Nature', *Annals of the Association of American Geographers*, 94(4), December.

[26] Meadows, Donella H., Dennis L. Meadows, Jørgen Randers and William W. Behrens III (1972). *The Limits to Growth* (Universe Books).

[27] Ostrom, Elinor, Gardner, Roy and Walker, James (1994). *Rules, Games, and Common-Pool Resources* (Ann Arbor: University of Michigan Press).

[28] Paavola, Jouni (2007). 'Institutions and Environmental Governance: A Reconceptualization', *Ecological Economics*, 55: 93-103.

[29] Peet Richard, Paul Robons and Michael Watts (Eds) (2011). *Global Political Ecology* (Abingdon, Routledge).

[30] Pretty, Jules, Andrew S. Ball, Ted Benton, Julia S. Guivant, David R. Lee, David Orr, Max J. Fefferand Hugh Ward (eds) (2007). *The SAGE Handbook of Environment and Society* (Los Angeles, Sage Publications).

[31] Rao, P.K. (2010). *The Architecture of Green Economic Policies* (Heidelberg, Springer).

SECTION 1

Approaches and Challenges

2

The Politics of Environmental Science: Recent Trends and Important Questions

Tim Forsyth

For many social and political analysts of environmental change, the links of environmental science and political values have been clearly established for some time (e.g. Thompson et al., 1986; Leach and Mearns, 1996; Forsyth, 2003). But, for many physical scientists, these links are not so apparent, and discussion on them is resisted because scientists fear it will weaken the veracity of the truth claims coming from science. For example, at the height of public discussions on whether anthropogenic climate change was happening or not, the Executive Secretary of the United Nations Framework Convention on Climate Change, Michael Zammit Cutajar, announced:

> The science has driven the politics… if the science is to continue guiding the politics, it is essential to keep the politics out of the science (Cutajar, 2001:1).

This chapter argues three key points. First, it is important to persist in demonstrating the social and political influences on scientific knowledge, in order to make science more useful and fairer, in addressing urgent environmental problems. Second, politicizing science in this way, does not mean that scientific knowledge is useless or unrelated to biophysical changes, but that all knowledge produced about environmental change will reflect some social influences. And third, that social and political analysts of environmental change needs to change from focusing on its current emphasis on the *social interests* of science (or who benefits) towards a newer, and more practically useful focus on the *explanatory potential* of science (or, how we explain problems).

How can social and political science achieve these objectives? This chapter proposes some ways ahead, by summarizing recent trends in the politicization of environmental science, and then by suggesting alternative ways to politicize environmental explanations. In effect, the chapter argues that historic work on the sociology of scientific knowledge now needs to be matched by a more politicized understanding of environmental cause-and-effect, in order to make the findings of political ecology more useable among environmental scientists and policy makers.

The chapter uses a case study from Thailand, and different approaches for explaining soil erosion, in order to illustrate this more politically situated environmental science.

Why is "Science" Political?

Most environmental explanations invoke the use of "science" as a "hard" biophysical explanation of how environmental problems occur, which in turn have implications for how they can be addressed. Usually, "science" in this context is considered to be a universal "law", or assumed cause-and-effect, that reflects the mainstream use of positivist forms of scientific explanation. Positivist science is usually understood as a scientific method that seeks to create universal laws based on careful sampling and inference. For example, the statement that "clean drinking water freezes at 0° Centigrade at sea level" is a positive statement that is easily demonstrated, which is considered universally true by most people.

But, positivism itself has changed over time. Early positivists – such as the German physicist, Mach (1838-1916) – established "laws" by identifying trends in existing datasets. The so-called Vienna School of the 1920s developed the so-called Logical Positivism by advancing Mach's approach by using *verification* – or, by arguing that laws only existed when trends in one dataset could be identified in other datasets. Karl Popper (1902-1994) advanced this approach further, by replacing verification with *falsification*. Under Popper's approach (also called "critical rationalism") scientists would first make *hypotheses* based on observed trends, and, second try to *falsify* hypotheses by seeking to identify these trends in new datasets under controlled experiments. Hypotheses should be considered true, if it was not possible to falsify them. Clearly, all of these approaches have important differences, but Popper's approach is popularly called "positivism", even though it is the most ambitious means of establishing scientific laws than preceding forms of positivism (Harré, 1993).

Social and political analysts have also criticized positivism. Perhaps most importantly, sociologists of scientific knowledge have pointed out that all empirical investigation reflects a viewpoint of what "are" problems, or which kind of information is useful. The German theorist, Habermas (1974), has described this form of knowledge creation as "technical cognitive interest". Hajer (1995) also used the term "problem closure", to indicate how a definition of a problem will also pre-determine what kind of information (and for whose benefit), knowledge is collected. For example, "deforestation" is commonly considered to be a problem. But various researchers, including groups as diverse as hydrologists and anthropologists have pointed out that "deforestation" – as a term – is far too general and imprecise, to describe all forms of logging, or forest disturbance that occurs (indeed "forest" itself may also be too general) (Hamilton and Pearce, 1988). More attention is needed in defining which impacts create what kinds of problems for various people. But in general, many governments, scientific bodies, and environmental activists refer generally to "deforestation", and seek to apply predefined solutions to various contexts.

Politicizing Environmental Science

Many workers in environmental science have pointed out how positivist environmental science has led to universal laws and explanations that are inaccurate, or, which do not reflect the interests of many affected people. For example, much early work within cultural ecology, found examples where local people in supposedly fragile ecological zones were able to forge livelihoods – and protect environment simultaneously – through the use of conservation practices and risk-sharing strategies, such as sharing access to rice terraces, diversifying tasks within households (e.g. Conklin, 1954; Geertz, 1963).

This kind of detailed analysis of local practices provided important challenges to explanations that tended to describe environmental risk in terms of physical changes alone, or which assumed that people (or population growth), would necessarily threaten environments. In this sense, early cultural ecology work provided some of the seminal studies of how local institutions (or shared behaviour), could provide a successful adaptation to environmental scarcity.

But in addition, some political ecologists have also studied social institutions underlying different environmental "science", or authoritative knowledge claims.

One turning point came with one study by Thompson et al. (1986), that showed how the predictions of deforestation in the Himalayas by different scientific, or advocacy organizations, varied by a factor of 67, even ignoring some apparent typing errors. This study argued that organizations will always select, or represent data, in ways to support their worldviews, or political agendas. Rather than asking "what are the facts?", the authors suggested we should ask "what would you like the facts to be?" Later, Thompson would elaborate this approach as Cultural Theory, which divided social solidarities into egalitarians (e.g. NGOs), individualists (e.g. businesses), hierachists (the state), and fatalists (people with little power such as hill farmers) (e.g. Thompson et al., 1990).

Cultural Theory is attractive to social scientists, because it provides a fast explanation for how different analysts might shape diverse physical facts into explanations that suit their own worldviews. Yet, Cultural Theory has also been criticized for being too reductionist – or, for suggesting there are four main worldviews – and because Cultural Theory does not necessarily help environmental managers make decisions on what should be done. Instead, it is a theory of how worldviews differ, rather than about how to cut through these different worldviews.

As an alternative, some social scientists began to analyze environmental explanations in terms of historical "narratives" (Leach and Mearns, 1996) or "storylines" (Hajer, 1995).

> Storylines are devices through which actors are positioned, and through which specific ideas of "blame" and "responsibility" and "urgency" and "responsible behavior" are attributed (Hajer, 1995: 64-5).

Or, similarly:

> Development narratives tell scenarios, not so much about what should happen, as about what will happen according to their tellers – if the events or positions are carried out as described (Roe, 1991: 288).

This way of analyzing environmental explanation differed from positivism, because it emphasized the historic and culturally embedded evolution of supposedly factual explanations. For example, Fairhead and Leach's (1996) study of deforestation in Guinea, West Africa, indicated that the "received wisdom" about forest loss mentioned earlier was partly the result of colonial French scientific influences, coupled with government agendas to extend control over rural areas. Consequently, changing the participation and framing of scientific explanations often showed that explanations were not immutable "laws" at all.

The social analysis of knowledge claims has been applied in scientific practice in various ways. Bruno Latour (2004), for example, echoing the work of the seminal philosopher of science, Willard Quine (1908-2000), argued that scientific laws always reflect two questions: how many are we? And, can we live together? These questions indicate that constructions of "reality" are functions of who participates in creating these images, and how well they remain rooted to this vision. For example, the old narratives of deforestation in Guinea rose through the rise of dominant social groups under colonial and post-colonial times, and through the continued exclusion of social groups that might challenge the dominant views of nature.

In a similar vein, the sociologists of science, Functowicz and Ravetz (1993) also argued that scientific "certainty" reflected the fixity of scientific disciplines, or professional networks. They argued that "certainty" (as opposed to "uncertainty") arose, when outside opinions, or experiences, were excluded from discussion.

And so-called semantic and institutional realists within philosophy of science have argued that truth claims are dependent on how social groups organize diverse events and processes, to match their own experience. For example, John Searle (1995) argued that truth statements (i.e. scientific explanations), can only arise when they are organized like a sentence, with a subject, object, beginning, middle and an end. On this basis, floods could be explained through the collective experience of lowland farmers who witness the co-existence of upland agriculture and deforestation with lowland flooding. But, a more accurate explanation of floods may involve more complex factors than this framing – and the resulting solutions may also intervene less in upland agriculture.

All of these approaches have aimed to locate truth claims (or environmental explanations) within social and political contexts, and with the social solidarities – or networks – that uphold them. But, despite their success in linking knowledge to social contexts and solidarities, some political ecologists have argued there is still a need to make these approaches more useable in day-to-day environmental management. In particular, one long-term concern is that linking knowledge to social solidarities is too relativist (the assumption that all truth claims are equally valid), often associated with postmodern approaches to science and knowledge (Levitt, 1999).

As Blaikie (1995: 11) noted:

> A counterweight to the deconstruction of science must also be provided. A case could be made that the bulk of what is styled as political ecology has been written by social scientists, who have paid little attention to what natural scientists have had to say about their environments, usually with embarrassing results.

And then later, he wrote:

> By adopting an epistemology which avoids relativism and unreconstructed pluralism, it may be possible to address specific audiences in languages they recognize, to identify real and feasible choices (Blaikie, 1999: 144).

Can a situated environmental science really address audiences that are used to employing the positivist style of generalizations? The following case study illustrates one way of linking social solidarities and truth claims more transparently. The example compares a positivist approach to political ecology, with a focus on social solidarities alone, and then an approach that aims to use these solidarities, in order to achieve progress in terms of explaining problems.

Example: Explaining Soil Erosion in Northern Thailand

Positivism: The Universal Soil Loss Equation (USLE)

The Universal Soil Loss Equation (USLE) is the world's primary device for explaining and predicting soil erosion. It was developed in the central plains of the US, following the serious problems of erosion of the "Dust Bowl" of the 1930s, as a guide to help farmers keep soil loss within acceptable levels (USDA 1961):

$$A = R \times K \times LS \times C \times P$$

where A is potential soil loss;
R is rainfall and runoff;
K is soil erodibility;
LS is the slope length-gradient factor;

C is the crop/vegetation and management factor; and
P is the support practice factor (such as soil conservation measures).

But is the USLE really "universal"? The equation was developed in a location where rainfall intensity, slope length and land-use practices are not always the same, as in the tropics (Hallsworth, 1987: 145). Moreover, is it right to adopt "erosion" as the "problem closure" (after Hajer, 1995)?

The highlands of northern Thailand, are one location to assess these questions. This region commonly inspires images of teak forests, Buddhist temples, lush green rice fields and remote hillside villages inhabited by colorful "hill tribes". It has also occupied an unusual position of being one of the most researched regions in Asia, on account of its diverse problems, and it being a frontier zone, between capitalist democracies and communist zones during the Cold War.

Soil erosion has been described as a problem in this region for a long time. Deforestation is blamed for erosion, for it reduces the canopy cover of soil and disturbs soil. Cultivation also takes place on steep slopes, encouraging erosion, and potentially leading to sedimentation in lowland dams, rice fields and rivers. Erosion of soil is also considered to reduce its water-holding properties, which is seen to exacerbate lowland water shortages. Often, erosion is blamed on upland agriculture. Classically, the region of northern Thailand has contained two main ethnic groups: the lowland Thai (*khonmuang),* who traditionally inhabited irrigated intermontane basins; and upland minorities (so-called "hill tribes" or *chao khao),* who historically practiced forms of shifting cultivation in the uplands. In recent decades, these distinctions have become blurred, as both Thai and minorities inhabit the uplands. Shifting cultivation has also been replaced by more permanent and commercialized agriculture.

Accordingly, the Thai government has addressed the potential erosion problem in Thailand based on the USLE. It has published maps showing where annual rates of erosion are estimated to be many times above sustainable limits (Jantawat, 1988: 13), estimated soil erosion in northern Thailand to be "higher than the world and Asian averages" at the remarkably precise figure of 933.67 tonnes per square kilometer per year. Manu Srikhajon, and Ard Somrang (1980) estimated less precise categories of "severe" and "very severe" erosion on 16.9 per cent and 5.8 per cent of northern Thailand respectively.

Experts using the USLE have also claimed that many local farmers do not perceive erosion to be a threat, because they never experienced long-term erosion under historic shifting cultivation. In the late 1980s, for example, Harper and El-Swaify (1988) found that 37 per cent of farmers studied, explained that the reason they did not use conservation was, because they did not believe erosion to be a serious problem. Similarly, Pahlman (1990: 99) noted that 43 per cent of the upland (ethnic Thai) farmers she interviewed in Nan Province "did not perceive they had a problem of soil erosion at all" while only 23 per cent considered it to be a serious problem. To illustrate the argument, Pahlman (1990: 82) showed how farmers were keen to identify problems such as weeds, insects/pests, and lack of water or land, whereas "soil erosion" came last, in problems mentioned by farmers. As a result, the government and some development agencies have urged planting grass (vetiver) strips to reduce erosion on steep slopes. Sometimes, cultivation on steep slopes is also banned.

But, alternative studies have provided different findings to those of the USLE. First, we consider how social groupings have affected the perception of erosion as a problem. Then, we look at how perceptions and biophysical research can be combined, to indicate a more grounded understanding of environmental change.

Different Perceptions of Erosion

Jones (1997) studied perceptions of erosion among the Lahu upland people in Chiang Mai province. The Lahu are an ethnicity who previously practiced shifting cultivation, and at this time were cultivating rice, maize, pumpkins and potatoes at an altitude of some 630-700 m.

Previous research by the Thai government, had indicated that some soil conservation measures had reduced erosion rates from 1,104 to 54 kg per hectare. These measures were based on using alley cropping methods of cultivation, at the same time as selecting special crops such as pigeon pea. The government researchers assumed that farmers would both perceive erosion to be a problem, and would want to adopt soil conservation techniques such as grass strips.

Jones, however, found that most farmers already avoided using steep slopes, because they knew erosion would occur. Accordingly, most farmers described other problems such as declining soil fertility, the increased labor demands of weeding, and the growing need to use weedkiller. Consequently, most farmers discussed problems of land shortage, or a lack of agricultural productivity, rather than erosion explicitly.

Jones, therefore, argued that the belief that erosion is the most serious problem, blinds researchers to how the Lahu perceive soil degradation. She wrote:

> ...local knowledge is oriented towards problems solving... [The Lahu] do not consider the changing status of soils to be a problem (rather weeds are the reason they migrate). It is more important that they find fertile ground to move to, and hence have accumulated a greater knowledge of indicator species (Jones, 1997: 264).

Consequently, the awareness of soil *fertility,* and the means to identity and manage fertility, are more important to the Lahu, than simply focusing on erosion alone. Moreover, the Lahu had accumulated useful knowledge of plant species, to indicate which land was more fertile than average.

Similarly, Turkelboom (1999) studied the perception of erosion among the Akha people in the Chiang Rai province. The Akha are another migrant highland people, who generally arrived in Thailand during the last 100 years from Burma. Typically, Akha agriculture in the highlands tends to remove all vegetation, and then use plots of land exhaustively until crops begin to decline. In this village, farmers cultivate irrigated and rain-fed rice, as well as cabbage, beans and tree crops at 700-900 m altitudes.

According to this study, farmers agreed soil fertility was declining (Turkelboom 1999: 172, 190). Some Akha elders told the mythological story of a giant, underground snake, or pig-like monster (*pjengcha*), that caused landslips and political havoc every 13 years. This period of time could coincide with how long it takes for yields to decline significantly, after continuous cultivation.

Other villagers reported "you can see the bones through the soil now" or that "the land is becoming like old people – they are not strong enough to hold anything anymore".

This kind of research provides a rich analysis of how upland farmers perceive and adapt to environmental change. They provide useful counterpoints to the universalistic generalizations of positivist explanations, that local farmers do not perceive erosion to be a problem. But, the downside to assessing local perceptions alone, is that it does not necessarily reform the cause-and-effect statements, that underlie the uncritical use of positivism. The next section considers an alternative approach.

Combining Perceptions and Biophysical Explanations

Other studies have combined local perceptions and physical monitoring in order to provide alternative explanations of environmental change. In effect, this approach does not use a definition of a "problem" from outsiders, but instead allows local people to define the problem they experience, as a guide to gathering empirical information about these problems.

For example, Turkelboom's study of the Akha used various approaches to re-framing empirical research of erosion, in order to reflect local experiences of environmental problems. The study showed, in particular, that erosion was divided differently between households. Farmers owning higher slopes tended to lose soil fertility, because of higher rates of erosion. But, those on lower slopes, often *gained* soil fertility, because of sedimentation from above. Turkelboom (1999: 208-211) identified five levels of entrepreneurialism, or concern for soil conservation, within the village. These ranged from so-called secure investors (who owned paddy fields and fruit plantations); profit maximizers (adopting high-risk crops such as cabbage); diversifiers (farmers who mix rice cultivation with limited cash crops); survivors (those who cultivated only rice on a short-term basis); and dropouts (who relied solely on wage labour and petty business). The survivors accounted for some 30 per cent of the village. The point of this classification is to acknowledge that soil and crop management does not take place uniformly across single ethnic groups, but that there is great diversity between, and within households.

This analysis also led to some important clarifications of narratives about soil erosion in Thailand. Research showed that only about one third of agricultural slopes led to stream networks (the remaining two thirds were on slopes that were not connected to streams). This finding showed that upland agriculture need not always lead to lowland sedimentation.

Second, the study also suggested that erosion from new commercial crops is not as bad as suggested. Rain-fed rice (the most "traditional" Akha crop), had the highest rates of erosion: 60 tonnes per hectare per crop cycle. Maize and beans were least erosive, with median soil losses of respectively 19 and 10 tonnes per hectare per crop cycle. These rates are certainly high, and are likely to cause declining soil fertility.

But, erosion under cabbage (a new, commercial crop) was less than expected. Research showed that erosion under cabbage lay in between the two extremes already described. But, the cropping systems used by the Akha, meant that most cabbage was planted before the start of the rainy season. Consequently, the months when cabbage had only a small surface area were generally during the dry season, when rainfall erosion was least. Moreover, if the price of cabbage fell, farmers would abandon fields, allowing them to be invaded by grass and hence be further protected against erosion.

Reframing empirical research, in order to reflect the local perceptions of problems, therefore helped understand the origin of these problems better. Moreover, by so doing, it also produced helpful information to update existing cause-and-effect statements (or narratives), about the nature of erosion in general.

A further study by Forsyth (1996, updated by fieldwork, 2004-05) also adopted this approach. This study focused on the Mien in Chiang Rai province, who cultivate dry and irrigated rice, corn, soya, ginger, peanuts, and limited coffee, oranges and lychee at an altitude of 700-800 m. This study asked how farmers responded to soil degradation, and used historic aerial photographs, Geographical Information System (GIS), soil-erosion measurements, and interviews with farmers.

As with other studies, most erosion occurred on steep slopes. Overall erosion was measured between 24 and 64 tonnes per hectare per year, which at its highest level, is generally considered very high. But, as with other studies, farmers said they were aware of the risk of erosion on slopes, and so tried to avoid using the steepest slopes. Problems of declining soil fertility, therefore, might not result only from soil erosion *per se*, but from the repeated use of flatter slopes, where the exhaustion of soil nutrients is a more likely cause of declining soil fertility, than erosion.

Furthermore, research also indicated that many gullies pre-existed agriculture, and occurred under forest land, as well as on agricultural land. It was likely, these gullies were the result of long-term weathering of underlying granite. When asked, villagers said they preferred to keep gullies vegetated, in order to harvest plants (and in particular banana trees, which were fed to pigs). These gullies, rather than overland flow from agriculture, might therefore be important contributors to lowland sedimentation. Moreover, the gullies were not necessarily problems to local land users, and the decision to keep these gullies vegetated, might even limit the flow of sediment from them.

As with Turkelboom's study, this research updated existing narratives about erosion in Thailand, by using local perceptions to frame empirical research. This new empiricism then uncovered new insights about how erosion might occur, which presents new opportunities for addressing this problem. At no point, was there any suggestion that we could not find out more scientific knowledge about erosion, and how to manage it. But, throughout these studies, it was clear that using pre-existing narratives about the cause-and-effect of erosion, without acknowledging the role of social values, would not explain how problems occur, or how they can be solved.

Conclusion

This chapter has argued that environmental science needs to look more closely at how scientific knowledge, and social values, are inherently linked. This statement does not suggest that "science" can only be biased, or that truth claims can only be limited to whoever frames the research. Instead, this chapter argues that the most useful scientific progress can occur when we consider who (and for whose benefit), we collect scientific information and create scientific "laws", rather than assume that "laws" exist neutrally, for everyone, without social influence.

Scientific explanations need to be seen as directly related to the social networks and institutions that created them. This chapter has shown that some explanations of soil erosion are rooted in outsiders' expectations; and the operations of models such as the Universal Soil Loss Equation also create their own expectations of what is supposed to exist. Instead, we need to see each environmental explanation as a function of who has created it to date, and at what scale, and with which objectives. Some analysts call these memberships "networks", but many other words such as institutions, assemblages, or solidarities may also denote the same meaning.

The philosopher of science, Steve Fuller has claimed that many social studies of science have been based on what he calls "interest-oriented social epistemology" – or the analysis of who makes different knowledge claims. But, he also argues that scientific analysis can be made more socially progressive (and less relativistic), if we adopt a "politically-oriented social epistemology" based on *a priori* normative grounds, for directing the generation of knowledge (Fuller, 2000; Remedios, 2003:

11, 21). This politically-oriented epistemology, might be more useful in research concerning international development, or poverty alleviation, because it starts from a normative belief about *who* should be included in environmental explanation, or *why* we would want to include them. This approach to science might be preferable to uncritical positivism – where there is no discussion of how values shape knowledge – or unlimited relativism – where different viewpoints are compared equally.

The point of this argument is not to suggest that science cannot help us understand transferable truth claims about complex problems, such as soil erosion. Rather, it is to show that perhaps the purpose of this research, and the social inclusion about it, should be just as important as the generation of knowledge. By applying these lessons, political and social research into environmental change might be able to achieve a more politicized, and more powerful challenge to the simplifications and unexamined political agendas, supported by positivist environmental science.

References

[1] Blaikie, P. (1995). "Understanding Environmental Issues", pp. 1-30 in Morse, S. and Stocking, M. eds., *People and Environment*, London: University College London Press.

[2] Blaikie, P. (1999). "A Review of Political Ecology: Issues, Epistemology and Analytical Narratives", *Zeitschrift fur Wirtschaftsgeographie*, 43 (3-4):131-147.

[3] Conklin, H. (1954). An Ethnoecological Approach to Shifting Agriculture, *Transactions of the New York Academy of Sciences*, 77, 133-142.

[4] Cutajar, M.Z. (2001). "Notes for Closing Session", *Global Change Open Science Conference* (IGBP – IHDP – WCRP), Amsterdam, 10-13 July 2001, Bonn: International Human Dimensions Program on Global Environmental Change.

[5] Geertz, C. (1963). "Agricultural Involution: The Processes of Ecological Change in Indonesia", Berkeley, CA: University of California Press.

[6] Fairhead, J. and Leach, M. (1996). "Misreading the African Landscape: Society and Ecology in a Forest-Savanna Mosaic", Cambridge: Cambridge University Press.

[7] Forsyth, T. (1996). "Science, Myth and Knowledge: Testing Himalayan Environmental Degradation in Northern Thailand", *Geoforum*, 27(3): 75-392.

[8] Forsyth, T. (2003). "Critical Political Ecology: The Politics of Environmental Science", London: Routledge.

[9] Fuller, S. (2000). "The Governance of Science", Buckingham and Philadelphia: Open University Press.

[10] Funtowicz, S. and Ravetz, J. (1993). "Science for the Post-normal Age", *Futures*, September, pp. 739-756.

[11] Habermas, J. (1974). *Theory and Practice*, translated by John Viertel, Boston: Beacon Press.

[12] Hajer, M. (1995). "The Politics of Environmental Discourse", Oxford: Clarendon.

[13] Hallsworth, E. (1987). "Anatomy, Physiology, and Psychology of Erosion", New York: Wiley.

[14] Hamilton, Larry S. and Pearce, A.J. (1988). "Soil and Water Impacts of Deforestation", pp. 75-98 in Ives, J. and Pitt, D. eds., *Deforestation: Social Dynamics in Watershed and Mountain Ecosystems*, Routledge, London.

[15] Harré, R. (1993). "Laws of Nature", London: Duckworth.

[16] Harper, D. and El-Swaify, S. (1988). "Sustainable Agricultural Development in North Thailand: Conservation as a Component of Success in Assistance Projects", in Moldenhauer, W. and Hudson, N., eds., *Conservation Farming on Steep Slopes*, Ankeny, Iowa: Soil and Water Conservation Society of America.

[17] Jantawat, S. (ed.) (1987). *Proceedings of the International Workshop on Soil Erosion and its Counter Measures*. November. 11-19, 1984, Chiang Mai. Bangkok: Chuan Press.

[18] Jones, S. (1997). "An Actor-level Analysis of the Constraints on Sustainable Land Management in Northern Thailand: A Study from Chiang Dao District", *South East Asia Research*, 5(3): 243-267.

[19] Latour, B. (2004). "The Politics of Nature". Cambridge MA: Harvard University Press.

[20] Levitt, N. (1999). "Prometheus Bedeviled: Science and the Contradictions of Contemporary Culture", New Brunswick: Rutgers University Press.

[21] Manu Srikhajon and Ard Somrang (1980). "Soil Erosion in Thailand", Bangkok: Land Development Department.

[22] Pahlmann, C. (1990). "Farmers' Perceptions of the Sustainability of Upland Farming Systems of Northern Thailand", MSc. Thesis, Department of Resource Management, University of Canberra.

[23] Remedios, F. (2003). *Legitimizing Scientific Knowledge: An Introduction to Steve Fuller's Social Epistemology*. Kentucky: Lexington Books.

[24] Searle, J. (1995). "The Construction of Social Reality", New York: Free Press.

[25] Thompson, M., Warburton, M. and Hatley, T. (1986). "Uncertainty on a Himalayan Scale", London: Ethnographica.

[26] Thompson, M., Ellis, R. and Wildavsky, A. (1990). "Cultural Theory", Boulder: Westview.

[27] Turkelboom, F. (1999). "On-farm Diagnosis of Steepland Erosion in Northern Thailand: Integrating Spatial Scales with Household Strategies", Ph.D. Thesis, Katholieke Uniersiteit Leuven, Belgium.

[28] USDA United States Department of Agriculture (1961). "A Universal Equation for Predicting Rainfall-Erosion Losses", USDA-ARS Special Report: US Department of Agricultural Research Service.

3

Segmented Knowledge, Integrated Environmental Assessment and Governance

Richard B. Norgaard

Introduction

People are both smart and social, but the particular ways in which smartness and sociality have unfolded, with some ways becoming more dominant, stem from beliefs originating in Europe during the past few centuries that have become institutionalized only quite recently. These beliefs frame not only how we understand but also how environmental science, policy, and management have been structured in institutions. These beliefs help to explain why some environmental governance has been successful, as well as why other environmental problems remain unsolved. Taking an historical perspective helps us to see how dominant beliefs are intertwined with our environmental problems so that we can move beyond them to new institutional solutions, to new ways of being smart and social.

The Millennium Ecosystem Assessment (MA) has helped expose the nature of modern beliefs and their consequences very clearly. The MA was a review extending over five years by some 1400 scientists from around the world, of what is known about how people transform ecosystems, how ecosystem services promote human well-being, and what are the prospects for human well-being in the future. The MA entailed a participatory, deliberative process that provides an example of why dominant historical beliefs about the nature of reality, science, and management are incomplete. It also provides some interesting lessons on how the dominant framework might be dramatically expanded.

In this chapter, provided a historical context for this critically important expansion in how we do science and think about governance, describe the MA as an example of this new development in science, and draw lessons from the MA for reframing environmental governance.

Historical Context

For the vast majority of human history, people lived as hunter-gatherers in small groups of 50 to 200. Each person did nearly the same things, for there was relatively little specialization in tasks. They shared the same myths passed down from their ancestors. With very little hierarchy, or differentiation, it was relatively easy to act together, because they saw the same things together and interpreted their meaning together. People were hunter-gatherers for 99.5 per cent of human history, until the rise of agriculture began some 15,000 years ago.

Agriculture brought a surplus of production that facilitated investments in physical structures, and the rise of social hierarchy and diversification. Thus, along with irrigation projects, defensive walls, temples, and castles, we begin to see the rise of full-time leaders, and their differentiation into rulers, priests, and philosophers. Specialization in craftsmanship and the arts also arose, as well as full-time warriors. Nevertheless, the vast majority of people worked the land, and through this shared experience, they retained a common understanding of the natural world.

The transition to agriculture facilitated a tremendous increase in human population, from some five million people worldwide 15,000 years ago, to 1200 million people around 1850. Thus, before the implementation of modern science in agriculture, human population increased by a factor of 240. People slowly occupied different niches around the globe, with novel approaches to agriculture. Well-being and longevity increased as well. People did this through experiments and mistakes, observing outcomes, and adjusting how they interacted with nature. We now denigrate this as *trial and error*, yet *learning-by-doing* still plays an extremely important role in the age of modern science and technology. Indeed, with respect to the indirect consequences of technology, and the social and environmental consequences, this is especially true. The surplus from traditional agriculture supported early explorations and conquests across Asia, Europe, and Northern Africa; European voyages of discovery and imperialism through colonization; and the beginnings of Western science.

Five critically important complementary transitions took place in Western Europe and North America during the middle of the 19th century, 99.995 per cent of the way through human history.

First, the idea of material progress went from being a possible scenario explored by a few utopians, to becoming both a widely accepted aspect of modern life, and a dominant expectation for the future. It also became common wisdom that material abundance would reduce the wants that drive theft, the conflicts that drive war. In this way, the idea of material progress complemented long-standing, Western religious hopes for moral progress. Yet, material progress also soon became an end in itself, flooding out the moral.

Second, the industrial revolution got fully underway as Europeans and North Americans switched from using renewable energy – animal, biomass, water, and wind power – to non-renewable fossil hydrocarbons. The increases in population and well-being ever since, around the globe, have come largely through technologies that deplete coal, petroleum, and natural gas, the fossil stocks of solar energy captured over millennia by life itself. Historically, life processes took carbon dioxide from the atmosphere; environmental processes sequestered it as fossil hydrocarbons, changed the greenhouse effect, and created the environment we know today. People have literally been reversing the historical processes that made the environmental conditions in which today's life forms and ecological systems evolved.

Third, the role of markets in people's lives became increasingly important, the economic philosophy of markets arose, and markets were more systematically institutionalized. The rise of markets, combined with fossil-fuel-driven industrialization, facilitated the rise of specialization in the economic lives of increasing number of people.

Fourth, natural philosophy divided into separate specialized sciences of physics, chemistry, geology, and other disciplines we know today. Moral philosophy split into the social sciences. And it became standard practice for individual scholars to learn more and more about less and less. No mechanisms were established to bring the splintering sciences into a coherent whole.

And fifth, progressive governance was invented. In the second half of the 19th century, scientists and engineers were brought into the process of governance, as agents of progress. Americans created agricultural schools, departments of agriculture, and agricultural extension services, and during the 20th century, these were replicated around much of the globe.

It is important to acknowledge two beliefs about progressive governance that are widely known, but rarely fully addressed. First, modern peoples believed that agencies could be separately established along professional and disciplinary lines with agricultural scientists, water engineers, and fisheries experts, for example, housed in different agencies, and yet still working systematically together. This belief was rooted in the idea that the sciences would naturally fit together into a unified whole. In fact, historic problems that fit the foci of the original agencies are handled reasonably well. Problems that fall between their mandates, as well as some of the consequences of their projects that were outside their purview, become known as "environmental" problems. In fact, environmental problems are not a separate and distinct type of problem. Rather, they are the problems that remain insufficiently addressed due to the divisions created by the gains of specialization both in science, i.e. the disciplines, and in social institutions, i.e. the organizational advantages of charging particular branches of government with solving particular types of problems.

The second belief is that the agencies provide expert advice to the policy process and implement public projects in a manner that is value free. At least in democracies, values are supposed to come from the people, not through the progressive agencies and their scientists. Both the divided structure of science, and progressive governance, and the presumption of the objectivity of science and progressive governance have proven highly problematic, yet they remain dominant modern beliefs embedded in political discourse about science and environmental governance.

A key point here, however, is that modern beliefs about nature, and about science were only institutionalized in the structure of science, our social organization, and the relations between them a mere century and a half ago, a mere wink of time in any serious gaze at human history. Of course, during this "mere wink", material well-being, mostly in Europe and North America, advanced tremendously, but so did serious environmental problems advance tremendously. Since many now see environmental problems foreclosing options for material well-being for future generations, one of the conclusions of the Millennium Ecosystem Assessment, a deeper analysis of modern beliefs about nature, science, and environmental governance is in order.

Embracing Universal Principles or the Complexity of Evolved Systems

Early Greek and Roman philosophers argued that everything was composed of a few basic components such as earth, water, air, and fire. Some argued that the complexities of the universe got reduced to geometric golden means. The idea that everything can be explained in terms of underlying basic parts, and a fairly simple rule book for their assembly and operation, is a part of Western tradition.

Having spent a fair amount of time among physicists, I am accustomed to the phrase "you can deduce that from first principles". Some things can be deduced from the laws of thermodynamics, the properties of materials, and a few empirical constants. A little over a century ago, Svante Arrhenius determined from first principles, and a few parameters, how the doubling of carbon dioxide in the atmosphere would affect the temperature of the earth. With far more sophisticated global circulation models, also running on a few first principles, climate scientists have added a few important details to Arrhenius's initial estimates, but they are still just additional details. However, now that climate science is beginning to incorporate the dynamics of ocean currents, and the interactions of diverse terrestrial ecosystems over time, our understanding of climate change is becoming immensely more complicated, and no longer reducible to first principles at all.

Underlying the claim that one can deduce the complex nature of reality from "first principles", is the belief, that all science builds up from a relatively few basic principles. Once we know these, everything will fall into place. So far, however, this has not been the case. Physics explains some things about chemical phenomena, but one cannot derive the periodic table from physics. And how different types of atoms combine into different types of molecules, is the very essence of chemistry. Similarly, organismal biologists are constantly complaining that ecology neither builds on principles of organismal biology, nor incorporates its substantive knowledge. So, the idea that underlying principles explain complexity at higher levels simply has not been borne out. Some accept that at new levels, new basic principles must be introduced. But, the nature of science thus far suggests, that multiple new theories emerge at higher levels of complexity, and that each only explains different parts of the greater complexity. Thus, ecology has many frameworks of analysis: population biology, food webs, energetics, biogeochemical cycles, hierarchy analysis, ecosystem ecology, evolutionary ecology, behavioural ecology, and landscape ecology, etc. Similarly, a diversity of ways of thinking about people and social systems, can also be found in the social sciences. While the first principles of physics and chemistry hold at higher levels of complexity, new first principles have not emerged to explain these higher levels.

When we speak of biological diversity, we quickly point out that biodiversity can only be understood as genetic diversity, organismal diversity, and ecosystem diversity working together. This is because the way we understand genetic biodiversity is not nested in organismal and ecosystem diversity. Rather, our understandings of the three levels of biodiversity are interactive. Some scientists who acknowledge that biological systems are tightly interlinked with social systems, also argue that biological diversity can only be understood as interactive with social diversity. While Western and Westernized minds may strive for simplicity, for first principles, the nature of the diverse ways we understand higher levels of complexity, has important implications. If our social and economic systems operate on the same beliefs and rules globally, social diversity will be reduced, the range of human pressure on biological diversity is narrowed but greatly intensified, and the possibilities for biological diversity are greatly reduced.

Thus, we need to embrace diversity and complexity at each of these levels, including diversity and complexity in human systems, and see them as interrelated. While this is increasingly understood among biologists, we also live in an age of rising fundamentalism, in the search for first principles, whether from science or religion. While we need to accept that some things can be explained by universal underlying principles, we need to realize that underlying principles do not explain everything. Yet arguments from first principles carry strong appeal. Economists argue the case for globalization from underlying principles of exchange alone, universally applied. Western and Westernized minds have strongly embraced the principle of exchange, and transformed economic organization in spite of everything else we know, from the social sciences and practical understanding. Why do modern people build organizations that end up pushing particular underlying principles, rather than organizations that embrace the diversity of our world and of how we understand it? How can we organize ourselves, so that we can use the multiple frameworks and information from the multiple disciplines, and combine this with experiential knowledge?

The Renewal of Shared Learning and Collective Understanding

During the 1980s, the philosophy of sustainable development arose, a realization that real progress could only be made through a resolution of material differences between the rich and the poor and the present and the future. Sustainable development requires a shared understanding between the rich and the poor, urban and rural, and scientific and traditional people.

The parable of the three blind men touching different parts of an elephant, teaches young people that we see different things from different positions. This is important, but not sufficient. The message of the parable for adults is surely that we need even more hands on the elephant, that we had better talk together and feel some more, to move beyond the differences in what we are feeling, and determine that we have an elephant on our hands. The philosophy of sustainable development encourages a pragmatic reaching across different communities of scientists, practitioners, and interest groups to come to such a shared understanding.

For a few years, the philosophy of sustainable development and the importance of bringing different peoples into a collective understanding of development, dominated our thinking. Then the continued rise of free market fundamentalism, a phenomenon that had begun only somewhat before the emergence of the concern with sustainability, grew sufficiently strong to out-compete the more holistic philosophy. Sustainable development has not been forgotten, but free market fundamentalism reigned, bolstering the ideas that markets can solve everything, individual choice is almost always better than collective choice, and the burden of proof for exercising collective responsibility lies on those who are concerned about the direction development was headed.

Yet, even as free market fundamentalism gained strength, another phenomenon also emerged. Scientists began to deliberately work together in a new way to understand the climate system on which all depend. Atmospheric physicists thinking in milliseconds and microns, evolutionary ecologists thinking in continental scales and millennia, and economists thinking in dollars and discount rates, began to talk together. These ways of thinking do not naturally fit together. Large computer models help scientists think through the systemic complexities, while smaller models help them see the whole system. Climate scientists appeal to their models for scientific credibility, but, in fact, the big global circulation models are very incomplete, in that neither economic, nor ecological feedbacks are built in, while the more comprehensive models are incredibly simple. Much of the shared understanding of the scientists, actually comes through talking together, then doing their individual research around new assumptions, and learning how to interpret their results in the context of what those in other disciplines know. Furthermore, the process of understanding climate science has not simply been one of joining the separate disciplines, but also of bringing in scientists from around the globe,

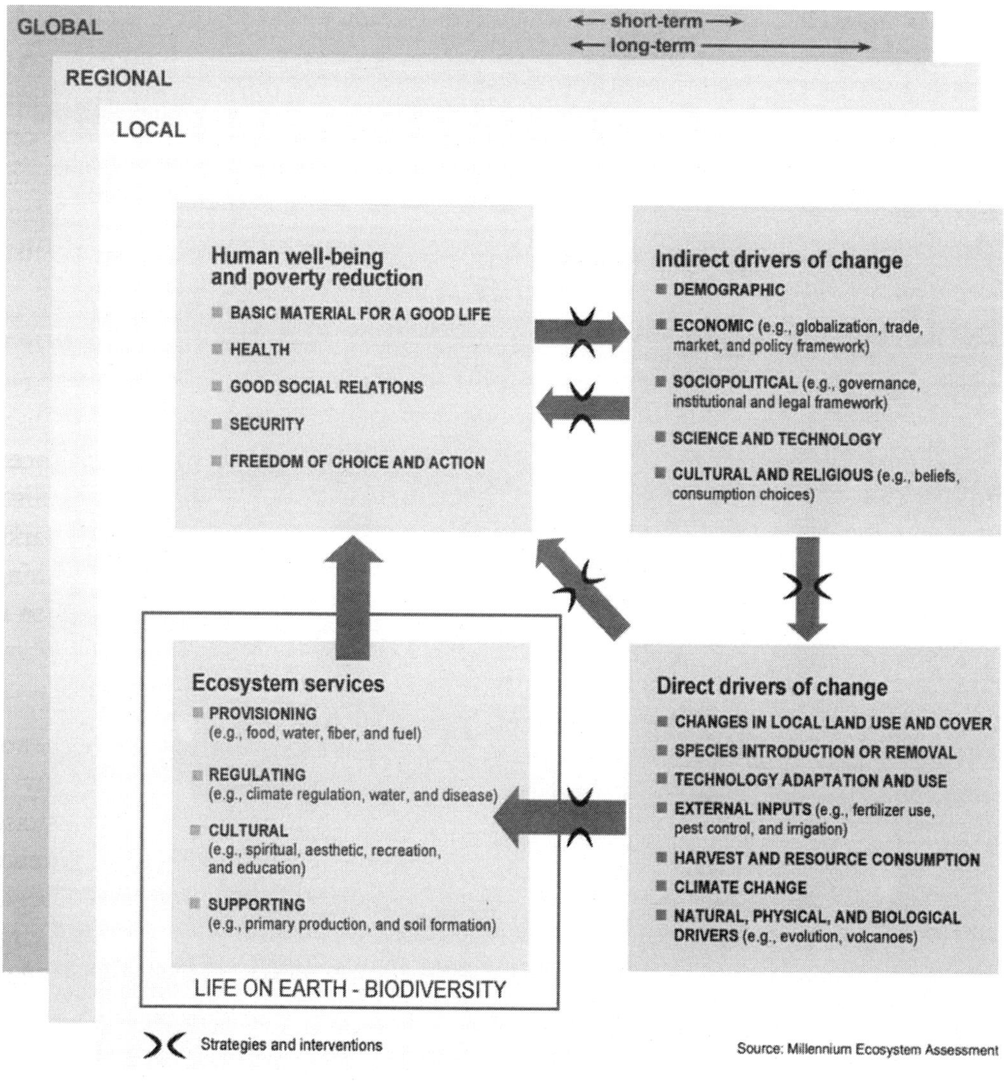

Fig. 1: A Framework for Understanding Ecosystem Services and Ecosystem Change

who can interpret the significance of climate science in their own environmental and social contexts. In this collective and interactive process, a large group of scientists have come to a shared understanding of climate change. Thus, climate science spans the disciplines, because there are scientists who are willing to spend time with each other, to learn from each other. In this way, they are building a collective understanding of the whole system, and what are thought to be its most important feedbacks.

The Millennium Ecosystem Assessment (MA) was even more phenomenal in that it tackled the interactive complexities from all of the multiple drivers of ecosystem change, not simply those primarily driving climate change. The MA scientists developed a systemic framework (Figure 1), assessed the scientific literature, and synthesized a four-volume report on the conditions and trends of ecosystems, social systems, and the interactions between them, and what these mean for human well-being over the next half century.

The general framework for the analysis was one of the most important accomplishments of the MA. It systemically illustrates the key issues, while at the same time, it highlights the difficulties of understanding ecosystem change in more than a qualitative way. Ecosystem change occurs through a great number of mechanisms. Few of the individual processes can be represented in a mathematical model; none with parameters that hold from one locale to the next, let alone around the globe. Ecologists have nothing comparable to the relationship between the stock of carbon dioxide in the atmosphere, and equilibrium global temperatures. Without a central relationship to build on, as in the IPCC assessments, computer models played a much smaller role in the MA. While climate scientists probably overemphasize the importance of formal models in their basic understanding of climate change, the role of formal models in the MA was so limited that no appeal could be made to them at all.

There is another important difference between the IPCC assessments and the MA. Economic organization and incentives are at the centre of the complementary unfolding disasters of both climate change and ecosystem change, yet the MA veered significantly from the approach taken in the IPCC. Economic growth models using gross domestic product (GDP) as a core metric, are central to the IPCC scenarios. Human well-being, technological responses, and levels of damage are all tied to GDP growth. While the nature and tightness of the tie of these variables to GDP are discussed in the IPCC assessments, the economic models themselves remain at the core of the analysis, on a par with the physical science models that relate the accumulation of greenhouse gases to climate change. Indeed, the whole approach of scenarios with quantitative projections of GDP evokes "predictable precision" that climate science cannot deliver. The MA took a decidedly different approach by decoupling human well-being, as well as technological change and other phenomena, from GDP. With human well-being uncoupled from GDP in the MA, economic reasoning with its formal models did not dominate the discussions of well-being. Indeed, other social scientists probably had a comparative advantage at "looking around" the economy, and thinking directly about ecosystem services and human well-being.

The MA picked up where the IPCC had gotten to after a decade, and started with scientists from the developed and the developing countries participating almost equally, exposing tensions over equity and Western visions of the future, right from the beginning. Interpretive social scientists were never able to append themselves to the core climate models, and hence worked apart from the IPCC process, while interpretive social scientists were welcomed from the beginning into the MA. Thus, feedbacks from "softer" analyses of social change were treated with as much respect as the analyses economists had quantified for the IPCC. While climate scientists are now becoming serious about the complexities of feedbacks from diverse terrestrial ecosystems, and are incorporating the dynamics of ocean currents, the MA started with such complexity and more, yet dealt with the different feedbacks in a less formal way. In short, climate assessment reflects the initial framing and order in which additional frames of analysis were added, while the MA reflects what happens when complexity and the need for multiple frames are acknowledged from the start.

For solid scientific reasons, the MA had to be methodologically pluralistic. Ecologists have multiple ways of framing relations and dynamics between species. The multiple ways economists understand economic systems were brought into the MA from the beginning. The Millennium Ecosystem Assessment, once it had been accepted that all frames of analysis come to the table on an equal footing, had to be a deliberative process of learning together. Let me highlight the reasons why deliberation was a necessity.

First, the literature that was assessed reflects the fragmented, disciplinary nature of science. Environmental scientists rarely make the linkages identified in the MA general framework to the social system, while social scientists rarely make adequate linkages in their analyses to the environmental system. Thus, natural scientists and social scientists had to interpret each other's literatures together, clarify the linkages from what they each knew through experiential knowledge, and come to a common understanding of the significance of the literature to the more systemic questions being addressed by the MA.

Second, ecology consists of formal frameworks such as food web models, more interpretive frameworks such as landscape ecology, and metaphors such as "environmental engineer". The different ecological ways of thinking do not fit together within an overarching meta-model of an ecosystem. Which framing seemed most powerful was case specific, and in many cases, several framings were important. Similarly, the literature on the relations between the environment and human well-being are framed by neoclassical as well as Marxist political economists, anthropologists from cultural ecology and ethnobiology, geographers of different schools of thought, and political ecologists whose original training could have been in anthropology, geography, political science, or sociology.

Third, neither social systems nor ecosystems have "inherent" scales for analysis. While many social models are applicable at any scale, the situation in ecology is much messier. Researchers select the spatial and temporal extent, and the grain of an analysis depending on the problem focus, ecological or other framework chosen, and the constraints of obtaining appropriate data. The differing spatial and temporal extents and grains of analysis of the cases assessed, made it very difficult to summarize the literature as a whole, and interpret its general applicability globally, including to situations not yet analyzed.

Fourth, MA participants became increasingly aware of the historical contingencies and local contextualities of the dynamics between social and ecological systems. Everything had multiple causes and multiple effects, while particular analyses typically emphasized, but one or two. The variety of factors and their interrelations across spatial and temporal scales that could have contributed to a crash of a population, or shift in the structure and processes of an ecosystem, could not be documented. There were parallel difficulties for explaining social system change.

Fifth, and closely related to the fourth, we know very little about ecosystem thresholds due to the complex nature of ecosystems and their dynamics. Identifying thresholds, a concept critical to both popular notions and formal stock-flow models of sustainability, was not possible, because no ecosystem and the ways it is embedded in larger systems has been so completely modelled, and empirically calibrated, that the distinction between sustainable flows and degradation can be made. Thus, neither the MA conceptual framework, nor the empirical literature reviewed distinguished between ecological services generated by sustainable ecosystem flows from those that were generated through degrading ecosystem properties that would result in reduced future flows. While participants were well aware that populations crash, and ecosystems go through transitions, that are difficult if not impossible to reverse, the shared concern that future generations would have fewer ecosystem services, a concern that seemed to have increased for most participants through the MA, could not be deduced scientifically.

Sixth, while concern was shared, values, especially those rooted in economics, were actively disputed. While the relative impacts of different greenhouse gases can be compared and aggregated reasonably well, with respect to their impact on warming, it was impossible to compare, or aggregate drivers of ecosystem change. Some biologists were intrigued by the possibilities of solving the need for relative weights through economic valuation, and some economists were prepared to use valuations in the literature. Participants from developing countries, however, argued that economic valuation methods weigh the dollars the rich spend on ecotourism the same, as the dollar-equivalents the poor spend on food and bus fare. The MA addresses future generations out of a concern that the current socioeconomic system does not weigh them adequately. Thus, it would be illogical to use current preferences, behaviour, or replacements costs from a system on the wrong course, to weight and aggregate details, to inform new policies to protect the future. Others pointed out that, for there to be any rationality to relying on stated preferences or human behaviour, one would have to assume that lay people were sufficiently informed of the very complexities the MA scientists were struggling to understand. This assumption contradicted the objective of the MA to provide much needed knowledge to decision makers. In short, the problems of using monetary values to weight phenomena are tightly embedded in the very socioeconomic system driving the problems of ecosystem degradation the MA sought to understand, in order to design new policies.

Thus, for clear scientific reasons, to the extent that the MA put scientists' fragmented knowledge together into a coherent whole, it was through collaborative learning and collective judgement. This is a new way of doing "big science". The three blind men are not simply announcing their separate findings about the elephant, but many scientists are feeling, talking to each other, thinking together, going back to feel again, and expanding the number of people participating in the process.

Expanding Science, Shifting Governance

Reductionist science assumes that scientists can address smaller and smaller questions without losing time, linking what they are learning to the other sub-fields of their disciplines, let alone other disciplines. The vast majority of scientists still believe the parts will all come together "naturally", and if not, it will be someone else's responsibility to bring them together. Of course, we now know this is not true. The Millennium Ecosystem Assessment provides documentation as to why this is not true and what can be done to overcome it. Yet, our universities and research institutions continue to be structured as if the separate sciences will somehow merge into a coherent whole, long after empirical evidence has documented otherwise, and new approaches have emerged, for which scientists could be better prepared.

Similarly, environmental management institutions are largely structured around historic notions of how science works. The expanded way that science is working to understand complex environmental problems raises serious questions with respect to bureaucratic accountability. Environmental agencies derive authority from science, are held accountable for basing their decisions on the best science, and have found themselves in a power vacuum when the science is not clear. And standards of clear science are historic, i.e. coherent combinations of established laws, or unchallenged theories backed by empirical documentation. Judgement is regarded with suspicion. As scientists become more deliberate and deliberative, in how they collectively understand complex systems, and public consciousness of this new way of doing big science increases, environmental policy and management agencies will probably be able to adapt to it. But a systematic effort needs to be made.

On the positive side, these relatively recent developments in science complement experiments initiated somewhat earlier to bring user groups and traditional people with experiential knowledge into a participatory role with science. Action research, participatory research, rapid rural appraisal, citizen science, and related efforts entail experiential knowledge, deliberation, and judgement comparable to that used by scientists in the IPCC assessment and MA process. To be sure, scientists have an edge in interpreting the scientific literature, but local people have an edge when it comes to local conditions.

We think of ourselves as the smartest and most social of all species. I do not know whether either of these qualities is more characteristic of people, than porpoises, or whales. Perhaps the key distinction is that people also have opposable thumbs for many other species, from ants to wolves are social. But, I am certain that people's smartness and sociality needs to work more effectively together. Our ability to communicate and organize ourselves in disparate tasks, as social beings, and our ability to understand as smart beings, are inseparable. They cannot be described, measured, analyzed, or evaluated separately. Our system of being smart only works through the ways we communicate, organize, and build knowledge together. The particular approach we took starting around 150 years ago, to being smart and social is not working, we need to change the institutional structures and understandings of science that guide our smartness and sociality, but we should not give up on being smart and social.

Yet, unfortunately, the lure of answers rooted in first principles remains strong. We have scientific fundamentalists who interpret reality through the lenses of particular realms of science. We have free market fundamentalists who see everything in economic terms. Others rely on religious fundamentalism. Yet surely each of these and any combination of fundamentalist approaches will hasten the collapse of the very multi-levelled ecological, socio-economic, and cultural diversity on which we depend.

This paper is a particular synthesis of some of the arguments elaborated more fully where references to the broader literature can also be found.

References

[1] Lélé, Sharachchandra and Richard B. Norgaard. 1996. Sustainability and the Scientist's Burden. *Conservation Biology* 10: 354-65.

[2] Lélé, Sharachchandra and Richard B. Norgaard. 2005. Practicing Interdisciplinarity. *BioScience* 55(11): 967-975.

[3] Norgaard, Richard B. 2004. Learning and Knowing Collectively. *Ecological Economics* 49(2): 231-241.

[4] Norgaard, Richard B. 2007. Deliberative Economics. *Ecological Economics* 63(2-3): 375-82.

[5] Norgaard, Richard B. 2008. Finding Hope in the Millennium Ecosystem Assessment. *Conservation Biology* 22(4): 862-69.

[6] Norgaard, Richard B. and Paul Baer. 2005. Collectively Seeing Complex Systems: The Nature of the Problem. *Bioscience* 55(11): 953-960.

[7] Norgaard, Richard B. and Paul Baer. 2005. Collectively Seeing Climate Change: The Limits of Formal Models. *Bioscience* 55(11): 961-966.

4

Climate Change and Environmental Governance

Nitin Desai

Environmental Governance

The challenge of environmental governance can be looked at from four distinct but related perspectives – the ecological, the economic, the ethical and the decision-making challenges that need to be addressed by the governance mechanism.

From an ecological point of view, the challenge is that of reflecting systemic interactions in mindsets dominated by disciplinary or geographical boundaries. Ecological interdependence has always existed in the form of energy and material flows and species exchange between ecosystems. That interdependence is the very basis for the existence of life on earth. The geographical scale of this interaction can range from neighbouring ecosystems to the earth as a whole and the time scale between cause and effect can stretch into decades or centuries. There are also thresholds and discontinuities, which, if crossed, can lead to a sudden change.

The reason for concern now is the increase in the scale and depth of the human impact on ecosystems. The proportion of river waters impounded and the share of human emissions in the nitrogen cycle are examples where the scale of intervention is well beyond the marginal. As for depth, we are now manipulating life forms at the genetic level and even creating exotic substances unknown in the natural world. A further development is that increasingly, the geography of interdependence is global. The challenge for environmental governance is that of devising methodologies of analysis and decision-making procedures that require these interactions to be taken into account.

From an economic point of view, we can see these interactions as externalities where one person's welfare depends on consumption decisions made by another, one entity's production possibilities are affected by the decisions made by another and one generations' options are constrained (or enhanced) by decisions made by another. A thermal power plant emitting hot water into a river affects fisher folk downstream, a chemical plant disposing off wastes increases disease risks for residents, a generation that cuts down forests reduces options for future generations. The market mechanism in most instances does not provide an opportunity for those who are affected by such externalities to signal their preferences to others. The challenge is that of designing policies that correct these market failures with appropriate regulatory controls and economic instruments that convey the costs of these externalities to today's decision makers.

From an ethical point of view, the issue can be seen as one of equity. An environmental problem generally involves some injustice between groups, regions or generations. The central issue is that of fixing responsibility. But in doing so, one must recognize both meanings of the word "responsibility" – as "culpability" in the sense that a polluter is responsible for a problem because he caused it and as "duty" in the sense that all who are concerned and affected have a duty to contribute to resolving the problem. Redressing the injustice requires the allocation of responsibility as culpability with a rigorous application of the "polluter pays principle". It also requires the recognition of responsibility as duty. The challenge is to do this in a global and national political context in which power is distributed unequally and to give practical expression to the principle of "common but differentiated responsibility".

From a decision-making point of view, the difficulty is that of coping with risk and uncertainty. Environmental governance requires balancing known costs and unknown benefits or unknown costs and known benefits. This has led to the formulation of the precautionary approach which requires taking measured actions to anticipate and mitigate risks without waiting for full certainty. Yet, there is a need for proportionality in response to potential threats so that those that are more likely receive more urgent and more substantial attention compared to those where there is much uncertainty. The challenge for governance is that of better monitoring and assessment so that scientific resources are deployed rationally taking account of the imminence and gravity of the threat. But risk and uncertainty also pose a challenge for creating regulatory measures and incentives to shift the behaviour agents to reduce risk and that hold agents liable for the risks that their behaviour poses for others.

> "Ecological interdependence involves uncertainty, long-range cause and effect relationships, thresholds and discontinuities, a scale of impact that is reaching limits in some areas, a close connection with the processes of economic globalization, a geography of impact that cuts across national jurisdictions and an incidence of impact that reflects power relations. For all of these reasons, it requires a qualitatively different form of global response."
>
> – Nitin Desai[1]

The Challenge of Climate Change

The basic facts about the threat of climate change are well known. There is now a near consensus amongst scientists that global warming is already under way and that it is due to human activities in the form of emissions of greenhouse gases, mainly, but not solely, from the massive increase in the burning of fossil fuels since the start of the industrial revolution in the eighteenth century. For example, the concentration of carbon dioxide has gone up from 275 to 285 ppm in the pre-industrial era (*circa* 1750) to 379 ppm in 2005. Additionally, synthetic greenhouse gases like CFCs and HCFCs are also getting accumulated in recent times in the atmosphere.

The issue is not the greenhouse gas effect – without it the earth would be a cold rock, some 32°C colder than its present average temperature of 14°C. Nor is it the variability of climate. That also has happened due to natural causes in the past, and life on earth has adapted to these ice ages and interglacials. Our current concerns arise because the greenhouse blanket has become thicker, raising the equilibrium temperature level to a point at which catastrophic changes are threatened, that this change is likely to take place at an unprecedentedly rapid rate, posing major challenges for adaptation and because it is manmade we can act to reverse the trend for adoption. Since the processes involved are human induced, we can act to reverse the trend.

For the purposes of identifying the challenge that this poses for environmental governance, it is useful to distinguish between two scenarios – one, involving a moderate increase (2°C) and the second exposing us to a catastrophic increase (5°C+). A moderate increase will affect hydrology, coastal zones, mountain ecosystems and biodiversity with significant impacts on agriculture, health and settlements. A catastrophic increase will amplify all of these impacts and could activate certain tipping points that fall in three broad groups. The first involves the impact of large temperature increases on the water that is trapped in the gigantic ice sheets in the Arctic, Greenland and the Antarctic. If global warming starts approaching the 5°C+ level, we run the serious risks of these melting and leading, among other things, to a sea level rise that is much higher than in the moderate scenario. The second set of tipping points involve the impact of temperature increase on some processes that could lead to run away climate change, the main candidate for concern being the melting of the permafrost and the consequent release of vast quantities of methane. The third set involves the impact on certain delicately balanced climate systems like the Indian Ocean monsoon and the Gulf Stream.

A moderate increase is probably unavoidable given the accumulation of GHGs that has already taken place and the momentum of continuing increases that cannot be slowed down very quickly. But the risks of a catastrophic increase can be greatly reduced. Hence, the challenge for governance is twofold – slow down the pace of change in GHGs and even reverse it to avoid catastrophic climate change and start providing for the adaptation to the consequences of the moderate scenario which is unavoidable.

The challenge for decision making that these risks of climate change pose comes from several factors. First, the time frame is very long relative to the usual time frame of governments, corporations and households. Most major impacts will be felt 50, even 100 years from now and the potential catastrophic impacts even later than that and over long periods. But action is required now if these catastrophic impacts are to be avoided. Waiting till the consequences are closer in time would not only add to the costs of action but may also be too late to prevent the effects.

The second issue is that of equity. Those with the highest culpability, the industrial countries of the Northern Hemisphere may well be the least affected. In fact, some like Russia or Canada may even benefit from moderate increase. On the other hand, those who are most affected, the developing countries in the tropics, are the least culpable and also less developed and poorer. In this situation, the challenge for governance is that of securing agreement on goals for mitigation. Here, the focus on measures targeted at preventing catastrophic change may help as this would be in the interests of all countries, including the Northern developed world. There is also the challenge in getting an agreement on the fair sharing of costs of mitigation and adaptation.

What does economics have to say about how this challenge should be approached? Economists will look at this problem in terms of their understanding of how externalities should be handled. Climate change is the mother of all externalities: it is global, long-term, and highly variable in its impact in different geographies and involves risks of major irreversible changes in the ecosystems. The normal economist's approach of looking for policies that in effect "internalize the externality" requires global agreements that touch energy production and use which lies at the very core of any economy. The variable impact of the externality and the very large differences in the degree of culpability for the problem pose issues of intra-generational equity.

The choices that we make now will involve big differences in potential utility between generations separated by a century or more. These choices will be affected by judgements about the value that today's generation places on the welfare of future generations relative to their own. The issue here is not that future generations will be wealthier and, therefore, a rupee accruing to them as a benefit is less valuable than a rupee of cost incurred today. The issue is about the pure rate of time preference, the discount on future utilities simply because they arise in the future even if the future were not any richer than the present. Analytically, to argue that such a discount is justified is like saying that one jurisdiction is justified in placing a lower value on benefits accruing to another jurisdiction simply because it is different. An alternative view looks at it in terms of opportunity costs and uses the current marginal productivity of capital as the rate at which the current and future costs and benefits are made commensurate.

A further complication arises because all of these economic assessments have to be performed for a problem where there is a substantial uncertainty about the scale of the impact, its timing and its geographical spread. The actions required now are mainly precautionary measures to prevent future disasters rather than compensatory measures to take care of realized externalities only to a limited extent; more about potential risks.

Many economists have written about the economics of actions to mitigate climate change risks. Unlike the underlying climate science, there is as yet no consensus view from economists. There are some well-known skeptics, like Bjorn Lomborg, who have argued that the costs and benefits of action on climate do not compare favourably with other priorities like health care.[2] An intermediate position is taken by economists like William Nordhaus, who argues for a policy ramp with a slow start to mitigation in which policies involve modest rates of emissions reductions in the near term, followed by sharp reductions in the medium- and long-term.[3] A more radical approach is advocated in the influential Stern Review.[4] Nicholas Stern has argued forcefully for a goal of 50 per cent reduction in GHG emissions.

> "Our estimate of the optimal emissions-reduction rate for CO_2 relative to the baseline is 15 per cent in the first policy period, increasing to 25 per cent by 2050 and 45 per cent by 2100. This path reduces CO_2 concentrations, and the increase in global mean temperature relative to 1900 is reduced to 2.4°C for 2100 and 3.4°C for 2200... these calculations measure the emissions-reduction rates relative to the calculated baseline or no-control emissions scenario."
>
> – William Nordhaus[5]

> "Avoiding the risks of dangerous climate change requires that global greenhouse gas emissions peak within the next fifteen years are halved relative to 1990 by 2050, and then decline to less than 10 giga tonnes (GT) of emissions (1 tonne per capita)."
>
> – Nicholas Stern[6]

Economists look at issues like this in terms of costs and benefits and that is the case both for Nordhaus and for Stern. The difference in their proposals reflects the difference not so much of methodology as about assumptions, particularly regarding discount rates. But there are certain things which are quite clear. The costs of mitigation will depend on when we start – the later we start, the higher the cost. They also depend on the goal for permissible temperature increase (and ambient GHGs) that is considered acceptable.

The costs of adaptation will depend on the extent of temperature increase. There is a big difference between the moderate and catastrophic scenarios defined above, with adaptation costs being prohibitively high in the high temperature increase scenario. The geography of incidence is also expected to be very uneven between coastal/inland areas, high latitudes/low latitudes, etc. Many of these costs of adaptation will have to be borne well into the future and it is tempting to argue that a poor country has to focus on addressing current poverty and building the economic capacity to address these problems when they are more imminent. But this argument must take into account the very real possibility that the costs of action will rise more rapidly than economic capacity the later we start the mitigation and adaptation effort.

Before proceeding further, one must note the weakness of cost estimates. We lack knowledge about high temperature impacts, particularly with regard to the probabilities attached to possible catastrophic changes. There is a lack of adequate assessments from developing countries where the most adverse impacts are expected. There is also a certain ambiguity about the extent of adaptation assumed. Will we just learn to live with a warmer, more uncertain climate or will we need to spend to protect ourselves from this more adverse climate?

From Analysis to Action

The messages from current scientific assessments of climate change for environmental governance are very clear. The time to act is now as the costs of inaction are far greater than action and costs will go up if action is delayed. Every country must aim at a transition to low carbon economy. There is another more difficult message and that is that mitigation actions are not enough. A certain measure of global warming and resultant climate change is unavoidable. Early action on programmes and which focus on adaptation of land and water use and human settlements are as necessary.

The case for action from an economic perspective rests on an assessment of costs and benefits. According to the Stern Review, inaction would mean loss of consumption equivalent to a reduction of 5–10 per cent now and forever. As against this, the costs of mitigation actions to stay within the moderate increase scenario would cost the equivalent of 1 per cent of consumption now and forever. Clearly, this is a very attractive cost benefit ratio and would justify the strong response favoured by the Stern Review. A further argument for strong action is that it is needed as an insurance to prevent a catastrophic increase that could activate tipping points that would involve costs as high as the equivalent of 20 per cent of consumption, now and forever.

The uncertainties actually reinforce the case for action. The available evidence suggests a certain asymmetry and the downside risk is greater than the upside gain. If the outcome turns out to be worse than expected, there are huge costs. But, if it turns out to be less bad than there is not much gain and the loss of premature expenditure on mitigation is modest. This is particularly true for the early action which will focus on energy efficiency and forestry. The McKinsey Study[7] gives a cost curve identifies specific options for saving 27 giga tonnes of CO_2e costing Ä40/tCO_2e or less. Of this, 5 giga tonnes of saving can be secured at zero or negative cost. The curve also identifies a large potential in forestry (deforestation accounts for 20 per cent of CO_2 emissions). It also suggests that much of the potential exists in developing countries.

Action to manage climate change risks must be guided by three strategic imperatives: innovate, integrate and anticipate. The importance of innovation can be illustrated by the required increases in carbon productivity. Between now and 2050, carbon emissions have to halve according to most projections. But global GDP will rise by a factor of five or so. That means that carbon productivity must increase tenfold by 2050 ($740GDP/t$CO_2e$ to $7300GDP/t$CO_2e$ according the McKinsey estimate[8]). An increase of this order is comparable to the increase in labour productivity during the industrial revolution and will not come without a profound change in the way in which energy is produced, distributed and consumed. This will require innovations in technology and business models that are as yet unknown.

The case for integration can be seen in forestry. Deforestation accounts for 20 per cent of CO_2 emissions and actions to address this as one of the quick win routes to mitigation. But forests cannot be managed simply as carbon sinks. They fulfil many other ecosystem functions like biodiversity conservation, water and sol management, which have to be protected. This requires the integration of climate change mitigation and adaptation with other objectives. One must also recognize that in some cases, there is a synergy between actions to address climate change and other objectives. For instance, renewable energy and energy efficiency promotion may also help to address objectives about widening energy access and enhancing energy security. Forest conservation may deliver other benefits while sequestering carbon.

The importance of anticipation can be illustrated in the case of adaptation. This requires that climate risks which are not yet evident are taken into account in water, land use, agriculture and settlement planning. The investments being made in housing, urban infrastructure, water resource development, transport, energy and other infrastructure will last for many decades and will have to cope with some of the anticipated consequences of climate change on ambient temperatures, rainfall, sea levels, river water flows, adverse weather events well within their lifetime. Prudence requires that the risks of climate change are taken into account in their design at the very start rather than postponing adaptation to some expensive retro designing at a later stage.

The modalities of intervention to secure the mitigation efforts can take many forms. There is a general preference in economics for price type measures, say through carbon taxation because they can ensure Pareto optimality. But the quantitative impact of such price signals is uncertain as the response of corporations and households will be clouded even more by uncertainty. More than that, the real difficulty is the near impossibility of securing an international agreement that would ensure that all producers and consumers all over the world received similar price signals. The large differences that prevail in energy prices at present testify to this. The alternative is quota type measures in the form of carbon caps on major emitters or in the form of carbon emission standards for equipment. With such quotas, quantitative impact is ensured if compliance is good. But they may lead to departures from Pareto optimality unless they are combined with trade as in cap and trade systems with carbon permit trading In fact, both approaches may be needed. At the micro level, quotas are implementable for big point sources which account for large proportion of emissions. In certain other cases like road transport and electrical appliances, legally enforced efficiency standards may work. But, price/tax type measures are required to reach diffuse sources like household use and road transport. Nor can one rely only on quotas and price signals. Public funding is necessary to finance compensatory payments to ensure equity and as support for long gestation activities necessary because of centennial time frame.

Securing Global Co-operation

The greenhouse gas mantle surrounds the earth as a whole and the ecological cycles that affect the concentration of greenhouse gases in the atmosphere are global. Emissions by one country affect every other. Hence, actions to mitigate climate change have to be based on a global agreement which engages all the major emitters. The elements of an international agreement that is needed to address the issue are basically as follows:

- The acceptable limit for the likely temperature increase.
- The implied time profile of global carbon dioxide and other GHG emissions.
- The distribution of allowable global emissions between countries.
- The mechanisms that would allow flexibility in fulfilling commitments.

- The mechanisms that would support adaptation actions.
- The financial and technology transfer arrangements for compensating countries which take on more than their fair share of obligations.

The world is still far from such a comprehensive agreement. But the process started in the form of the Inter-governmental Panel on Climate Change (IPCC) which brings together thousands of scientists from all parts of the world and the UN Framework Convention on Climate Change (UNFCCC) which was opened for signature at the Rio Earth Summit in 1992. The UNFCCC is only a framework and in the mid-nineties, a Kyoto Protocol was negotiated and this established quantitative caps on GHG emissions by the industrial countries, which are basically the OECD plus Russia and Eastern Europe. But the biggest emitter, the USA never ratified the Protocol and has consistently refused to accept legally binding obligations on its emissions.

The first Phase of the Kyoto Protocol ends in 2012 and the countries of the world are, as of end 2010, still in the midst of a negotiating process that addresses several things – the next phase of the Kyoto Protocol, a Long Term Cooperation Agreement (LCA) that seeks to engage all countries and dilutes to some extent the differentiation between developed and developing countries that characterized the first phase of climate diplomacy, an agreement on Reducing Emissions from Deforestation and Degradation (REDD), an agreement on the funding of adaptation and agreements on finance and technology.

The world faces a carbon constraint on all future production and consumption if it is to avert the risk of uncontrolled climate change. The central issue for securing a global agreement is that of equity in the sharing of this scarce environmental space. The UNFCCC recognizes the principle of "common but differentiated responsibility", the historical culpability of industrial countries who account for the bulk of the increase in ambient GHGs since the industrial revolution and the primacy of development for developing countries. All of these are an attempt to translate the principle of fairness into the language of rights and obligations.

The degree of fairness in the sharing of environmental space can be assessed in terms of the share of carbon emission in relation to population. One concept under discussion in seminars if not in the negotiations is convergence to equal per capita emissions by a target date, say 2050, at a level consistent with containing emissions to ensure a 50 per cent chance of keeping the average global temperature increase to 2°C. India has already offered that it would ensure that its per capita emissions never exceed the average for the developed countries, so that any action by them to reduce their emissions very substantially would act as a brake on India's emission growth. Another concept that has received some attention lately is that of carbon budgeting where the available room for carbon emissions, given agreed goals on temperature increase risks, would be shared as a stock on the basis of population. A more contentious proposal would do this but would also take account of cumulative use from past emissions.

The real issue is not just the analytics of fairness. It is the adequacy of the process that we have to secure to achieve the cooperation that we need. The politics of cooperative action have been studied by social scientists and one such survey suggests the following conditions for success in securing cooperation[9]:

- *There is a reasonable presumption that cooperative management can improve the resource and that all users will benefit:* with open access resources like atmosphere, the history of unequal use challenges this.
- *The extent to which participants agree on the data and the dynamics underlying projections of the future state of the resource:* the IPCC process helps in the development of a consensus on the science but there is no process for securing a consensus on the economics or the ethics of climate change.
- *The ability of participants to take a long-term view and the willingness to accept short-term costs for resource recovery:* governments are moved by short-term political costs and benefits and by influential lobbies and these do not as yet give sufficient regard to the rights of future generations.
- *A perception by each participant that the others care for his interest, will reciprocate concessions and can be trusted to observe commitment:* this unfortunately has suffered because of failures of compliance and attempts to reopen agreed principles of fairness.

> "Environmental agreements are sovereignty bargains in which states surrender some autonomy of action in order to acquire some influence on the policies of other states which impinge on them."
>
> – Nitin Desai[10]

In the final analysis, what we need is a changed mind set. Every country has to recognize that global cooperation and agreement are necessary. No country should be satisfied with the absence of an agreement or a weak agreement simply because it leaves it off the hook. Such a policy is truly short-sighted. A strong and effective global agreement is in everyone's interest. The normal framework of reciprocal concessions that dominates international negotiations and a mindset that starts from the ethical premise that national interest trumps all other considerations cannot deliver an adequate global agreement on climate change. In the final analysis, the worst risks of climate change can only be avoided by the acceptance that we are in one life boat and that steering it to safety requires that those who are most able put in a greater effort and those who are less able do what they can to avoid destabilizing the boat.

Notes

1. Desai, Nitin (2005). 'Global Environmental Security' in *Emerging Global Order and Developing Countries,* University Press Limited (UPL), Dhaka.
2. Bjorn, Lomborg (2001). *The Skeptical Environmentalist*, Cambridge: Cambridge University Press, 2001, pp. 305–17.
3. Nordhaus, William (2007). *The Challenge of Global Warming: Economic Models and Environmental Policy*, Yale University, September 2007.
4. Stern, N. (2006). *The Stern Review on the Economics of Climate Change*, Cambridge: Cambridge University Press, 2006.
5. Nordhaus, William (2007). pp. 16-17.
6. Stern, Nicholas (2008). *Key Elements of a Global Deal on Climate Change*, London School of Economics & Political Science, London, UK, p. 3.
7. McKinsey Global Institute (2008). *The Carbon Productivity Challenge*, McKinsey & Co.
8. McKinsey Global Institute (2008). p. 7.
9. Sarah, Gillinson (2004). *Why Cooperate? A Multi-Disciplinary Study of Collective Action,* Overseas Development Institute, Working Paper 234, London: ODI, pp. 13-14.
10. Desai, Nitin (2005). Op. cit.

5

Environmental Governance and IPCC

N. Sundararaman

Effective and timely environmental governance, in the specific instance of global warming, was the driving idea behind the establishment of the IPCC in 1988 (environmental governance was not a term current in those days).

Climate Change and Global Warming

One word of caution here: global warming – the current concern – is a subset of climate change. It is confusing to use the two terms interchangeably.

Climate change is a generic term. Climate has changed and is changing naturally on many time scales (night and day, seasonal, inter-annual, decadal and longer, geologic) and space scales (micro, regional, global). The support to our climate is the solar energy input into the earth-ocean-atmosphere system. This input is modulated in nature by the rotation of the earth on its axis (night and day), orbital journey of the earth around the sun during the year and annual changes in the earth's surface properties – e.g. annual crop cycles, forests/deserts, wet/dry land areas (seasonal), differing responses of the solid earth and the oceans to the solar input and the interactions between the two (inter-annual and decadal and longer) and the orientation (precession) of the earth's axis in space (geologic).

The way in which the earth-ocean-atmosphere system reflects back or absorbs and uses the solar input is the primary determinant of climate as we know it. Climate is expressed by numbers such as temperature and precipitation averaged over some specified duration.

In addition to the geographical/astronomical factors mentioned above, over the last century or so, the changing composition of the atmosphere is having an effect on climate change. This specific phenomenon is global warming and it refers to the observed increase in global average surface temperature (and other meteorological variables) since we began observing temperatures directly (seriously since about mid-nineteenth century with instruments). This warming is now understood to be largely due to human-induced changes to the atmospheric composition.

Factual Information and Decision-Making

Climate is a global common. Hence, the current trend in climate – global warming – is a global issue. This has also been argued and accepted in the scientific literature for over a century. The warming has consequences to human health and welfare everywhere. Hence, any action – to contain it or other – has to be collectively taken by humanity as a whole.

Any decision is based on a set of known and reliable facts. The less reliable the facts, the less definitive the decision-making. Thus, the facts need to be assembled, scrutinized, tested for reliability and stated in clear terms. Facts so arrived are needed to be acknowledged as such by all stakeholders. Then decisions can be arrived at, by negotiations among the stakeholders or by other means, and more importantly, their implementation becomes widely and readily accepted. Where facts are unavailable or are inadequate or less reliable, the situation needs correction through research. The assembled facts themselves can point to further research requirements and priorities. Unless all the stakeholders agree on the facts, policy-building cannot use a common ground.

Bird's Eye View of the Relevant History

Before the IPCC, there had been a number of scientific assessments on acid rain in north-eastern North America, ozone depletion and global warming by national and international bodies and results of much research in published literature. An international meeting in Villach, Austria, in October 1985 (International Conference on the Assessment of the Role of Carbon Dioxide and of other Greenhouse Gases in Climate Variations and Associated Impacts), jointly organized by the United Nations Environment Programme (UNEP), the World

Meteorological Organization (WMO) and the then International Council of Scientific Unions (ICSU), now renamed the International Council for Science, on global warming pointed to the importance of including non-CO_2 greenhouse gases and the need for a more formalized international endeavour on the subject.

It was clear that any formal international mechanism would need to be connected to the WMO for atmospheric and oceanic sciences and to UNEP for biospheric and socio-economic impacts. It was also clear that a separation should be scrupulously maintained between fact-finding and policy-formulation. The former should be an objective, policy-neutral assembling of facts and assessment of their reliability. It was also important that all stakeholders, speaking through their governments, agree on the results of fact-finding. Then all governments could formulate their policy options starting from the same base.

The Tenth World Meteorological Congress in 1987 requested its Executive Council "in cooperation with the governing bodies of UNEP and ICSU ... to arrange appropriate mechanisms to undertake further development of scientific and other aspects of greenhouse gases". I had done the first straw-man draft of the resolution and passed it onto Gene Bierly, the then Director of the Atmospheric Sciences Division of the US National Science Foundation (and a delegate to the Congress). This, after debate and modification, became the Congress resolution.

The Council, in turn, "requested the Secretary-General (*of WMO*), in coordination with the Executive Director of UNEP, to explore and, after appropriate consultation with members of the Executive Council, to establish an ad hoc intergovernmental mechanism to carry out internationally coordinated scientific assessments of the magnitude, timing and potential impact of climate change. The mechanism developed should avail itself of balanced scientific expertise and provide for participation by governments and organizations".

The 14th session of UNEP Governing Council, a few days later, "urged the Executive Director to respond positively to the decision by the Tenth Congress of the World Meteorological Organization requesting its Secretary-General, in cooperation with the Executive Director of the United Nations Environment Programme to explore and, after appropriate consultation with Governments, to establish an ad hoc intergovernmental mechanism to carry out internationally coordinated scientific assessments of the magnitude, timing and potential impact of climate change".

The Institution

The WMO Secretary-General established the IPCC Secretariat, jointly with UNEP Executive Director, and designated the author the Secretary of the IPCC in May 1988. He also sent out invitations to governments for a meeting of the IPCC later that year. In the event, the IPCC met in its first session in Geneva in November 1988.

As has been mentioned, it was important to assess known science and impacts as well as to give some guidance – options – on what to do. The IPCC in its first session, established three Working Groups and a Bureau. The Working Groups were on science (Working Group I), on impacts (Working Group II) and on response strategies (Working Group III). It elected Prof. Bert Bolin of Sweden as its Chairman and Dr. A. Al Gain of Saudi Arabia as its Vice-Chairman. The IPCC also established, in its second session in Nairobi in June 1989, the Special Committee on the Participation of the Developing Countries. Working Group I was chaired by Sir John Houghton of the UK, Working Group II by Prof. Yuri Izrael of the-then USSR, Working Group III by Dr. Frederick M. Bernthal of the USA and the Special Committee by Ambassador Jean Ripert of France. Algeria, Australia, Brazil, Canada, India, Indonesia, Japan, Kenya, Malta, the Netherlands, Nigeria and Venezuela were also elected as vice-chairs/rapporteurs of various working groups and the Special Committee.

The report was completed in 1990 (this has come to be known since as the First Assessment Report).

Accepted Facts on the Science of Global Warming

At the outset, let it be understood that all the figures and statistics cited in this chapter are from the Report of the IPCC, 2007, hereinafter referred to as IPCC 2007. A Report of the IPCC is by definition the overall synthesis report based on the Summaries for Policymakers (SPM) and the underlying full reports of IPCC Working Groups I, II and III; it is approved section by section – almost line by line – by governments with the concurrence and in the presence of experts who participate in the writing of the Working Group reports and the SPMs.

Effective management of global warming depends on how well two dilemmas are handled: one is based on scientific evidence and the other on scientific evidence and geographically uneven socio-economic consequences. Both need to be well understood to help policy formulation by individual governments.

The first dilemma is founded in the cause of the observed increase in global mean surface temperature (0.74°C in the 1906–2005 period, IPCC 2007) – especially that over the past half a century (0.13°C per decade which is almost twice the rate over the century). The cause is well understood to be directly found in human activities associated with (a) the need to feed the world population and (b) the need to meet the aspirations of the world population for better living standards (Panel 1).

Panel 1

CURRENT GLOBAL WARMING CAUSED BY HUMAN ACTIVITIES FOR:

- PROVISION OF FOOD
- IMPROVING LIVING STANDARDS INCLUDING PROVISION OF ENERGY

The observed increase in temperature is due (see below) to the increasing atmospheric concentrations of the so-called greenhouse gases (GHGs): carbon dioxide (CO_2), methane (CH_4), nitrous oxide (N_2O) and a group of mostly human-made fluorinated gases or F-gases (e.g. PFCs, CFCs, HCFCs, SF_6) (Panel 2). Of these, methane and nitrous oxide result substantially from food production; carbon dioxide emissions are from activities related to power generation, transport, warming and cooling of buildings and industry and deforestation (Figure 1). More than half of the carbon dioxide is from fossil-fuel use (Figure 2; pie diagram [c] here shows sources of carbon dioxide).

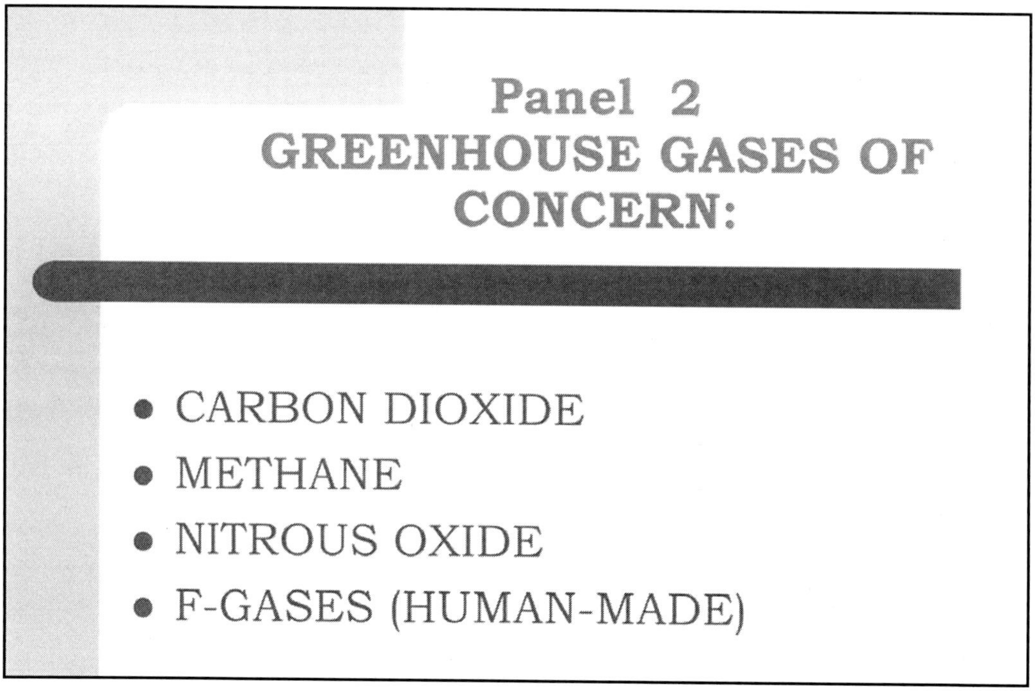

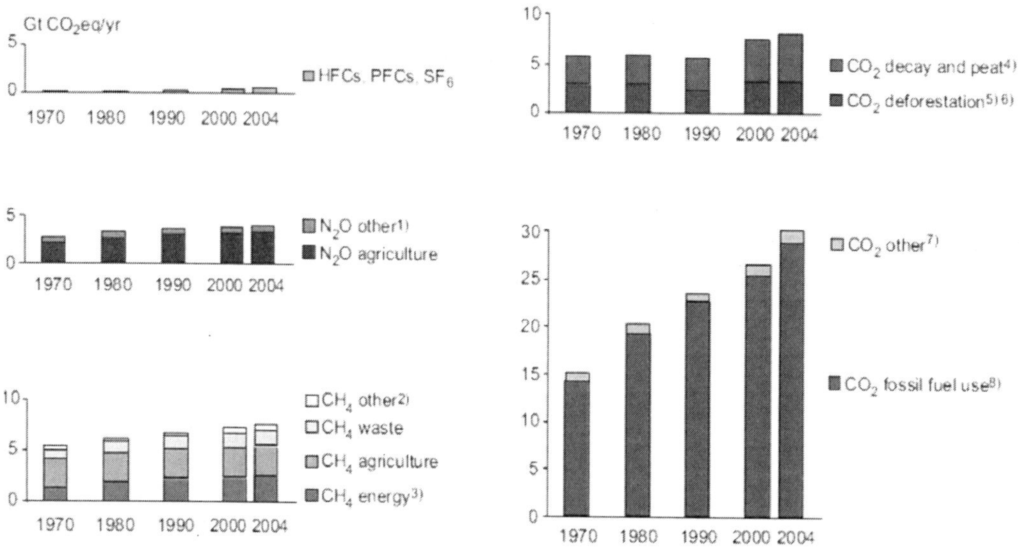

Fig. 1: GHG Emissions

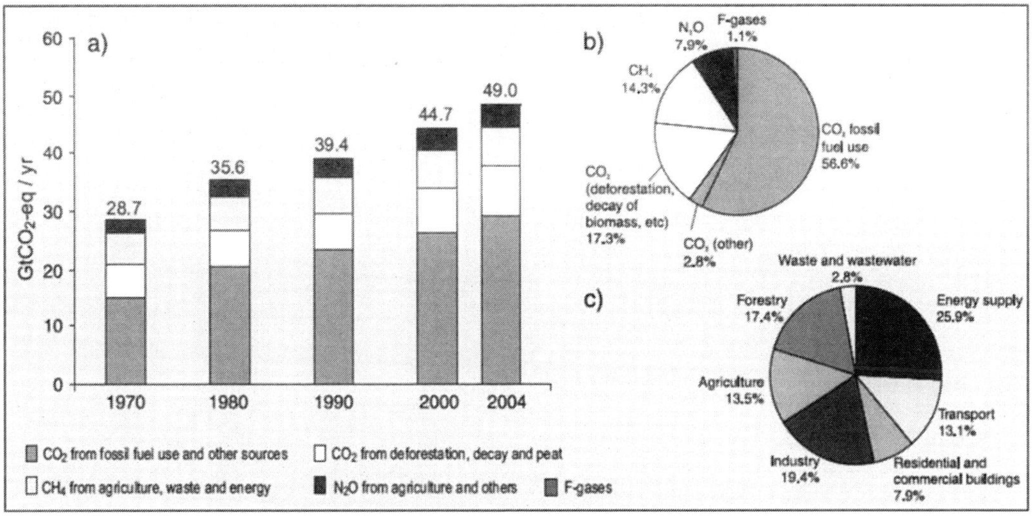

Fig. 2: Global Anthropogenic GHG Emissions

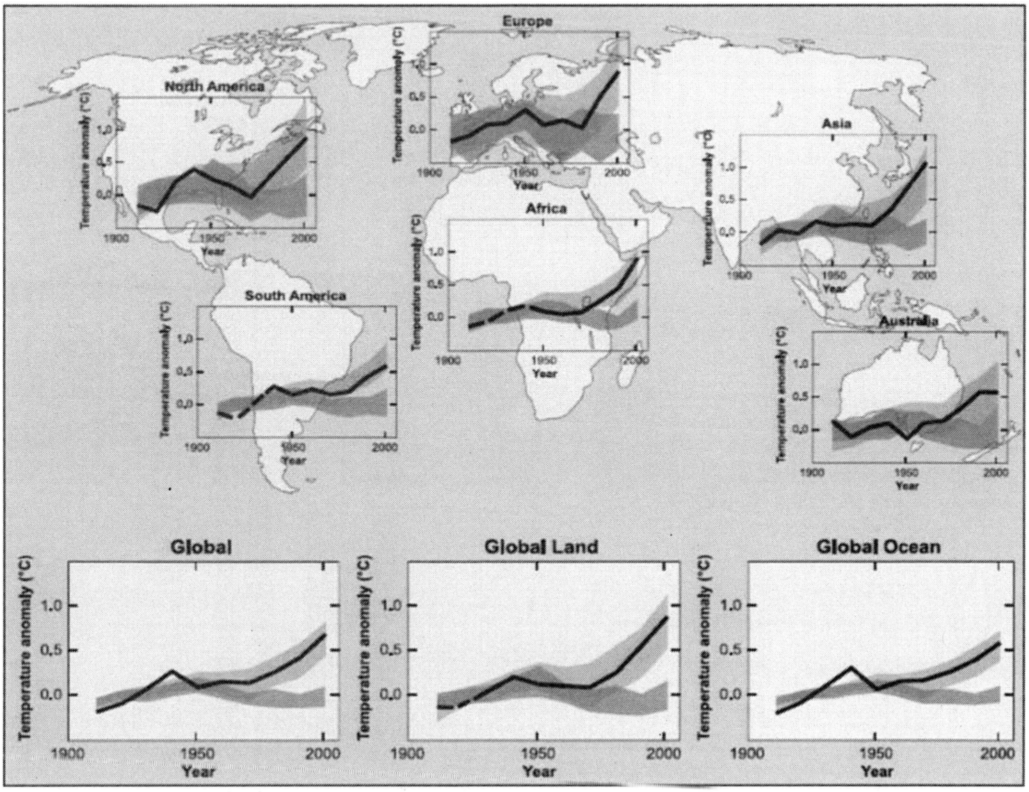

Fig. 3: Observed Temperature Increase

How has the Temperature Changed?

Figure 3 (black line) shows the observed temperatures in different parts of the globe. One can see a generally increasing trend (the exception is Australia in recent years).

How can We Conclude that Human Activities are Causing the Observed Temperature Trend?

It is done by calculating temperature change over the observational period and comparing the calculated value with that observed.

In order to arrive at calculated temperature changes, scientists calculate respective contributions to the so-called radiative forcing of the earth's atmosphere, from natural and anthropogenic causes. Among anthropogenic causes, as may be seen from Figure 4, carbon dioxide is the largest contributor followed by methane plus

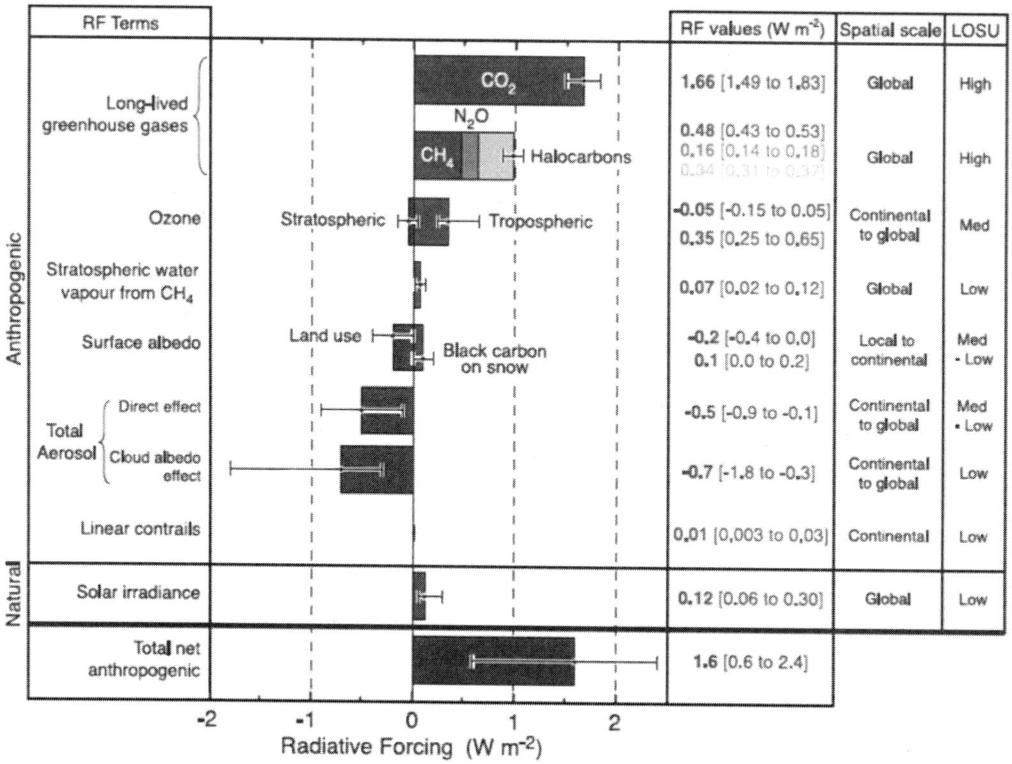

Fig. 4: Radiative Forcing Components

nitrous oxide and F-gases in that order. There are other contributors to radiative forcing, particularly the aerosols (suspended particles), whose contributions can be both positive and negative. The net anthropogenic contribution, however, is positive.

The calculations are done using elaborate and well-tested, coupled ocean-atmosphere numerical models. These models have been tested satisfactorily (e.g. Mt. St. Helens, Pinatubo eruptions).

When one takes into account natural forcing alone (solar radiation and naturally-generated aerosols from volcanoes and dust), the model-generated temperature trends do not agree well with those observed (blue coloured curve in Figure 3). When anthropogenic forcing (green house gases as well as anthropogenic aerosols – e.g. soot from forest fires, sulphate and nitrate particles generated from industrial activity) are included along with natural forcing (pink coloured curve in Figure 3), the agreement is far better. Major forcing comes from the green house gases, as has been pointed out (Figure 4). This is the central argument for the IPCC conclusion that human activity has caused the global warming.

Why should One be Concerned about this Global Warming?

No cause for worry would attach to the warming trend if there are no consequences for human living conditions. Such is not the case. Water security, food security, energy security, sea level rise and attendant coastal zones management, forest, mountain and glacier ecosystems, and the continued existence and health of natural ecosystems, entire small islands and biodiversity would all be affected in a warmer world, to varying degrees within nations and among nations.

Population is the major stress on water security. But, with temperature increase, the changing snowfall/rainfall patterns in space and time (seasonal flooding in some areas and seasonal droughts in the same and other areas), the character of precipitation (increasing intense shower activity dumping much water over a short duration affecting the potential to replenish underground aquifers), loss of soil moisture (due to temperature increase), runoff changes (earlier spring runoff in glacier and snow-fed rivers), inherent time lags and water-related health issues (infectious diseases, malaria) all would add to the difficulties in achieving water security.

Polewardly or upwardly migrating climate zones and warmer tropical and softened-soil boreal/austral regions would affect food security, forest and other ecosystems and biodiversity. The threat to biodiversity comes from habitat stress which arises from human populations and climate change. Diversion of land use for producing biofuels (as one of the alternative fuels in low or no carbon economies) would adversely impinge on food production.

With increased water temperatures, and changes occurring in ice cover, salinity, oxygen levels and ocean circulation, algal, plankton and fish abundance in high-latitude oceans would shift in range. Fish would migrate earlier in rivers.

Finding primary fuel sources in sufficient abundance in the face of rapidly growing demand worldwide to replace fossil fuels would require intense mid- to long-term planning, very large investments, and lifestyle changes; this would affect energy security in the short- to medium-term and competitiveness and related aspects of international trade regimes and employment opportunities.

These consequences and the associated uncertainties form the scientific part of the second dilemma.

What does the Future Hold?

One can make projections of future emissions of green house gases and anthropogenic aerosols (the so-called emissions scenarios) by making educated

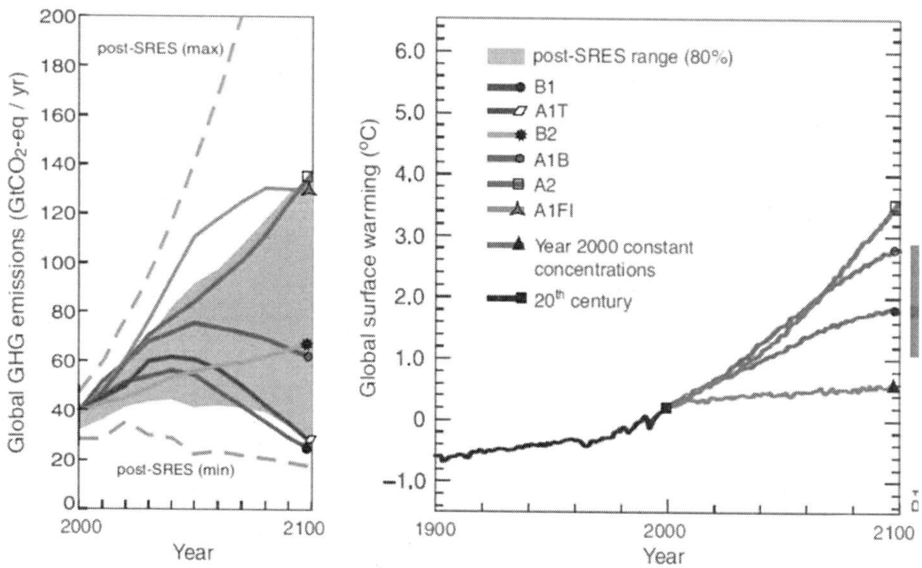

Fig. 5: Scenarios of Projected T

guesses for assumptions over a few decades on population trends, potential technology changes and geographically even or uneven economic development, etc. A large number of emissions scenarios has been developed. Several representative scenarios have been looked at (for temperature estimates). These are shown in Figure 5. The corresponding projections in temperature are also shown in the same figure. These projections give increases ranging from 1.6 to 4°C (IPCC 2007), that is, from about twice to about five times the current (and hence the current rate of) observed temperature increase.

Such changes in temperature would have key impacts:

Key Impacts as a Function of Increasing Global Average Temperature Change

(Impacts will vary by extent of adaptation, rate of temperatue change, and socio-economic pathway)

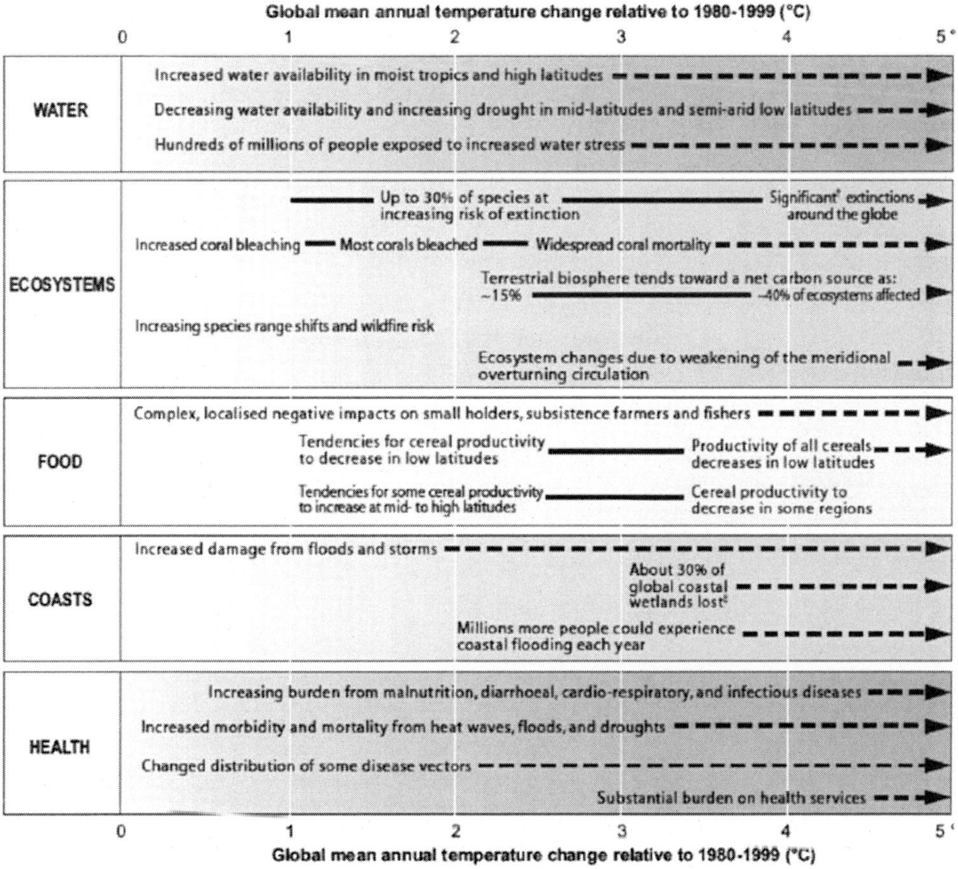

The vulnerability of different sovereign states to the various security and other stresses enumerated above would be different. The adaptability of the different geographical regions and their populations to the stresses – both intra-regional and inter-regional – would very much depend on the state of their socio-economic development and availability of adequate financial and other resources. Segments of already vulnerable populations would become more vulnerable due to their lack of adaptation resources. This is the socio-economic part of the second dilemma.

What can the World Community Do?

Formulation of national policies in this context would necessarily focus on national interests. However, agreements on international protocols within the United Nations Framework Convention on Climate Change (UNFCCC) would be much harder to achieve. The atmosphere responds through changed radiative forcing regardless of where a greenhouse gas molecule comes from, implying that collective action by all is imperative for lowering or eliminating global emissions. A middle ground will have to be found among precautionary principle on environmental grounds, polluter pays principle on equity grounds and demands for absolute certainty in the science on grounds of economic, employment and international commerce exigencies.

Non-Annex 1 countries (i.e. developing countries in the UNFCCC), while they have no obligations for mitigation under the Convention, could in their own national self-interest undertake actions such as improving efficiencies in the generation, delivery and end-use of power, switching to alternative and renewable primary energy sources, enhancing literacy and health care, better water and forest management and promotion of more beneficial agricultural practices; these are also the same kind of actions that considerations of sustainable development would demand. Annex 1 countries could in addition to these same measures reduce GHG emissions by the various tools available under the Kyoto Protocol. They could also actively seek to capture and store carbon.

The way forward globally lies in a combination of mitigation (by Annex 1 countries under the Convention) and adaptation actions and improvements in the knowledge base by all. Every one of these has economic implications. Estimates of costs of damages (adaptation costs) are far less robust than forecasting temperatures, ten, fifty, hundred years from now or calculating the cost of a new non-fossil fuel power plant or transportation system.

The time lags in the chain from emissions to secular temperature changes to their socio-economic impacts to adequate and timely response actions, all would require clearer definition and understanding. Such understanding needs to go far beyond specialist and government policy makers, executive and legislative branches, academic entities such as schools and universities and the media, and should extend to the public at large in a serious and sustained manner. It appears to me, in this context, that widespread dissemination of information to the women populations of the world can play a decisive role. But whatever the target group, we should remember "to tell the truth, the whole truth and nothing but the truth" refraining from scoring brownie points to buttress a pet policy initiative.

IPCC Role in Environmental Governance

The 1990 IPCC report played a decisive role in the negotiations leading to the signing of the United Nations Framework Convention on Climate Change. The 1996 report contributed decisively to the formulation and signing of the Kyoto Protocol. This was because of the acceptance by the governments of the world of the IPCC findings and conclusions. This acceptance came due to the governments sitting in plenary sessions, along with the experts writing the reports, and approving the reports. This is a necessary step for the governments – stakeholders – to "own" the IPCC conclusions. The IPCC procedures that were developed since 1990 – the selection of experts from lists submitted by governments with c.vs to draft the Working Group reports and their SPMs, the selection of reviewers in a similar fashion, the response to the reviews, the submission at every stage (chapter stage, SPM stage, Synthesis Report stage) of drafts for review and finally, the approval of all drafted reports by governments – this process is vital in building consensus and helping all governments with the same database to make decisions and implement them.

As long as the IPCC maintains its objectivity and strictly avoids all "policy taint", it can continue to contribute positively to global warming governance.

The 2001 IPCC report established that GHGs and aerosols resulting from human activities are causing the observed global warming. The 2007 report reaffirmed this conclusion and adduced evidence of observed changes in the natural ecosystems and socio-economic systems.

6

Judicialization of Environmental Governance in India and its Implications

Geetanjoy Sahu

Over the past three decades, the Indian Supreme Court has not only played a significant role in environmental protection, it has also secured a firm foothold in the environmental governance arena. The environmental judgements of the Court,[1] in many cases, have significant impacts on the overall environmental governance process in India. Obviously, a certain amount of judicialization is not exclusive to environmental issues, since, for a host of different reasons, judicial intervention has become decisive in different aspects of governance in India. In fact, its role has become crucial and significant in every sphere of governance, which includes prisoners' rights, child labour, inmates of various asylums, ensuring the rights of the poor to education, shelter and other essential amenities, sexual harassment of women at the workplace, preventing corruption in public offices, accountability of public servants, and utilization of public funds for development activities.[2] Nevertheless, judicialization of environmental governance appears to have assumed greater proportions than in other arenas of governance and, therefore, it could prove interesting to study the dynamics of this phenomenon and, more specifically, its implications for environmental governance in India. In this chapter, I discuss the increasing judicialization of environmental governance in India. In doing so, I begin by defining judicialization of environmental governance and then highlight different forms of judicialization of environmental governance through some illustrative environmental judgements of Indian Supreme Court and finally analyse its implications for environmental governance in India.

Defining Judicialization of Environmental Governance

The role of the Indian Supreme Court in resolving environmental disputes has increasingly come to be recognized as a feature of environmental governance in India. Ever since its constitution, Indian Supreme Court is an important political actor, in the sense that it is contributing to define some public policies.[3] This fact contradicts the traditional idea of judges making decisions only for particular cases. From a political science perspective, this has led to an increasing scholarly interest on the role of Indian Supreme Court in governance in general and in environmental governance in particular, departing from a traditional environmental governance process with legislature and executive playing the major role. In environmental governance, studying the role of Indian Supreme Court has become a feature of political analysis since 1980s, in part linked to the increasing role of Indian Supreme Court in the post-emergency period, which has not only included judicial reform, but also in relation to the concern with principle of social justice and fundamental rights construction as part of the Supreme Court initiative to protect from the democratic majoritarianism.[4]

While conventionally, the executive and the legislature play the major role in the governance process, the Indian experience, particularly in the context of environmental issues, is that the Court has begun to play a significant role in environmental governance. Besides the assigned role of interpretation and adjudication[5] of environmental law, the Court has laid down new principles to protect the environment, reinterpreted environmental laws, created new institutions and structures, and conferred additional powers on the existing ones through a series of illuminating directions and judgements. The Court's directions on environmental issues involve not just general questions of law – as is usually expected from the Court of the land – but also the technical details of many environmental cases. Indeed, some critics of the Court describe it as the 'Lords of Green Bench' or 'Garbage Supervisor'.[6] International legal experts have recognized unequivocally the Indian Courts of law as pioneer, both in terms of laying down new principles of law, and also in the application of innovative methods in the environmental justice delivery system.[7] Although it is not unusual for Courts in the Western democracies to play an active role in the protection of the environment, the way the Indian Court has been engaged since the 1970s in interpreting and introducing innovative principles in the environmental jurisprudence is unique. Not a single week passes without an environmental judgement either by the Supreme Court or

High Courts somewhere in the country directing the implementing agency to protect and improve the environment.

The increasing "judicialization of environmental governance" refers to the fact that certain environmental matters that were traditionally dealt through legislation and administrative actions, and that were considered belonging to legislature and executive branch, begin to be decided increasingly more so by judges, or at least become far more dependent on judicial decisions, meaning that, in turn, many environmental groups/NGOs begin to formulate their demands in legal and judicial terms.[8] The judicialization of environmental governance suggests first a greater presence of judicial processes and Court rulings in resolving conflicts around environmental issues. Second, it is a manifestation that conflicts over ownership of natural resources is increasingly resolved in the Court. Third, it is the consequence of the process by which environmental groups increasingly see advantage in invoking legal strategies and the arbitration of judges to advance certain environmental interests. The mobilization of legal strategies by environmental groups to some extent empowers judges in environmental decision-making process. The judicialization of environmental governance, thus, indicates a greater involvement by judges in environmental law-making and natural resource management. Its increasing presence also suggests that state agencies to implement the environmental law have failed to discharge their constitutional duties, and in some cases, may even be violating the laws which increase environmental degradation.

Forms of Judicialization of Environmental Governance

This being the case, India has, over the past three decades, witnessed some important forms of judicialization of environmental governance, but perhaps the most significant have been the following: (a) liberalization of judicial process to resolve disputes around environmental issues; (b) implementation of environmental laws and judgements through Court appointed committees; and (c) evolution of environmental laws and policies. I shall now briefly describe each of these elements of judicialization of environmental governance in India.

Liberalization of Judicial Process in Resolving Environmental Litigation

The increasing judicialization of environmental governance is being seen as part of the pro-active role of the Supreme Court in the form of continual creation of successive strategies to uphold rule of law, enforce fundamental rights of the citizens, and constitutional propriety aimed at the protection and improvement of the environment. Unlike other litigations, the frequency and different types of orders passed periodically by the Supreme Court in environmental litigation, and its continuous engagement with environmental issues through innovative methods, has expanded the sphere of judicial decision making on environmental issues. These innovative methods, for instance, include entertaining petitions on behalf of the affected party and inanimate objects, taking *suo moto* action against the polluter, expanding the sphere of litigation, expanding the meaning of existing Constitutional provisions, making spot visits to assess the environmental problem at the ground level, appointing *amicus curiae* to speak on behalf of the environment, and encouraging petitioners and lawyers to draw the attention of the Court about environmental problems through cash award. The following section gives a brief summary of the key innovations in each category and highlights how these innovative methods have expanded the judicial process in resolving environmental litigation.

The most important procedural innovation for environmental governance has been the relaxation of traditional process of standing in the Court and introducing the concept of Public Interest Litigation (PIL).[9] Until the early 1970s, litigation in India was in its rudimentary form because it was seen as a pursuit for the vindication of private vested interests. During this period, initiation and continuance of litigation was the prerogative only for the individual aggrieved party. A complete change in the judicial process took place in the 1980s, with efforts made by Justice P.N. Bhagwati and Justice V.R. Krishna Iyer. The ambit and extent of PIL was expanded in the 1980s, from the initial prisoners' rights concerns, to others like bonded labour, child labour, inmates of various asylums, ensuring the rights of the poor to education, shelter and other essential amenities, sexual harassment of women at the workplace, preventing corruption in public offices, accountability of public servants, and utilization of public funds for development activities.

The Court's approach to entertain PIL for environmental protection, however, is significant in many ways. First, prior to the emergence of the concept of PIL, Criminal Law provisions as contained in the Indian Penal Code, Civil Law remedies under the law of Torts and provisions of the Criminal Procedure Code existed to provide remedies for public nuisance cases, including air, water and noise pollution. However, due to the lack of people's awareness about environmental problems and limited knowledge of environmental laws, there were problems in drawing the attention of the Court towards environmental problems. Again, there was no provision in the environmental legal framework for allowing the third party to seek the help of the Court, if the party was not directly affected by environmental problems.[10] Hence, the biggest hurdle in the path of litigation for environmental justice had been the traditional concept of *locus standi*. Earlier, when the third party approached the appellate Court for seeking relief against an injury they did not incur directly, the action was not maintainable, as the appellate Court focused its attention on the identity of the petitioner rather than the subject of petition.[11] But, now the Court's approach has changed and it has been ruled that any member of the public having sufficient interest, may be allowed to initiate the legal process in order to assert diffused and meta-individual rights. Generally, in environmental litigation, the parties affected by pollution are a large, diffused and unidentified mass of people. Therefore, the question arises as to who ought to bring such cases to the Court's notice where no personal injury, in particular, has been noticed. In such situations, the Court has emphasized that any member of the public having sufficient interest may be allowed to initiate the legal process in order to assert diffused and meta-individual rights in environmental problems.[12]

A number of cases on environmental issues have been initiated through PIL. Beginning with the Dehradun lime stone quarrying case[13] in 1983, followed by the Ganga Water Pollution case, Delhi Vehicular Pollution case, Oleum Gas Leak case, Tehri Dam case, Narmada Dam case, Coastal Management case, industrial pollution in Patancheru, and T.N. Godavarman case, all of them came to the Court's attention through PIL. These cases have been initiated by Non-Governmental Organizations (NGOs), and environmental activists on behalf of other individuals and groups or the public at-large, to ensure the implementation of statutory acts and constitutional provisions aimed at the protection of the environment and enforcement of fundamental rights. It has been found from Indian Supreme Court Case reports that out of 104 environmental cases[14] from 1980–2000 in the Supreme Court of India, 54 were filed by individuals who were not directly the affected parties, and 28 were filed by NGOs on behalf of the affected parties. This suggests that the instrument of PIL has provided an opportunity to the third party to represent on behalf of the affected people and the environment itself.

The Court has also shown a willingness to alter the rules of the game wherever necessary to entertain environmental cases. For example, where there are a wide variety of offenders, the Court has chosen to treat a particular case as a representative action and issued orders binding on the entire class. In one case, concerning massive pollution of the river Ganga, the Court has published notices in the newspaper drawing the litigation to the attention of all concerned industries and municipal authorities inviting them to make an appearance.[15] In this case, the petition was filed against the Kanpur tanneries and Kanpur Municipal Council to stop polluting the river Ganga. The Court, however, asked all the industrialists and the Municipal Corporations and the town Municipal Councils having jurisdiction over the areas through which the river flows in India, to appear before the Court. Similarly, in 1995, T.N. Godavarman Thirumulpad filed a writ petition with the Supreme Court of India to protect the Nilgiris forest land from deforestation by illegal timber operations.[16] The Court expanded the Godavarman case from a matter of ceasing illegal operations in one forest into a reformation of the entire country's forest policy.

The positive impact of the Court's approach to environmental litigations through third party representation has been such that it has dramatically transformed the form and substance of environmental governance in India. Recourse to judicial proceedings is a costly exercise for those who suffer substantial injuries from environmental pollution. Even if the aggrieved party takes recourse to judicial proceedings, the Court may only settle disputes between the appellant party and the polluter, and the rights of other aggrieved persons remain unsettled. Judicial remedies for environmental maladies would have effective results only if the remedies benefit those who are not parties to the litigation. By entertaining petitions on behalf of the poor and disadvantaged sections of the society, from different NGOs and public-spirited people, the Court has attempted to ensure the rights of people in terms of deciding compenzation and providing other remedies to the affected people. Allowing a third party to bring environmental problems to the Court's notice has also an important bearing on inanimate objects, which cannot represent themselves in the litigation process. The voice of the inanimate objects has been represented by concerned NGOs and environmental activists through the instrument of PIL. The polluter has been asked to pay for the damage done to the natural objects and restore the environment to its natural state.[17]

The intervention of the Court in resolving environmental litigation has also expanded the meaning and ambit of fundamental Right to Life in the Indian

Constitution. The six fundamental rights of Indian citizens are specified in Articles 14-32 of the Indian Constitution, such as right to equality (Articles 14-18), right to freedom (Articles 19-22), right against exploitation (Articles 23-24), right to freedom of religion (Articles 25-28), cultural and educational rights (Articles 29-31) and right to Constitutional remedies (Article 32). There are four Constitutional provisions that are directly relevant to protect the fundamental rights of citizens. Under Article 13, the Court is granted power to judicially review legislation, so that the laws inconsistent with the fundamental rights may be held void. In addition, Article 32 confers on every citizen the Court's original jurisdiction for the enforcement of his or her fundamental rights. Through this provision, individuals can approach the Court to seek the protection of their fundamental rights. Article 32 and Article 226 of the Indian Constitution grant wide remedial powers to the Supreme Court and High Courts of each Indian State in Constitutional cases. Under Article 136, the Supreme Court has discretionary power to grant special leave to appeal from any judicial order, judgement, or decree in the land, thereby providing another route for judicial review.

The earliest understanding of these provisions had been a narrow procedural one where fundamental rights and other Constitutional provisions were interpreted as procedure established by law.[18] Moreover, inconvenient Court decisions on the Constitutionality of state action were simply overturned by amending the Constitution until the 'basic structure' of the Constitution was declared unalterable.[19] In 1978, the Court breathed substantive life into Article 21 by subjecting state action interfering with life or liberty to a test of reasonableness; requiring not only that the procedures be authorised by law, but that they are 'right, just and fair'.[20]

An account of the interpretation of right to healthy environment as part of fundamental right to life would illustrate the efforts of the Court to expand the scope of existing fundamental right to life. For instance, in the Ratlam Municipal case, the Court has upheld that public nuisance is a challenge to the social justice component of the rule of law. Decency and dignity are non-negotiable facets of human rights and are a first charge on local self-governing bodies.[21] Likewise, in the Dehradun Lime Stone Quarrying case, the Court has made it clear that economic growth cannot be achieved at the cost of environmental destruction and the peoples' right to healthy environment. In the Doon Valley case, concerning mining environment, the Court has interpreted Article 21 to include the right to live in a healthy environment with minimum disturbance of ecological balance and without avoidable hazard to them and to their cattle, house and agricultural land and undue affection of air, water and environment.[22] This aspect has been further emphasized in the Ganga water pollution case by Justice Venkataramiah, who has extended the right to life to include the right to defend the human environment for the present and future generations.[23] In M.C. Mehta vs Union of India,[24] the Court has accepted that environmental pollution and industrial hazards are not only potential civil torts, but also a violation of the right to health. In this way, through the interpretation of Article 21, the Court has sought to convert formal guarantees into positive human rights.

The above Court's interpretations in expanding the meaning of right to life have brought new dimensions, not only in environmental governance, but also in the discourse on human rights in India. The credit for the creation of a host of environmental rights and enforcing them as fundamental rights goes to the Supreme Court of India. This is a significant contribution for environmental governance in India, if one learns from experiences elsewhere. The legal system may guarantee a Constitutional right to environment and statutes may accord the right to participate in environmental protection for citizens. However, when no methods for their participation are made available, then they are as good as non-existent. This is the experience in Spain, Portugal, Brazil and Ecuador.[25] Importantly, Indian experience contrasts very significantly from these countries. There is no direct articulation of the right to environment anywhere in the Constitution or, for that matter, in any of the laws concerning environmental management in India. But this has been seized from below, by environmental groups, motivating the Court to find and construct environmental rights from the available legal material. What the Court has achieved since 1980, is to view the fundamental right to life to include different strands of environmental rights that are at once individual and collective in character.

Another important innovation of the Court in resolving environmental disputes has been found in judges' personal interest to have first-hand information through spot visits to understand the nature of the environmental problem and the issues revolving around it. In the Ratlam Municipal vs Vardhichand case,[26] before arriving at a decision, Justice V.R. Krishna Iyer[27] visited the Ratlam town and assessed the problem and then directed the Ratlam Municipality to take appropriate measures to construct a proper drainage system in the city. Similarly, in the Doon Valley case, Justice P.N. Bhagwati[28] visited the area and found that the environmental litigation involved certain complex issues, including the rights of the workers, traders and fragile ecology of the area. He then appointed an independent committee to assess the problem and based on the recommendation of the committee, the Court directed the state government of Uttar Pradesh to close down certain mining units, which were illegally operating, and allowed other mining units to operate only with certain conditions to ensure the protection of environment. In the Narmada Dam case, the visit of Justice S.P. Bharucha to the dam site also made a difference in his interpretation of the case.[29] In his dissent judgement, Justice S.P. Bharucha expressed dissatisfaction with the rehabilitation process and the way environmental clearance was given to construct the dam in the river valley.[30] The spot visits of judges enabled them to assess the environmental problem on the ground and hence, the decisions given by these judges have made a difference in the outcome of the case. However, most of the judges share the view that it is neither feasible nor possible for them to make spot visits to arrive at a decision always. Therefore, the innovative method to arrive at a decision through spot visits has become a part of individual interest of judges, rather than a standard practice in the decision-making process.

It is important to note that these judicial innovations have become part of the larger Indian environmental governance process ever since the Court has started intervening in the affairs of the executive in the post-emergency period.[31] The innovative methods initiated in resolving environmental litigation have expanded the judicial process in dealing with different aspects of environmental problems and have contributed immensely to the evolution of environmental jurisprudence principles in India.

Implementation of Environmental Laws and Policies

At the theoretical level, the advocates of the theory of separation of power between legislature, executive and judiciary argue that the Court should not have any role in the implementation of its own decisions. Its function is confined only to the adjudication of laws and policies. The implementation of its judgements solely depends upon the implementing agencies of the state. The Court's intervention in the implementation of its judgements would violate the principle of separation of power and go against the spirit of democracy. The question then arises as to how the orders made by the Court in environmental litigation can be enforced. The orders made by the Court are obviously not self-executing. They have to be enforced through state agencies, and if the state agencies are not enthusiastic in enforcing the Court orders and do not actively cooperate in that task, the object and purpose of the environmental litigation would remain unfulfilled. The consequence of the failure of the State machinery to secure enforcement of Court orders in environmental litigation would not only be to deny effective justice to the affected people of pollution on whose behalf the litigation is brought, but it would also have a demoralizing effect and people would lose faith in the capacity of environmental litigation to deliver environmental justice. The success or failure of environmental litigation would necessarily depend to the extent to which it is able to provide actual relief to the pollution affected people and restore the damage done to environment at the grassroots level. If the Court orders passed in environmental litigation are to remain merely paper documents, then the innovative method of allowing PILs for resolving environmental problems by the Supreme Court would be robbed of all its meaning and purpose. It is, therefore, absolutely essential to the success of the PIL that a methodology should be found for securing enforcement of Court orders in environmental litigation.[32] It is in this situation that the Court has introduced an important innovative method to ensure the implementation of its directions through Court-Appointed Monitoring Committee.

The case on point is the one concerning forest conservation in the T.N. Godavarman vs Union of India. It started in 1996 as a case seeking directions from the apex Court for stopping the felling of trees in Nilgiris forest and to regulate indiscriminate cutting of timbers in the Nilgiris Forest. The case is yet to be finally decided. Instead, a series of orders passed by the Supreme Court that concern protecting forest, wildlife, preserving biodiversity, national parks, evicting encroachers including tribal, is still in different stages of implementation.[33] The Court adopted a novel method in making the administration work. It made the government create a think tank like Central Empowered Committee, make preparations for implementation of directions and report at every stage the progress made in achieving the objective. It was indeed an effort by the Court to assist, partner and guide the administration in protecting the forest across the country and present a model for the rest of the county to emulate. In this process of implementation and in its enthusiasm to present such a model, however, the Court has got itself mired in the complexities of a problem that was at once managed by the bureaucracy, local institutions and through traditional form of forest management.[34]

Similarly, the role of Indian Supreme Court in implementing its directions in the Dahanu Thermal Power Plant case through monitoring committee is worth mentioning. Dahanu is situated 120 km north of Mumbai, in the Thane district of Maharashtra, and is one of the last green belts along the country's rapidly industrialising western coast. In 1989, the State Government of Maharashtra approved a proposal of the Bombay Suburban Electricity Supply Company (BSESC), to set up a coal-based thermal power plant in the Dahanu Taluka[35] of Thane District. On 29 March 1989, two local environmental activists: Nergis Irani and Kityam Rustom (Members of the Dahanu Taluka Environment Protection Group) along with Bombay Environmental Action Group filed writ petitions first in the Bombay High Court and then in the Supreme Court challenging the decision of the Central Government to build the power plant.[36] They lost the case, with the Court citing the necessity of energy to power the city of Mumbai as strong grounds to sanction the project. To allay petitioners' apprehensions of environmental damage, the Court directed that the condition requiring the installation of a Flue Gas Desulphurization (FGD)[37] plant should not be relaxed without a full consideration of the consequences.

It is also important to mention that Dahanu was 'notified', or classified, under the Indian Coastal Regulation Zone (CRZ) by the MoEF on 19 February 1991.[38] The CRZ bans any new construction and development activities within 500 metres of the high tide line. Dahanu was also declared 'eco-fragile' by a government notification of 21 June 1991[39] (Notification under the Environment Protection Act, 1986, restricts the development of industries, mining operations and other development in the region). Even though Dahanu had been declared an ecologically fragile area, political and industrial interests continued to bring forward development projects in Dahanu Taluka, sidelining both the eco-fragile notification and the CRZ notification of the Government of India. This led environmentalist Bittu Sehgal to file a writ petition in the Supreme Court in 1994, asking the Court to implement the notifications in Dahanu Taluka.[40] The Supreme Court then appointed the National Environmental Engineering Research Institute (NEERI) to investigate the issues set forth in the petition. Based on the NEERI report, the Supreme Court upheld the Dahanu Notification prohibiting any change of land-use in the region and ordered that a committee of experts be formed under Section 3 of the Environmental Protection Act of 1986 to ensure implementation of the environmental laws protecting Dahanu's eco-fragility. The MoEF appointed the

Dahanu Taluka Environmental Protection Authority in 1996 under the chairmanship of retired Mumbai High Court judge, Justice C.S. Dharmadhikari and supported by a team of eleven expert members. The Authority is empowered to ensure the implementation of Court directions as well as the eco-fragile notification of 1991. When contacted to know about the implementation status of the Court orders, the Dahanu Taluka Environmental Protection Authority Chairperson, Justice C.S. Dharmadhikari confirmed that the FGD has been installed and the Dahanu power plant is operating as per the orders of the Indian Supreme Court.[41]

It is also observed that the Dahanu Taluka Environmental Protection Authority has been quite open to ideas and viewpoints of different stakeholders in dealing with various environmental issues. The Dahanu Taluka Environmental Protection Authority has conducted regular meetings and public hearings giving sufficient notice to each and every party to the dispute. In this way, the local communities from different sections have found their voice with regard to any development issues in Dahanu through their participation in the DTEPA meeting and public hearing. The Authority has responded to all public appeals within a stipulated time frame. There is no discrimination in this regard. Thus, the work of the Dahanu Taluka Environment Protection Authority was of value, not necessarily because of its instrumental success in protecting Dahanu but also because its multi-disciplinary structure and highly independent mode of operation created a new deliberative space, which was open to the arguments of the local community. Rather than being vilified as interfering in the affairs of the executive, the DTEPA has shown how useful a multi-disciplinary environmental monitoring committee can be to implement Court directions on environmental issues and to empower local people.[42]

Like the T.N. Godavarman and Dahanu Thermal Power Plant cases, the Indian Supreme Court has also appointed monitoring committees in other cases to ensure the implementation of Court directions, such as Loss of Ecology Authority in the Vellore Leather Industrial Pollution Case, Supreme Court Monitoring Committee on Hazardous Pollution Cases, and Bhurelal Committee in the Delhi Vehicular Pollution Case. Few would argue today that court should not intervene in the implementation process. Instead, today's debates focus on how legitimate is court's intervention? Why today's court is engaged in implementing its own directions to such an extent is also a heated debate. Yet generally, there is an agreement that court is not singularly responsible for the alleged intervention in thc implementation process. Other governmental institutions and society in general, share responsibility for the marked increase in judicial intervention in the implementation of its directions.

Evolution of Environmental Laws and Policies

The Court of India, while administering environmental justice, has evolved certain principles and doctrines within and, at times, outside the framework of the existing environmental law. Environmental principles, such as the polluter pays principle,[43] precautionary principle[44] and public trust doctrine[45] have been adopted by the Court in its concern to protect the environment from further degradation and improve the same. It is important to note that these principles have been developed in various international agreements and conferences to control and prevent further environmental degradation.

Drawing inference from international environmental principles, the Court of India has applied various principles to resolve domestic environmental problems. For example, the Polluter Pays Principle was invoked by the Court of India in the Indian Council for Enviro-Legal Action vs Union of India. Giving the judgement, the judges held that 'we are of the opinion that any principle evolved in this behalf should be simple, practical and suited to the conditions obtaining in this country. Once the activity carried on is hazardous or inherently dangerous, the polluter carrying on such activity is liable to make good the loss caused to any other affected party by the polluter's activity, irrespective of the fact whether the polluter took reasonable care while carrying on his activity.'[46] In this case, the Court has stated that the 'Polluter Pays Principle' means that the absolute liability for harm to the environment extends not only to compensate the victims of the pollution, but also the cost of restoring the environmental degradation. Subsequently, the 'Polluter Pays Principle', as interpreted by the Court, has been recognized as a fundamental objective of government's environmental policy to prevent and control pollution.[47]

The precautionary principle, as applied by the Court in the Vellore Citizens' Welfare Forum vs Union of India,[48] imposes an obligation on every developer, industry and governmental agency to anticipate, prevent and attack the causes of environmental degradation. The Court also held that if there are threats of serious and irreversible damage, then any lack of scientific certainty should not be used as a reason for postponing measures to prevent environmental degradation. Finally, the Court emphasized that the onus of proof shall be on the actors or the industrialists to show that their action is environmentally benign. The precautionary principle had also been emphasized in cases such as M.C. Mehta vs Union of India and A.P. Pollution Control Board vs M.V. Nayudu case.[49]

To further justify, and perhaps extract, the state initiative to conserve natural resources, the Court also enunciated the doctrine of 'public trust,' thereby obligating conservation by the state. The 'public trust' doctrine has been referred to by the Court in M.C. Mehta vs Kamal Nath case.[50] The doctrine extends to natural resources, such as rivers, forests, sea shores, air, etc., for the purpose of protecting the ecosystem. The State holds the natural resources as a trustee and cannot commit breach of trust. In the above case, the State's order for grant of a lease to a motel located on the bank of the river Beas, which resulted in the Motel interfering with the natural flow of the water, has been quashed and the public company which received the lease has been directed to compensate the cost of restitution of environment and ecology in the area.

Implications of Judicialization of Environmental Governance

The dominant understanding of judicial functioning in the common law world is that it can be rendered compatible with liberal democratic principles only if adjudication remains distinct from legislation. Indeed, ever since Montesquieu clearly formulated for the first time the theory of separation of powers in 1748, it has been argued that for the smooth functioning of democracy, judicial power needs to be separated from the legislative and the executive. The impossibility of having a rigid separation of powers has, however, been illustrated in the Constitution of the UK, America and India.[51] For example, under the American Constitution, the President has legislative powers in his right to send messages to Congress and the right to veto, while Congress has the judicial power of trying impeachments and the Senate participates in the executive power of making treaty and appointments. Similarly, in the UK, the emergence of the Cabinet system of government presents a standing refutation to the doctrine of separation of powers because Great Britain has a very closely connected legislature and executive, with further links to the Court.

The framers of the Indian Constitution have not incorporated a strict doctrine of separation of powers, but have rather envisaged a system of checks and balances.

However, the Indian Supreme Court, in the Delhi Laws Act case[52] has noticed that the Indian Constitution does not vest the legislative and judicial powers in the Legislature and the Court in clear terms. The framers, in effect, have imported the essence of the modern doctrine of separation of powers, applying the doctrines of Constitutional limitation and trust. Therefore, none of the organs of government such as, legislature, executive and the Court under the Constitution can usurp the function or powers which are assigned to another organ by the Constitution.

Importantly, the most visible aspect of the doctrine of separation of powers in India has been reflected in the Indira Gandhi vs Rajnarain case in 1975. It was held by the Court that 'though the doctrine of rigid separation of powers in the American sense does not obtain in India, the principles of checks and balances, underlying that doctrine constitutes a part of the basic structure of the Constitution or one of its basic features which cannot be impaired even by amending the Constitution; if any such amendment of the Constitution is made, the Court would strike it down as unconstitutional and invalid.'[53] The Court has elevated this feature of separation of powers to the basic inviolable structure of the Constitution in the landmark judgement of the Court in Kesavananda Bharti vs Union of India.[54] The separation of powers is accepted so as to preserve the freedom and independence of the organs of the state, whose independence is necessary for their proper functioning and also for the smooth functioning of democracy.[55]

Significantly, the application of the theory to modern governments has shown consistently that the separation of powers has to be reconciled with the need for their cooperation with each other.[56] Nevertheless, for free and efficient working of government, it is crucial that there be a balance and equally felt need for the cooperation and dependence amongst the three distinct organs of governance. A closer look at the Indian political system in general and the judicial system in particular, shows that this balance might have been lost. As indicated earlier, the judicial power has surged ahead in recent times and its presence is felt in every arena of governance, such as environmental protection, human rights protection, protection of prisoners' rights, and workers' rights, which are supposed to be dealt by the executive and the legislature. As in the case of other governance problems, the role of the Court in resolving environmental disputes, through interpretation and expansion of existing policy and creation of additional structure for environmental protection, has become an important part of environmental governance in India.

This raises the question as to why there is a need for judicial intervention in resolving disputes revolving around environmental problems. In view of the Stockholm Conference on Human Environment and growing awareness of the environmental crises in the country, India has amended its Constitution and added direct provisions for protection of the environment.[57] The Constitution (Forty-Second Amendment) Act, 1976 has made it a fundamental duty to protect and improve the natural environment. Article 48-A states that the state shall endeavour to protect and improve the environment and to safeguard forests and wildlife of the country. Corresponding to the obligation imposed on the state, Article 51-A (g), which occurs in Part IV (A) of the Constitution dealing with Fundamental Duties, casts a duty on every citizen of India. Article 51-A (g) provides that it shall be the duty of every citizen of India to protect and improve the natural environment, including forests, lakes, rivers and wildlife, and to have compassion for living creatures.

In the subsequent years, India has also enacted a number of statutory acts for the protection and improvement of the environment. The enactment of the Water (Prevention and Control of Pollution) Act of 1974 has given the statute book its first real foundation for environmental protection. Other major enactments that have followed are the Forest Conservation Act (1981), the Air Prevention and Control of Pollution Act (1986), the Environmental Protection Act (1986), the National Environment Tribunal Act (1995), the National Environment Appellate Act (1997) and the Biodiversity Protection Act (2002).[58] In this way, India has enacted a range of regulatory instruments to preserve and protect its natural resources. Unfortunately, the plethora of such enactments and the Constitutional provisions has not resulted in preventing environmental degradation in the country. Noticeably, the last two decades have been a period of rapid degradation in the Indian environment. The enactment of a number of laws both by the Central and State governments relating to the environment has not made much headway in controlling the environmental degradation process and the laws, by and large, have remained unenforced, misadministered or mismanaged. In such situations, the environmental activists and NGOs have approached the Court for suitable remedies and the Court's intervention has resulted in reminding and compelling the implementing agencies to perform their statutory obligations towards the protection of environment. This process of judicial intervention in resolving environmental disputes is viewed as judicial activism in present days. Judicial activism means essentially that the judiciary expands its own scope and jurisdiction and goes into matters not normally considered to be within its own domain. In other words, the judiciary often goes beyond giving of judgements and issuing of specific directions for executive action and sometimes even monitoring the progress of action, resorting to what is known as 'continuing mandamus'.[59]

The expansion of judicial activism through environmental cases, in particular, is widely debated and discussed in India. On the one hand, critics of the theory of separation of power view this kind of judicial activism as a sign of hope to correct shortcomings on environmental issues. They argue that the approach of the Court in intervening in the affairs of the executive is to ask whether the implementation or non-implementation of the policy results in a violation of the fundamental rights or not. If the Court finds a violation of the Constitutional provisions, then it can direct authorities to discharge their duties. In M.C. Mehta vs Union of India,[60] the Court has explained how, despite the enactment of the Environment Protection Act, 1986, there had been a considerable decline in the quality of environment. The Court has noted that despite several PILs, required attention has not been paid by the authorities concerned to take the steps necessary for the discharge of duty imposed on the state. Any further delay in the performance of duty imposed by the Central Government cannot, therefore, be permitted. Suitable directions by the Court to require performance of its duty by the Central Government need to be mandated by the law. The Court, however, required the Central Government to indicate what steps it had taken thus far and also place before it the national policy, if any, drawn up for the protection of the environment.

The Court's directions to the implementing agencies to effectively enforce the environmental laws, or when it asks the polluter to pay the compenzation for the damage it has done to the environment and to the people, has been welcomed. This process of judicial interpretation of existing law and policy to ensure better quality of life and an attempt to check governmental lawlessness are said to have 'transformed the Supreme Court of India into a Supreme Court for Indians'.[61]

On the other hand, the advocates of theory of separation of power argue that the intervention of the Court in the affairs of the implementing agency to protect the environment and enforce fundamental rights is violating the principle of separation of powers, as the theory of separation of power suggests that each organ of the government has to perform within the prescribed limits as designed by the Constitution of India. In a number of cases, the Court has gone beyond its adjudication function to protect the environment, thereby violating the principle of separation of powers and creating problems for other organs of the State. Its continuous intervention in the affairs of executive, questioning the validity of government policy and resuming administrative powers to protect the environment aggressively has invited steadfast resistance from administrative branches. For example, in the Delhi Vehicular pollution case, the Court directions to convert all commercial vehicles into Compressed Natural Gas (CNG) has witnessed protest, not only from the private companies, but also from the Government of India and the Delhi state government. Steadfast resistance from the agencies responsible for enforcing the Court order has raised serious questions about the wisdom of this decision.[62] Many opponents have disputed the reliability and practicality of CNG, arguing that the technology is still in development, making the conversion both risky and costly. By disregarding the pleas of the Delhi government and insisting upon the implementation of its orders, the Court seems to be usurping the authority of the existing pollution control structures to execute their duties independently.[63] This raises both institutional and Constitutional questions, as the Court wrestles to determine which branch of government is best suited to handle pollution control matters.

Similarly, in the T.N. Godavarman Thirumulpad vs Union of India case, the Supreme Court has gone beyond the scope of its jurisprudence. In this ongoing case, the Supreme Court has extended the scope of the petition from a matter of ceasing illegal operations in Nilgiris forest land from deforestation by illegal timber operations into a reformation of the entire country's forest policy. The Court held that the meaning of 'forest' is to be as per dictionary definition, irrespective of ownership, and its orders are to apply to all lands entered in any government record as 'forest'. The paradox of this order has been a further centralization of power over the country's forest lands in the hands of the same bureaucracy against whose mismanagement the original PIL was filed. This has seriously impacted millions of forest dwellers' customary, as well as legal rights to forest lands and resources for their very survival.[64] One indication of the importance of forest lands in people's lives is the fact that more than 2,000 interlocutory applications (IAs) have been admitted in the case,[65] ranging from the North East to the Andamans to Madhya Pradesh.

As far as tribal rights over their customary resources, as well as their self-governing institutions, are concerned, the Constitution of India provides specific protection to tribal rights, particularly in Schedule V and Schedule VI areas.[66] Surprisingly, the Supreme Court has overlooked all these dimensions with its environmental activism governed by a vision of 'forests' existing in isolation and out of context. The Court's definition of 'forest' itself, and the assumption that forests are best managed by state bureaucracies, is highly problematic, given the long history of forest degradation under state control and serious conflicts with forest dwelling tribal and other communities over access to forest resources for survival. It does not seem to have been brought to the notice of the Court that in states like Orissa, West Bengal and Jharkhand, villagers, on their own initiative, are regenerating and protecting their forests, often from corrupt forest officials and timber mafias, in several thousand villages. Even in its own judgement in the *Samatha vs State of Andhra Pradesh*,[67] a five-judge bench of the Supreme Court recognized that for tribals, forests are their traditional source of sustenance. They have a historical right to minor forest produce and to communal residence on forest land. These rights of tribals have been neglected in the *Godavarman* orders.

These efforts of the Court are, without doubt, unprecedented. The measures appear to be an invasion over the administrative terrain. The Court, however, has denied any such usurpation. In its pronouncements, the Court has justified its action either under a statutory provision[68] or as an aspect of their inherent powers.[69] It is undeniable that the devices employed by the Court helped it to get detailed facts, understand complexities of social, economic and scientific issues revolving around environmental problems and accordingly arrive at a decision. But, the environmental governance process has become more complex through such judicial intervention and innovations.

Conclusion

The examination of the increasing judicialization of environmental governance through expansion of judicial process in resolving environmental litigation; implementation of environmental judgements through court appointed monitoring committee; and evolution of environmental laws and policies reveals that the Indian Supreme Court has been playing an important role in the current environmental governance process in India. While the procedural innovations have widened the scope for environmental justice through recognition of citizens' right to a healthy environment, entertaining petitions on behalf of affected people and inanimate objects and creative thinking of judges to arrive at a decision by making spot visits, substantive innovations have redefined the role of the Court in the decision-making process through application of environmental principles and expanding the scope of environmental jurisprudence.

Given the failure of the executive and legislature in discharging their Constitutional duties, the Supreme Court's increasing intervention in environmental protection and improvement has made an attempt to arrest the dysfunctional trend of other organs and has forced them to implement the environmental laws in an effective manner. However, in reminding other organs about their Constitutional duties and enforcing fundamental rights of citizens, the Supreme Court has, at times, crossed its boundaries and started interfering in the very basic affairs of environmental management. In resolving more than 100 environmental cases since 1980, the Supreme Court has continuously engaged itself in the management and resolution of environmental conflicts, and thereby has increased the country's dependence on the Court for environmental protection. This dependence on a judicial institution that has already exceeded the boundaries of its responsibilities has been further complicated by the lack of monitoring of the Supreme Court's orders and the vagueness of the legislative and executive roles regarding environmental issues. There has been no uniform cooperation from the implementing agencies to effectively enforce the Court directions. It is also observed that most of the innovative methods introduced by the Court have neither been followed consistently nor been institutionalized to make a long-term impact for the environmental governance process. In such a situation, how long will the Supreme Court monitor the implementation of its decisions? As the opposition to judicial intervention in the affairs of other organs increases, what will happen if the implementing agencies and people disobey Court decision for the protection of environment?

This analysis leads to a conclusion, therefore, that while judicialization of environmental governance has significant impact on the overall environmental governance process in India, it also has created structural and institutional problems in the effective management of environment. The challenge then is how to institutionalize and democratise its merits and minimize its negative implications and unwanted effects, which, from an academic point of view, should prompt us to investigate more specifically which forms of judicial intervention in environmental protection and improvement is effective for environmental governance and which, in contrast, are not healthy for environmental governance in India.

Notes

1. All instances of the term 'the Court' refer to the Supreme Court of India.
2. For more details, see Prashant Bhushan (2004), 'Supreme Court and PIL', 39(18), *Economic and Political Weekly*, p. 1770.
3. See H.G. Gadbois, Jr. (1985), '*The Supreme Court of India as a Political Institution*', in R. Dhavan, R. Sudarshan and S. Khurshid, eds., 'Judges and the Judicial Power: Essays in Honour of Justice V.R. Krishna Iyer', Bombay: N.M. Tripathi Private Limited.
4. For more details on the role of judiciary in Indian democracy, see S.P. Sathe (2001), '*Judicial Activism in India*', New Delhi: Oxford University Press. Also, see Upendra Baxi (2000), '*The Avatars of Indian Judicial Activism: Explorations in the Geographies of [In] Justice*', in K. Verma, ed., *Fifty Years of Supreme Court of India: Its Grasp and Reach*, New Delhi: Oxford University Press.
5. Speaking constitutionally, the role of the Supreme Court as proclaimed under Article 141 of the constitution of India is to 'declare' the law that shall be binding on all courts in India. As such, it does not envisage interaction, much less a direct dialogue, with the executive government of the day.
6. *See* S.S. Prakash and P.V.N. Sarma, 'Environment Protection vis-à-vis Judicial Activism', 2 *Supreme Court Journal* 56 (1998).
7. *See* G.L. Peiris, 'Public Interest Litigation in the Indian Subcontinent: Current Dimensions', 40(1), *International and Comparative Law Quarterly* 66 (1991). *See also* M.R. Anderson, 'Individual Rights to Environmental Protection in India', *in* A.E. Boyle and M.R. Anderson, eds., *Human Rights Approaches to Environmental Protection*, pp. 1–24 (United Kingdom: Oxford University Press, 1998).
8. See Smitu Kothari (2001), '*Social Movements in India: Institutions, Interests and Identities*', in Atul Kohli, ed., The Success of India's Democracy, UK: Cambridge Press.
9. In the Indian context, some of the legal scholars prefer the expression 'Social Action Litigation' to 'Public Interest Litigation', as this tool for justice to protect basic rights of individuals and communities has, through innovations of the higher Court in India, for greater positive impacts on the social lives of the people in India than the United States, where the PIL movement took roots. For more details, see Upendra Baxi, 'Taking Suffering Seriously: Social Action Litigation in the Supreme Court of India', in Tiruchelvam and Coomaraswamy, eds., *The Role of the Court in Plural Societies* (New York: St. Martin's Press, 1987).

10. *See* Atiyah Curmally, '*Environmental Governance and Regulation in India*' 96 (New Delhi: Indian Infrastructure Report, 2002).
11. *See* Peiris, note 7 above at 68.
12. *RLEK vs State of Uttar Pradesh and Others*, Supreme Court of India, Judgement of 19 December 1996, AIR 1985 SC 652.
13. The Dehradun lime stone quarries litigation filed by the Rural Litigation and Entitlement Kendra in 1983 was the first PIL on environmental issue in the country before the Supreme Court.
14. The information is based on the All India Reporter from January 1980 till December 2000, Supreme Court Cases.
15. *M.C. Mehta vs Union of India*, Supreme Court of India, Judgement of 22 September 1987, AIR 1988 SC 1037.
16. *T. N. Godavarman vs Union of India*, Supreme Court of India, Judgement of 12 December 1996, AIR 1997 SC 1228.
17. *Indian Council for Enviro-Legal Action vs Union of India* (Bichhri village industrial pollution case), Supreme Court of India, Judgement of 13 February 1996, 1996 (3) SCC 212.
18. *A.K. Gopalan vs Union of India*, Supreme Court of India, Judgement of 19 May 1950, AIR 1950 SC 27.
19. *Kesavananda Bharti vs Union of India*, Supreme Court of India, Judgement of 24 April 1973, AIR 1973 SC 1461.
20. *Maneka Gandhi vs Union of India*, Supreme Court of India, Judgement of 25 January 1978, AIR 1978 SC 597.
21. *See Ratlam Municipality vs Vardhichand and Others*, Supreme Court of India, Judgement of 29 July 1980, AIR 1980 SC 1629.
22. *See RLEK vs State of Uttar Pradesh and Others*, Supreme Court of India, Judgement of 19 December 1996, AIR 1985 SC 656.
23. *See M.C. Mehta vs Union of India*, Supreme Court of India, Judgement of 22 September 1987, AIR 1988 SC 1045.
24. In this case, the Court declined to determine whether or not the defendant in this case was sufficiently under government control to be an authority, and therefore susceptible to constitutional control.
25. Article 45, Article 66, Article 335 and Article 19 (2) of the respective countries such as Spain, Portugal, Brazil and Ecuador contain specific provision for the

enjoyment of the fundamental right to live in a healthy environment, but no substantive methods exist for their protection. *See* S. Douglas-Scott, 'Environmental Rights in the European Union-Participatory Democracy or Democratic Deficit' *in* A.E. Boyle and M.R. Anderson, eds., *Human Rights Approaches to Environmental Protection*, pp. 109–28 (United Kingdom: Oxford University Press, 1998).

26. *Ratlam Municipality vs Vardhichand and Others*, Supreme Court of India, Judgement of 29 July 1980, AIR 1980 SC 1622.
27. Interview with Justice V.R. Krishna Iyer, Cochin, 21 August 2005.
28. Interview with Justice P.N. Bhagwati, New Delhi, 23 September 2005.
29. Interview with Justice S.P. Bharucha, Mumbai, May 2010.
30. *Narmada Bachao Andolan vs Union of India and Others*, Supreme Court of India, Judgement of 18 October 2000, AIR 2000 SC 3753.
31. *See* Gobind Das, 'The Supreme Court: An Overview', in B.N. Kripal et al. (eds), *Supreme But Not Infallible* (New Delhi: Oxford University Press, 2001). The author argues that the Indian Supreme Court had always been uncomfortable with former Prime Minister of India, Mrs. Indira Gandhi's regime; during the late sixties, her economic and political policies were struck down in the Bank Nationalization and Privy Purse cases; in the early seventies, the Court was locked in the Kesavananda battle and again in her election cases; when the Court supported her emergency in the Shukla case and Detenu case, it was execrated by public opinion; and during the Janata rule, the Court was confirming legal attempts for her political extinction in the Special Courts Bill and Assembly Dissolution cases. Whenever the Court opposed her policies, it had to pay the penalty in the form of suppressions of judges and constitutional amendments. In the post-emergency period (1975-77), the Court decided not to interfere with the major political and economic decisions of government and opened up new fields of interest and different areas of judicial activities; it chose the poor, the helpless, the oppressed in the name of social justice, constitutional conscience, and the rule of law.
32. For more details on the role of judiciary in Indian democracy, see S.P. Sathe (2001), *Judicial Activism in India*', New Delhi: Oxford University Press. Also, see Upendra Baxi (2000), '*The Avatars of Indian Judicial Activism: Explorations in the Geographies of [In] Justice*', in K. Verma ed. Fifty Years of Supreme Court of India: Its Grasp and Reach, New Delhi: Oxford University Press.
33. Some of the significant orders issued by the Court are the following: the Order of 12.12.96 clarified certain provisions of the Forest (Conservation) Act, 1980 and also extended the scope of the Act. The Court held that the word 'forest' must be

understood according to the dictionary meaning; all ongoing activity within any forest in any state throughout the country, without the prior approval of the Central Government, must cease forthwith; the Court order of 9 May 2002 constituted an Authority at the national level called the Central Empowered Committee and assigned it the task to monitor the implementation of the Court orders, removal of encroachment, implementations of working plan, compensatory afforestation plantations and other conservation issues.

34. For a more detailed analysis of the case, *see* Armin Rosencranz, Edward Boenig and Brinda Dutta (2007), The Godavarman Case: The Indian Supreme Court's Breach of Constitutional Boundaries in Managing India's Forests (Washington DC: Environmental Law Institute.

35. In the Indian governance structure, Taluka refers an administrative division at the district level.

36. *Dahanu Taluka Environment Protection Group vs Bombay Suburban Electricity Supply Company Ltd.* with *Bombay Environmental Action Group vs State of Maharashtra and Others*, Supreme Court of India, 1991 (2) SCC 539.

37. A Flue gas de-sulphurization unit performs the important role of reducing the sulphur dioxide emissions from the thermal power plant.

38. For more details, *see* Government of India, Ministry of Environment and Forests, Notification dated 19 February 1991.

39. *See* Government of India, Ministry of Environment and Forests, Notification dated 20 June 1991.

40. See *Bittu Sehgal vs Union of India*, Supreme Court of India, W.P. (Civil) No. 231 of 1994.

41. Interview with Justice C.S. Dharmadhikari, Chairperson of DTEPA, 28 September 2008.

42. For more details, see Geetanjoy Sahu and Armin Rosencranz (2009), Court-Appointed Monitoring Committee: The Case of the Dahanu Taluka Environment Protection Authority', 5/2 *Law, Environment and Development Journal.*

43. The Polluter Pays Principle is a principle in *International Environmental Law* where the polluting party pays for the damage done to the *natural environment.*

44. The Precautionary Principle aims to provide guidance for protecting public health and the environment in the face of uncertain risks, stating that the absence of full scientific certainty shall not be used as a reason to postpone measures where there is a risk of serious or irreversible harm to public health or the environment.

45. The Public Trust Doctrine is the principle that certain resources are preserved for public use, and that the government is required to maintain it for the public's reasonable use.

46. See *Indian Council for Enviro-Legal Action vs Union of India* (Bichhri village industrial pollution case), Supreme Court of India, Judgement of 13 February 1996, 1996 (3) SCC 215.

47. *See* Government of India, National Environmental Policy, 2006, available at http://www.envfor.nic.in/nep/nep2006.html

48. *Vellore Citizens' Welfare Forum vs Union of India*, Supreme Court of India, Judgement of 28 August 1996, AIR 1996 SC 2716.

49. *Andhra Pradesh Pollution Control Board vs Prof. M.V. Nayudu*, Supreme Court of India, Judgement of 27 January 1999, AIR 1999 SC 812.

50. *M.C. Mehta vs Kamal Nath*, Supreme Court of India, Judgement of 13 December 1996, 1997 (1) SCC 388.

51. *See* Durga Das Basu, *Introduction to the Constitution of India* (New Delhi: Princeton Hall of India, 1986).

52. In re: Article 143, Constitution of India and Delhi Laws Act (1921) etc., Supreme Court of India, Judgement of 23 May 1951, AIR 1951 SC 332.

53. *Indira Gandhi vs Rajnarain*, Supreme Court of India, Judgement of 7 November 1975, AIR 1975 SC 2299.

54. *See Kesavananda Bharti vs Union of India*, Supreme Court of India, Judgement of 24 April 1973, AIR 1973 SC 1461.

55. For a comprehensive analysis on the approach of the Court towards infrastructure projects, *see* Videh Upadhyay, 'Changing Judicial Power', 35(43 and 44), *Economic and Political Weekly* 3789 (2000).

56. *See* Durga Das Basu, *Administrative Law* (New Delhi: Prentice Hall of India, 1986).

57. *See* Atiyah Curmally, *'Environmental Governance and Regulation in India'* 96 (New Delhi: Indian Infrastructure Report, 2002).

58. For more details on Indian Environmental Law, *see* Sanjay Upadhyay and Videh Upadhyay, *Handbook on Environmental Law: Forest Laws, Wild Life Laws and the Environment*, Volume I & II (New Delhi: The Lexis Nexis Group of Companies, 2002).

59. *See* Ramaswamy Iyer 'Some Constitutional Dilemmas', 41(21), *Economic and Political Weekly* 2064 (2006).

60. *M.C. Mehta vs Union of India*, Supreme Court of India, Judgement of 18 November 1997, 1998 (9) SCC 589.

61. *See* Upendra Baxi, 'The Avatars of Indian Judicial Activism: Explorations in the Geographies of [In] Justice', *in* K. Verma ed., *Fifty years of Supreme Court of India: Its Grasp and Reach* (New Delhi: Oxford University Press, 2000).

62. Kuldeep Mathur, Battling for Clean Environment: Supreme Court, Technocrats and Popular Politics in India, Working Paper/03-01 (New Delhi: Centre for the Study of Law and Governance, 2001).

63. PT Armin Rosencranz and Michael Jackson, The Delhi Pollution Case: The Supreme Court of India and the Limits of Judicial Power, 2003, available at http://www.cleanairnet.org/caiasia/1412/articles-69423_delhi_case.pdf.

64. *See* Madhu Sarain, 'Who is Encroaching on Whose Lands?' *Seminar*, October 2002, p. 70, available at http://www.india-seminar.com/2002/519/519 comment.htm.

65. *See* Forest Case Update, October 2007, available at http://www.forestcaseindia.org/f14/Iss%2039%20Oct%2007.pdf

66. *See* N. K. Behura and Nilakantha Panigrahi, *Tribals and the Indian Constitution* (New Delhi: Rawat Publictions, 2006).

67. *Samata vs State of Andhra Pradesh and Others*, Supreme Court of India, Judgement of 11 July 1997, 1997 (8) SCC 191.

68. The power to appoint commissioners in matters of civil nature is found in Order XXVI Civil Procedure Code and Order XLVI Supreme Court Rules, 1966.

69. Inherent power of the Supreme Court under Article 32 and of the High Courts under Article 226 of the Constitution.

SECTION 2

Imperatives and Instances

7

Ecological Distribution Conflicts and Economic Growth

J. Martinez-Alier

Introduction

> *"We are certainly not in a 'post-material' age. Activists of the Environmental Justice movement in the United States emphasized the links between the globalization of the economy, the increasing flows of energy and materials, and the environmental degradation of habitats for many of the world's people: "In many places where Black, minority, poor or Indigenous peoples live, oil, timber and minerals are extracted in such a way as to devastate eco-systems and destroy their culture and livelihood. Waste from both high- and low-tech industries, much of it toxic, has polluted groundwater, soil and the atmosphere. Environmental degradation such as this, and its concomitant impact on human wealth and welfare, is increasingly seen as violation of human rights".*[1]

The teaching of economics is still based on an image of the economy as a merry-go-round between consumers and producers. They encounter each other in markets for consumer goods or in markets for the services of production factors (like selling labour time for a wage). Prices are formed, quantities are exchanged. This is Chrematistics. Macroeconomic accounts (GDP) aggregate the quantities multiplied by the prices. The economy may be described however in a different way, as a system of transformation of (exhaustible) energy and materials (including water) into useful products and services, and finally into waste. This is Bioeconomics or Ecological Economics (from N. Georgescu Roegen, 1966, 1971; Herman Daly, 1968; A. Kneese and R.U. Ayres, 1969; Kenneth Boulding, 1966). Now, it is the moment to substitute GDP by social and environmental indicators at the macro-level.

Several UNRISD reports (Ghai and Vivian, 1992; Friedman and Rangan, 1993; Gadgil and Guha, 1995) and other authors (Taylor, 1995; Rocheleau, 1995; Peet and Watts, 1996; Bryant and Bailey, 1997; Goldman, 1998) described over ten years ago, the new tide of global environmentalism born from conflicts on the burdens of pollution, on the sharing of uncertain environmental risks, on the loss of access to natural resources and environmental services. In such conflicts, the poor (whether indigenous peoples or not, whether women or men) are often on the side of resource conservation and a clean environment even when they do not call themselves "environmentalists". The increased use of energy and materials in the world economy means that tribal areas around the world (though not only tribal areas) become "commodity frontiers" where bulk commodities essential to the metabolism of the rich economies (oil, coal, gas, bauxite, copper, timber, hydroelectricity) or preciosities (diamonds, gold, mahogany, aquaculture shrimp) are supplied.

In this chapter, first, an explanation of calculations of energy and material flow will be offered so that the concept of "social metabolism" is understood (Ayres, 1989; Fischer-Kowalski, 1998; Haberl, 2001; Cleveland, 1987, 1998). Second, some complaints related to mining in indigenous or non-indigenous territories will be interpreted in the light of a worldwide environmental justice movement that uses diverse idioms. Third, the links between metabolic profiles of countries (and regions) and ecological distribution conflicts will be traced more systematically. Fourth, the use of the language of indigenous territorial rights in such conflicts will be discussed, in a context of pluralism of values. Although the defence of indigenous groups against oil extraction, mining, large dams or logging, and the movements for environmental justice insofar as they fight against "environmental racism", could be seen as manifestations of *identity politics*, it will be argued that it is rather the other way around, identity being one idiom in which ecological conflicts are expressed.

It may be that a multilateral bank involved in an ecological conflict wants to do a cost-benefit analysis of a dam or mining project, ready to compensate in money terms for the negative externalities produced. It may be that the Net Present Value of the commercial and non-commercial products and environmental services of a particular forest is calculated, so as to count the real costs of a hydroelectric dam that will flood this forest. It may be also that other actors, while not necessarily adverse to obtaining monetary compensation, insist on the sacredness of the land, or on territorial rights (protected through Convention 169 of ILO or national legislation), or on ecological or landscape values, or on human rights to livelihood. There is a diversity of languages of valuation. Who has the power to simplify complexity by imposing a method of resolution of such conflicts? Who has the power to impose one single language of valuation?

Social Metabolism

The economy may be described in terms of economic indicators such as growth of GDP, savings ratio, budget deficit as percentage of GDP and current account balance in the external sector. Social factors may be taken into account, as in demographic and public health statistics, and in the Human Development Index. The economy may also be described in terms of physical indicators. Economic, social and physical indicators are non-equivalent descriptions. The economy of a country or a region may be described in the following terms: it provides 230 GJ of energy per person/year, its HANPP is 35 per cent, material flow amounts to 21 tonnes per person/year of which fossil fuels account for 5 tonnes. Of the material flows, 6 tonnes are imported and 1 tonne is exported. Income per capita is US$ 30,000. This country occupies place ninth in the Human Development Index. Of another economy, we say that it provides only 25 GJ person/year, its materials flow amounts to only 3.5 tonnes person/year, its HANPP is 60 per cent (a heavily populated country, relying on biomass, with little external trade). Foreign trade is less than 0.3 tonne per capita/year of exports or imports. Income per capita is only US$ 2,100 (at purchasing power parity). It occupied place 137th in the HDI. Different classes of people in such countries have different metabolic profiles.

It should be obvious that the study of the use of energy in the economy (Cottrell, 1955; Debeir et al., 1986) is more relevant than ever as we anticipate the patterns of economic growth of India, China and other countries, their effects on oil and gas prices, the increased human use of biomass as fuel to the detriment of other species, the immediacy of peak oil, the increased use of coal and its effects on the greenhouse effect, the growth of nuclear power. At the world level, all sources of energy go up (McNeill, 2000). Biomass energy (as food, feedstuffs and fuelwood), must have increased over four times in the twentieth century, coal increased six times, oil increased much more. The notion of energy return on energy input (EROI) was applied in the 1970s to the economy by Charles Hall and other ecologists (Odum, 1971), noticing the increasing energy costs of obtaining energy (in different systems: wind energy, tar sands, fuel-biomass ...).

One fundamental notion of human ecology is the distinction between the endosomatic use of energy (as food) and the exosomatic use of energy as fuel for cooking and heating, and as power for the artefacts and machines produced by human culture. This distinction was first traced by A.J. Lotka (1911). Thus, one person per day must eat equivalent to 1500, 2000 or 2500 kcal. Since one calorie is equal to 4.18 joules, a daily food intake of 2400 kcal is equal to 10 MJ (megajoules), a convenient round number. If a person is five or ten times richer than the average of her society, she is not for this reason going to consume five or ten times the average food energy. In some cultures, being somewhat fat is still a desirable social attribute, a sign that poor people have difficulties in getting the minimum amount of food energy, some indeed starve because of lack of calories or malnutrition. In affluent societies almost nobody starves, and poor people are (as in the United States) fatter on average than rich people, probably the first time this happens in human history. As regards the exosomatic use of energy, humans have developed in the course of history many artefacts and machines that use energy for production or amusement. While endosomatically, the energy consumption of one well-fed person per day is 10 MJ and, therefore, per year is 3.65 GJ, the exosomatic use of energy varies very much. Poor people use some energy for cooking (perhaps more than for eating, if they cook in open fires), also some energy to feed domestic animals (one or two cows per family), and for making some clothes and repairing their house. They might have a pump for the well, if they are better off – if not, they will use human work to get water, such work being a transformation of the food energy intake. They will also do some travel in overcrowded buses or trains. Altogether, perhaps another 5 or 6 GJ of energy per person/year will be used exosomatically (we are not counting here the warmth provided directly by the sun and indeed the other environmental services, such as the rain and the carbon cycle, driven by solar energy). Consider now a citizen of a rich suburb, going to work every day by car, driving 50 km (25 each way), spending, therefore, at least 3 litres of petrol (30,000 kcal). Only for travel to work, the expenditure of energy is over ten times more than the direct food energy intake of a well-fed person.

In poor countries, food energy is a substantial part of the total use of energy. In other words, the exo/endo energy use ratio (Giampietro, 2003) is two or three. In the wealthiest countries of the European Union, the energy use per person per year is of the order of 200 GJ, in the United States almost double than this. The exo/endo ratio reaches 100. The unequal exosomatic use of energy largely explains the differences in the per capita production of carbon dioxide, and therefore, it explains the international conflict on the property rights on the carbon sinks (oceans, soils, new vegetation) and on the atmosphere as a temporary reservoir.

The relations between poverty and environment have different facets (Jodha, 1998, Nadkarni, 2000). Indira Gandhi seems to have declared in Stockholm in 1972 that "poverty is the worst form of pollution". In India, if current rates of economic growth are maintained over ten or twenty years, as seems likely, then this will make a very significant contribution to the decrease of the existing poignant poverty. In order to increase their standard of living, poor people must increase their exosomatic energy use. Water consumption, the flow of materials, and some environmental and health risks (nuclear industry, motorized transport) also increase with economic growth. As the Indian economy locks itself over the next decades into a pattern of carbon emissions similar to the European per capita level, with a population of 1.3 billion people, then India by herself will increase by 40 per cent the total of today's world emissions, while what is required at world level is 60 per cent decrease of today's emissions.

Another facet in the relation between poverty and environment is that the poor, because of their direct reliance on natural resources outside the market (perhaps in the form of Common Property Resources), are often careful environmental managers. Notice also that economic accounting distorts the importance of the environment for human welfare. In India, there are figures showing that Common Property Resources contribute a larger amount of money per year than foreign assistance. Beyond this, economic valuation is irrelevant in order to assess the *livelihood value* of water, firewood, soil fertility, pastures that are essential for adivasi and other poor people who have no money to buy substitutes for them. The cost of one litre of bottled in India is 12 rupees (2004), about one-fourth of a daily rural wage. A part of income growth goes simply to compensate for the loss of free resources no longer available because of environmental degradation and population growth.

There is one type of economic growth that increases both poverty and environmental degradation, for instance, the expropriation of tribal people to the benefit of open cast mining. There might be a contrary situation: economic growth allows the rural people to move up in the domestic energy "ladder" (Foley, 1985). Use of firewood and dung for domestic fuel might decrease in India over the next years as LPG becomes more affordable (in 2004, a 14 kg bottle of LPG cost about 270 rupees, while the rural daily wage was in many regions 60 rupees, i.e. about one euro).

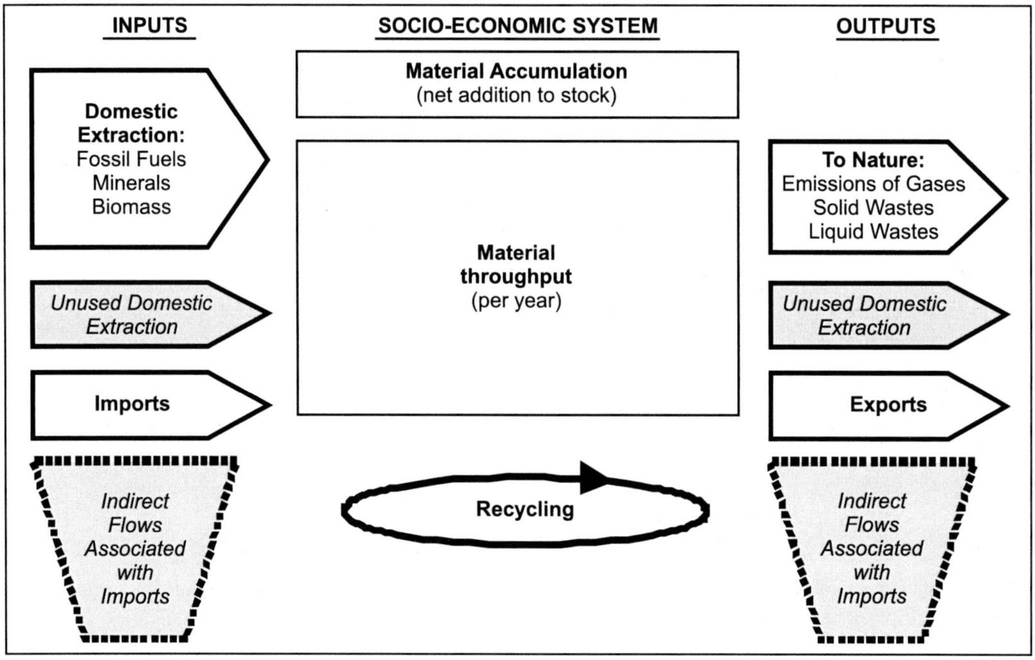

Fig. 1: Economy-wide Material Balances (excluding air and water)

Social metabolism comprises not only the energy flow but also the flow of materials. Research on material flows has made much progress (Brigenzu and Schütz, 2001; EUROSTAT, 2001; Adriansee et al., 1997; Matthews et al., 2000). Eurostat statistics for European countries follow an agreed methodology, with a complete balance of the economy (Fig. 1). Material flows are domestic, if extracted from the system, or imports, if coming from the rest of the world. In the Eurostat methodology, material flows are classified into three main material groups (minerals, fossil fuels and biomass) and into three main categories (imports, exports and domestic extraction). The net accumulation of materials can be calculated as the difference between what enters the system and what goes out as waste – this is inevitably produced (as carbon dioxide for instance), part of it is recycled outside markets by natural cycles, a small part is recycled by markets (some paper, metals). Material flows can be used or unused. The latter represent materials extracted or discarded during the production of a good, i.e. mining overburden, while the term "used" refers to an input for use in the economy.

The level of economic development, the geography of each region, the population density, the commercial relations, the changing technologies and environmental regulations explain the specific metabolic profiles that are established in terms of material flows and in terms of energy flows. Both are needed. Fossil fuels and biomass will show up both in the material and energy statistics, but nuclear energy and hydroelectricity are not in the material flows.

The HANPP, on its side, uses biomass statistics (which can be counted also as energy or materials). HANPP also incorporates land-use data on soil that does not produce biomass. The HANPP is calculated in three steps. First, the potential net primary production (in the natural ecosystems of a given region or country), NPP, is calculated. Then, the actual NPP (normally, less than potential NPP, because of agricultural simplification, soil sealing) is calculated. The part of actual NPP used by humans and associate beings (cattle, etc.) relative to potential NPP is the HANPP, meant to be an index of loss of biodiversity (because the higher the HANPP, less biomass available for "wild" species). This assumed relation is itself a topic for research (Kraussman et al., 2003; Haberl et al., 2003, 2005). In India, more use of kerosene or LPG for domestic cooking and heating might lead to a decrease in HANPP, and therefore, to less pressure on forests (this would be good for the tigers). In the European Union, HANPP decreased after the 1950s, it will now perhaps grow again: substitution of biofuels for fossil fuels, reduces net emissions of carbon dioxide but it increases HANPP.

Water is excluded from MFA because its weight is of the order of one hundred times more than the material flows, and it would overshadow all trends.[2]

Environmental Justice

"Environmental Justice" has come to mean since the late 1980s and early 1990s an organized movement against "environmental racism, i.e. the disproportionate allocation of toxic waste to Latino or African-American communities in the United States. It is also relevant for Indian reservations in the United States, particularly in the context of uranium mining and nuclear waste (Erickson et al., 1993, 1994;

Kuletz, 1998). In October 1991, the First National People of Color Environmental Leadership Summit took place in Washington D.C., the Principles of Environmental Justice were proclaimed. The Environmental Justice movement (Bullard, 1990, 1993; Pulido, 1991, 1996; Bryant and Mohai, 1992; Bryant, 1995; Sachs, 1995; Gottlieb, 1993; Szasz, 1994; Schwab, 1994; Westra and Wenz, 1995; Dorsey, 1997; Faber, 1998; DiChiro, 1998; Camacho, 1998 and Taylor, 2000) is quite different from the two previous environmentalisms in this country, namely, the efficient and sustainable use of natural resources (in the tradition of Gifford Pinchot), and the cult of wilderness (in the tradition of John Muir). Of course, one could think that, in America, the movement started not in the Warren County in North Carolina in 1982 but in the struggles against mining in Wisconsin conducted by alliances of Indian tribes and environmentalists in the 1970s and 1980s (Gedick, 1993), and in many other struggles by Native Americans, from Alaska to Tierra del Fuego including the complaints in Nevada against the proposed nuclear waste deposit in Yucca Mountain (Erickson et al., 1993, 1994 and Kuletz, 1998).

Which will be the worldwide First of May or Eighth of March of Environmental Justice? Chico Mendes' assassination day, Ken Saro-Wiwa's, or the day when Karunamoi Sardar died defending her village in Khulna, Bangladesh, against the shrimp industry on 7 November 1990?[3]

The Environmental Justice movement in the United States shifted the NIMBY image of grassroots environmental protests by turning them into NIABY protests (not in anyone's backyard). The uncertainties of environmental risk (for instance, dioxin), and the statistical difficulties in separating racial and economic factors in toxic waste location decisions, gave rise to a rich practice of "popular epidemiology" (Novotny, 1998). It might be difficult to prove that race more than poverty correlates with toxic waste, but if this is convincingly shown then the chances of redress are high. By emphasizing "racism", the movement for Environmental Justice also emphasizes incommensurability of values. Money and human dignity are not commensurate. When Gandhi, as a young lawyer, was thrown out of a first-class carriage in South Africa, it was not acceptable to argue that the injury to dignity was compensated by the lower cost of a third-class fare.

Environmental racism becomes a useful language for conflicts which have been fought under the banner of indigenous territorial rights. Activists in the class action suit under ATCA against Texaco from Ecuador, blamed Texaco in advertisements in US newspapers in 1999 for "environmental racism" (*New York Times*, 23 September 1999): "The lawsuit alleges that in Ecuador, Texaco dumped the poisonous water produced by oil drilling directly onto the ground, in nearby rivers, and in streams and ponds. The company knowingly destroyed the surrounding environment and endangered the lives of the indigenous people who had lived and fished there for years. These are people of color, people for whose health and well-being Texaco shows only a cavalier disregards... It's time that Texaco learns that devaluing the lives and well-being of people because of the colour of their skin is no longer acceptable for any American company". Notice that this language, so effective in the United States, was not used when the case started in 1993, and it would be problematic to apply it to Texaco's successor, Petroecuador. Perhaps "internal colonialism" (Adeola, 2000) could be used against Petroecuador, as against the Nigerian authorities, while "racism" could be reserved for Texaco (or Shell, in the Niger Delta). In the famous case of the U'Wa in Colombia against Occidental Petroleum (Oxy) in the late 1990s, an additional language was used, both the soil and the subsoil of the territory were considered sacred. The U'Wa argued moreover that their land was protected as indigenous territory (*resguardo indígena)* under the Constitution. Oxy insisted that in Colombian law, the riches of the subsoil belong to the State, and that eventual damages to U'Wa property would be compensated for.

In South Africa (Bond, 2000, 2002), the environmental impacts which the racist apartheid regime left behind, surfaced later. International litigation was initiated by victims of asbestosis against British companies, particularly Cape. The company was aware of the dangers of asbestos at least from 1931 onwards, when Britain asbestos regulations were introduced. Nevertheless, production continued in South Africa with the same low safety standards. Given the chance, workers and their families would have complained, not so much because they were environmentalists but because their health was threatened. The law firm which represents the asbestosis victims also brought actions in London for damages to workers at Thor Chemicals in KwaZulu-Natal on behalf of victims of poisoning by mercury, and on behalf of cancer victims from Rio Tinto's Rossing uranium mine in Namibia.[4] In April 1990, massive concentrations of mercury had been detected in the Umgeweni River near the Thor Chemicals' Cato Ridge plant. "Why did Thor, a British company, decide to build the world's largest toxic mercury recycling plant on the borders of KwaZulu in a fairly remote part of South Africa? Why not build it closer to the sources of the waste mercury in the United States or in Europe?" (Cock and Koch eds., 1991: 82–84). The Basel Convention of 1989 forbids the export of hazardous waste from rich countries except for recovery of raw materials or for recycling. However, the issue is far from over. The logic of Lawrence Summers' Principle still remains compelling.[5]

At the Frontiers of Metal Extraction

One could argue that the world environmental justice movement started long ago at different dates and places, as a cross-cultural movement with an untold history in many countries. Thus, in the Central Sierra of Peru, one hundred years ago, indigenous peasant communities defended themselves against expanding haciendas (Mallon, 1983). They also had to struggle on another related front, against mining companies, and they still do. Therefore, a new network called CONACAMI arose in Peru in the late 1990s. Going back to 1900, there was a world boom in copper. In 1901, the Peruvian government allowed private property of mining deposits (Dore, 2000: 13–15). The Cerro de Pasco Corporation, from New York, started a large scale underground mining operation. It built roads, railroads, dams, hydroelectric plants, mining camps, at 4000 m above sea level. It first built several small smelters, and then in 1922, a big smelter and refinery at La Oroya, the effects of which became a cause celèbre. "The new smelter polluted the region's air, soil and rivers with arsenic, sulfuric acid and iron-zinc residues" (Dore, 2000: 14). The pastures withered, people became ill. A legal case was brought against the company by communities and by hacienda owners. The company was forced by the court to buy the lands it had polluted, as a form of indemnity. When in later years, the La Oroya smelter became less pollutant (at least with respect to the air, because of the scrubbers, if not with respect to the rivers), the property of all this land became a valuable asset for the company, which then started a large sheep ranching business, getting into border conflicts with surrounding communities. The enormous ranch (of about 300,000 ha) was expropriated in 1970 by the Land Reform.

Mining in Peru was long dominated by the Cerro de Pasco Copper Corporation, but in the 1950s and 1960s, copper moved southward, towards Cuajone and Toquepala, large open-pit mines. The Southern Peru Copper Corporation owned by Asarco and Newmont Gold subjected the city of Ilo of 60,000 inhabitants in the late 1990s, to water and air pollution for thirty years. The smelter was built in

1969, 15 km north of Ilo, it spewed daily almost two thousand tonnes of sulfur dioxide, while tailings and slag were discharged without treatment on land, and also on the coastline. The actors at this time were speaking on both sides an explicitly environmental language (Diaz Palacios, 1988 and Balvin, 1995). The Southern Peru Copper Corporation was Peru's major single exporter. The conflict did not involve indigenous peasant communities as in the central Sierra. A class-action suit under the ATCA was initiated at the District Court for the southern District of Texas, Corpus Christi Division, in September 1995, but it was dismissed.

Copper mining keeps growing worldwide, though not without conflicts. In the island of Bougainville, the Rio Tinto Zinc company got into trouble because of local opposition despite the agreement the company had made with the government of Papua New Guinea, which has sovereignty over Bougainville, in order to exploit what was described as the most profitable copper and gold mine in the world. Back in 1974, it was reported that "the natives of Bougainville have stopped throwing geologists into the sea even since the company declared itself willing to compensate them for the land it had taken with cash and other material services". However, it was also reported that monetary compensation was not enough: "The village communities affected gave the highest importance to land as the source of their material standard of life. Land was also the basis of their feelings of security and the focus of most of their religious attention. Despite continuing compensation payments and rental fees, local resentment over the taking of the land remains high, and there is strong opposition to any expansion of mining in Bougainville, whether by the existing company, the government, or anyone else" (Mezger, 1980: 195). Finally, the tiny island of 160,000 inhabitants erupted into a secessionist war at the end of the 1980s.

Not far from Bougainville, the copper extraction frontier reached West Papua under Indonesia's sovereignty, thirty years ago at a copper and gold mine called Grasberg owned by Freeport McMoRan from New Orleans.[6] Rio Tinto has a participation in this mine. The plans were in 2000 to mine *daily* 300,000 tonnes of ore, of which 98 per cent would be dumped into the rivers as tailings. The total copper content to be finally recovered would be nearly 30 million tonnes of copper, three years of world production. This open cast mine is at high altitude, next to a glacier. Water pollution in the Ajkwa river has been the major complaint, and acid drainage is an increasing problem. In 1977, at the initial stages of operation, some Amungme rebelled, and destroyed the slurry pipeline carrying copper concentrate to the coast. Reprisals by the Indonesian army were terrible. Many complaints against Freeport McMoRan led to a class-action suit under the ATCA in New Orleans in April 1996 by Tom Beanal and other members of the Amungme tribe. Tom Beanal declared (at a speech at Loyola University, New Orleans, 23 May 1996): "These companies have taken over and occupied our land.... Even the sacred mountains we think of as our mother have been arbitrarily torn up, and they have not felt the least bit guilty.... Our environment has been ruined, and our forests and rivers polluted by waste.... We have not been silent. We protest and are angry. But we have been arrested, beaten and put into containers: we have been tortured and even killed". The best-known representative of the Amungme became Yosepha Alomang.[7]

The company was deeply involved with the regime, having given shares in the company to relatives and associates of President Suharto. Freeport is also the biggest source of tax revenue for Indonesia. Which line will the separatist movement in West Papua (Organisasi Papua Merdeka, OPM), take towards Freeport? The circumstances in West Papua (or Irian Jaya, this being the official Indonesian name) with both a very rich mine and a separatist movement, explained the heavy military presence. It would be a cruel joke to say that an environmental policy implementing the "polluter pays principle" would have allowed externalities to be internalized into the price of exported minerals.

The metabolism and the social structure of the copper supplying regions have been altered. The supply of recycled copper is less than half of the total world demand, hence the need to move into new frontiers. In many conflicts, the language of money compensation does appear. Indigenous identity was an issue in the central highland of Peru and in West Papua but not in the conflict in coastal southern Peru. The language of indigenous territorial rights (whose official acceptance would be a novelty in Indonesia), and the even stronger language of a separate national identity (which is historically relevant, since West Papua was annexed by Indonesia after the departure of the Dutch), may be used in the case of Freeport McMoRan, as it was in Bougainville where sacredness was reportedly also brought into play.

Meanwhile, Indonesian authorities seemed to be going ahead with a criminal law suit (in Indonesian courts) against the world's biggest gold producer, the Newmont Mining Corporation, for disposal of poisonous material into the water in Buyat Bay on Sulawesi island, damaging the inhabitants' health (*Int. Herald Tribune*, 3 December 2004). There is no space here to describe so many other conflicts on gold mining, such as the conflict between the Yanacocha mine and local communities in Cajamarca, Peru (where Atahualpa met Pizarro). The gold mine is owned by Newmont, and also by a local company, with a five per cent share belonging to the International Finance Corporation of the World Bank. Another conflict is currently taking place in the KiloMoto mines where gold was first discovered in 1903 by a Belgian expedition in what was then the Congo Free State, run as a domain of King Leopold II. The mines produced much gold until 1960 and civil war. Anglo Gold Ashanti has a vast exploration zone, in dense rainforest. A Human Right Watch report of 2005, "The curse of gold", complained against this South African company controlled by Anglo American which is the second biggest gold producer, because of payments to militia group responsible for atrocities in north-east Congo. This company is moving into new frontiers. "With South Africa high grade mines running out of ore and becoming unprofitable, the company has been seeking new reserves in high-risk countries such as Congo and Colombia" (*Financial Times*, 2 May 2005).

In Sipakapa, near San Marcos, west of Guatemala, there was a public consultation in June 2005 under Convention 169 of ILO against gold mining by the Montana company. In other recent gold mining cases in Latin America (Tambo Grande in the northern coast of Peru, Esquel in Patagonia in Argentina), public consultations have also been held, but not under Convention 169 since they are not indigenous territories.

In contrast to oil or copper, gold is a preciosity, rather irrelevant for the metabolism of the importing societies. To buy gold is a habit of the human species in which the East and the West truly meet. Gold mining is destructive both when it is small-scale (*garimpeiros* in Brazil) and when it is large-scale by corporations. The participants at a Peoples' Gold Summit in San Juan Ridge, California, which was held on June 2-8, 1999, asked for a moratorium on the exploration for gold, arguing that: "Life, land, clean water and clean air are more precious than gold. All people depend on nature for life. The right to life is a guaranteed human right. It is, therefore, our responsibility to protect all of nature for present and future generations. Large-scale gold mining violently uproots and destroys the spiritual, cultural, political, social and economic lives of peoples as well as entire ecosystems. Historic and current destruction created by gold mining is greater than any value generated.[8] Commercial gold mining projects are mainly on indigenous lands. By violating their land rights, mining companies are denying the right to life of those indigenous peoples, whose relationship to land is central to their spiritual identity and survival. We need to support the self-determination of indigenous peoples and the recovery, demarcation and legal recognition of campesinos, tribal and indigenous peoples' lands.... Large-scale and small-scale, toxic chemical-dependent gold mining damages landscapes, habitats, biodiversity, human health and water resources. Water especially is contaminated by cyanide, acid mine drainage, heavy metals and mercury from gold mining. Additionally, the hydrological cycle is changed and water sources are grossly depleted by pumping water from aquifers."

What are the teachings of such cases? How do cases on mining conflicts in the so-called "tribal belt" of India differ from those in other countries?

Metabolic Profiles and Ecological Conflicts

Ecological distribution conflicts number in the thousands (Schnaiberg, 1986; Martinez-Alier and O'Connor, 1996, 1999). Links can be traced between social metabolic profiles and conflicts at different scales. Conflicts are classified here according to the different points in the "commodity chains" where they occur, in extraction, in manufacture and transport, or finally in waste disposal.

Conflicts on the Extraction of Materials and Energy

Mining and Oil Extraction Conflicts

Complaints over mines and smelters because of water and air pollution, and land occupation by open-cast mining and slag (many such conflicts are historical, e.g. Ashio in Japan or Rio Tinto in Southern Spain *c.* 1900, Central Peru *c.* 1920). Also, conflicts on oil and gas extraction. For instance, in the growing economy of India, there are conflicts on the mining of coal, iron ore, uranium, bauxite located mainly in adivasi territories in Orissa and Jharkhand (*Down to Earth,* 15 April 2005, 26–35), by national public or private companies but also by transnational companies (e.g. the Alcan and Vedanta projects in Orissa). There are also conflicts on the extraction of building materials (including deaths of revenue officials who try to stop the quarrying of sand by "sand mafias" in Tamil Nadu, *The Hindu,* 17 December 2004).

Biopiracy

The appropriation of genetic resources ("wild" or agricultural) without adequate payment or recognition of peasant or indigenous ownership over them (including the extreme case of the Human Genome project against which many indigenous peoples complained). The word "biopiracy" was introduced by Pat Mooney, of RAFI, c. 1993. The facts are old; the new name reveals a sense of injustice.

Land Degradation

Soil erosion caused by unequal land distribution, or by pressure of export production. Blaikie and Brookfield (1987) introduced the crucial distinction between pressure of population and pressure of production on the sustainable use of land.

Plantations are not Forests (Carrere and Lohman, 1996; Lohman, 1991, 1996)

Around the world, complaints arise against eucalyptus, pine, acacia plantations for wood or paper pulp or cellulose production (often exported) (www.wrm.org.uy). Increased use of the biomass leads to such conflicts (e.g. resistance by indigenous peoples against Aracruz in Brazil, or the conflict on the ENCE cellulose plant in Uruguay in 2005-06).

Mangroves vs Shrimp

Conflicts arise over the appropriation of the biomass of mangroves by the shrimp industry, hence the movement to preserve the mangroves for livelihood against the shrimp export industry in Thailand, Honduras, Ecuador, Colombia, Brazil, India, Philippines, Bangladesh, Sri Lanka, Indonesia... (see the Environmental Justice Foundation's reports, London, www.ejfoundation.org).

National/Local Fishing Rights

Other forms of use of biomass give rise to other conflicts. Thus, there are national and local fishing conflicts. Hence, the attempts to stop open access depredation by imposing (since the 1940s in Peru, Ecuador, Chile) exclusive fishing areas. The language here is international public law. Another conflict is that of the defence (or introduction) of local communitarian fishing rights against industrial fishing by trawlers (as in coastal India).

Conflicts on Transport

- Complaints over oil spills from tankers or pipelines, over new motorways, harbours and airports, also over "hidrovías" (such as Paraguay-Paraná), e.g. the

Sethusamundram Ship Canal Project between Tamil Nadu and Sri Lanka that shortens navigation time between the east and west coasts of India but constitutes a threat to the local fisheries because of dredging. Physical indicators for transport (tons-km) grow faster than GDP, and than the material and energy throughout the economy.

- Bioinvasions is the introduction and establishment of alien species, deliberate, or accidentally caused by trade or human travel. There are often social asymmetries in the burdens from bioinvasions. European pathogens, and animals such as sheep, caused havoc in the Americas and Australia in colonial times (Melville, 1994 on the Mezquital Valley in Mexico and the Otomi people). There are less dramatic examples. Thus, some escaped species of trees in South Africa (black wattle) diminish local water availability.

Conflicts on Waste and Pollution

Toxic Struggles

A name given in the US to fights against hazards from heavy metals or dioxins (Gibbs, 1981 and Hofrichter, 1993). It describes also older cases in other countries, such as Minamata mercury poisoning in Kumamoto Prefecture in Japan caused by the chemical manufacturer Chisso Corporation in the 1950s and 1960s, where complaints continue to be put forward still today.

Waste Dumping

Thus, the ship breaking yards at Alang (Gujarat) have a devastating environmental impact. This situation is periodically in the news. In 2005, the Danish authorities called back a toxic Danish ship sent there (*Down to Earth*, 31 May 2005, 16-17). On 15 February 2006, Greenpeace won a court case in Paris forcing the government to bring back the aircraft carrier *Clemenceau* headed for dismantling in Alang. Also, "thousands of tonnes of electronic and electrical waste (e-waste) are being illegally exported every year from Britain to the developing Asian countries, including India, Pakistan and China". ("The trade is absolutely illegal and against the spirit of the Basel Convention, said Kishore Wanhade of Toxics Link in Delhi." – *The Hindu*, 18 December 2004). Greenpeace used *Toxic Imperialism* in 1988 for waste dumping in poorer countries.

Transboundary Pollution

Applied in the 1970s and 1980s mainly to sulphur dioxide crossing borders in Europe, and producing acid rain. Also between areas in the USA (New England polluted by western winds), and from China to Japan.

Equal Rights to Carbon Sinks

The proposal for equal per capita use of oceans, new vegetation, soils and atmosphere as sinks or temporary reservoirs for carbon dioxide (Agarwal and Narain, 1991). The disproportionate emissions of carbon dioxide have given rise to a "carbon debt" (www.deudaecologica.org), as Andrew Simms calls it.

Consumers' and Citizens' Safety

Struggles over the definition and the burden of uncertain risks from new technologies (nuclear, GMO). They also affect producers (agro-toxics). Some conflicts are new (BSE). Others are old, and regulatory authorities failed to apply what is now called the "precautionary principle". Ulrich Beck (1992) focused on surprises (such as Chernobyl) more than on older technological conflicts (asbestos, DDT, CFC...) or on the effects of trends of metabolic flows (e.g. the enhanced greenhouse effect).

Links between local and global are established. For instance, Oilwatch provides information on conflicts on oil extraction in fragile tropical areas. Every oil well stopped, every pipeline delayed, is a contribution to the fight against climate change, argues Oilwatch. What is needed is a programme to provide energy to the two billion poorest people for their livelihood needs, not a continuous expansion of oil extraction and consumption. Stopping oil production in some wells (as it sometimes happens), and an oil extraction moratorium, would make a global contribution against climate change, perhaps deserving "carbon credits".

Ecologically Unequal Exchange

The trade pattern consisting in specialization in the export of raw materials has given rise to the notion of *Ecologically Unequal Exchange*. Such plunder economy was called *Raubwirtschaft* by German and French geographers one hundred years ago. In a theory of ecologically unequal exchange, attention is drawn to physical accounting, focusing on the unequal amounts of energy (or exergy, i.e. available energy), or materials (in tonnes), or land used up. Then, more of the original exergy and materials have been dissipated in producing the final products or services (in the metropolis), the higher the prices of these final products or services will have to be (Hornborg, 1998; Naredo and Valero, 1999 and Naredo, 2001). Thus, "market prices are the means by which world system centres extract exergy from the peripheries" (Hornborg, 1998). This would also apply to trade between the regions of a large country such as Brazil, India or China.

At the beginning of European colonization, the goods imported were what Wallerstein called "preciosities", for instance, silver and pepper. The means of transport at the time made bulky trade impossible. Indeed, preciosities (high chrematistic value per kilogram) are still traded. Gold is like shrimp, in this regard, or Sierra Leone's diamonds. Similarly, consider the local ecological impacts of exports of ivory or tiger body parts compared to the irrelevance of such trade for the importing countries' metabolism. Also, sugar was initially a preciosity. Later, based on the slave plantations, it became a bulk commodity playing a role (as Sidney Mintz showed) in the bio-metabolism (endosomatic energy) of the English working class. Other early bulk commodities (such as guano, wood, cotton) had a role in the techno-metabolism of the importing countries. While in the nineteenth and early twentieth centuries, the countries of today's European Union depended on their own coal and biomass as energy sources, now they have become large net importers of oil and gas. They might resort also to large-scale biofuels imports from Brazil, Argentina and Canada. Taking all materials together (energy carriers, minerals, metals, biomass), the European Union (15 countries) was importing in 2000 about four times more tonnes than it was exporting. Meanwhile, Latin America appears to be exporting six times more tonnes than it imports (Giljum and Eisenmenger, 2004). Moreover, Southern exports carry heavier "ecological rucksacks" than the imports, as shown by research on the energy dissipated and the carbon dioxide produced by each dollar of exports and of imports of Brazil (Machado et al., 2001), and by research on the "environmental pollution terms of trade" for metals (Muradian et al., 2002). Pengue (2005) has computed the hidden flows in the soybean trade of Argentina, in the form of loss of nutrients, the soil erosion and the "virtual water". Also, Pengue mentions the new resistance against pesticides acquired by some weeds which become invaders. Pérez-Rincón (2006) gives figures in the early 2000s for Colombia of 70 million tonnes of exports per year compared to 10 million tonnes of imports.

True, some rich countries with high material and energy use per capita are net resource-exporters because of low populations (Canada, Australia), successfully following the path of Harold Innis' "staple theory of growth". The United States was also a net exporter of natural resources. However, in the 1970s, it reached the Hubbert curve oil peak. Oil imports are now over 10 mbd, i.e. 500 million tonnes or 2 tonnes per person per year. For comparison, material flow in very poor countries is 3 tonnes/person/year (mostly biomass). Whatever the historically changing positions of different countries or regions, the metabolic processes that maintain the world system centres are guaranteed by ecologically unequal exchange, deteriorating terms of trade for natural resources, cheap labour and cheap human lives in the peripheries, and, when needed, by military power.

There are then claims for repayment of the so-called *Ecological Debt* from North to South, bringing together the "carbon debt", i.e. damages from rich countries on account of past and present excessive per capita emissions of carbon dioxide, and claims because of biopiracy, ecologically unequal exchange, and also environmental liabilities by private companies.

Conclusion

The metabolic perspective illuminates the ecological contents of conflicts "disguised" under different headings, e.g. *workers' actions for occupational health and safety* are struggles (in the framework of collective bargaining or outside it) to prevent damages to workers in mines, plantations or factories (they are, so to speak, "red" outside and "green" inside). Also, *urban activism for clean air, green spaces, sanitation, cyclists' and pedestrian rights* has inspired old or new struggles outside the market in order to improve conditions of livelihood or to gain access to recreational amenities. Ecological conflicts also give rise to what Bina Agarwal (1992) called *social ecofeminism* or *environmental feminism*, meaning the environmental activism of women, motivated by their social situation. The idiom of such struggles is not necessarily that of feminism and/or environmentalism. The *Environmentalism of the Poor* describes social conflicts with an ecological content, today and in history, of the poor against the relatively rich, not only but mainly in rural contexts (Guha, 1989; Martinez-Alier, 1991, 1992; Guha and Martinez-Alier, 1997).

In resource extraction or in waste disposal conflicts, some actors deploy the language of *indigenous environmentalism*, that is, the use of territorial rights and ethnic resistance against external exploitation, for instance in Yucca Mountain, Nevada. Convention 169 of ILO is used in such cases in some countries, or in India, the protection of adivasi peoples by the Constitution and by court decisions (Samata, 2003). As we saw, in the United States, *Environmental Justice* arose against "environmental racism", also in South Africa, in Brazil, and elsewhere (Dunion, 2003 and Acselrad et al., 2004). The fights against "environmental racism", or the conflicts in defence of native agricultural varieties against biopiracy or against the intrusion of transgenic crops (as in Mexico), or the defence of indigenous groups against oil extraction, mining, large dams, industrial pollution or logging, could be seen as expressions of an *identity politics*. This is mistaken because there are common causes to such conflicts and there are cross-cultural similarities in resistance. Not isolated NIMBYs but a collective NIABY. Thus, in the struggles around the world for biomass and against the privatization of common property lands, the eucalyptus or other undesired plantation trees are pulled out, and other locally useful trees are put in. Because of unequal property rights, and inequalities of power and income among humans (both international and internal to each state), the pollution burdens and the access to natural resources are unequally distributed. Capitalism (or, in general, the industrial system) advances into commodity frontiers because it uses more materials and energy, therefore, it produces and displaces more waste, undermining the conditions of livelihood and existence of peripheral peoples who complain accordingly. Therefore, to see in ecological conflicts, mainly a reaffirmation of identity is not convincing. It is rather the other way around, identity being one idiom in which such conflicts are expressed.

Whenever there are unresolved ecological conflicts, there is likely to be not only a discrepancy but incommensurability in valuation (Faucheux and O'Connor, 1998; Funtowicz and Ravetz, 1994; Martinez-Alier, Munda and O'Neill, 1998; Martinez-Alier and O'Connor, 1996, 1999; O'Connor and Spash, 1999). Environmental conflicts are expressed as conflicts on valuation, either inside one single standard of valuation, or across plural values. In other words, "semiotic resistance" (O'Connor, 1993) to environmental abuse may be expressed in many languages. For instance, it can be stated that while humans have different economic values (Lawrence Summers' Principle) they all have the same value in the scale of human dignity. When we say that someone or something is "very valuable" or "not very valuable", this is a statement that elicits the further question, in which standard of valuation? (O'Neill, 1993; Munda, 1995; Martinez-Alier, Munda and O'Neill, 1998).

The increased use of energy and materials in the world economy means that tribal areas around the world (though not only tribal areas) become "commodity frontiers" where bulk commodities essential to the metabolism of the rich economies (oil, coal, gas, bauxite, copper, timber, hydroelectricity) or preciosities (diamonds, gold, mahogany, aquaculture shrimp) are supplied. If the economy was "dematerializing" in an absolute sense (and not only, as in some countries, relative to GDP growth), then many of the conflicts considered here would be less pervasive and intense. Different languages of valuation are used. People who are poor and whose health and lives are cheap, often appeal to non-chrematistic languages of valuation. The question is not whether economic value can only be determined in existing markets, in as much as economists have developed methods for the monetary valuation of environmental goods and services or of negative externalities outside the market. Rather, the question is: must all evaluations in a given conflict (e.g. on extraction of bauxite in Orissa, on a hydrolectric dam in the north-east of India, on the destruction of a mangrove in Honduras to the benefit of shrimp exports, on the determination of the suitable level of carbon dioxide emissions by the European Union), be reduced to a single dimension? (Funtowicz and Ravetz, 1994). Who has the power to determine which is the bottom-line in an environmental discussion? The critique of conventional economic accounting often emphasizes the forgotten current values of environmental services from ecosystems. The environmental services from coral reefs, mangroves, tropical rainforest may be given a notional money value per hectare per year, and then the lost hectares are translated into virtual economic losses. This approach is good in order to impress the public with the importance of environmental losses but it is certainly insufficient in order to grasp the relations between economy and environment. Our economy depends on the photosynthesis of millions of years ago for our main energy sources. It depends on ancient biochemical cycles for other mineral resources that we are squandering without replacement. In the case of oil, the extraction peak will be reached soon. We are taking about 87 mbd – in terms of calories, the world average is equivalent to about 20,000 kcal per person/day (ten times the food energy intake), and in the USA, it is equivalent to 100,000 kcal per person/day. In exosomatic energy terms, oil is then far more important than biomass. Oil at US$ 90 a barrel is still cheap from the point of view of its fair inter-generational allocation and the externalities it produces.

There is a historic trend towards increasing energy costs of obtaining energy (a lower EROI). Coming down from the peak of the Hubbert curve will be politically and environmentally difficult. Conflicts arise in the Niger Delta and in the Amazonia of Peru and Ecuador against companies such as Shell, Repsol and Oxy. Appeal to some other energy sources (agro-fuels, nuclear energy) will compound the difficulties. Wind and photovoltaic energy are fortunately increasing. They will help to compensate for the dwindling supplies of oil over the next few decades. Coal supplies are increasing (they already grew seven times in the twentieth century) but coal is noxious locally and also globally because of carbon dioxide emissions.

One may readily agree that conventional economic accounting is misleading. The experience that Pavan Sukhdev (with Haripriya Gundimeda and Pushpam Kumar) gained in India trying to give economic values to non-timber products from forests, and to other environmental services (such as carbon uptake, water and soil retention), has been an inspiration for the TEEB process (The Economics of Ecosystems and Biodiversity) sponsored by DG Environment of the European Commission and by UNEP in the years 2008-10. As the TEEB team states, a monetary representation of the services provided by clean water, access to wood and pastures, and medicinal plants, does not really measure the essential dependence of poor people on such resources and services. In National Income Accounting, one could introduce valuations of ecosystem and biodiversity losses either in satellite accounts (physical and monetary) or in adjusted GDP accounts ("Green Accounts"). The economic valuation of losses might be low compared to the economic gains of projects that destroy biodiversity. However, which groups of people suffer most by such losses? In their project "Green Accounting for India" they found that the most significant direct beneficiaries of forest biodiversity and ecosystem services are the poor, and the predominant impact of a loss or denial of these inputs is on the well-being of the poor. The poverty of the beneficiaries makes these losses more acute as a proportion of their "livelihood incomes" than is the case for the people of India at large. Hence, the notion of "the GDP of the Poor": for instance, when water in the local river or aquifer is polluted because of mining, they cannot afford to buy water in plastic bottles. Therefore, when poor people see that their chances of livelihood are threatened because of mining projects, dams, tree plantations, or large industrial areas, they complain not because they are professional environmentalists but because they need the services of the environment for their immediate survival. This is the "environmentalism of the poor".

In *Down to Earth* (15 August 2008), Sunita Narain gave some current examples from India: "In Sikkim, bowing to local protests, the government has cancelled 11 hydro-electric projects. In Arunachal Pradesh, dam projects are being cleared at breakneck speed and resistance is growing. In Uttarakhand last month, two projects on the Ganga were put on hold and there is growing concern about the rest. In Himachal Pradesh, dams are so controversial that elections were won where candidates said they would not allow these to be built. Many other projects, from thermal power stations to "greenfield" mining, are being resisted. The South Korean giant Posco's iron ore mine, steel plant and port are under fire. The prime minister has promised the South Korean premier that the project will go ahead by August. But local people are not listening. They do not want to lose their land and livelihood and do not believe in promises of compensation. In Maharashtra, mango growers are up in arms against the proposed thermal power station in Ratnagiri. In every nook and corner of the country where land is acquired, or water sourced, for industry, people are fighting even to death. There are wounds. There is violence. There is also desperation. Like it or not, there are a million mutinies today.... After I visited Kalinganagar, where villagers died protesting against Tata's project, I wrote this was not about competition or Naxalism. These were poor villagers who knew they did not have the skills to survive in the modern world. They had seen their neighbours displaced, promised jobs and money that never came. They knew they were poor. But they also knew modern development would make them poorer. It was the same in prosperous Goa, where I found village after village fighting against the powerful mining lobby...."

These movements combine livelihood, social, economic and environmental issues, with emphasis on issues of extraction and pollution. They set their "moral economy" in opposition to the logic of extraction of oil, minerals, wood or agro-fuels at the "commodity frontiers", defending biodiversity and their own livelihood. In many instances, they draw on a sense of local identity (indigenous rights and values such as the sacredness of the land) but they also connect easily with the politics of the left. However, the traditional left in some southern countries still tends to see environmentalism as a "luxury of the rich" .

While conventional economics looks at environmental impacts in terms of externalities or lost environmental services which should be internalized into the price system, one can see externalities (following Kapp) not as market failures but as cost-shifting successes which nevertheless might give rise to environmental movements (Leff, 1986 and O'Connor, 1988). Such movements cannot be gagged by cost-benefit analysis. In conclusion, conflicts on the access to natural resources or on the exposure to environmental burdens may be expressed:

(a) Inside one single standard of valuation. How should the externalities caused by a firm be valued in money terms, when demanding compensation in a court case? How could an argument for conservation of a natural space be made or contested, in terms of the number and biological value of the species it contains? An appeal to the particular experts is here appropriate.
(b) Through a value standard contest or dispute, as when losses of biodiversity, or in cultural patrimony, or damage to human livelihoods, or infringements on human rights, or loss of indigenous territorial rights, are compared in non-commensurable terms to economic gains from a new dam or from a mining project or from oil extraction (O'Connor and Spash, 1999: 5).

REFERENCES

[1] Acselrad, H., S. Herculano and J.A. Padua, eds., *Justiça Ambiental e Cidadania*, Relume Dumará, Rio de Janeiro, 2004.

[2] Adeola, Francis O., Cross-National Environmental Injustice and Human Rights, *American Behavioural Scientist*, 43(4): 686-706, 2000.

[3] Adriaanse, A., Brigenzu, S, Hammond, A., Moriguchi, Y., Rodenburg, E., Rogich and D. Schütz, H., *Resource Flows. The Material Basis of Industrial Economies.* Washington DC: World Resources Institute, 1997.

[4] Agarwal, A. and S. Narain, *Global Warming: A Case of Environmental Colonialism*, Centre for Science and Environment, Delhi, 1991.

[5] Agarwal, B., The Gender and Environment Debate: Lessons from India, *Feminist Studies*, 18(1), 1992.

[6] Ahmed, Faris, *In Defence of Land and Livelihood. Coastal Communities and the Shrimp Industry in Asia*, Consumers' Association of Penang, CUSO, InterPares, Sierra Club of Canada, Ottawa and Penang, 1997.

[7] Ayres, R.U., Industrial Metabolism, in J. Ausubel ed., *Technology and Environment*, National Academy Press, Washington DC, 1989.

[8] Ayres R.U. and B. Warr, Accounting for Growth: The Role of Physical Work, in S. Ulgiati ed., *Advances in Energy Studies*, SGEditoriali, Padova, 2003, also in *Structural Change and Economic Dynamics* 16: 181-209, 2005.

[9] Balvin, Doris, with Juan Tejada Huaman and Humberto Lozada Coastro, *Agua, mineria y contaminacion. El caso Southern Peru*, Labor, Ilo, 1995.

[10] Beck, U., *Risk Society: Towards a New Modernity*, Sage, London, 1992.

[11] Blaikie P. and H. Brookfield, *Land Degradation and Society*, Methuen, London, 1987.

[12] Bond, P., *Unsustainable South Africa*, Merlin Press, London, 2002.

[13] Bond, Patrick, Economic Growth, Ecological Modernization or Environmental Justice? Conflicting Discourses in Post-apartheid South Africa, *Capitalism, Nature, Socialism*, 11(1): 33-61, 2000.

[14] Brigenzu, S. and Schütz, H., *Total Material Requirement of the European Union.* In: European Environmental Agency (ed). *Technical Report No. 55*, EEA, Copenhagen, 2001.

[15] Bryant, Bunyan and Paul Mohai, eds., *Race and the Incidence of Environmental Hazards, Westview*, Boulder, 1992.

[16] Bryant, Bunyan, ed., *Environmental Justice. Issues, Policies and Solutions*, Island Press, Washington DC, 1995.

[17] Bryant, Raymond and Sinead Bailey, eds., *Third World Political Ecology*, Routledge, London, 1997.

[18] Bullard, R., *Confronting Environmental Racism: Voices from the Grassroots*, South End Press, Boston, 1993.

[19] Bullard, Robert, *Dumping in Dixie: Race, Class and Environmental Quality*, Westview, Boulder, 1990.

[20] Camacho, David E., ed., *Environmental Injustices, Political Struggles. Race, Class and the Environment*, Duke University Press, Durham and London, 1998.

[21] Carrere, R. and L. Lohman, *Pulping the South: Industrial Tree Plantations and the World Paper Economy*, Zed, London, 1996.

[22] CASI, Velippalayam, Nagapattinam, Tamil Nadu. *Struggles Against Shrimp Industries and the Role of the Campaign Against Shrimp Industries. An Update*, January 2004.

[23] Cleveland, C.J., Biophysical Economics: Historical Perspectives and Current Recent Trends, *Ecological Modelling*, 38: 47–73, 1987.

[24] Cleveland, C. and M. Ruth, Indicators of Dematerialization and the Materials Intensity of Use, *Journal of Industrial Ecology*, 2: 15–50, 1998.

[25] Cock, Jacklyn and Eddie Koch, eds., *Going Green: People, Politics and the Environment in South Africa*, Oxford University Press, Cape Town, 1991.

[26] Cottrell, F., *Energy and Society: The Relations between Energy, Social Change and Economic Development*, McGraw Hill, New York, 1955.

[27] Debeir, J.C., Deléage, J.P. and Hémery, D., *Les servitudes de la puissance. Une histoire de l'energie*, Flammarion, Paris, 1986.

[28] Diaz Palacios, Julio, *El Peru y su medio ambiente. Southern Peru Copper Corporation: una compleja agresion ambiental en el sur del pais*, IDMA, Lima, 1988.

[29] DiChiro, Giovanna, Nature as Community. The Convergence of Environmental and Social Justice, in Michael Goldman, ed., 1998.

[30] Dore, Elizabeth, Environment and Society: Long-term Trends in Latin American Mining, *Environment and History* 6: 1–29, 2000 (previous version in Spanish in *Ecologia Politica*, 7, 1994).

[31] Dorsey, Michael, El movimiento por la Justicia Ambiental en EE.UU. Una breve historia, *Ecologia Politica*, 14: 23-32, 1997.

[32] Dunion, K., *Troublemakers: The Struggle for Environmental Justice in Scotland*, Edinburgh U.P., Edinburgh, 2003.

[33] Emmanuel, A., *Unequal Exchange: A Study of the Imperialism of Free Trade*, Monthly Review Press, New York, 1972.

[34] Erickson, Jon. D and Duane Chapman, Sovereignty for Sale. Nuclear Waste in Indian Country, *Akwe:kon Journal*, Fall 1993, 3–10.

[35] Erickson, Jon D., Duane Chapman and Ronald E. Johny, Monitored Retrievable Storage of Spent Nuclear Fuel in Indian Country: Liability, Sovereignty, and Socioeconomics, *American Indian Law Review*, University of Oklahoma College of Law, 1994, 73–103.

[36] EUROSTAT, *Economy-wide Material Flow Accounts and Derived Indicators – A Methodological Guide*. Luxembourg: Office for Official Publications of the E.C., 2001.

[37] Faber, Daniel, ed., *The Struggle for Ecological Democracy. The Environmental Justice Movement in the United States*, Guildford, New York, 1998.

[38] Faucheux S. and O'Connor M., eds., *Valuation for Sustainable Development. Methods and Policy Indicators.* E. Elgar, Cheltenham, 1998.

[39] Fischer-Kowalski, M., Society's Metabolism. The Intellectual History of Material Flow Analysis, Part I, 1860–1970, *J. of Industrial Ecology*, Vol. 2 (1), 61–78, 1998.

[40] Fischer-Kowalski, M. and W. Huettler, Society's Metabolism. The Intellectual History of Material Flow Analysis, Part II, 1970–1998, *J. of Industrial Ecology*, Vol. 2 (4), 107–136, 1998.

[41] Foley, G., Wood Fuel and Conventional fuel in the Developing World, *Ambio* 14(4-5): 253-57, 1985.

[42] Friedman, John and Haripriya Rangan, eds., *In Defense of Livelihood. Comparative Studies in Environmental Action*, UNRISD, Kumarian Press, Hartford CT, 1993.

[43] Funtowicz, S. and J. Ravetz, The Worth of a Songbird: Ecological Economics as a Post-normal Science, *Ecol. Econ.*, 10(3), 197–207, 1994.

[44] Gadgil, M. and R. Guha, *Ecology and Equity. The Use and Abuse of Nature in Contemporary India*, Routledge, London, 1995.

[45] Gedicks, Al, *The New Resource Wars. Native and Environmental Struggles Against Multinational Corporations*, South End Press, Boston, 1993.

[46] Ghai, Dharam and Jessica M. Vivian, eds., *Grassroots Environmental Action. People's Participation in Sustainable Development*, Routledge, London, 1992.

[47] Giampietro, M., *Multiple-scale Integrated Assessment of Agroecosystems*, CRC Press, Boca Raton, FL, 2003.

[48] Gibbs, L.M., *Love Canal: My Story*, State Univ. of New York Press, Albany, 1981.

[49] Giljum, S. and Eisenmenger, N., North-South Trade and the Distribution of Environmental Goods and Burdens, *Journal of Environment and Development*, 13(1), 2004.

[50] Goldman, Michael, ed., *Privatizing Nature: Political Struggles for the Global Commons*, Pluto, London, 1998.

[51] Gottlieb, Roger, *Forcing the Spring: The Transformation of the American Environmental Movement*, Island Press, Washington DC, 1993.

[52] Greenpeace, *International Trade in Toxic Waste*, Brussels, 1988.

[53] Greenpeace, The Database of Known Hazardous Waste Exports from OECD to Non-OECD Countries, 1989–94, Washington DC, 1994.

[54] Guha, R. *The Unquiet Woods: Ecological Change and Peasant Resistance in the Himalaya,* Oxford U.P., Delhi, 1989.

[55] Guha, R. and J. Martinez-Alier, *Varieties of Environmentalism*, Oxford U.P., Delhi, 1997.

[56] Guha, R. and J. Martinez-Alier, Political Ecology, the Environmentalism of the Poor, and the Global Movement for Environmental Justice, *Kurswechsel* (Vienna), Heft 3, 1999: 27–40.

[57] Haberl, H., The Energetic Metabolism of Societies. Part I: Accounting Concepts, The Energetic Metabolism of Societies, Part II: Empirical Examples, *J. of Industrial Ecology* 5(2), 2001.

[58] Haberl, H., Fischer-Kowalski, M., Krausmann, F., Weisz, H., and Winiwarter,

V., Progress Towards Sustainability? What the Conceptual Framework of Material and Energy Flow Accounting (MEFA) can offer. *Land Use Policy* 21(3), 2004.

[59] Haberl, Helmut et al., Human Appropriation of Net Primary Production as Determinant of Avifauna Diversity in Austria, *Agriculture, Ecosystems and Environment*, 110: 119–131, 2005.

[60] Hall, Ch., Cleveland, C.J. and Kaufman, R., *Energy and Resources Quality: The Ecology of the Economic Process*, Wiley, New York, 1986.

[61] Hofrichter, R., ed., *Toxic Struggles: The Theory and Practice of Environmental Justice*, foreword by Lois Gibbs, New Society Publishers, Philadelphia, 1993.

[62] Hornborg, A., Toward an Ecological Theory of Unequal Exchange: Articulating World System Theory and Ecological Economics, *Ecol. Econ.*, 25 (1): 127–36, 1998.

[63] Jodha, N.S. (1998), Poverty and Environmental Resource Degradation. An Alternative Explanation and Possible Solutions, *Economic and Political Weekly*, 33 (36-37): 238490.

[64] Khagram, S., *Dams and Development. Transnational Struggles for Water and Power*, Oxford UP, Delhi, 2005.

[65] Krausmann, F., Haberl, H., Schulz, N.B., Erb, K.H., Darge, E. and Gaube, V., Land-Use Change and Socio-Economic Metabolism in Austria, Part I: Socio-Economic Driving Forces of Land-Use Change 1950–1995. *Land Use Policy*, 20 (2003), 1, 1–20.

[66] Krausmann, F., Haberl, H., Erb, K. and Wackernagel, M., Resource Flows and Land Use in Austria 1950–2000: Using the MEFA Framework to Monitor Society-Nature Interaction for Sustainability. *Land Use Policy* 21(3), 2004.

[67] Kuletz, Valerie, *The Tainted Desert. Environmental and Social Ruin in the American West*, Routledge, New York, 1998.

[68] Leff, Enrique, *Green Production. Toward an Environmental Rationality*, Guilford, New York, 1995.

[69] Lohman, Larry, Peasants, Plantations and Pulp: The Politics of Eucalyptus in Thailand, *Bulletin of Concerned Asian Scholars*, 23(4), 1991.

[70] Lohman, Larry, Freedom to Plant. Indonesia and Thailand in a Globalizing Pulp and Paper Industry, in Michael J.G. Parnwell and Raymond L. Bryant, eds., *Environmental Change in South-East Asia. People, Politics and Sustainable Development*, Routledge, London and New York, 1996.

[71] Lotka, A.J., Die Evolution von Standpunkte der Physik, *Annalen der Naturphilosophie*, 10: 59–74, 1911.

[72] Low, Nicholas and Brendan Gleeson, *Justice, Society and Nature. An Exploration of Political Ecology*, Routledge, London and New York, 1998.

[73] Machado, G., R. Schaeffer and E. Worrell, Energy and Carbon Embodied in the International Trade of Brazil: An Input-Output Approach, *Ecol. Econ.*, 39(3): 409–424, 2001.

[74] Mallon, Florencia, *The Defense of Community in Peru's Central Highlands*, Princeton U.P., Princeton, 1983.

[75] Martinez-Alier, J. with K. Schlüpmann, *Ecological Economics. Energy, Environment and Society*, Blackwell, Oxford, 1987.

[76] Martinez-Alier, J., Ecology and the Poor: A Neglected Issue in Latin American History, *Jour. of Latin American Studies*, 23(3), 1991: 621–640.

[77] Martinez-Alier J. and E. Hershberg, Environmentalism and the Poor, *Items*, Social Sciences Research Council, New York 46(1), March 1992.

[78] Martinez-Alier J. and M. O'Connor, Ecological and Economic Distribution Conflicts, in R. Costanza, O. Segura and J. Martinez-Alier, eds., *Getting Down to Earth: Practical Applications of Ecological Economics*, ISEE, Island Press, Washington DC, 1996.

[79] Martinez-Alier J. and M. O'Connor, Distributional Issues: An Overview, Chapter 25 in J. van den Bergh, ed., *Handbook of Environmental and Resource Economics*, E. Elgar, Cheltenham, 1999.

[80] Martinez-Alier, J., Munda. G. and O'Neill, J., Weak Comparability of Values as a Foundation for Ecological Economics, *Ecol. Econ.*, 26: 277–86, 1998.

[81] Martinez-Alier, J., *The Environmentalism of the Poor. A Study of Ecological Conflicts and Valuation*, E. Elgar, Cheltenham, Northampton MA, 2002, New Ed. Oxford U.P., Delhi, 2005.

[82] Martinez-Alier, J. and H. Schandl, Introduction to the Special Section: European Environmental History and Ecological Economics, in *Ecol. Econ.* 41(2), 2002, 175-6.

[83] Matthews, E., Amann, C., Brigenzu, S., Fischer-Kowalski, M., Hütler, W., Kleijn, R., Moriguchi, Y., Ottke, C., Rodenburg, E., Schandl, H., Schütz, H. van den Voet, E. and Weisz, H. (2000), *The weight of nations. Material outflows from industrial economies.* Washington DC: World Resources Institute.

[84] McCully, P., *Silenced Rivers: The Ecology and Politics of Large Dams*, Zed, London, 1996.

[85] McNeill, J.R., *Something New under the Sun. An Environmental History of the Twentieth-Century World*, Norton, New York, 2000.

[86] Melville, E. *The Plague of Sheep*, Cambridge U.P., Cambridge, 1994.

[87] Mintz, S., *Sweetness and Power. The Place of Sugar in Modern History*, Penguin, London, 1985.

[88] Metzger, D., *Copper in the World Economy*, Heineman, London, 1980.

[89] Moody, Roger, *The Gulliver File. Mines, People, and Land: A Global Battleground*, Minewatch-WISE-Pluto Press, London, 1992.

[90] Munda, G., *Multicriteria Evaluation in a Fuzzy Environment. Theory and Applications in Ecological Economics*. Physika Verlag, Heidelberg, 1995.

[91] Muradian, R., M. O'Connor and J. Martinez-Alier, Embodied Pollution in Trade: Estimating the "Environmental Load Displacement" of Industrialized Countries, *Ecol. Econ.*, 41(1): 51–67, 2002.

[92] Nadkarni, M.V., 'Poverty, Environment and Development: A Many Patterned Nexus', *Economic and Political Weekly*, 35 (14): 1184–90, 2000.

[93] Naredo, J.M. and Valero, A., *Desarrollo económico y deterioro ecológico*, Argentaria-Visor, Madrid, 1999.

[94] Naredo, J.M., Quantifying Natural Capital: Beyond Monetary Value, in M. Munasinghe and O. Sunkel, *The Sustainability of Long-term Growth: Socioeconomic and Ecological Perspectives*, E. Elgar, Cheltenham, Northampton MA, 2001.

[95] Novotny, Patrick, Popular Epidemiology and the Struggle for Community Health in the Environmental Justice Movement, Chapter 5 in D. Faber, ed., 1998.

[96] O'Connor, James, Introduction, *Capitalism, Nature, Socialism*, 1, 1988.

[97] O'Connor, Martin, On the Misadventures of Capitalist Nature, *Capitalism, Nature, Socialism*, 1993.

[98] O'Connor M. and Spash C., eds., *Valuation and the Environment. Theory, Methods and Practice*. E. Elgar, Cheltenham, 1999.

[99] Odum, H.T., *Environment, Power and Society*, Wiley, New York, 1971.

[100] O'Neill, J., *Ecology, Policy and Politics*, Routledge, London, 1993.

[101] Peet, R. and M. Watts, eds., *Liberation Ecologies*, Routledge, London, 1996.

[102] Pengue, Walter A., Transgenic Crops in Argentina. The Ecological and Social Debt, *Bull. of Science, Technology and Society*, 25(4): 314–322, 2005.

[103] Pérez-Rincón, M.A., Colombian International Trade from a Physical Perspective: Towards an Ecological "Prebisch Thesis", *Ecol. Econ.*, in press (2006).

[104] Pulido, Laura, *Environmentalism and Economic Justice: Two Chicano Struggles in the Southwest*, Univ. of Arizona Press, Tucson, 1996.

[105] Rocheleau, D. et al., *Feminist Political Ecology*, Routledge, London, 1995.

[106] Sachs, Aaron, *Eco-justice: Linking Human Rights and the Environment*, Worldwatch Inst., Washington DC, 1995.

[107] Samata, *Surviving a Minefield. A Landmark Supreme Court Judgement Restoring the Rights of Tribals*. Hyderabad, January 2003.

[108] Schnaiberg, A. et al., *Distributional Conflicts in Environmental Resource Policy*, E. Elgar, Aldershot, 1986.

[109] Szasz, A., *Ecopopulism: Toxic Waste and the Movement for Environmental Justice*, Univ. of Minnesota Press, Minneapolis, 1994.

[110] Taylor, B.R., ed., *Ecological Resistance Movements. The Global Emergence of Radical and Popular Environmentalism*, SUNY Press, Albany, 1995.

[111] Taylor, Dorceta, The Rise of the Environmental Justice Paradigm, *American Behavioral Scientist,* 43(4), January 2000.

[112] Westra, Laura and Peter Wenz, *Faces of Environmental Racism: Confronting Issues of Global Justice*, Rowman and Littlefield, Lanham MD, 1995.

Notes

1. Deborah Robinson, International Possibilities Unlimited, Washington DC, "Environmental Devastation and Home & Abroad: The Importance of Understanding the Link", 1999, www.preamble.org/environmental_justice
2. However, water use should be added to the metabolic profiles in a separate account. The political ecology of water focuses on conflicts on dams (Mc Cully, 1996 and Khagram, 2005) such as in India the Narmada Bachao Andolan, also new conflicts in the North-East, and complaints against the "interlinking of the rivers". Also, conflicts on the use and pollution of aquifers (of which the Plachimada conflict in Kerala between farmers and the Coca-Cola company became world famous). In Brazil, there is an organized movement of atingidos por barragens. In 2005, a successful civic resistance movement stopped water transfer from the Sao Francisco river (see www.irn.org). The political ecology of water also studies the dumping of waste into water, or the energy and environmental impacts of new desalination projects, or the use and prices of water. There is also a new discussion on "virtual water" (i.e. the water "cost" of different products). Cf. Hoekstra, A.Y. and P.Q. Hung (2002), Virtual water trade: a quantification of virtual water flows between nations in relation to international crop trade. Value of Water Research Report Series n. 11, UNESCO-IHE, Delft (see: www.waterfootprint.org).

3. "Horinkhola and the surrounding villages have been declared a "Shrimp-Free Zone", and every 7 November, thousands of landless peasants gather here in a show of solidarity with this community's resistance against the shrimp industry" (Ahmed, 1997: 15).
4. Ronnie Morris, "UK court demolishes double standards", Business Report, 4 March 1999, and subsequent information downloaded from www.saep.org.
5. Internal World Bank memo, as reported in *The Economist*, 8 February 1992, under the title "Let them eat pollution".
6. Documentation on this case comes from the files from the Permanent People's Tribunal on Global Corporations and Human Wrongs organized by the Lelio Basso Foundation at the School of Law, University of Warwick, Coventry, 22-25 March 2000. See also Eyal Press, "Freeport-McMoRan at Home and Abroad", The Nation, July 31-August 7, 1995, and Robert Bryce (from the newspaper Austin Chronicle), "Spinning Gold", Mother Jones, Sept.-Oct. 1996.
7. Survival for Tribal Peoples (London), Media Briefing May 1998, "Rio Tinto critic gagged".
8. I would frame the issue in terms of incommensurability of values rather than the value being larger or smaller.

8

Role of Ecological Economics in Policy-Making

Kirit S. Parikh

Introduction

Policy-making in a democratic country like India with its cultural, linguistic, climate and environmental diversity requires striking many balances. Not only the interests of various stakeholders have to be balanced, but also the interests of present and future generations have to be balanced. The economic growth needed for furthering human development has to factor in the potential impact on environment that might adversely affect human development in future. The notion of sustainable development advanced by the Bruntland Commission has to be operationalized.

Policy makers facing periodic elections have a short horizon and tend to undervalue future. Environmental consequences of economic development often take time to manifest themselves and so they get neglected. Ecological economics can help us bring awareness about the costs and benefits in a more holistic manner and lead to better decisions.

The fundamental notion of environmental economics is to value environmental consequences of an action. Valuation is generally done with an anthropocentric perspective. What would a deterioration in environmental quality cost to human being in economic terms. There is often an underlying assumption that natural capital can be substituted by man-made capital. This is not acceptable to many ecologists who argue, and rightly so, that some things are priceless and cannot be valued. How do we value tigers for example? The environmental economists' notion of existence value tries to capture this concern but then the economists' penchant for quantification dominates and methods of contingent valuation are used. However, this is again an anthropocentric valuation. By recognizing the limitation of environmental economics and setting certain aspects as invaluable and defining 'go' – 'no go' boundaries clearly can reconcile the difference.

The strong sustainability criteria is a step in this direction. The ecologist's concern is the sustainability of eco systems. The idea of resilience is useful in reconciling the ecologist's concerns with the economist's need for valuation. Resilience can be characterized by the largest shock that ecology can bear without losing its ability to recover its steady state and without tipping into another phase space (Parikh Kirit, 1989). An ecological system can be described by the levels of various state variables. The maximum tolerable shock will define the minimum values of some state variables. Thus, by requiring that these values must not be allowed to fall below these levels while working out economic strategies, we can to a great extent bridge the gap between ecological and economic viewpoints.

Valuation is helpful in policy-making. This is best illustrated by looking at major policy issues facing India and seeing where environmental economics can help in making a better policy.

How Important is it to Account for the Environment?

The first question is how important is it to account for environmental quality change? In 1988, the MOEF had set up a committee under M.S. Swaminathan, of which I was a member, to chalk out an action plan for sustainable development (MOEF, 1990). An important recommendation of the committee was that we should introduce natural resource accounting. Subsequently, at the behest of MoEF, we at IGIDR prepared a frame work (K. Parikh et al., 1993). I was also involved in preparing for UNEP a simple guide for preparing accounts as per the SEEA framework of UN-STAT. This was followed by a primer for UN-ESCAP with case studies (J. Parikh and K. Parikh, 1997 and 1998) of natural resource accounting.

The idea behind natural resource accounting is that almost all economic activities have some impact on the environment. The degradation of natural resources, or a loss in the quality of the environment, imposes a burden on the present and future generations. It may not be wrong to borrow from the coming generations if we leave them richer and more able to deal with the problems we leave behind. However, they should not have their options closed. Thus, we need to know how much of resources we have used up and how much of a burden we leave behind. Accounting of environmental resource use does not normally take place in the process of economic activities because the costs of environmental degradation and resource depletion are not borne by the economic actors who cause them.

That natural resource capital contributes to production just as man-made capital does has been well recognized by the classical economists. Thus, land rent constituted a part of value-added. Alfred Marshall recognized the contribution that natural capital made to production of goods and services considering it as a factor of production. Thus, accounting for natural capital and its depreciation is but a logical extension of the ideas of national income accounting.

With natural resource accounting, one becomes aware what the true growth is, say, 3 per cent rather than 7 per cent. When one accounts for the value of natural resource degradation, one realizes that policies need to change. A greater appreciation of the value of natural resources occurs.

Of course, there are many problems and data limitations in doing such accounting. Yet, once the usefulness and importance of missing data is demonstrated, such data might get collected.

The estimate of such accounting made for India illustrate this. We had estimation of environmental degradation of four key resources in India, air, forest, soil and water for the year 1994–97.

Pulling the four estimates together, we get the economy wide cost of environmental degradation which we should consider applicable to mid 1990s. These are summarized in Table 1.

Table 1: Annual Cost of Environmental Degradation in India, 1994—97

(Per cent of GDP)

Resource	Range
Air	0.4
Forests	1.1 – 1.6
Soil	0.30 – 0.80
Water	1.70 – 2.1
Total	3.5 – 4.9

Table 1 shows that we should subtract an additional 3.5 per cent to 4.9 per cent of

GDP from our NDP to obtain an environmentally adjusted NDP. What does this imply for the growth rate of India's environmentally adjusted NDP?

It would depend on whether damage to environment and natural resources is accelerating or not? If, as a per cent of NDP, the cost of environmental degradation has remained the same in past years, then the growth rate is not affected.

On the other hand, if the cost of degradation was nil five years ago and is now 5 per cent of GDP, the growth rate of NDP over the five years has to be reduced by 5 percentage points.

It should, however, be emphasized that the estimated costs are partial and the cost to social welfare is likely to be much larger.

Also costs of other types of degradation, such as due to solid wastes, due to hazardous wastes, due to loss of scenic beauty or natural ecosystems and biodiversity, were not accounted for. All these would increase the costs significantly.

Thus natural resource accounting using many ideas and techniques of environmental economics can bring greater awareness of the importance of natural resources and hopefully guide national developmental policies.

Sectoral Policies

Environmental economics have even a greater role in sectoral polices. When environmental economists assess the cost of air pollution in a city in terms of higher incidence of diseases and deaths, cost of health care, value of working days lost, lower value of properties, etc., the affected citizens get empowered to demand action. We have seen how this led to CNG for buses, taxis and three wheelers in Delhi and other metros in the country. Way back in 1991 an IGIDR study (Parikh Jyoti and Painuly J, 1991) had argued for CNG buses for energy efficiency and on economic grounds. This did not buy traction but environmental economics got results.

Land Degradation

Another example where sectoral-level analysis can provide important insight for policy is land degradation.

Despite the fact that the share of agricultural GDP has gone down from 57 per cent in 1950-51 to 18 per cent in 2008-09, agriculture sector is still an important sector on which the economy and vast number of rural inhabitants depend.

It is important to examine how soil resources are used. Have farmers degraded soils by overuse of fertilizer or irrigation? Have they maintained quality of cultivated lands? If not what is the depreciation in its value?

If land were actively traded and land markets perfect, then the market would determine the loss in the value of soil due to degradation such as salination, water logging or erosion. Unfortunately, agricultural land is hardly traded in India and cannot provide us this loss in value of soil. It is, therefore, necessary to develop a method to value changes in soil quality.

Degraded land has been variously estimated in India. Some of the estimates (Alvares and Billorey, 1988) show that from 1947 till 1997, degraded land increased by 112.8 M.Ha to 200 M.Ha which is 35 to 60 per cent of the country's geographical area (TERI 1998). These data are somewhat hard to use as they do not define clearly what is meant by degraded and so any land can be called degraded.

National Remote Sensing Agency (NRSA) based on satellite data estimates total degraded land to be much less at 41 M.Ha in 1988-89, Reddy Ratna V. (2000). This estimate is much more systematic and has well defined measures of degradation. However, it does not provide information on to how much of this is in cultivated land.

If one were to ask farmers in a village how good a particular piece of land is, one would get a subjective valuation as, eight annas or twelve annas (there were 16 annas to a Rupee before we changed to the metric system in 1957). Such rating was used to assess land revenue in the past. One would also generally find a consensus among farmers on the rating of a piece of land.

We use the productivity approach to calculate the value of cultivated land. Lutz et al. (1994) and Norse and Saigal (1992) have used other approaches to value soil quality. Based on data from a nationwide survey carried out by NCAER (National Council of Applied Economic Research) in 1975-76 of cultivated land, Parikh K. and U. Ghosh (1991) have estimated statewise soil quality multiplier functions defining production function as follows:

$$\text{Yield} = g\ (\text{physical and chemical parameters of soil}) \cdot f\ (\text{inputs})$$

Thus, the subjectively assessed soil quality g, is estimated to be a function of soil type (sand, loam, light clay, heavy clay), colour (red, black, gray, yellow), depth (less than 1 foot, between 1 to 3 feet, greater than 3 ft.), salinity (nil, moderate, high), drainage (good, moderate, poor), and percolation (high, moderate, low).

The estimated functions were used to find out the elasticity in average soil quality multiplier for the state for salinity and soil erosion (see Table 2).

Table 2: Elasticity of Change in Land Quality Due to Soil Erosion and Salinity

State	Average Land Quality[@]	% Change in Average Land Quality of the State over Base Case Values	
		1% Land Changed from > 3 Ft to < 1 Ft Depth	1% Land Changed from Nil to High Salinity
Andhra Pradesh	9.339	–0.142	–0.134
Assam	9.734	–0.083	–0.285
Bihar	9.972	–0.049	–0.015
Gujarat	9.231	–0.187	–0.237
Haryana	12.505	–0.077	–0.106
Karnataka	9.307	–0.227	–0.155
Kerala	11.006	–0.188	–0.173
Madhya Pradesh	9.204	–0.162	#
Maharashtra	8.583	–0.229	–0.187
Orissa	8.351	–0.076	#
Punjab	10.663	#	–0.368
Rajasthan	9.370	–0.102	#
Tamil Nadu	10.387	–0.214	#
Uttar Pradesh	10.642	–0.013	–0.089
West Bengal	9.303	–0.081	–0.464

Notes: # The values for these states were not calculated as the coefficient were of perverse sign due to too few observations in the data set.)

@ On a scale of 1 to 16.

Source: Based on Parikh K. and U. Ghosh (1991).

Valuing Soil Degradation

More recent data of soil quality is available from data of remote sensing satellite imagery with ground truthing published by National Bureau of Soil Survey & Land Use Planning (NBSSLUP) of ICAR. Unfortunately, these also do not separate data for cultivated and other soils. Nonetheless, making plausible assumptions we obtain what might be called upper bounds of degradation of cultivated lands for two attributes, salinity and depth of soil for selected states. This was possible to do only for some states. Table 3 and Table 4 give these data:

Table 3: Prevalence of Salinity (Per cent of Cultivated Land)

State	1975-76 Salinity Level			1995-96 Salinity Level		
	Nil	Moderate	High	Nil	Moderate	High
Andhra Pradesh	58.4	38.6	2.8	54.9	38.6	6.3
Gujarat	40.4	49.1	10.5	29.5	49.1	21.4
Haryana	67.9	31.5	0.6	65.3	33.1	1.6
West Bengal	45.8	53.5	0.7	43.7	53.5	2.8

Source: Analysis by author based on NBSS & LUP publications concerning soils of different states.

Table 4: Depth of Soil in Selected States (Per cent of Cultivated Land)

State	1975-76			1995-96		
	< 1'	1' – 3'	> 3'	< 1'	1' – 3'	> 3'
Andhra Pradesh	34.4	40.2	25.4	39.9	40.2	19.9
Gujarat	13.9	54.14	34.7	21.5	44.6	33.9
M.P.	9.7	53.6	36.6	22.9	40.5	36.6
Maharashtra	20.3	34.8	44.9	33.9	29.1	37.0
Tamil Nadu	21.5	47.8	30.7	26.8	45.1	28.1

Source: Same as Table 4.5.

Table 5: Percentage Change in Soil Quality Multiplier over 1975 to 1995

State	Due to Changes in Soil Depth (per cent)	Due to Changes in Salinity (per cent)
Andhra Pradesh	–0.78	–0.47
Gujarat	–1.34	–2.57
Haryana	–	–0.16
Madhya Pradesh	–0.14	–
Maharashtra	–0.2.45	–
Tamil Nadu	–0.10	–
West Bengal	–	–0.10

Based on Tables 3, 4 and 5, we estimate the changes in soil quality multiplier that have occurred over the period 1975 to 1995 (see Table 5). Assuming we can add these two up, the highest change has taken in Gujarat, which is –3.91. In other states, it is much less. We take 4 per cent as an upper bound of production loss to assess the loss in value of soil that has taken place over the 20 year period between the two surveys. The steps in the process are as follows:

Table 6: Loss of Agricultural Output (₹ million) 1995-96

State	State Domestic Product in Agriculture, 1995-96	Value of Output in Agriculture@	Loss in Agriculture, Income Due to Soil Loss	Loss in Agriculture, Income Due to Salinity
Andhra Pradesh	217670	296030	231	1020
Gujarat	116540	158490	212.4	3000
Haryana	96800			210
Madhya Pradesh	174440	237240	24.4	
Maharashtra	242830	330250	809	
Tamil Nadu	108330	147330	14.7	
West Bengal	200660			270
Total Selected states		1169340 (100)	12910 (1.1)	4500 (0.61)

Note: @ Using Output/Value added ratios from EPW data book on NAS.

- The value added in agriculture in the country as a whole in 1995-96 was ₹ 2,556,130 million at current prices. The ratio of value of output to value added in 1995-96 was 1.36. This gives the value of agricultural output to be ₹ 3,976,340 million.
- All of the 4 per cent loss of output would be loss in value added as this is the loss in output for the same level of input. Thus, the loss comes to ₹ 159,050 million (= 0.04 * 3,976,340). If instead of 4 per cent which is the highest figure for loss, we use the average loss coefficient of 1.71 per cent as seen in Table 4.8, the loss amounts to ₹ 68,000 (= 0.0171 * 3,976,340) million. Note that this is the loss due to degradation that has taken place over 20 years.
- If we assume the soil degradation to have occurred uniformly over the 20 year period, the loss in agricultural income due to one year's degradation will be one twentieth, and range from ₹ 68,000/20 = ₹ 3,400 million to ₹ 159,050/20 = ₹ 7,950 million.
- The loss in the value of soil due to one year's degradation is the present

discounted value of the annual loss in income. At a discount rate of 10 per cent it is ₹ 37,460 million to ₹ 87,510 million.

- The range of loss in the asset value of cultivated lands due to degradation of agricultural land for 1995-96 is thus, estimated to be ₹ 37,460 millions to ₹ 87,510 million.
- The national GDP at factor cost at current prices in 1995-96 was ₹ 9,857,870 million. Thus, the depreciation of cultivated lands amounts to 0.38 per cent to 0.89 per cent of GDP. This is what should be subtracted from GDP to obtain NDP that is adjusted for degradation of cultivated land.

What this shows is that it is important to define clearly what one means by land degradation. Degradation is a serious problem but not as alarming as some make it out to be. Also why would farmers let their land get degraded? Some degradation they cannot control, but some they can. One of my Ph.D. students (Sharma, Sudhir, 2000) had examined the question: Are farmers irrational in their land cultivation practices when soil quality changes and future yields are accounted for? He found that from the perspective of maximizing present discounted value of income over time, Punjab farmers, given their constraints, were quite rational.

Environmental economics can thus provide guidance as to what policy measures should one take to incentivize farmers to minimize the social consequences of land degradation.

Microlevel Analysis

Understanding obtained through environmental economics of how people get affected at microlevel can guide policies. Indoor air pollution due to the use of biofuels such as wood and dung for cooking cause lot of health problems (Smith, K., 1994).

A study based on an integrated survey covering 15,293 rural households from 148 villages in three states of rural north India and one state in south India, carried out in 1999 (Parikh, Jyoti et al., 2005), shows the importance of clean fuels. Symptoms of diseases related to air and water pollution, expenditure on health, person days lost, demographic and socio-economic information, measurements of air quality in the kitchen, outside the kitchen and the attributes of the home were collected. A questionnaire on symptoms was administered as per the protocol of British Medical Association and diseases inferred. As an indicator of respiratory function, (Peak Expiratory Flow) was measured for most of the adults present at the time of the survey. Medical doctors examined a sub-sample of individuals for confirmation of diseases.

The study estimated that

- Ninety 6 per cent of households use *biomass energy*, 11 per cent use *kerosene* and 5 per cent use *LPG* for cooking. Most of them use multiple fuels.
- Forests contribute 39 per cent of the fuel wood need.
- A total of 314 Mt of biofuels are *gathered* annually.
- Eighty five million households spend 30 billion hours annually in fuel wood gathering.
- Respiratory symptoms are prevalent among 24 million adults of which 17 million have serious symptoms.
- Five per cent of adults suffer from Bronchial asthma, 16 per cent from Bronchitis, 8.2 per cent from Pulmonary TB and 7 per cent from Chest infection.
- Risk of contracting respiratory diseases and eye diseases increases with longer duration of use of biofuels.

Total economic burden of dirty biomass fuel was estimated to be ₹ 299 billion using a wage rate of ₹ 60 per day, comprising opportunity cost of gathering fuel, working days lost due to eye infections and respiratory diseases, and the cost of medicine.

As women are the primary sufferers of the adverse impact of use of biomass fuels, there is a close linkage between gender and energy. Gender and energy issues have remained on the periphery of energy policy, and require greater attention and backing.

These social and economic costs obtained using environmental economics got reflected in the Integrated Energy Policy report (Planning Commission, 2006) that recommended as follows:

> Energy security at the individual level implies ensuring supply of such a lifeline energy need. India cannot be energy secure if her people remain without secure supply of energy for lifeline needs. (Ensuring this would require targeted subsidies as many households would be unable to pay for safe, clean and convenient commercial energy to meet lifeline needs.) This requires:

— *Electrification of All Households*: The government has announced its commitment to ensure this by 2009-10.
— *Provision of Cooking Energy*: We may set a goal to provide clean cooking energy such as LPG, NG, biogas or kerosene to all within 10 years. It may be noted that the requirement of cooking energy does not increase indefinitely with income. Thus, the total amount of LPG required to provide cooking energy to 1.5 billion persons is around 55 Mtoe.
— *Other Sources*: We may provide fuel wood plantations within one kilometre of all habitations. Those who do not have access or cannot afford even subsidized clean fuels, rely on gathering wood. Neighbourhood plantations can ease their burden and the time taken to gather and transport wood.

These recommendations were accepted by the cabinet and are now part of our national IEP (Govt. of India, 2009).

Conclusion

These examples show the importance and use of environmental economics and with our increased appreciation of ecological services, that of ecological economics in policy-making. While much needs to be done to refine methodologies and to collect needed data as also to understand the dynamics of ecosystems, we can still make a difference to push for policies that lead to sustainability.

References

[1] Alvares Claude and Ramesh Billorey (1988), "Damming the Narmada: India's Greatest Planned Environmental Disaster", *Third World Network Pennang*, Malaysia.

[2] Government of India (2009), *Integrated Energy Policy*, 1989.

[3] Lutz, Earnst, Stefano Pagiola and Carlos Reiche, Eds. (1994), *Economic and Institutional Analyses of Soil Conservation Projects in Central America and the Caribbean*, World Bank, Environment Paper 8, Washington D.C.

[4] MOEF (1990), *Report of the Core Committee for the Preparation of a National Environment Policy* (M.S. Swaminathan Committee), Ministry of Environment and Forests.

[5] National Bureau of Soil Survey & Land Use Planning (NBSSLUP) of ICAR.

[6] Norse David and Saigal Reshma (1992), "National Cost of Soil Erosion – The

Case of Zimbabwe", Contribution by FAO at the Cidie workshop on Environmental Economics and Natural Resource Management in Developing Countries, Washington D.C.

[7] Parikh Jyoti and Parikh Kirit S. (1997), *Accounting and Valuation of Environment: A Primer for Developing Countries,*. New York, United Nations, 1997.

[8] Parikh Jyoti and Parikh Kirit S., Eds. (1998), *Accounting and Valuation of Environment: Case Studies from the ESCAP Region*, New York, United Nations, 1998.

[9] Parikh Jyoti et al. (2005), "Lack of Energy, Water and Sanitation and its Impact on Rural India" in Parikh Kirit S. and R. Radhakrishna (eds.), *India Development Report 2004-2005*, Oxford University Press, New Delhi.

[10] Parikh Jyoti and Painuly J. (1991), "Compressed Natural Gas (CNG) in Transport Sector: Techno-Economic Assessment for India", Discussion Paper No. 49, IGIDR, March, 1991.

[11] Parikh Kirit S. (1989), "An Operational Measurable Definition of Sustainable Development", *C.N. Vakil Memorial Lecture* delivered at the 72nd Annual Conference of Indian Economic Association, Trivandrum, December 30, 1989.

[12] Parikh K. and U. Ghosh (1991), "Natural Resource Accounting for Soils: Towards an Empirical Estimate of Costs of Soil Degradation for Cultivated Land in India", IGIDR-DP-48, Indira Gandhi Institute of Development Research, Mumbai.

[13] Parikh Kirit S., Jyoti K. Parikh, V.K. Sharma and J.P. Painuly (1993), *Natural Resource Accounting: A Framework for India*, Report prepared by IGIDR for MOEF, November 1993.

[14] Parikh Kirit S. (2002), *Environmental Governance for Sustainable Development in Asia and the Pacific*, Report Prepared for ESCAP and UNDP, United Nations, New York, 2002.

[15] Planning Commission (2006), *Report of the Expert Committee on Integrated Energy Policy, 2006* (Kirit Parikh Committee).

[16] Reddy Ratna V. (2000), "Land Degradation in India: Extent, Costs, Determinants and Trends", Part of the project report on "Sustainable development Framework for India", Centre for Economic and Social Studies, Hyderabad.

[17] Sharma, Sudhir (2000), *Soil Nutrient Availability and Sustainability of Agriculture in Punjab*, Ph.D thesis, Indira Gandhi Institute of Development Research (IGIDR), Mumbai.

[18] Smith, KR. (1994), "Health, Energy and Greenhouse-Gas Impacts of Biomass Combustion in Household Stoves", *Energy for Sustain Dev* 1994; 1(4): 23–29.

[19] TERI (1998), *Green India 2047: Looking Back to Think Ahead*, Tata Energy Research Institute, New Delhi.

9

The Future of Indian Agriculture

Yoginder K. Alagh

The future of Indian agriculture is a subject which unfolds many possibilities and some major environmental concerns. Most of these lie outside agriculture, and agricultural actors will have to relate with them. The story will be in an iff – then mode or conditional forecasting made famous by my teacher the Nobel Laureate Lawrence Klein.

Indian agriculture is becoming increasingly demand driven. This will accelerate in the future. It has been argued, by the present author and others that agricultural diversification in India is basically driven by domestic demand, (Y.K. Alagh, Shastri Memorial Lecture, reprinted in ICAR, *Agricultural Transformation in India*, 1989/1995.) The major impact of faster income growth was on domestic demand leading a process of demand diversification in a big way.

Expansion and diversification of the consumption basket was basically driven by a higher growth performance since the 1980s. The agro-based items of consumption are important in the demand baskets of different income groups. These consumer items are not for elite consumption alone. As people are better off, they eat more eggs, drink more milk and eat vegetable, fruit and cheese. This has happened in the nineties and by now, this diversification of the food basket is well-known.

Demand will depend largely on income growth, taste patterns and population growth. The Eleventh Plan does not have a separate population projection exercise but in one of its sections, the numbers given are the following:

2011/12 1208 million
2016/17 1283 million

Source: GOI, 2008, Eleventh Plan, Vol. 1, p. 75.

As compared to these estimates, India's most experienced demographer, Marie

Bhat estimated that the growth rate of population would go down to 1.52 per cent annual in the decade 2001-11 to 1.25 per cent annual in the decade 2011-21. This would imply a population level of 1202.98 million by 2010 and 1345.38 million by 2020, which is higher. The demographer Tim Dyson who has been working on India's demography in his Standard projection estimates India's population at 1271 million in 2020 and his High projection is close to Marie Bhat's figures (T. Dyson, 2003a, 2003b). These alternate estimates suggest that population and, therefore, future demand projections have a degree of uncertainty to them. However, it has to be noted that India's population is now seen as an asset for its growth process discussed below (Y.K. Alagh, 2006b).

As compared to these figures, some FAO publications recently have used slightly higher projections as the following estimates show:

Population (billions)	1.0 (2000)	1.2(2015)	1.4(2030)

Source: F.A.O., 2006 as quoted in F.A.O., 2008, p. 24.

Economic Growth

To put it in a somewhat stylized manner:

India will grow between 6 to 8 per cent annually and will become the third or fifth largest economy of the world in this period. (For a model based on which, these projections are derived after some modifications, taking into account recent experience, see V. Pandit, 2004 and Y.K. Alagh, 2000.) The investment rate and productivity growth will be the drivers. For example, around a third of India's GDP growth in 97/07 is technology driven. Factor productivity growth will rise from 3.5 per cent annual to 5 per cent. Trade will also matter – it will become around 4 per cent of the World Trade.

Demand

Population and Income Growth will give us the base for demand. Decadal Growth of cereal demand is 13 per cent. On the other hand, growth of demand of fruits and vegetables, eggs, chicken and milk is much higher. The decadal growth figures for potatoes is 24 per cent, 30 per cent for vegetables, 40 per cent for milk, 200 per cent for eggs and 250 per cent for chicken. Demand for beef, mutton and pork also goes up but given religious reasons, the absolute figures are low. The low growth of cereal demand is compensated by very high demand growth of non-cereal based and non-crop based agricultural goods. There are these two perspectives on the relative importance of grains in India's agricultural demand projections.

G.S. Bhalla and Peter Hazell (IFPRI, 1997) find that feed demand is 'low' in India as compared to other countries like China. In fact, this is a feature of India's taste patterns. The argument that India will consume a lot of meat when it grows richer is false since rich households in India consume much less meat as compared to their counterparts in other countries. In fact, in 1975, the US Think Tank, The Hudson Institute had argued that India will not be able to feed itself since it will not have the land and water to meet demand for meat. It was shown that if Indians, as they grow rich, consume as rich Indians did in the seventies, then shortages of land and water would not emerge in the future even with the available agricultural technologies in the mid-seventies. However, undeterred by these taste pattern arguments, Bhalla and Hazell project huge demands of grains. Their projections of foodgrain demand in 2020 are as follows:

Indian Feed Coefficients: 278 to 370 million tonnes
Chinese Feed Coefficients: 375 to 616 million tonnes

In a later projection, they have moderated these numbers to 325 million tonnes (Bhalla, Hazell and Kerr, 1999). P.C. Bansil (1998) and K.N. Murthy (1998) have convincingly argued that these projections are on the high side since they do not capture the diversification of the food basket away from grains with rising incomes. Also the feed assumptions of the IFPRI model are absurd since they do not capture inter-country and intercultural differences in food tastes and structure of animal husbandry industry. The IFPRI Bhalla Hazell argument on Indian food demand, particularly of meat determined by 'global (metropolitan) styles of living' or a kind of Macdonald Global Taste Standard is particularly weak.

P.C. Bansil points out that Bhalla and Hazel have erroneously rejected P. Kumar's work (op.cit., Paroda and Kumar) because it is better founded in consumer behaviour derived from A Food Characteristic Demand System. In this system, energy, variety and tastes of individual food are additive in the utility space and the utility of one food depends on the level of consumption of every other food. Once the consumption of cereals is stabilized, the income calorie elasticity is zero. Bansil notes that as poverty rates were going down, the percentage of households reporting eating two square meals a day was going up and the average consumption of cereals had exceeded the ICMR norm of 165 kgs of cereals a day. He also systematically demolishes the Bhalla Hazel feed projections. K.N. Murthy, a student of R. Radhakrishna shows that since the Bhalla Hazel projections are based on a log inverse Engel curve, the elasticity of demand varies with the level of income, which is a reasonable specification for food demand. But Bhalla and Hazel only use the mean level constant elasticity for projections over a very long period which leads to very significant upwards biases. Murthy shows that "BPH have overpredicted the aggregate cereal demand by 20 million tonnes (14 per cent) by 1993-94 itself" (K.N. Murthy, 1998, p. 2944) and "BPH have overpredicted the aggregate demand for cereals in India by 80 million tonnes, a staggering 42 per cent error in the year 2020" (ibid., p. 2944).

My projections contained in Table 1 for the UN, include diversification away from grains and are lower for cereals and foodgrains as compared to the IFPRI and other normative projections. However, the non-foodgrain projections are much higher than those of the High Foodgrain Indian Projections. Our projections from the UN Alagh model (Y.K. Alagh, 2000, 2001, 2006) are as follows:

Table 1: Agricultural Projections for India 2020

Commodity	2020 (mn. tonnes)
Foodgrains	225
Edible Oil	19
Sugar	42
Potato	40
Fruits and Vegetables	176
Milk	128
Meat	6
Eggs	5
Fish	14

On Markets and Strategies

Recently, UN studies have established through international comparisons, a point we have made that India is urbanized more than what it says and its non-farm employment growth is globally comparable. The FAO bring out that in a global comparison and analysis, FAO and World Bank "distinguish three categories of countries: agriculture-based, transforming and urbanized. India is found in the transforming country category, with a clear historical trajectory of moving from being agricultural-based" (FAO, 2008, p. 4).

The FAO note that according to popular statistics, India is less urbanized, but they point out that:

> "On the other hand, what constitutes 'rural' is in fact somewhat subjective and what is considered urban or rural varies considerably among countries. The Brazilian definition, which is currently a political controversy, is partly based on administrative divisions, and shows a rural population of 19 per cent. The OECD on the other hand, uses a simple measure of population density of over 150 people per square kilometre, which, for Brazil would give a figure of 25 per cent. If we apply this to India, where only a small proportion of people live in areas below this density, it would give a rural population of only 9 per cent – quite a contrast to the normal Indian view of being 70 per cent rural. Although as we have seen, Brazil is much more urbanized, 20 per cent of the population lives in areas with fewer than 50 inhabitants per square kilometre; in India less than 1 per cent do" (FAO, 2008, p. 5).

The following picture illustrates:

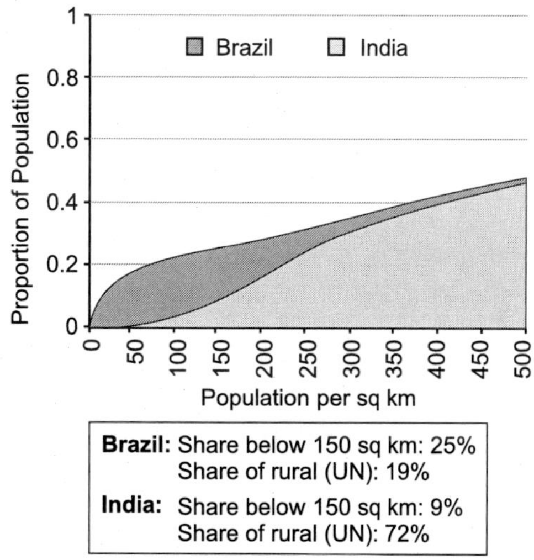

Source: Centre for International Earth Science Information (2004).

The FAO go on to add:

> "This is particularly important, discussed in more below, when we look at the village-level economies. If we measure how isolated the rural population is in terms of market access, using a definition of more than five hours of

> travel time to reach a market town of more than 5,000 people, only 5 per cent of South Asians live in 'remote areas' whereas more than 30 per cent of Africans are in this situation. Similar characteristics hold true for the percentage of the population living in higher potential agricultural areas, as shown below" (FAO, 2008, p. 4).

Our argument therefore is that urbanization is proceeding much faster than earlier estimates of scholars like A. Kundu, who worked with the low urbanization growth rates of the Census 1991/2001 period. For example, for Gujarat, Yoginder K. Alagh and P.H. Thakkar worked out that a number of habitations which met the Census 2001 criteria of urbanization were still classified as 'villages'. It was found that in the decade 1991-2001, in Gujarat, rural non-agriculture main workers increased more than urban non-agriculture main workers. As per the 2001 Population Census, there were 122 big villages in Gujarat, each of them satisfying the three Census criteria of non statutory towns. These villages had a total population of 11.21 lakhs. If this is taken as a correction factor, then the revised estimate of degree of urbanization of Gujarat for the period 1991-2001 will be nearly 39.57 per cent (earlier estimate being 37.36 per cent and the correction factor being 2.21 per cent).

The level of urbanization in Gujarat has, therefore, not increased by 2.87 per cent points, but 5.06 per cent points, which is close to double the earlier estimated change and makes a big difference in policy and forecasting work, since it is well-known that urban projections are based on urban-rural growth differences, and changes in first differences of the magnitudes considered can make big impacts on outcomes. The 2011 census shows that urban populations for Gujarat were underestimate by exactly the percentages estimated in the Alagh-Thakkar paper. Earlier, land use studies found little effect of urbanization on land use. For example, decadal release of land for urbanization was generally less than 5 per cent. This has now changed.

Increasingly in global work and expert studies, higher estimates of urbanization are being projected as compared to the urban pessimist projections. Thus, the International Water Management Institutes Strategic Analysis of the National River Linking Project has a demographic projection by A. Mahmood and A. Kundu (Amarasinghe, Shah and Malik, 2008, paper 6). However, they examine sensitivities to higher urbanization rates in the three volume study on water futures as compared to official figures. According to them as stated in the following quote:

> "According to others, this is even a conservative estimate of population growth in India (Y.K. Alagh cited by Amarasinghe and Sharma, 2008)" (U. Amarasinghe, T. Shah and P.S. Malik, ed., 2008, p. 12). The IWMI studies quote a higher figure of urbanization of 45 per cent by 2025 as compared to a lower figure of 37 per cent for that year (S. Verma and S. Phansalkar, 2008, in Amarasinghe, Shah and Malik, 2008, ed., p. 29 and also discuss the 21st century as an urban century, p. 40).

The United Nations has also recently reproduced the Alagh version of the Krugman model of urbanization as estimated for India as detailed above (see United Nations, 2008). To conclude, therefore, for this study, we project that the rural population share will go down to 58 per cent in 2020 and 55 per cent in 2025. This compares with the official projection of 68 per cent in 2020 and 64 per cent in 2025 (GOI, 2006, Table 10, p. 56).

Rural Population in 2020 will, therefore, be 738 million out of the total population of 1273 million projected above. The Eleventh Plan has projected the rural labour force as 45.7 per cent by 2016-17, the last year for which they have given projections (GOI, 2008, Vol. 1, p. 75, Table 14A). An earlier projection by G.S. Bhalla and P. Hazell (Bhalla and Hazell, 2003, p. 3478) using age specific participation rates separately for rural areas was 46.9 per cent. We assume a participation rate of 46 per cent and get a figure of 340 million as the labour force. This is much lower than the figure of 404 million estimated by Bhalla and Hazell on account of a much lower estimate of urbanization.

The Vision

In the next two decades, Indian agriculture will meet the requirements of food security and will rapidly diversify itself. It will function in a rural urban continuum, with rapid developments of markets and shifting of working populations from villages to linked small towns and also from crop production to value added activities. Employment growth will be high in these activities chasing a high rate of economic growth. All this will happen if the institutional structure gives the appropriate signals in term of technology and organizational support, and the necessary economic support in terms of pricing and infrastructure support. Otherwise, there will be rising food prices chasing few goods and immiserization. (For a numerical model illustrating these two alternative outcomes see Y.K. Alagh, 2012.)

There are other issues apart from two two big questions. They relate to non-renewable resources, particularly land and water.

Land for Agriculture

In a book authored with Uma Lele of the World Bank, I had predicted wrongly that the net area sown would be stuck at 141 million hectares and growth needs would need to be sourced from productivity and more intensive cropping. Growth in net area sown at around 1 per cent annual in the early period of planning fell to around 0.6 per cent and then to 0.3 per cent in subsequent decades and was now not growing at all. It was reasonable to assume that the geographical area of the country or the extensive land frontier for exploitation had reached its limits and some of us, while at the Planning Commission had correctly projected that the net area sown or arable land of the country would remain constant. But now, for the first time in Indian economic history, we are told that the net area sown, rising slowly earlier and constant since the early nineties has gone down by eight million hectares. The last year in which NAS was less than the 2002/03 number was in 1958/59. The models used for discussion in India, including the National Commission on Perspectives for Water Development do not take this factor into account and, therefore, are outdated for discussion.

Water

There is an intimate relationship between cropping intensity, land use and water development. Irrigation permits the possibility of multiple cropping by bringing additional land under cultivation and the same land to be used more than once. Application of new technologies in the past was related to assured water supply. The new technology obviously raises productivity. But on account of photo insensitivity properties, newer technologies permit shorter duration crops, which also is associated with increase in cropping intensity. The use of these kinds of relationships has been common in Indian agricultural policy and plan models, since the mid-seventies when the first agricultural sub-model of Indian planning was formulated for grain self-reliance and is used in the current generation of water forecasting models also (Chopra, 2005).

In the nineties, arable area had stopped growing and so the land constraint was far more severe. Growth was seen as now to be sourced from double cropping and yields. This fundamental relationship was used to project the intensive resource base of the economy. It was projected that by the end of the decade, India would have used up most of its balance water reserves, with the irrigated area reaching around 114 million hectares by 2010. Projections for 2020 were a requirement of irrigation of 122 million hectares. The projections assume a vastly improved performance on the land and water management frontiers. It needs to be remembered that the balance groundwater reserves are now more limited. A very dramatic effort will be needed to harvest and carefully use the available water.

Meanwhile, in reality, irrigated area has stopped growing In this decade (Table 2).

Table 2: Irrigated Area in India 1998/99-2002/03 (mn.hec.)

Sl. No.	Year	Net Irrigated Area	Gross Irrigated Area	Irrigation Intensity
0	1	2	3	4
1.	1998/99	56.51	77.64	121.13
2.	1999/2000	56.76	77.99	121.23
3.	2000/01	54.83	74.29	119.46
4.	2001/02	55.88	77.00	121.12
5.	2002/03	53.07	70.67	117.60

Source: Government of India, Ministry of Agriculture, November 2005, Agricultural Statistics at a Glance: 2005, Table 14.2, p. 176.

People like me were wrong in forecasting that cropped area would remain constant, but are right in the warning we gave. The decline in canal irrigated area is equally recent and shocking, having been discovered by Tushar Shah of the International Water Management Institute in this neat little picture copied from the IWMI website.

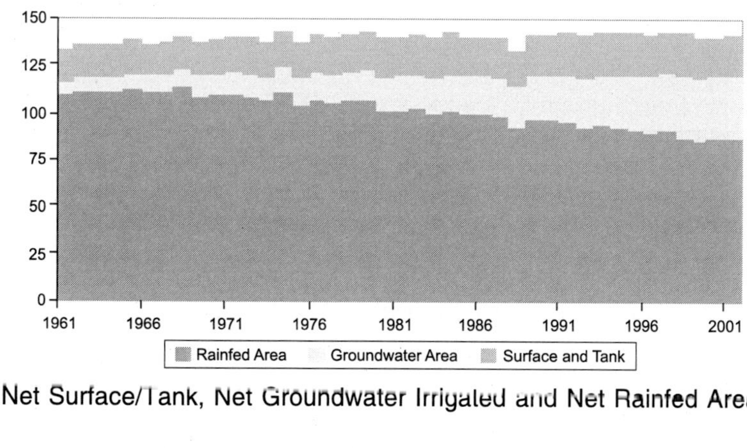

Net Surface/Tank, Net Groundwater Irrigated and Net Rainfed Area

We really do not have a detailed analysis of the debacle in irrigation. The first issue is the failure of the Advanced Irrigation Benefit Programme (AIBP). This programme for completing ongoing irrigation projects was started when I was the Planning Minister. It was started because we have a long history of successes with such programmes. The first such programme was started in 1975/76, when we had formulated a plan for food self-reliance. Table 5 shows that the worked and irrigated area went up by 5 million hectares and irrigation intensity from 108.77 to 110.25. We then reinvented it in 1987/88 when the late Rajiv Gandhi wanted a Plan for stepping up stagnating agricultural production. As member in the Planning Commission, I saw it work again and over a brief period, the irrigated area went up by around 5 million hectares and irrigation intensity from 113.15 to 115.15. There has been very little progress since. These earlier programmes and the critical role they played have been described elsewhere,[7] but the real issue is why did the AIBP fail? We need a serious professional evaluation, but having been involved with planning and monitoring of such programmes for over three decades, I suspect that not including a Canal component to cover the last mile of water deliveries is one reason and the other is bringing in a loan component and not keeping it a Central Plan scheme.

There are, however more basic factors at play. As compared to relief against rainfall failure, the farmer now wants yield enhancing water supplies for water stress periods of diverse crops grown with modern technology. Access to groundwater gives them this facility, badly planned and inefficiently managed canals don't. Farmers and their communities now want control on water deliveries. We have just started canal systems which employ, for example, hydraulic controls up to distributory levels and the successful examples are few and far between. In a recent critique of the Ken Betwa project put on web by the Interlinking of Rivers Project, we have described how the soil scientists have shown that the area is unsuitable for paddy, and irrigation would enhance yields from oilseeds, pulses and fodder crops, but the system is designed largely for flood irrigated paddy. We have also described the alternatives now possible, like the computer controlled delivery systems being constructed in the Sardar Sarovar Command (see Alagh, 2006, below).

Are Small Projects and Groundwater the Answer?

Tushar Shah has shown that this is not the solution. In fact, according to him, groundwater use in a hundred Districts is the problem and needs a special programme of replenishment I would suggest link with surface water use. I have been pushing this both at the Planning Commission and I hope the next budget would address the problem.

According to Shah, "There are 100 districts which account for over 60 per cent of India's 'critical' and over-exploited blocks. These also happen to have the highest concentration of dug-wells in the country; here is where the falling water tables have the most disastrous impact on drying up wells and forcing farmers to revert to rainfed farming. Outside Punjab, most recent farmer suicides are reported from these districts; groundwater stress is an important source of agrarian distress in these regions.

Table 3: Groundwater-Stressed Hard-Rock States of India

States	Annual Ground-water Draft (billion m^3)	Total Number of Irrigation Dug Wells in Use and Disuse ('000)	% of India's Critical and Over-exploited Blocks	Area Irrigated by Ground-water (m ha)	% of Wells and Tubewells with Electric Pumps	Potential for Increased Recharge through Well Modification (b m^3)
Andhra Pradesh	14.90	1185	296	1.68	93.5	5.9
Gujarat	11.50	936	43	2.39	54.5	4.7
Karnataka	10.71	328	68	0.86	96.1	1.64
Madhya Pradesh	17.12	1277	30	3.50	85.5	6.4
Maharashtra	15.09	1659	8	1.57	96.1	8.3
Rajasthan	12.99	1172	190	3.66	47.4	5.86
Tamil Nadu	17.65	1656	175	1.41	82.5	8.28
Total for seven states	99.96	8213	810	15.07	82.6	41.1
Seven states as % of India total	43.3	85.4	70.9	48.9	65.2	
India	231	9617	1142	30.8	61.0	

Source: Tushar Shah.

Much of this distress can be alleviated – and at a relatively low cost to the society – by mounting a well-designed programme of groundwater recharge. It is sometimes suggested that small watershed development programmes are an effective answer to groundwater depletion; however, according to Tushaar Shah, this is only partly so. In arid and semi-arid areas of India, tanks, small water harvesting structures with poor surface-area-to-depth ratio act as evaporation pans; they lose much more water to non-beneficial evaporation than is available for recharging the aquifers. In old times, when groundwater withdrawal was a small fraction of today, irrigation tanks made sense; but today, they need to be reinvented. This is evident from the fact that on their own, farmer communities in many of these districts are converting their centuries-old irrigation tanks into percolation tanks to increase recharge to their wells." While Tushaar Shah does not mention this, this will require development in the framework of watershed development, in the sense that the aquifer characteristics will have to be the bedrock of the regeneration process and it will involve the interaction of the efforts of multiple stakeholders. Tushar Shah's point, however, is that individual effort will be required and this then becomes a case of the point made early in the watershed project experience of aligning individual rights with limited and focused cooperation. Also, there are synergies in combining this programme with canal modernization.

By their very nature, hard-rock areas have a profusion of dug-wells and tanks while sandy-alluvial aquifer areas are dominated by tubewells and have few tanks for irrigation. The groundwater recharge strategy in hard-rock areas should therefore focus on modifying dugwells and tanks for maximizing groundwater recharge.

The implications of these trends are not being realized with the urgency they deserve, since at a basic level resource constraints of a more severe kind faced by certain East Asian economies are now being approached in India. Organizations, communities, households and individuals will have to grasp this fact and live with it. The severity of the blow will take time to sink in. But time India does not have. A few years ago I had warned that we are getting close to the kind of land and water shortage East Asian societies like China, Japan and Korea have grappled with, but have built up institutions through the centuries to cope. I had argued that we need to hasten. We would we hoped harvest water and improve irrigation deliveries.

By 2020, Chopra and Goldar estimate a BAU Scenario:

> In such a scenario, overall water shortage or deficit is only of 2 per cent. This is accompanied by an under utilization of surface water capacity of

> 21 per cent (due to low water use efficiency) and an over-extraction of groundwater of 25 per cent. Such an unbalanced growth shall itself be the source of a considerable amount of unsustainability.

The second interpretation of the BAU scenario is motivated by the need to estimate regional shortages or surpluses. The BAUST or the business – as usual with the state level estimates is made by assuming that surface and groundwater development follow the trend extrapolated from the past.[1] The regional analysis reveals that over-extraction of groundwater shall emerge in eight states. In addition to Gujarat, Haryana, Punjab and parts of Uttar Pradesh which are characterized as areas with overuse of groundwater, Andhra Pradesh, Maharashtra and Tamil Nadu are also expected to be subject to over-extraction. Surface water shortages may start emerging in some states such as Gujarat, Bihar, Maharashtra and Orissa and again taking population projections and the energy models as developed by the AITD urbanization study and suitable assumptions they estimate:

> The total requirement for households, power and industry is 103.62 BCMs in the BAU scenario. Adding evaporation loss and ecological requirement we obtain a total requirement of 223.62 BCMs for requirements other than agriculture.

Chopra and Goldar also estimate a high growth scenario. Then:

> The high-growth scenario at the national level implies a rate of growth of agriculture of 4.98 per cent per annum with the foodgrain sector growing at 2 to 2.4 per cent p.a. and the non-foodgrain sector at 7.69 to 9.22 per cent p.a. Irrigated land requirement increases to 122 million hectares. With present levels of water use efficiency, water requirement increases to 804.2 BCMs. This implies a shortfall/water deficit of 22 per cent. The manner in which this translates into over-extraction of groundwater or other indices of unsustainability depends on policies pursued and cannot be ascertained. It is, however, clear that both the high growth and BAU scenarios are likely to result in unsustainable demand for water of one kind or the other in the absence of specific investments and policies directed at improvement of water-use efficiency and other sustainability promoting measures.

The requirements of the households, power and industry sectors likewise add up to 120.57 BCMs in the HG scenario as against 103.62 BCMs in the BAU scenario.

Regarding the quality of water they say,

> An important issue which our analysis brings out is, at present levels of urban wastewater and effluent treatment, water quality will deteriorate significantly, impacting availability as well, in certain areas. The reduction in water availability due to quality problems is expected to be substantial. We use this evidence to underscore the need for and the corresponding benefit from sustainability investments.

Chopra and Goldar then develop a sustainable policy scenario:

> It is clear from the above analysis that, in order to achieve sustainable water development, consistent with sectoral requirements arising from a sustained 7 to 8 per cent annual growth in GDP and other accompanying changes in the economy, a large number of interventions shall be required. These interventions could be technological, institutional, or supply augmenting possibilities. Table 4 list some interventions for sustainability we suggest, including watershed management, drip irrigation, and institutional arrangements, such as water users' associations, that help in more efficient use of water. Some of these have been experimented with in different contexts and we estimate (on the basis of existing studies) the extent to which they can be expected to spread over the next twenty years. Corresponding costs are also worked out. These are, in other words, the costs to be borne for ensuring sustainable use of water. Other interventions suggested involve costs which are either difficult to measure, involve uncertainty or are not only economic costs but also perhaps political in nature. Further, interventions are also classified according to whether they are to be undertaken on presently irrigated land which is privately owned,

Table 4: Nature of Interventions under Sustainable Scenario

Nature of Interventions	Sector	Water Saving/Addition (in BCMs)
Demand Management/ Recycling Technology	Households	22.51
	Power sector	7.29
	Industry	13.86
	Agriculture	35.83
Supply Supplementing	Additional Runoff Capture	142.00
Total Water Saving/ Augmentation		221.49

or consist of interventions on land (possibly under private, common or government ownership) to be brought under irrigation.

Conclusion

The prospects for Indian agriculture are good. Demand will grow fast and if we create the correct incentive and organization systems the Indian farmer will not fail us as he has responded well in the past when our policies were supportive.

Research systems will have to concentrate on a much larger cafeteria of crops and support to non crop agriculture, including animal husbandry, fish and forests.

The real dangers apart from anti agricultural policies are in running into real resource constraints. Again, here the strategies for land and water management are known and agricultural research can fill in the gaps. Unfortunately, the Eleventh Plan is the first plan without a chapter on the Perspective of the Economy and we have to rely on the efforts of people concerned on India's future outside the government like me. We may hope for a more serious effort in the mid-term review of the Eleventh Plan. As a member of the Planning Commission it was my good fortune to develop his vision of a detailed agro climatic strategy for India. It is more urgent now.

References

[1] Alagh, Yoginder K., 1989/1995, Planning and Policies for Indian Agricultural Research, Shastri Memorial Lecture, Reprinted in ICAR. *Landmarks in Indian Agriculture.*

[2] Alagh, Y.K., 1991, *Indian Development Planning and Policy: An Alternative View*, "Wider Studies in Development Economics", Delhi: Vikas Publishing House.

[3] ———, 1994, "Macro Policies for Indian Agriculture", in FAO, *Economic Liberalization and Indian Agriculture*, New Delhi, ISID, pp. 23-54.

[4] ———, 1996, "The Theory of Not Hastening Slowly", *Indian Journal of Labour Economics.*

[5] Alagh, Yoginder K., 2000, *Global Sustainable Future and Developing Countries*, in Fu chen Lo et al., ed., below.

[6] Alagh, Yoginder K., 2001, *Sustainable Development India: 2020*, UNU/IAS.

[7] ———, 2002, "Poverty Food Security and Human Security, Rajiv Gandhi Foundation, Special Issue", *Journal of Global Management.*

[8] ———, 2004, *State of the Indian Farmer: An Overview*, Delhi, Academic and Ministry of Agriculture.

[9] ———, 2005, The Economics of Forestry in India, *Anvesak.*

[10] Alagh, Yoginder K., 2006a, India 2020, *Journal of Quantitative Economics*, New Series, Vol. 4, No. 1, January, pp. 1—14.

[11] Alagh, Yoginder K., 2006b, "Demographic Dividend: Possibilities and Realities", Seminar on Global Imbalances and their Impacts on Emerging Economies, Denpasaar, Bali, Bank Indonesia, IMF and ADB, 16-17 November.

[12] ———, 2009, *The Indian Poverty Debate – Measurement and Strategy*, forthcoming Volume of IHD.

[13] ———, 2012, *The Future of Indian Agriculture*, Delhi, National Book Trust.

[14] Alexandratos, Nikos, 1995, *World Agriculture Towards 2010*, An FAO Study, Chichister, Wiley.

[15] Bansil, P.C., 1998, Demand for Foodgrains by 2020, *Economic and Political Weekly*, March 7, pp. 546–547.

[16] Bhalla, G.S. and P. Hazell, 1997, "Foodgrain Demand in India 2020: A Preliminary Exercise", *Economic and Political Weekly*, December 27.

[17] Bhalla, G.S., P. Hazell and J. Kerr, 1999, *Prospects for India's Food Supply and Demand to 2020*, Washington, IFPRI Discussion Paper 29.

[18] Bhat, Mari P.N., 1998. "Demographic Estimates for Post Independence India: A New Integration", *Demography India*, Vol. 1, pp. 23–57.

[19] ———, 2000. *General Growth Balance Method as an Integrated Procedure for Evaluation of Completeness of Censuses and Registration Systems: A Case Study of India 1971-1991.* Delhi: Institute of Economic Growth.

[20] R. Dyson, T., 2003a, *New Population Projections for India*, Welcome Trust India Project Paper No. 1, London, L.S.E.

[21] ———, 2003b, *India's Population: The Future*, in T. Dyson, R. Cassen and L. Visaria (ed.), below.

[22] Dyson, T., R. Cassen and L. Visaria (ed.), 2003, *Population, Environment and Human Development*, Oxford, OUP.

[23] F.A.O., 1993, *Agriculture Towards 2010*, Rome, F.A.O., for final published version see, N. Alexandratos.

[24] F.A.O., 2006, *State of Food and Agriculture in Asia and the Pacific 2006*, FAO Regional Office for Asia and the Pacific, Bangkok.

[25] F.A.O, 2008, *Accelerating Agricultural Growth in India*, New Delhi, MOA, GOI.

[26] Lo, Fu chen, H. Tokuda and N.S. Cooray, 2000, *The Sustainable Future of the Global System*, Tokyo, UNU-OECD.

[27] Government of India, Planning Commission, 1979, *Report of The Task Force on Projections of Minimum Needs and Effective Consumption Demand*, New Delhi, Perspective Planning Division.

[28] Government of India, Planning Commission, 1980, *Draft Sixth Five-Year Plan*, New Delhi.

[29] ———, 1998, NCIWRDP, Report of the Working Group on Perspective of Water Requiremnts, New Delhi.

[30] ———, 1999, NCIWRDP, *Water Resources Development Plan of India*, New Delhi.

[31] ———, Planning Commission, 2008, *Eleventh Five-Year Plan: 2007/2012*, Delhi, Oxford University Press.

[32] ———, 2006, National Commission on Population Projection, *Report of the Technical Group on Population Projections*, Delhi, Census of India.

[33] Government of India, Planning Commission, 1980, *Draft Sixth Five-Year Plan*, New Delhi.

[34] Lele, U., N. Kumar, N.C. Saxena, Y.K. Alagh and Kinsuk Mitra, 2000, *India: Alleviating Poverty Through Forest Development*, Washington, World Bank, Operations Evaluation Department.

[35] Mukherjee, Robin, Manabendhu Chattopadhyay and Chiranjib Neogi, 2001, *Productivity, Human Development and Basic Needs in India*, Calcutta, Indian Statistical Institute.

[36] Murthy, K.N., 1998, "Foodgrains Demand in India to 2020: A Comment", *Economic and Political Weekly*, November 14, pp. 2943-2944.

[37] Pandit, V., 2004, "Sustainable Economic Growth for India: An Exercise in Macro Economic Scenario Building", *Journal of Quantitative Economics*, January, pp. 1–24.

[38] Paroda, R.S. and Praduman Kumar, 2000, "Food Production and Demand in South Asia", *Agricultural Economic Research Review*, Vol. 13, No. 1, pp. 1–24.

[39] Planning Commission, July 2005, "Mid Term Appraisal of Tenth Five Year Plan, 2002/2007".

[40] Radhakrishna, R. and Indrakant, S., 1988, Evaluating Rice Market Intervention Policies. Manila, Asian Development Bank.

[41] Radhakrishna, R. and C. Ravi, 1990, *Food Demand Projections for India*, Hyderabad, CESS.

[42] Ravi, C., 2001, *Complete Demand System, Welfare and Nutrition:An Analysis of Indian Consumption Data*, Ph.D. Dissertation, Centre for Economic and Social Studies, Hyderabad.

[43] UNU, 2001/02, *Improving the Management of Sustainable Development – Towards a New Strategic Framework for Large Developing Countries: China, India, and Indonesia*, Tokyo, UNU-IAS.

[44] UNU, 2001, *The Sustainable Future of the Global System: Endeavours from RIO to Johannesberg: Summary Report*, Tokyo, UNU/IAS.

10

Is JFM Really Helping Communities and Forests?

Need to Focus on Institution Building

Rucha Ghate, Harini Nagendra and Deepshikha Mehra

Decentralization Initiatives in Forest Management

Decentralization of forest management in India began with the acceptance of people oriented forest policy in 1988, followed by the Joint Forest Management (JFM) programme in 1992. In the year 2000, the Government of India introduced a scheme for establishing Forest Development Agencies (FDA) at forest division level in various states, for federating the JFM committees. This indicated the government's commitment towards continuation and expansion of participatory forest management. Around the same time, the *Panchayat* Extension to Scheduled Areas Act (PESA) of 1996 took decentralization of management and ownership of natural resources, including forests, to areas beyond the Forest Department managed territory. This act gave power to the *gram sabha* (village assemblies) in scheduled areas over community resources, specifically over minor forest products. The latest passing of the "Scheduled Tribes and other Traditional Forest Dwellers (Recognition of Forest Rights) Act, 2006" (STOTFDA) by the Indian parliament in December 2006 was another major step forward in the process of recognizing and re-establishing indigenous people's symbiotic relation with forest. While the provisions of PESA are still to reach communities, and it is too early to comment on the impacts of STOTFDA, JFM has been found to be the most common operational form of the devolution policies for the 'inclusive' decentralized management of forests in India. But, have the local communities internalized JFM provisions? Has JFM resulted in regulated use of forest products by communities? What has been the role of forest department in ensuring this? These are some of the questions addressed in this article. We first discuss the experience of JFM as reflected in the writings of other scholars, to set the background for the study. This is followed by a discussion of impact of JFM on forest management based on a field study of three villages located in the poverty stricken, forest rich Gadchiroli district of Maharashtra state in India. The study concludes that there is a need for the Forest Department (FD), as the implementer of the programme, to shift its focus of investments, presently restricted to plantations, to institution building of JFM committees that are responsible for managing forests.

Background of JFM and its Critique

The JFM system envisages the involvement of local communities in the management of state-owned forests under partnership arrangements with the state Forest Department (FD). Usufruct rights on forest products for subsistence, restoration of degraded as well as preservation of well-stocked forest lands, sharing of benefits flowing in the long term, and making available other development funds for poverty alleviation (under FDA) are the broad incentives offered under the programme, with operational variations between states, and alterations/ modifications over time.[1] JFM is thus looked at as an attempt to reverse the process of forest degradation on the one hand, and meet people's needs for forest produce on the other.

There is a large body of literature on JFM. Research scholars have extensively studied various aspects of JFM – provisions, structure, working and impacts. The JFM programme, which is based on the Forest Policy of 1988, had incorporated suggestions made in the Report of Committee on Forest and Tribals in India (1982). The authors of the report had advocated a major turn towards a management strategy in which user groups were to play a much more active role than in the past (Baland and Platteau, 1996). Therefore, JFM was not just a response to pressure from donor agencies, but recognition of the failure of past approach of the state agencies (Thompson, 1995; Matta, 2006). From the outset, JFM has been looked upon as a unique approach that kindled a lot of hope, and at the same time, led to skepticism during the initial years. While Poffenberger et al. (1998: xi) had enthusiastically expressed that JFM had brought in "reversal of the alienation of forest people's rights, of institutional conflict, and of ecological patterns of forest degradation", and that "India's grassroots experience of ethno-forestry can be replicated across regions and nation-states, provided communities are allowed to regain management authority over the integral resources that sustain their livelihoods" (p. 13), other studies showed that JFM would suffer because in many instances, both the partners – Forest Department and the communities – were not ready for the new institutional arrangement (Parul, 2006). Similarly, the communities found it difficult to reconcile with the idea of being equal partners in managing a resource from which they were strictly kept away for so many years and whose use invited punishment (Sarin, 1998).

The early criticism of JFM was based on it being a typically top-down approach of the state; asymmetric power relationships between the state functionaries and the people; power imbalances within communities, and inadequate benefit-sharing provisions (Sundar, 2001; Conroy et al., 2000), and doubts were expressed about the department executing sharing of long-term benefits from timber (Arora and Khare, 1994). Another major limitation discussed in 1990s was in the context of 'tenure' being unclear, insecure and without unambiguous, exclusive rights of access to the resource (Lele and Rao, 1996). Absence of legal status to Forest Protection Committees (FPC), government's right to dissolve FPC, unilateral decision making, and inappropriate sharing of forest produce were some other aspects criticized by scholars (Pattnaik and Dutta, 1997).

Now, more than a decade later, many evaluation-based studies have been published offering both (few) positive and (more) negative outcomes of the JFM. The studies demonstrate that in most places, protection committees created under JFM do not last long, or end being unequal partners (Matta and Kerr, 2004). They become dysfunctional either after initial enthusiasm dies down or after the incentive money is exhausted (Kumar, 2002). In some cases, village level JFM committees exist only on paper and are ineffective in protecting the resource (Ghate and Nagendra, 2005). Some note that communities by and large have remained unconvinced about the benefits to be gained from accepting the state designed arrangements at considerable loss of autonomy, while there are also concerns over what is being perceived as covert attempts by the state to expand its authority over forests (Sarin et al., 2003), leaving no room for people's participation (Ballabh et al., 2002). Some studies are harsh at the attitude of forest officials towards JFM committees, which are looked at 'not as people's organization' but as 'a creature that works under the thumb of a forester' (Shah, 2003). It is alleged that forest officials have no real interest in the community and, therefore, in 'collective action' (Hill, 2000), and some find participation by local communities as 'puppetish', indicating that it is not 'participation' in true sense.

Upadhyaya (2003) feels that JFM continues to be on a weak legal footing as it fails to grant security of rights. He feels that the short-term benefits offered under JFM do not act as additional incentives because they are no different from the traditional *nistar* rights that were enjoyed by the communities before JFM. Studies have also brought out the fact that legislation is not enough to ensure participation. Even when representation of women and backward class in executive committee is made mandatory, they might feel too intimidated and inhibited to express their interests and concerns in any form in a public forum (Puri, 2004). Scholars have brought out problems with JFM treating each community as a homogenous entity right from the beginning. "JFM, like many other participatory projects, does not take into account the fact that the community, it is going to be working with, is made up of people placed very differently" (Kumar, 2005). It is assumed in most cases that once the provisions for participation have been made, people would participate (Puri, 2004). In a more recent study of JFM in Indian Shiwaliks, Balooni et al. (2010) find that similar institutional reforms can have diverse outcomes, and especially in case of hierarchical societies, vested interest at the local level may shape roles within or outside the institutional arrangements.

On the other hand, there are studies claiming that the forest committees in several instances are working not merely as the "sounding board for schemes that the department would wish to undertake in villages", but have successfully used the forum, both formally and informally, to secure forest usufruct (Tiwary, 2005). Shylendra (2002) has found that JFM in Gujarat has been able to incorporate and address various issues concerning the livelihood security of the local people. Another multi-state study indicates that biomass growth rate has been comparatively higher in JFM forests as compared to the national average (Murli et al., 2002). Similarly, a study on JFM in Gujarat has found that JFM forests are meeting substantial biomass needs of the community and contributing towards achieving sustainable forestry (Patel et al., 2006). Similar positive results have been quoted from Rajasthan as well (Aggarwal et al., 2006). In a study conducted in the Dehradun district of Uttarakhand, it was observed that the household income considerably increased due to alternative job opportunities, as well as agricultural production. There was reduction in distance travelled and time spent for fuel wood and fodder collection, and thus village women were financially empowered, and institution building had paved the way for sustainability of the whole process (Srivastava et al., 2004). According to Balooni et al. (2007: 1443) "Recent literature does suggest that the paradigm shift from centralized to decentralized forest management has increased the access of local communities to forest resources, increased internal social mobilization has helped communities challenge the traditional state authority and enabled them to create political capital, exposed the conflicts over resource interests, paved the way for positive changes and explored potentials for better forest management".

Our study, based on the working of JFM in three villages in rural Maharashtra, shows that the scenario is not as promising as mentioned in the preceding paragraph.

Provisions for Institution Building under JFM

JFM envisages the building of village-level institutions, popularly named as Forest Protection Committees (FPC). In a recent move, as has been mentioned earlier, the Central Government has encouraged the federation of JFM/FPC under Forest Development Agencies (FD) to strengthen them. Offering better livelihood opportunities through integration of development programmes of other government agencies to deal with rural poverty is an extended objective of FDA. Looking at the structure of JFM, it could be said that many of the design principles formulated by Ostrom (1990) are, in principle, incorporated in the JFM. The design principles are defined as essential elements or conditions that help to account for the success of institutions in sustaining common property resources (CPR). They are: clearly defined boundaries, congruence between appropriation and provision rules and local conditions, collective-choice arrangements, monitoring, graduated sanctions, conflict resolving mechanisms, and minimal recognition of rights to organize. While the first and seventh are supported by the Forest Department, communities under JFM are supposedly given the autonomy to deal with the rest, though irrespective of communities' capability to form operational rules, implement, monitor, sanction and resolve conflicts. Even if one is to look at commonly accepted conditions conducive for collective action, summarized by Baland and Platteau (1996: 289) as, "...user group must be small, live close to the CPR, and be free to set access and management rules in its own way; the CPR must be clearly defined and people must have high level of dependence on them; rules as well as techniques of calculation and control must be simple and fair; there must be well-established schemes of punishment (and these work best when they are graduated to fit the offence); cost of monitoring must not be too high, well-known and low cost conflict-resolution must be available; crucial decisions must be taken publicly, and some record-keeping accountability must be provided for", JFM seems to be programmed fairly well. If communities living in and around forest have the autonomy, as is the intention under the JFM, to develop rules of use, they are likely to be fair and simple. Community, traditionally or otherwise, can arrange to deal with infractions and sanctions. Further, the Forest Department has a mandate to provide help with record keeping and technical know-how. Emphasis of Wade (1994) on the resource being 'critical for the locals' and 'scarce', are both relevant in case of the JFM in forest-based rural communities, especially with degraded forest. It is now pertinent to ask, if JFM is thus structurally on sound footing, has it been successful in building robust institutions? It is with this basic query that a study of three communities was undertaken first in the year 2002, and the same communities were revisited in the year 2007.

JFM and FDA in Maharashtra

Maharashtra is one of the forerunners in JFM. It adopted JFM in the year 1992 and has modified it on the lines of Central Government regulations from time to time. According to the JFM cell of Forest Department of Maharashtra, of the 15,000 odd forest fringe villages in the State, 11,759 had come into the JFM fold by September 2006. Recognizing the important role that can potentially be played by JFM committees, Principal Secretary, the Government of Maharashtra instructed all the state government departments to implement development schemes in the villages with JFM committees, on priority.[2] In the year 2002, the Central Government issued necessary guidelines to all the states mentioning that the agency would function as the federation of all Joint Forest Management Committees within territorial /wildlife forest divisions under the Societies' Registration Act. The concept of FDA was construed on the fact that it is the Forest Department that has the maximum access to villages where staff or workers of other rural development departments cannot reach. Being in constant contact, forest officials know better than anybody else that it is the lack of alternative developmental activities that compels the villagers to encroach and use the forest unsustainably. Thus, using the network of the JFM registered communities, it was aimed that rural development activities would be routed through FDA in the forest fringe villages registered under the JFM programme. The decision to establish FDA and implement the

Samanvit Gram Vanikaran Samirddhi Yojana (SGVSY) in Maharashtra State was taken in January 2001.

The broad short-term and long-term objectives of the programme include regeneration of degraded forests, augmentation of fuel wood, fodder and grasses, people's participation in planning and regeneration efforts to ensure sustainability and equitable distribution, conservation and improvement of non-timber forest produce such as bamboo, employment generation, ecological restoration, environmental conservation and eco-development, and improvement in quality of life of people living in and around forest areas. To fulfil the above-mentioned objectives, it was proposed under the FDA that the respective divisional offices of Forest Department would create awareness about FDA, prepare micro plans in consultation with villagers, and undertake the activities proposed in micro plan with coordination between various district rural development departments.

Study Sites

For this study, we focus on Gadchiroli, one of the eleven districts of Vidarbha, in Maharashtra State (India). This district is rich in forest resources, with most of the forest cover in the state concentrated here. In fact, 61.34 per cent of the forest yield in the state comes from this district. Yet, more than half the population of the district is below the poverty line despite being surrounded by rich forest resources. The district is one of the poorest in Maharashtra, with the per capita income of Gadchiroli district being 48 per cent less than the State average. The district covers 14,412 square kilometres. The population density is very low, as only 0.99 per cent of the state's population resides in this district, and 38 per cent of its population is tribal. Markegaon, Deulgaon and Ranvahi are the three villages from Gadchiroli district selected for this study as they represented three institutional structures. The three forests have different histories. The villages differ on the issue of initiation of forest protection activity. While in case of Markegaon, the Forest Department had initiated the JFM programme, in Deulgaon and Ranvahi, forest protection had started much before the JFM reached these villages. In Ranvahi, an NGO had initiated its forest protection, while the protection activity in Deulgaon was self-initiated. As the three villages fall under the same bio-climatic zone, there are no perceivable differences in climatic conditions. The region receives around 1420 mm of rainfall annually. The forests belong to the dry deciduous category. The dominant floral species include *Cliestanthus collinus (garadi), Anogeissus latifolia (dhawda), Tectona grandis (sagwaan)* and *Terminalia alata (ain).*

Research Methods

Primary data for the three villages was collected with the help of ten research instruments developed by the International Forestry Resources and Institutions (IFRI) co-housed at the Workshop in Political Theory and Policy analysis, Indiana University and SNRE, University of Michigan, Ann Arbor, USA. The IFRI research programme was established in the mid 1990s. The research protocols combine study of socio-economic, institutional and biological factors in a long-term comparative programme of research. The data collected in the method involves biophysical measures of forest conditions by laying of temporary forest plots, climatic and soil conditions, demographic information, and socio-economic indicators along with details about institutions affecting the use of forest resources using rapid appraisal and traditional interview methods (Ghate and Nagendra, 2005; Ghate et al., 2009). IFRI has Collaborative Research Centres in Africa, Asia, Europe, Latin America and North America. Members of the IFRI network use the same methods, collect data on a common set of variables, and share it as an international database. This enables the researchers to conduct large N studies, and time series analyses (Ostrom and Nagendra, 2006).

In this chapter, we present an analysis of institutional data along with some data on botanical evidences.

Results

In this section, we explore the impact of JFM (year of visit 2002) and FDA (year of visit 2007) programme on three village communities. The impact would be captured through institutional and forest data.[3] Institutional variables, such as formation of rules for fodder and fuel wood collection, number of meetings, etc., will form the body of institutional data. Field observations regarding tree felling, grazing, encroachments, fire damage, charcoal making, insect damage and soil erosion, along with measures like tree and sapling density, frequency and DBH (diameter at breast height) will form forest data. For temporal comparison, 12 important species, namely, *Anogeissus latifolia* (main use for fuel wood), *Buchnania lanzan* (fruit extracted), *Butea monosperma* (leaves, flower, and fruit extracted),

Chloroxylon swetiana (fuel wood), *Cleistanthus colinus* (a fast growing specie, leaf litter used as manure, fuel wood), *Diospyros melanoxylon* (leaves as main source of livelihood), *Lagerstroemia parviflora* (a fast growing specie used for fuel), *Lannea coromandelica* (fuel wood), *Madhuca longifolia* (flower is a major source of livelihood), *Pterocarpus marsupium* (timber, implements), *Tectona grandis* (housing timber, implements) and *Terminalia alata* (timber, implements) are considered.

Case 1: Deulgaon Community

The village Deulgaon has not changed much in five years since no modern amenities, including an all weather road, have come to the village since 2002. Number of households has increased from 33 to 45, while the number of individuals in the community has increased from 173 to 182. The caste combination remains the same at 70 per cent Gond (a scheduled tribe) and 30 per cent Kunbi (an 'other backward class' community). The nearest market (Gilgaon village) is 6 kilometres away, while Dhanora (a bigger market and a sub divisional head quarter) is 17 kilometres away. Subsistence farming continues to be the major occupation and main crops grown remain the same – paddy and pulses. The community continues to depend on forest for its fuel wood, fodder and small timber needs, though only

Degraded Forest of Deulgaon

for subsistence and not for commercial gains. As any other rural community in central India, Deulgaon community too owns a large number of cattle and goats, which has increased further between 2002 and 2007. With all these animals grazing in forest, as it is the cheapest option, it has impacted the forest condition.

Institutional Indicators

Two individuals, convinced of the need to protect forest surrounding its village, took the initiative in convincing others in 1990. Protection work started informally, with villagers offering their time voluntarily. Formal governance structure of the committee of 12 members – 3 female and 9 male, under JFM came much later. The committee that was formed in 1998 remained the same even in 2007, with no change in the governance structure as well as the activity carried out by the association, which is mainly the coordination of work when plantations are taken up by the Forest Department. At the operational level, it is imperative for a committee under JFM to form specific rules for forest protection and forest use. This is not done in this village. Protection work in relation to poaching by outsiders has suffered because the dispute of boundary with a neighbouring village has not been settled. Election of office bearers as well as meetings, which were held once a month in 2002, became irregular by 2007. Patrolling of forest is only done in summer now, which was earlier done throughout the year. Dwindling seriousness regarding patrolling is also evident by the fact that selection of guards is now done by 'lots', while earlier, the community appointed the guards. The availability of minor forest products – gum, *moha, tendu* leaves, etc., has reduced. While in 2002, 20 per cent of the food needs were met from the forest, five years later, only 10 per cent of the needs are met with. Lack of support from the division office of FD is reportedly affecting the protection work in Deulgaon. An old bamboo plantation, which was reported in the first visit, is completely ruined due to lack of protection. New plantation of bamboo was taken up again in 2005 under FDA.

Although the community has traditional rights for harvesting timber for house construction and making of agricultural implements, there is a total ban on tree felling imposed by the FD, with some concessions been given to villages that have JFM committee. Each JFM committee is expected to make rules regarding the subsistence use of timber. The Deulgaon committee too has a rule for timber use that each household can harvest for housing and for preparing agricultural implements for personal use, but not for sale. In 2002, there was restriction on felling of timber below a particular girth, but this restriction had disappeared by

2007. In case of fuel wood, the most important rule is that only dry and fallen twigs or branches are to be picked by the villagers and no tree is to be cut or branches lopped for this purpose. There are no other restrictions on quantity for self-use, but no sale is allowed. Only axe is used for cutting small branches. Earlier, there was restriction on cutting of big and old trees, no such restriction remains now. As has been mentioned earlier, there is a large number of cattle that graze in this forest. In the five years since 2002, all restrictions on grazing have remained only on paper and this is evident from the survey of forest plots. Evidence of grazing was found in each plot taken in the forest of this village. Earlier there were rules regarding open grazing of cattle in forest area. Grazing was allowed on rotational basis in marked areas, with each area being kept open for five years. By 2007, even this rule was given up.

With the deterioration of rules and regulations, no infractions got reported, no penalties were imposed, no fines collected in case of all the three forest products. During our 2002 study, there existed a system of penalizing the infractions, although it did not go beyond issuance of warning or public shaming. But, as the forest indicators show, the level of monitoring has deteriorated between 2002 and 2007. There was slight improvement in the level of interaction between the villagers and forest officials due to introduction of FDA in 2003, but it soon became irrelevant with drying up of funds available under it.

State of Forest

Deulgaon's forest is a natural forest which is used by the community as well as two neighbouring communities for subsistence. The 'visit notes' taken in the year 2002 specifically mention that this ancient forest had degenerated due to overuse but good protection by the community is helping it regenerate. However, the revisit in the year 2007 clearly indicated the deterioration of the forest. There were evidences of rampant felling, grazing and pest infestation. Due to poor protection, the only plantation taken up by FD under the FDA programme in 2005, was found to be in a bad state with survival rate as low as 20 per cent. Forestry data collected by laying of 30 temporary plots showed the reduction in the total number of saplings and trees between 2002 and 2007. Earlier, the community had a plan for managing the forest. They had divided the forest into management zones with a system of rotational harvesting in place during the first visit. Forester's appraisal (included in the IFRI protocols) at that time had mentioned that Deulgaon forest was 'about normal for this ecological zone', which changed to 'somewhat sparse' in 2007.

Similarly, commercial value of forest too went down from 'normal' to 'below normal'. During both the visits, the forester found the type of conservation measures adopted in relation to this forest as 'too lax'.

Specific indicators of forest health are discussed below to give a clearer picture.

Overuse of the Resource

Indications of weakening of the forest-governing institution in Deulgaon can be seen from the increased evidences of grazing, tree cutting and encroachments in the sample plots of 2007 as compared to those sampled in 2002.

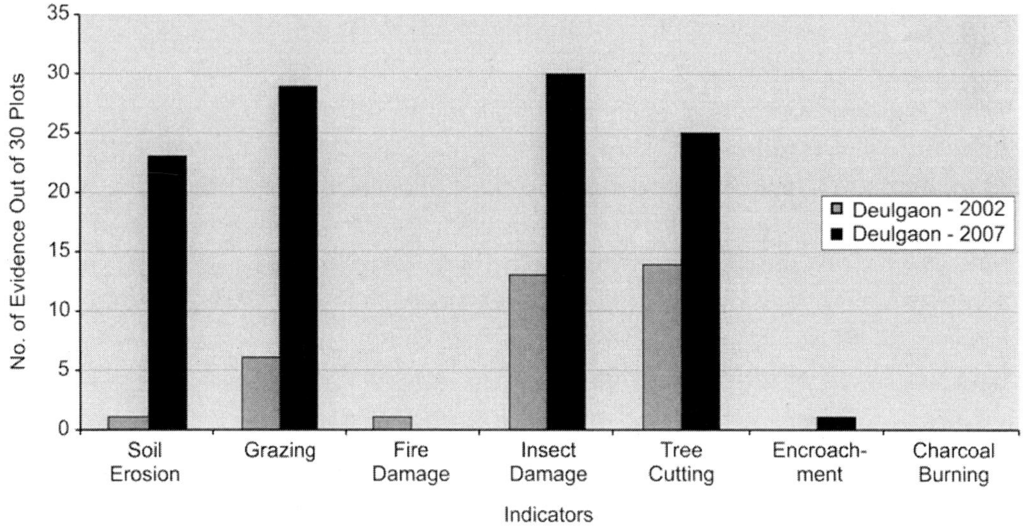

Fig. 1: Deulgaon – Indicators of Forest Condition

Declining Density of Saplings and Trees

Average number of saplings per plot has decreased in 2007 as compared to 2002. Saplings provide an important indicator of regeneration, and hence the future condition of the forest. In this region, saplings are often used as roof supporters. During the period between two visits, there seems to be an unregulated increase in the use of saplings, thus threatening the future growth of the forest. Saplings of six important NTFP species like *Madhuca longifolia* and *Buchanania lanzan,* did not appear in the sample plots of 2007 while these were recorded in 2002, indicating that the future survival of these species in this forest area is at risk. In case of timber species like *Terminalia alata* and *Diospyros melanoxylon*, density had reduced.

It is important to note that although this region is known for the valuable teak (*Tectona grandis)*, no saplings of this species were found in any of the plots in the two years of study.

At the tree level, 50 per cent of the species show a decline in density. This is especially true for timber specie such as *Tectona grandis, Terminalia alata,* and *Pterocarpus marsupium*, indicating that they are being harvested for timber. The NTFP species show very little change. Fast growing species record an increase in density in 2007 as compared to 2002. These species do not need protection to propagate. The DBH class distribution analysis substantiates these observations. The DBH distribution in Deulgaon shows a substantial decline in trees in the DBH class of 2.5 to 10 cms (saplings) in the year 2007. Only 4 out of 12 species appeared in this class in 2007 as compared to 9 species that appeared in 2002. While the distribution of tree species in all the DBH class was well-spread in 2002, it was sporadic in 2007. Trees were missing in the DBH class of 60.1 to 70 cms in 2007.

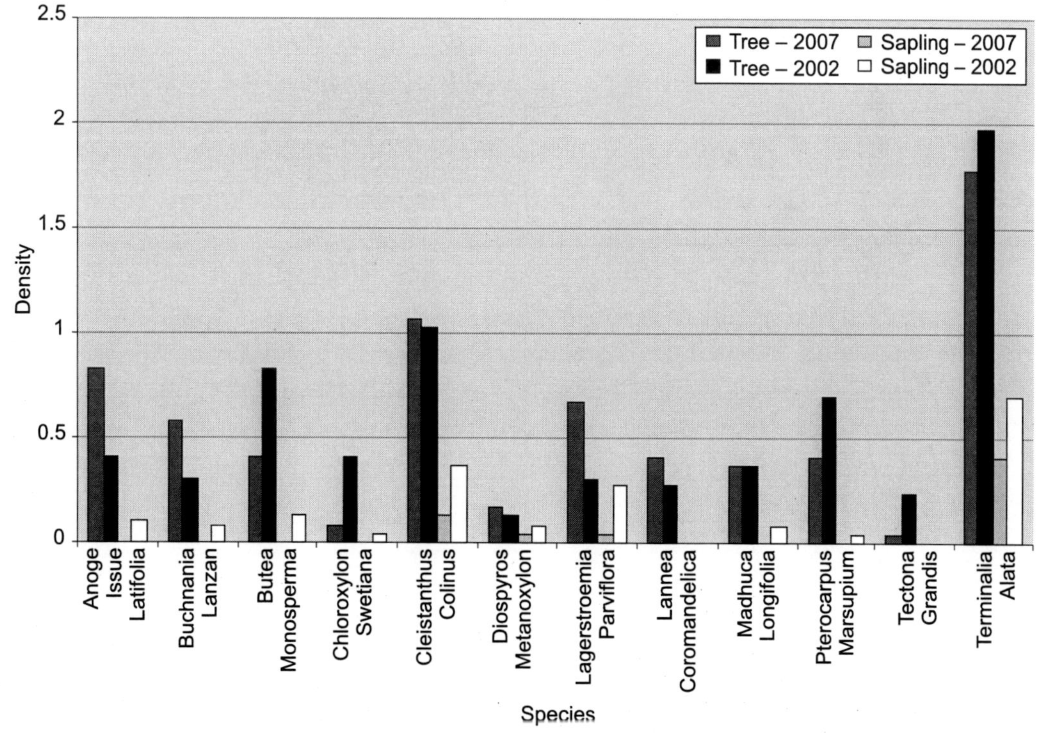

Fig. 2: Deulgaon – Change in Tree and Sapling Density

Case 2: Ranvahi

Ranvahi, which gets its name from a stream coming from a nearby forest and running alongside the village, has majority (96%) of its households belonging to the *gond* tribe. Number of households in Ranvahi increased from 81 to 89 in five years, and the number of individuals from 393 to 424. Increase in the livestock as well as number of households that own the livestock in the village has added pressure on forest due to open grazing. Malewada is the nearest market, which is 2.5 kilometres away, and Kurkheda is the larger market 27 kilometres away. For all the households in Ranvahi, subsistence farming is the main occupation, which provides them with paddy that lasts from seven to eight months. The only sources of cash income for the village are sale of *tendu* (*Diospyros melanoxylon)* leaves and *moha* (*Madhuca longifolia*) flowers. Although there is some employment generated through FD for forestry operations like singling, weeding and plantations, a nursery developed in the village for plantation work under JFM almost eight years ago, does not exist anymore.

Institutional Indicators

Forest protection in Ranvahi was introduced by an NGO in the year 1995, which later encouraged the community to join the JFM programme. Although the basis mandate of the NGO was to promote self-help groups of women in the village, to earn goodwill of the people, it helped the community to develop the constitution of the forest association, and helped them in getting funds under various schemes of the government. However, after the initial enthusiasm died down, activities of the association mainly got restricted to coordinating all the forest related activities. By the year 2007, the number of executive members increased to 10 from 7 in 2002. Waning interest of the community during this period also gets reflected in the irregular general body meetings as well as election of the committee members. Although the meetings of the EC takes place regularly as before, once a month, all the members do not attend these anymore. General body meetings, which were held once a month five years ago, are now held once in only three months, and now only half the members attend the meetings which was earlier attended by almost all members. However, the decisions taken in these meetings for determining the quantity of forest products required by various households, continue to be so.

The community has traditional rights for harvesting timber for house construction and making of agricultural implements – 20 poles and 50 bamboo poles. But to protect the diminishing forest close to the vicinity, FD encouraged the community to decrease this to 10 poles per households per year under JFM. This rule has remained till date. Although no infraction is on record, it is possible that due to poor monitoring, infractions go unnoticed. The most important rule for fodder collection is that only dry and fallen twigs or branches are to be picked by the villagers and no tree can be cut or branches lopped for this purpose. There are no other restrictions on quantity for self-use but no sale is allowed. These restrictions have not changed over the years. As mentioned earlier, there is a large number of cattle that graze in forest. In the past five years, all restrictions on grazing have remained only on paper and this is evident from survey of forest plots. Evidence of grazing was found in each plot in this village, even in plantations. Resultantly, survival of plantation has been adversely affected. Earlier, there were rules restricting grazing of cattle in forest area; grazing was opened in parts of forest and each area was kept open only for five years. But by 2007, there were no rules to restrict the grazing of cattle in forest.

All the necessary records to be maintained under FDA are maintained by the ex-officio member secretary, usually a forest guard or a round officer. The striking feature of this association is that it works in close association with the local forest office and because of this cooperation, it continues to receive funds more frequently than other forest associations. The Ranvahi community received INR 200,000 of funding for entry point activity, which is incentive money, under FDA. This is over and above the funding received for plantation work. The amount is much more than the amount received by any other village. However, these funds have not resulted in strengthening of the institution.

State of Forest

Although the forest condition continues to be 'normal for this ecological zone' as perceived by the community members, all the plantations taken up by the FD have failed. There were six plantations of useful species like Bamboo, *awala* (*Phyllanthus emblica)*, *shivan*, teak (*Tectona grandis*) (timber species) and fodder, taken up since 1998 in Ranvahi, for improving the quality of forest, but all of these failed without exception. The reasons given by the villagers, like, the poor quality of land, and fire kindled by the *tendu* contractors which destroys the forest, are not convincing enough. The main reason seen by the IFRI team is lack of

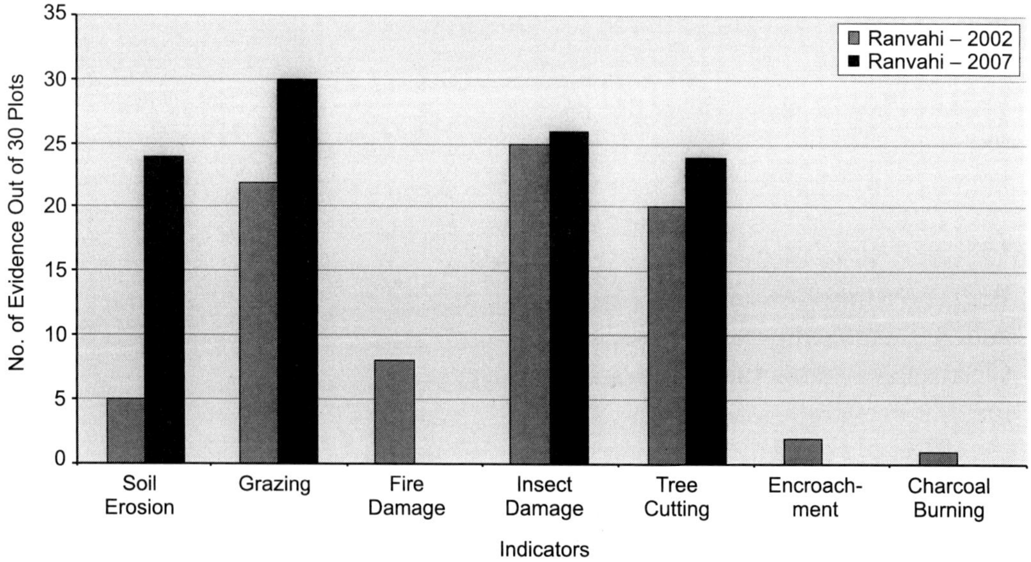

Fig. 3: Ranvahi – Indicators of Forest Condition

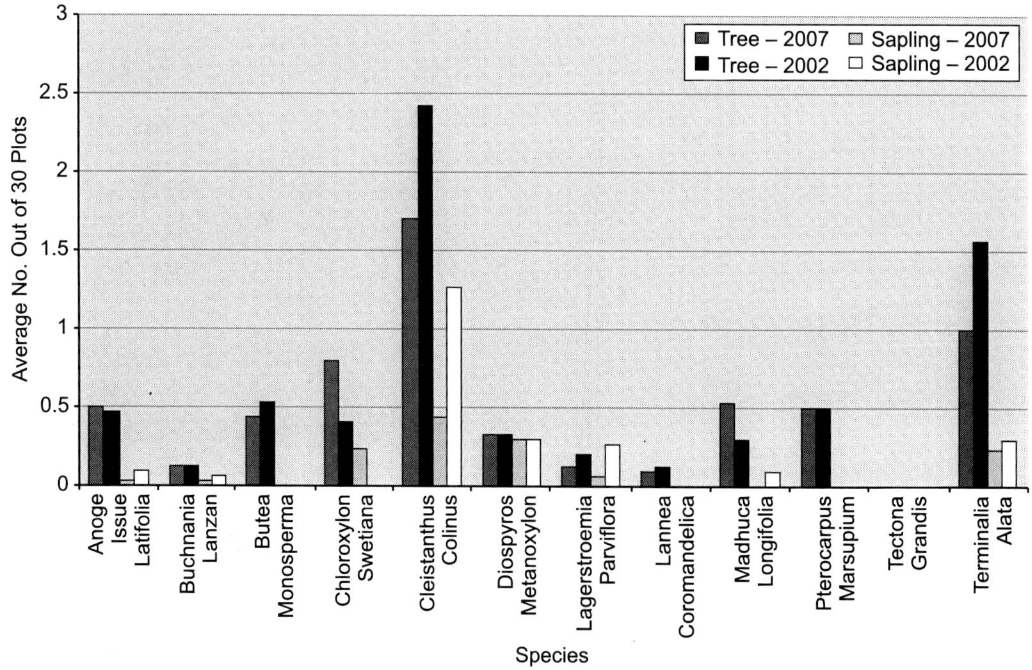

Fig. 4: Ranvahi – Change in Tree and Sapling Density

protection. Also, naxalite (extreme leftist) activity being rampant in the area, FD staff usually does not participate in any forestry activity directly. It is important to note that the number of staff at the FD division office has gone down from 401 in 2002 to 376 in the year 2007. FD has apparently played little role in the management of this forest.

Indicators of Forest Condition

Anthropogenic pressures like tree felling and grazing have increased between 2002 and 2007, resulting in severe soil erosion and a marginal increase in insect damage. On the other hand, there are instances of encroachments and evidence of charcoal-making in 2007.

Tree and Sapling Density

Most of the important timber and NTFP species have shown a decline in sapling density. A big difference (decline) was seen in the DBH class of 2.5 to 10 cms. Species like *Tectona grandis* seems to be on the brink of extinction from this forest as it neither appeared in the sapling or the tree stage in 2002 nor in 2007. In terms of numerical strength too, nine out of 12 species have shown a decline or have not appeared in the sample plots at all in 2007, indicating that regeneration of these species is severely affected, and their future survival is at risk.

Changes in tree density show mixed trends in Ranvahi forest. While important timber and fuel wood species have shown a decline in density, NTFP species like *Madhuca longifolia* have shown increased density in 2007 as compared to 2002. This indicates that the timber species have been harvested, but NTFP species have been well protected, with conversion of some of the saplings to trees between the two points of time.

Case 3: Markegaon

Markegaon is an old traditional village, located in naxal affected area, with 32 tribal households. It is almost a stagnant village with no increase in households between 2002 and 2007, though the population has marginally increased from 161 to 172. Dhanora town, which is also the sub-district headquarter, is the main market and is 7.5 kilometres away. Since there is no public transport, villagers go to the market on bicycles. There is little interaction with officials, even forest officials, especially after two villagers were killed by the naxalites in 2005. Villagers are very passive in receiving new information and do not open up with outsiders. Subsistence farming is the major occupation, and paddy, cereals and pulses are grown that are sufficient for households for eight months. Cereals and pulses are sold for cash income. All the households of Markegaon depend substantially on forest for a variety of things. Forest dependence in this village is varied and more extensive compared to the other two study villages (Ghate et al., 2003). Between the years 2002 and 2007, the number of cattle in this settlement has gone down from 150 to 140. But due to a tribal development scheme, the number of water buffaloes has increased from 30 to 42, and goats from 30 to 110. Farming and wage labour are the two occupations, while some cash income also comes from sale of forest products like *tendu* leaves, *moha* flowers, etc. Firewood collected from the nearby forest is the only source of cooking and cattle are grazed openly in forest. These adversely impact the resource.

Women in Markegaon

Institutional Indicators

JFM was introduced in this village only because of the initiative of FD in 1997. Each forest division in forested areas of Maharashtra were given targeted number of forest protection committees to be set up. Markegaon was one such village to join JFM without full knowledge of the programme. Therefore, it is not surprising to see that there are no activities undertaken collectively by the villagers in relation to forest. One person has been keen in mobilizing the community to take up protection work, and has been trying to bring the community together to formulate rules of forest use, but with little success.

This community has not undertaken forest protection seriously. The community insists that patrolling of forest has been going on since establishment of JFM, but it seems to be half-hearted and unreliable. Even the plantation that was taken under the FDA programme has failed due to neglect. There are 28 households that own land, while others have encroached on forestland with no ownership rights even after joining JFM. There are very few who attend meetings, and disinterested men and most of the women do not participate in rule making. There have been no reported infractions or conflicts, and no punishments have been imposed in the last five years. It is mainly because no misuse has been reported by anybody. Between 2002 and 2007, the Forest Protection Committee has passed rules regarding forest use. Although almost everyone in the village knows about the rules and has no complaints, it was clearly mentioned by the president of the JFM committee that these rules are not strictly implemented. There are eleven executive members, though the number of women has increased from three to five between 2002 and 2007. However, our team could easily see that the women were in the committee for namesake and did not really participate in the proceedings. The village being very small, most of the meetings are general body meetings because no one can be deterred from attending an executive meeting, and there is low attendance in any case.

The Markegaon community too has traditional rights for harvesting timber for house construction and making of agricultural implements, and there are no specific rules made in this regard. It was earlier decided that each household would bring timber from forest for subsistence use only after informing the committee, and no sale of timber would be allowed. However in 2007, it was reported that 10 per cent of timber harvested by the community was sold. It is quite clear that the community is lax about penalizing offenders. Regarding fuel wood, the most important rule is that only dry and fallen twigs or branches can be picked by the villagers and no tree can be cut or branches lopped for this purpose. In both the years, i.e. 2002 and 2007, there were no reports of fuel wood collection in excess of requirement. There were no other restrictions on quantity for self-use but no sale was allowed. No infractions were reported, no penalties imposed, no fines collected in case of this product in both the study periods. The picture is quite different in case of fodder. A large number of cattle grazed in the Markegaon forest in 2002 as well as in 2007. All restrictions on grazing in plantation area have remained only on paper, our forest survey also found evidence of grazing in each forest plot, even in plantations.

State of Forest

Markegaon's forest is old and natural. There are many big trees standing, and this forest is better than the other two forests studied. Plantations in this forest were undertaken twice, once under JFM and then under FDA. Yet, there seems to be gradual decline in the quality of forest, as is clear from the following analysis.

Indicators of Forest Condition

The local JFM institution of Markegoan has failed to develop stronger rules and implement them effectively. It can be seen from the increased evidence of grazing, encroachments, fire damage, soil erosion and tree cutting in sample plots of 2007

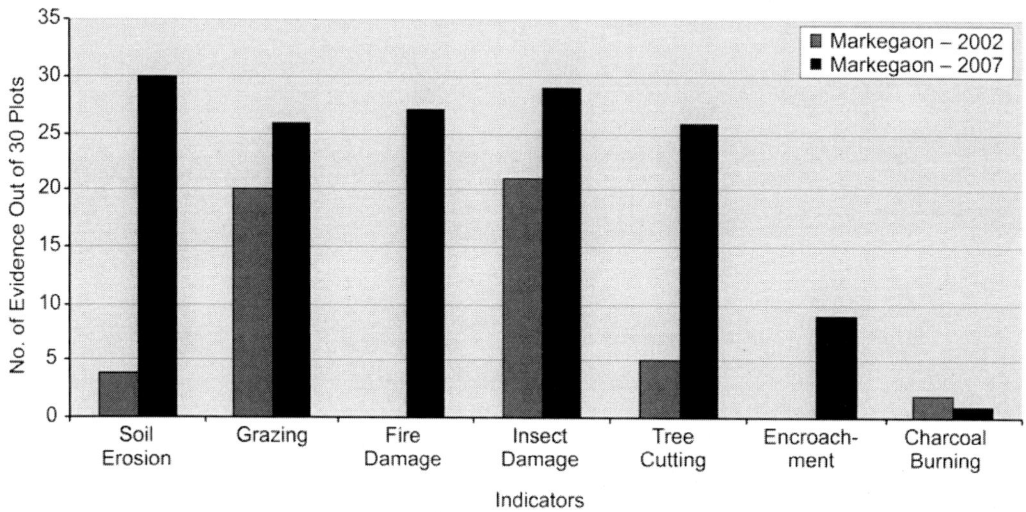

Fig. 5: Markegaon – Indicators of Forest Condition

as compared to the plots sampled in 2002. There is increased insect damage too. The institution seems to have deteriorated, as there has been increase in these activities since 2002.

Tree and Sapling Density

In 2002, only 10 per cent of the sample plots had no saplings, while by 2007, there was a dramatic increase in the number of sample plots, with over half (56.6 per cent) recording no saplings. This indicates the lack of protection. Saplings of species like *Lannea coromandelica* did not appear in either of the sample years. The density of saplings was reduced overall in 2007 as compared to the density in 2002. Thus, regeneration of many species has been impacted over the five year study period.

In 58 per cent of the 12 important tree species, there was reduction in density in 2007. These are important timber, NTFP and fuel wood species, indicating towards overall lack of protection. Some of the timber species like *Tectona grandis* and *Pterocarpus marsupium* show large reduction in numbers. This corresponds with the observation of the research team, who saw cartloads of timber trunks being carried by neighbouring villagers.

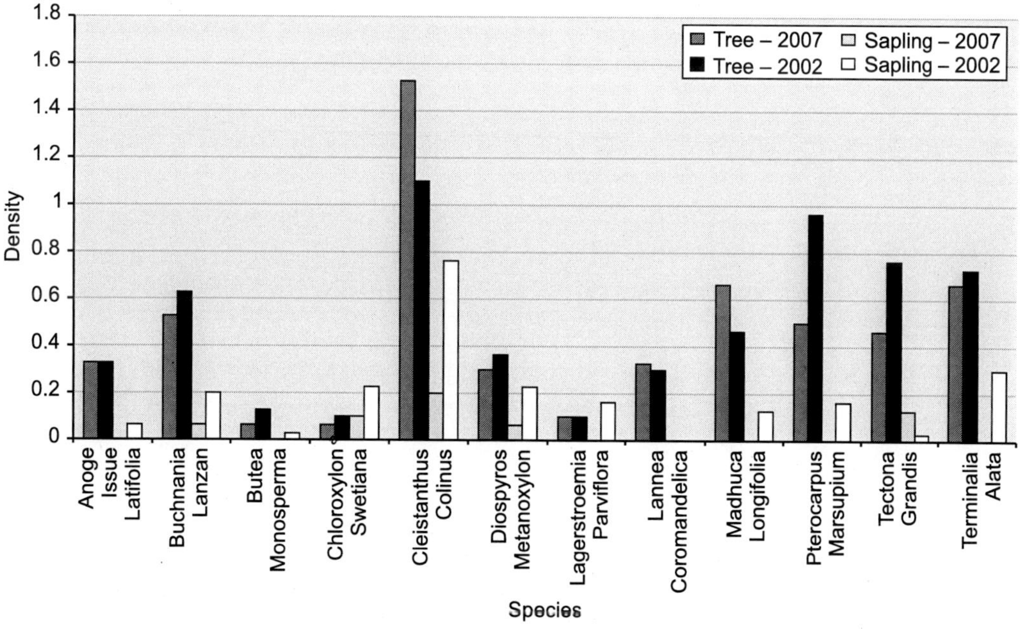

Fig. 6: Markegaon – Change in Tree and Sapling Density

To sum up, despite the official emphasis of the JFM and FDA programmes on forest plantation, vegetation analysis of forest condition brings out a different story. In all three forests, high levels of grazing, fire and other anthropogenic damages to forests are recorded, along with severe declines in regeneration. This does not bode well for the future of these forests. There is also significant felling of mature trees, especially of timber rich species, indicating the failure of the FDA and JFM plantation programmes.

Discussion

Participatory programmes like JFM and FDA are aimed at encouraging sustainable use of forest by communities by making them responsible for management of the resource, expecting this to lead to rural development. Accordingly, funds are allocated with maximum emphasis on plantations for restoration of degraded areas, along with incentive funds at the beginning of the programme. The basic expectation under JFM is that the communities joining the programme would formulate self-restrictive rules of forest product use, and follow them.

To analyse the three cases studied, we use Institutional Analysis and Development (IAD) framework, developed by Professor Ostrom and others at the Workshop of Political Theory and Policy Analysis, Indiana University, USA (Ostrom et al., 1994). The IAD framework is multi-dimensional, describing three levels of action: operational, collective choice and constitutional choice. At the operational level are day-to-day activities that affect the world directly. The collective choice level is where decision makers create rules to impact operational level activities. The constitutional level is where decision makers determine how collective choice participants will be selected and how the relationship among members of the collective choice body will be. In essence, constitutional choice outcomes affect collective choice decision making, which, in turn, affects operational level activities (Ostrom, 2005: 58). This analytical tool can be used at different levels, for example, at the level of analyzing specific Forest Protection Committee, or at higher level, the three levels of decision making being national (constitutional), state (collective), and local (operational). We chose the latter.

In 1990, the Government of India had accepted participatory policy in managing the forest. Individual states accepted the approach and formulated their own policy, to create local level institutions for joint management. Accordingly, village level

FPC were set up as institutions that would formulate their own rules of forest use, monitor them, deal with infractions and assist FD in implementing forest management plan. Either to maintain its control on the resource, or to help the community in performing its slated functions, the FPC has to have an ex-officio secretary belonging to the department. The post of secretary being the key post in administrative functioning of an organization, remained crucial for the functioning of FPC as well.

In our study villages, it can be clearly seen that FPC as the institution either remained inactive or deteriorated during the revisit period. This got reflected in the status of the resource as well. Despite funds being received under both the programmes, it did not result in either village development or improving forest quality through plantations and soil and moisture conservation works. Two factors seem to have played an important role here. At the collective choice level (State level), decision to create village level institutions was taken, but by making it mandatory to keep a forest official in the committee, the department did not give autonomy (found to be crucial by Behera and Engel, 2006) to the committees on the one hand, and made the community suffer due to the inefficiency of the secretary on the other. It is possible that the preference of the community towards individual ownership rather than communal ownership is gaining favour, as gets reflected in the increase of encroachments on forest land, especially in case of the small, traditional, completely tribal village of Markegaon. But this trend can be countered only by building robust institutions, the process aided by the FD. On the contrary, this study shows the FD is undertaking programmes like JFM and FDA without much conviction in people's participation. The FD staff itself is unaware of the basic purpose and provisions of the programme. Coordination between informal and formal efforts, that is, between the community and the Forest Department, which was the strength of Ranvahi community, now is turning into an unhealthy nexus. The Forest Department and NGOs need showpieces that can be used to convince funding organizations, and community wants to corner as much funding as possible. While multiple plantations have been taken up with huge costs, none has survived satisfactorily. While money is being pumped in through various programmes, the institution is getting weakened. These are alarm bells for programmes like JFM. With the Scheduled Tribes and Other Traditional Forest Dwellers (Recognition of Forest Rights) Act, 2006, coming into force, the use and misuse of forest resources would depend to a great extent on the maturity of communities. In these changed circumstances, building of strong local institutions should be the top priority, without which forests are likely to be the first casualty. As was found in a study of community management in Nepal, US and Kenya (Kellert et al., 2000), the objective of sustainable utilization is closely associated with biodiversity protection, with a clear focus on managing species for economic benefit. In most of the cases, sustainable utilization goals tended to be underemphasized and became the victim of mismanagement. In the present study also, we find that there has been consistent investment in forests (through plantations), but these have turned into bad investment due to lack of institutional strength. It only indicates that now there is increasing need for investment in institutions. An important dimension of the response of communities to social, economic and environmental pressures is the institutional dynamics, as Markandya (2001) puts it, for which relations of trust, participation of all stakeholders on decision making and a sense of ownership by all, are critical.

References

[1] Aggarwal, A., R.S. Sharma, B. Suthar and K. Kunwar, 2006. 'An Ecological Assessment of Greening of Aravali Mountain Range through Joint Forest Management in Rajasthan', India, *International Journal of Environment and Sustainable Development,* Vol. 5: 1, pp. 35–45.

[2] Arora, H. and A. Khare, 1994. 'Experience with the Recent Joint Forest Management Approach', paper prepared for the international workshop on India's Forest Management and Ecological Revival, New Delhi.

[3] Baland, J. and J. Platteau, 1996. *Halting Degradation of Natural Resources: Is There a Role for Rural Communities?* Oxford: Clarendon Press.

[4] Ballabh, V., K. Balooni and S. Dave, 2002. 'Why Local Resources Management Institutions Decline: A Comparative Analysis of Van (Forest) Panchayats and Forest Protection Committees in India', *World Development*, 30/12: 2153–2167.

[5] Balooni, K., V. Ballabh and M. Inoue, 2007. 'Declining Instituted Collective Management Practices and Forest Quality in the Central Himalayas', *Economic and Political Weekly*, April 21.

[6] Balooni, K., J.F. Lund, C. Kumar and M. Inoue, 2010. 'Curse or Blessing? Local Elites in Joint Forest Management in India's Shiwaliks', *International Journal of the Commons,* Vol. 4, No. 2, August 2010, pp. 707–728.

[7] Behera, B. and S.S. Engel, 2006. 'Institutional Analysis of Evolution of Joint Forest Management in India: A New Institutional Economics Approach', *Forest Policy and Economics*, 8(4): 350–362.

[8] Conroy, C., A. Mishra and A. Rai, 2000. 'Learning from Self-initiated Community Forest Management in Orissa, India', *Forests, Trees and People Newsletter*, 42: 51–56.

[9] Ghate, R., 2008. 'A Tale of Three Villages: Practised Forestry in India' in Rucha Ghate, Narpat Jodha and Pranab Mukhopadyay (eds.), *Promise, Trust, and Evolution: Managing the Commons of South Asia*, Oxford University Press, New York.

[10] Ghate, R., A. Chaturvedi and D. Mehra, 2003. 'Bio-diverse Economic Dependence of Indigenous Population: A Study from Gadchiroli District of Maharashtra', paper presented at Third Biennial Conference of the Indian Society for Ecological Economics (INSEE), at the Indian Institute of Management, Kolkata, 18–20 December.

[11] Ghate, R. and H. Nagendra, 2005. 'Role of Monitoring in Institutional Performance: Forest Management in Maharashtra, India', *Conservation and Society*, Vol. 3: 2 (509–532).

[12] Ghate, R., D. Mehra and H. Nagendra, 2009. 'Local Institutions as Mediators of the Impact of Markets on Non-timber Forest Product Extraction in Central India', *Environmental Conservation*, Vol. 36: 51–61.

[13] Hill, D., 2000. 'Assessing the Promise and Limitations of Joint Forest Management in a Era of Globalisation: The Case of West Bengal', paper presented at the eighth biennial conference of the IASCP – 'Constituting the Commons: Crafting Sustainable Commons in the New Millennium', Bloomington, Indiana University, USA.

[14] Kellert, S., J. Mehta, S. Ebbin and L. Lichtenfeld, 2000. 'Community Natural Resource Management: Promise, Rhetoric, and Reality', *Society and Natural Resources*, 13: 705–715.

[15] Kumar, C., 2005. 'Revisiting "Community" in Community-based Natural Resource Management', *Community Development Journal*, Vol. 40: 3 (275–285).

[16] Kumar, S., 2002. 'Does Participation in Common Pool Resource Management Help the Poor: A Social Cost-Benefit Analysis of Joint Forest Management in Jharkhand, India', *World Development* 30: 763–782.

[17] Lele, S. and R.J. Rao, 1996. 'Whose Co-operatives and Whose Produce? The Case of LAMPS in Karnataka', paper presented at the National Seminar on 'Rediscovering Co-operation', Institute of Rural Management, Anand, India, November 19–21.

[18] Markandya, A., 2001. 'Poverty Alleviation and Sustainable Development: Implications for the Management of Natural Capital', http://www.iisd.org/pdf/markandya_paper.pdf (accessed in January 2008).

[19] Matta, J.R. and J. Karr, 2004. 'Selling Environmental Services – Challenges and Opportunities for Sustaining Local Resource Management: Lessons from Joint Forest Management Experience in Tamil Nadu, India', paper presented at the 10th Biennial IASCP conference on 'The Commons in an Age of Global Transition, Challenges, Risks and Opportunities' at Oaxaca, Mexico, August.

[20] Matta, J.R. 2006. 'Transition to Participatory Forest Management in an Era of Globalization – Challenges and Opportunities', paper presented at the Eleventh Biennial Conference of the International Association for the Study of Common Property, Bali, Indonesia.

[21] Murali, K.S., I.K. Murthy and N.H. Ravindranath, 2002. 'Joint Forest Management in India and its Ecological Impacts', *Environmental Management and Health*, 13: 5 (512–528).

[22] Ostrom, E., 1990. *Governing the Commons: The Evolution of Institutions for Collective Action*, Cambridge: Cambridge University Press.

[23] Ostrom, E., 2005. *Understanding Institutional Diversity*, Princeton University Press, Princeton and Oxford.

[24] Ostrom, E., Roy Gardner and James Walker, 1994. *Rules, Games, and Common Pool Resources,* Ann Arbor: The University of Michigan Press.

[25] Ostrom, E. and H. Nagendra, 2006. 'Insights on Linking Forests, Trees, and People from the Air, on the Ground, and in the Lab', *Proceedings of the National Academy of Sciences USA,* 103(51): 19224–19331.

[26] Parul, R. 2006. 'Joint Forest Management in India: An Attitudinal Analysis of Stakeholders', *Resource, Conservation, and Recycling*, Vol. 51: 2 (345–354).

[27] Patel, R., M. Subhash, J.P. Tripathi, V. Kaushal and S. Mudrakartha, 2006. 'Regeneration of Teak Forests under Joint Forest Management in Gujarat', *International Journal of Environment and Sustainable Development,* Vol. 5: 1 (85–95).

[28] Pattnaik, B.K. and S. Dutta, 1997. 'JFM in South-West Bengal – A Study in Participatory Development', *Economic and Political Weekly,* 32/50: 3225–32.

[29] Poffenberger, M. and B. McGean, 1998. *Village Voices, Forest Choices: Joint Forest Management in India*, Oxford University Press, Delhi.

[30] Puri, E., 2004. 'Understanding Participation: Theoretical Foundations and Practical Implications', *Economic and Political Weekly,* June 12.

[31] Sarin, M., 1998. 'From Conflict to Collaboration: Institutional Issues in Community Management', in M. Poffenberger and B. McGean (eds.), *Village Voices, Forest Choices,* Delhi, India: Oxford University Press, 165–203.

[32] Sarin, M., N.M. Singh, N. Sundar and R.K. Bhogal, 2003. 'Devolution as a Threat to Democratic Decision Making in Forestry? Findings from Three States in India', Working Paper 197, Overseas Development Institute, London, UK.

[33] Shah, A., 2003. 'Fading Shine of the Golden Decade: The Establishment Strikes Back', Paper presented at GIDR national seminar on 'New Developmental Paradigms and Challenges for Western and Central Regional States in India', Gujarat Institute for Development Research, Ahmedabad, India.

[34] Shylendra, H.S., 2002. 'Environmental Rehabilitation and Livelihood Impact Emerging Trends from Ethiopia and Gujarat', *Economic and Political Weekly*, August 3, 2002.

[35] Srivastava, S.K., D. Kumar, R. Gupta, A.K. Mahendra and I. Pundir, 2004. 'Impact of Participatory Forest Management on Socio-economic Development of Rural People: A Case Study in Kodsi and Talaichittor Villages of Dehradun District', *Indian Forester*, Vol. 130: 3 (243–252).

[36] Sundar, N., 2001. 'Is Devolution Democratisation?', *World Development*, 29/12: 2007–2023.

[37] Thompson, J., 1995. 'Participatory Approaches in Government Bureaucracies: Facilitating the Process of Institutional Change', *World Development*, 23/9 (1521–1534).

[38] Tiwary, M., 2005. 'Panchayats versus Forest Protection Committees Equity and Institutional Compliance in Rural Development Forestry', *Economic and Political Weekly*, May 7, 2005.

[39] Upadhyay, S., 2003. 'JFM in India: Some Legal Concerns', *Economic and Political Weekly*, August 30, 2003.

[40] Wade, R., 1994. *Village Republics: Economic Conditions for Collective Action in South India*, Institute for Contemporary Studies, San Francisco, California.

Notes

1. No. 6.2/89-Forest Policy, June 1, 1990; No.22-8/2000-JFM(FPD), February 21, 2000; Strengthening of JFM Programme, Guidelines, by MoEF, on December 24, 2002; NAEB 25-1-1/99-B-2 Dated 4-01-2000 issued by Central Government to all States; Government Regulation No. MSC/2000/143/F-2, 25.4.2003 issued by Government of Maharashtra.
2. GR No. MSC/2004/lt.no. 20/F-2.
3. For further details on case studies, refer to Ghate, 2008.

11

Overseeing the Disappearance of an Ecosystem: Governance in West Bengal and the Wetlands to the East of Kolkata

Sudeshna Banerjee

This chapter engages with the theme of environmental governance, focusing on governmental attitude in West Bengal government to the wetlands to the east of Kolkata – a unique ecosystem, crucial to environmental sustainability and food security in West Bengal, but also to the sustainability of the planet as a whole in the face of global warming. Despite apparent governmental concern in West Bengal since the late 1980s to preserve the wetlands, despite the existence of a government department for the environment and despite the establishment of a state-funded Institute of Wetlands Management and Ecological Design (henceforth IWMED), massive encroachment on the wetlands as a whole not only continues unabated, but the rate of encroachment has, indeed, fiercely accelerated particularly since the 1990s.

The question is whether the glaring absence of any serious effort on the part of the West Bengal government to stop this decimation of the wetlands derives from bureaucratic short-sightedness and lack of coordination among government departments. After all, one important view is that in India, the environment is addressed symbolically by the government – whether at the centre or in the states – because of the role of the bureaucracy, which merely aims at managing problems and not solving them with a holistic, comprehensive and adequately informed commitment to conservation.[1] And it is undeniable that in the case of the concerned wetlands, the bureaucracy in West Bengal, far from being pro-active conservationists, has resorted to myopic, short-term, problem management exercises, largely ignoring the environmentalists' protests from the civil society and hardly caring to include any notable presence of earth scientists and biologists or other environmental scientists on the committees formed by the state. Thus, government has failed the conservation of the wetlands to the east of Kolkata, as this chapter will demonstrate.

However, this chapter raises the fundamental question as to whether such governance is not itself structured by the axes of power and power-laden ideologies that characterize the given socio-political context. The environmental governance of the wetlands to the east of Kolkata, we argue, should be ultimately contextualized in the political economy of mega-urbanization that the Government of West Bengal has come to strongly imbibe and mechanically apply – often at the cost of biodiversity and sustainability of the environment – in the trail of economic liberalization in India and primarily in the interest of real estate and infrastructure developers and private players in the education and health sectors. The area to the east of Kolkata, thanks to its proximity to all urban amenities, the airport and the recently constructed highway called the Eastern Metropolitan Bypass (henceforth EM Bypass), started becoming an exploitable asset for the Government of West Bengal, eager from the beginning of 1990s to court FDI and create a mega-urban agglomeration around Kolkata, commensurate with this agenda. Thus, the government's over-all insensitivity of 1980s towards the environment has given way since the 1990s to a more studied relegation of environmental considerations to the background whenever the latter have contradicted the prospect of a market-led agenda of urban development. This is matched by a studied governmental inaction regarding the development of such instruments as would have empowered the fishermen and peasants of the wetlands vis-à-vis the real estate developers and other private stakeholders in mega-urbanization, who have evidently received the blessing of the political establishment in West Bengal. It is not surprising, therefore, that the rhetoric of environmental governance in the state carefully elides the integrally related question of landownership in the wetlands even though the environmental sustainability of the region (maybe of the whole planet) demands that this anomalous land situation be immediately addressed and the peasants' and fishermen's occupancy right in the land and water bodies be somehow protected.

But the unavoidable question would be why such governance is passing off with very little protest from civil society, even environmental circles. Why the reason of urban neo-liberalism that legitimizes the West Bengal governments' handling of the wetlands to the east of Kolkata is managing to be the hegemonic reason precluding any significant pro-active pressure halting the pernicious evaporation of the wetlands is no less a question to be answered. After all, if any governance anywhere has been pinned down to responsibility towards the environment, it is usually as a consequence of environmental activism and strident interrogation of public policy from outside the sphere of the state.

A Unique Ecosystem Under Siege

The wetlands to the east (north-east, east and south-east) of Kolkata, named the 'Salt Lakes' by the British, struck the European traders, ship-captains and even the representatives of the East India Company in the eighteenth century as a sprawling marshy area in the form of a chain of salt water marshes and swamps stretching eastwards for more than seventy square miles from within three miles of the then Calcutta.[2] Though the area of this wetlands ecosystem have progressively dwindled since the late colonial period with successive waves in eastward of the city of Kolkata, it was once a vast area which stretched eastwards towards the Basanti-Gosaba-Canning (the threshold of the Sundarbans as they now stand) from areas which since the nineteenth or early twentieth centuries became integral parts of the city of Kolkata (Calcutta then) like Bagmari, Beliaghata, Entally, Ballygunge. The massive migration from East Pakistan in the 1950s and 1960s claimed many areas on the then eastern periphery of the city from the wetlands. However, eastern parts of some areas (like Dum Dum, Tangra, Topsea, Dhakuria, Jadavpur and Tollygunge) still retained their wetland topographical and ecological character. And even as late as the 1980s, the large areas of what are presently reckoned as South Dum Dum, Bidhannagar and Rajarhat municipalities were entirely wetlands in terms of its natural environment. Even what constitutes the easternmost wards of the Kolkata's municipal jurisdiction today, were in the early 1980s, parts of same wetlands ecosystem, along with several rural panchayats in the police station of Haroa, practically all of the rural panchayats in the present-day police stations of Rajarhat, South Bidhannagar, Bhangar and Sonarpur.

The distinctiveness of this ecological zone derives from its essential character as a low-lying spill basin of a tidal river system dominated by the tidal activity of the river Bidyadhari and embedded in the wider ecosystem of the Ganges-Brahmaputra delta within which this wetlands ecosystem is held in a biological and geomorphic continuum with the Sundarbans estuary to its south and east. Along with its distributary Piali, Bidyadhari, aided also by its numerous creeks, channels and canals, constitutes the main conduit whereby saline tide from the Bay of Bengal, finding an easy passage inland through the numerous estuaries of the Sundarbans and carried northwards by the river Matla (which Bidyadhari joins from the North) used to spill up to the early twentieth century over the vast area referred to as the Salt Water Lakes by the British.[3] Thus, it is Bidyadhari that has largely determined the environmental fundamentals of the vast marshy region in between the active part of the delta, i.e. the Sundarban estuary and the mature delta, i.e. the Basirhat-Barasat region. By spilling the tide from the bay over this vast stretch of lowlands, it is the Bidyadhari system that has created the marshes and swamps there and largely determined the biological foundations of this tidal ecosystem even though the ecosystem has transformed over time with land reclamation and the silting up of Bidyadhari. Again, it is Bidyadhari that has made the hydrological regime of the area saline – a salinity that has, however, gradually transformed into brackishness. Finally, if this wetlands terrain is inextricably related to the Sundarbans, it is because of the organically connecting role of the Bidyadhari. Indeed, it may be said that it is the history and tidal action of the Bidyadhari that acted as the ecological spur integrating this vast marshy terrain and also binding it with the Sundarbans in an intimate biogeochemical relationship which may be called a continuum. Henceforth in this chapter, therefore, we shall refer to this wetlands terrain as the Bidyadhari wetlands.

The environmental reasons against the rapid disappearance of the Bidyadhari wetlands under an expanding Kolkata's urban concrete are compelling, especially in the face of climate change due to global warming. These wetlands constitute the deltaic outlet for the entire subcontinental watershed and any interference with its waterways including the creeks, channels by concrete and metal structures can only be pernicious.[4] The nature of the Ganges delta which includes the Bidyadhari spill basin is aggrading and, therefore, the silt needs to move, as much as it is still possible for it to move despite the present-day sluggishness of the Bidyadhari. The Bidyadhari wetlands can ill-afford to have a rapidly expanding urbanization thwarting the movement of silt.[5] Indeed, any major anthropogenic alteration in any part of this dynamic natural entity is capable of upsetting the equilibrium of the entire Ganga-Brahmaputra basin and prove disastrous for the environmental sustainability of both eastern India and Bangladesh.[6] The wetlands region also has aquifers crucial for the water recharge of greater Kolkata and for the hydrological equilibrium of the delta.[7] Furthermore, this terrain is a site of immensely rich biodiversity that urbanization is threatening to destroy at the peril of the planet as a whole. Last but not the least, the sustainability of the fragile ecosystem of the Sundarbans depends on the environmental conservation of the Bidyadhari wetlands, as the latter not only bears the mark of its past inclusion in the Sundarbans but also acts as a ecological buffer zone to the Sundarbans with which it still retains considerable biogeochemical affinity.[8]

Apparently, it seems that in recent years, the state government has taken considerable strides towards the conservation of these wetlands. The wetlands area is protected by a 1992 verdict of the Calcutta High Court, which prohibits any change in the pre-existing land use. Filling up of water bodies in this area is prohibited under the West Bengal Town and Country (Planning and Development) Act, 1979 as well as under the West Bengal Inland Fisheries Act, 1984 (with amendment in 1993). Moreover, the East Kolkata Wetlands (henceforth EKW) – the waste-recycling zone within the wetlands – is a Ramsar site, protected under the Ramsar Convention,[9] to which India became a signatory in 1981. However, it should be pointed out in passing that the Ramsar area forms just a fraction of the Bidyadhari wetland system as evolved over thousands of years as merging/coalescing/shifting swamps and spill basins of multiple rivers in the process of the formation of the Ganga-Brahmaputra delta.[10]

If these safeguards are there on paper, the ground reality in the wetlands to the east of Kolkata is hardly encouraging for the survival of this ecosystem. Massive urbanization at the behest of agencies of urban development, on the one hand, and national and transnational majors in real estate development, health services, hospitality and retail, on the other, has already alarmingly reduced the expanse of the wetlands, particularly that stretch which is outside the boundaries of the Ramsar site. These changes in land use not only threaten the ecological balance of the area,[11] but also threaten to evaporate the wetlands ecosystem altogether with disastrous consequences for the Sundarbans multi-functional ecosystem.[12] Since the 1990s, environmentalists, NGOs, academics and social observers have frantically drawn attention to this development. The government – under the same political party since 1977 – has somehow never assumed the pro-active role needed to stop this rampant and ecologically disastrous encroachment beyond a superficial lip-service to the cause. The question is whether it is the archetypically bungling bureaucracy in a typically postcolonial administrative structure, with an evident colonial hangover and a lack of sensitivity, that is primarily responsible for this state of affairs.

An Environmental Cause Governmentalized: Bureaucratic Bungling

Governance in West Bengal, as elsewhere in India, has had to quickly imbibe an environment-sensitive rhetoric since 1976 with the amendment of the Indian Constitution to include environmental protection among the principles of ruling state policy, in the trail of 1972 United Nations Conference on Human Environment (Stockholm). The promulgation of the Environmental Protection Act of 1986 has further reinforced the trend. The West Bengal government, too, has had to fall in line and the West Bengal Department of Environment was established in 1982, while the West Bengal Pollution Control Board had come up in 1974 itself. Since the turn of the twentieth century, it has become mandatory for policy makers and planners in West Bengal to have an in-situ situation of wetlands ecosystem.[13] But governance is unavoidably implicated in bureaucracy, especially in postcolonial governmental structures. It is not surprising, therefore, to find that the bureaucratic machinery in West Bengal has its share in making environmental policy statements merely symbolic and tokenistic. Bureaucratic ineptitude is most graphically reflected in the webpage of the West Bengal Department of Environment itself, which in 2008 showed the name of Manabedra Mukherjee as the minister, whereas Mukherjee was the minister for environment in the previous cabinet which had ended its term in early 2006.

The department-bound and red-tape-riddled strain, said to be typical of the Indian bureaucracy, has characterized the environmental governance of the wetlands. Lack of interdepartmental coordination appears to be the most glaring of the bureaucratic lacunae determining the governmental failure to dam the tide of encroachment. Environmental governance, in particular, calls for a holistic idea of both the ecological reality and governmental practice as the interface between the two is complex and multi-ribbed. In the absence of such a holistic comprehension among most bureaucrats – even the environment-minded ones – the role of the state government in the wetlands issue has been ambiguous.[14] Its statements in different legal cases do not seem to be consistent. Some of its agencies propagate and devise conservation strategies,[15] while others tolerate and even promote environment-insensitive urbanization. And there are strong signs that administration as a whole is neither organized nor equipped to adequately deal with the delicate issue.[16] The mapping of the concerned wetlands is a case in point. Litigations regarding alleged encroachment on the wetlands has repeatedly brought to the fore the urgent need for accurate maps as an instrument for settling disputes regarding whether a given place is within the wetlands or not. And yet, the Department of Environment has not cared to come up with maps (of the wetlands) that can be regarded as adequately detailed.[17] The 'waste recycling region' is defined by a map prepared in 1985 by the State Planning Board, West Bengal. This definition, however, is ambiguous, the map is of inadequate scale and exists in various versions, none of which has been officially published by the authorities; there is lack of precision even regarding the boundaries of this region. [18]

It is public knowledge that all kinds of industries, including some of the gravely polluting ones, are flocking to set up shop on the eastern side of the EM Bypass. The immediate eastern side of the Bypass was, even in the beginning of the 1990s, evidently a part of the wetlands ecosystem. Today, with urbanization having forced the western boundary of the wetlands at many points almost two kilometres away from the Bypass, an intermediate stretch of about two kilometres has developed between the Bypass and the wetlands; this is effectively a buffer zone where no industry should be located which is pernicious for the fragile wetlands ecosystem. It is baffling, therefore, to find that between 2004 and 2008, marble processing companies, initially proliferating on the western side of the Bypass, has come to proliferate on the eastern side in the buffer zone, literally breathing [poison] down the neck of the wetlands. Interestingly, it was in the early 1990s itself that environmentalists had moved law courts about polluting industries entering the East Kolkata Wetlands (henceforth EKW) proper.[19] One would expect that the Department of Environment would closely coordinate with the West Bengal Industrial Development Corporation and the public authorities issuing trade licences to prevent polluting industries from entering EKW and its buffer zone. After all, the 2004 study of biodiversity, conducted by the government's IWMED itself has categorically brought out a clear decline in the biodiversity profile of the region.[20] It is, indeed, surprising that as late as 2008, when marble processing units had practically mushroomed all over the buffer zone and had stated encroaching on the EKW, the West Bengal Pollution Control Board (WBPCB) was not aware of the development.[21]

An Environmental Issue Governmentalized: Misleading Cartography and Erased Geomorphological History

However, even on the face of it, the governance of Bidyadhari wetlands is not just a story of bureaucratic ineptitude, bungling or red tape. The administrative attitude to the Bidyadhari wetlands seems to be curiously marked by a thread of consistency, too. Certain consciously adopted assumptions – assumptions that are contradicted by the natural history and geomorphology of the Bidyadhari spill basin – are being systematically applied to the governance of these wetlands over the last decade, even while this governance has also come to be structured of late in terms of a consciously chosen management-oriented paradigm of bureaucratic governance with important consequences for the sustainability of the wetlands.

The governmental discourse on wetlands to the east of Kolkata explicitly assumes, especially since the turn of the twentieth century, that the concerned wetlands somehow constitute a 'peri-urban fringe'.[22] Correspondingly the KMDA, the public nodal agency for administering the Mega City Programme pertaining to Kolkata, has made a clean sweep of the pre-existing perspective plans that had warned against any eastward expansion of the city of Kolkata into the low-lying wetlands. In tandem with these developments, the government's rationale of wetlands conservation has chosen to cultivate a studied silence about the kindred ecological relationship between the Bidyadhari wetlands and the Sundarbans ecosystem – a relationship that needs to be recognized and sustained if the Sundarbans are to be effectively conserved. Thus, the wetlands – even the issue of their conservation – are perceived from the vantage point of the city of Kolkata and its environmental sustainability. The 'peri-urban' wetlands are systematically represented in governmental discourse today as a peripheral marshy fringe that not only receives Kolkata's sewage and saves the city from the eventuality of choking under its own sewage but also recycles the sewage into manure for vegetables and food for a fish population that feed the city.[23] The relative inexpensiveness of such natural sewage disposal is also relieving for the West Bengal Government. The 'peri-urban wetlands', as configured by the government, has been named East Kolkata Wetlands. We need to pause here and consider the definition of 'peri-urban'. The exact definition of 'peri-urbanity' is debated by scholars, while the definitions of 'peri-urban interface' are thin and inconsistent.[24]

The simplest definitions of peri-urban are spatial, defining it as a zone around the built up area of a city where city and country land uses overlap. But in recent years, there has been a shift from simply spatial definitions to ones in which the element of time is introduced into the spatial in the form of social processes and other dynamics which supposedly create the 'peri-urban' by extending the town into the rural through a process of dispersion.[25] Now, whichever sense of 'peri-urban' the government might be seeking to invoke in relation to the wetlands to the east of Kolkata, the application of the term is problematic. There is no point denying that the EKW is indeed a zone into which the city of Kolkata is extending through a process of dispersion in terms of land use and livelihoods. But, the total terrain of tidal wetlands of the Bidyadhari – and not merely the EKW within it – stretches from within the eastern extremities of municipal areas of Salt Lake township, Kolkata and the Rajpur-Sonarpur municipality right up to the western extremities of Basanti and Canning on the threshold of the Sundarbans proper. Thus, in terms of built space, the Bidyadhari wetlands traverse the urban, the 'peri-urban' and the purely rural. Even if the processual sense of the term peri-urban is invoked, the eastern parts of the Bidyadhari spill basin, particularly in the rural panchayats in many parts of the police stations of Bhangar and Sonarpur were quite rural and did not experience any initiation of urban land use or livelihoods at least at the end of the 1990s when the state started applying the term 'peri-urban fringe' to the wetlands.

The government's representation of the 'peri-urban fringe' is baffling indeed. Of course, a crucial conceptual counterpoint would be that if Kolkata is not peri-wetlands in the government's reckoning, then the wetlands have no reason to be reckoned as peri-urban, particularly when ecosystemically the Bidyadhari wetlands were never fundamentally constituted by their proximity to the city of Kolkata; these wetlands were geomorphologically and biologically constituted by the tidal action of the Bidyadhari and affiliation to the Sundarbans, as we shall be detailing subsequently in this essay.

But the really curious assumption characterizing the recent governmental discourse is that this 'peri-urban fringe' is also an ecosystem;[26] obviously the EKW is being portrayed here as the concerned ecosystem. But the problem is, the moment the idea of ecosystem is invoked in relation to the region to the east of Kolkata, scholars with a comprehensive earth-scientific knowledge of the natural environment in West Bengal would justifiably identify the Bidyadhari wetlands as a whole and not merely the EKW as that ecosystem.[27] And the Bidyadhari wetlands is by no means a 'fringe' in any sense of the term; it is much bigger than the EKW that merely constitutes a part of it.

The state's description of the immediate eastern periphery of Kolkata as simultaneously a peri-urban fringe and a unique, autonomous ecosystem is based on the assumption that the EKW is a self-contained and isolable ecosystem. But this assumption is itself highly debatable.[28] The argument on which this particular representation of the EKW is based is that the inflow of waste water from the city of Kolkata, naturally recycled by the farmers and fisherfolk of the area to manure their vegetable farms and fishponds, has created an ecosystem out of a spill basin on which the Bidyadhari's tidal influx has no surviving signature, the river having silted up in the early twentieth century. It is evident that in characterizing the wetlands to the east of Kolkata, the official discourse exclusively emphasizes the waste recycling zone. No wonder, it sees the wetlands ecosystem as entirely man-made, non-saline and sewage-fed. It is also important to note that such an understanding of the wetlands is obviously techno-centric, even while it interprets the nature of the wetlands in the light of a history less than hundred years old.[29] The exclusive official attention to the EKW, in tandem with the invention of East Kolkata Wetlands as a nomenclature also betrays the urban-centric – indeed Kolkata-centric – bias of wetlands governance. The name, indeed, gives the impression that wetlands to the east of the city somehow would not have existed had it not been for the city of Kolkata, whereas the reality is that long before the region now known as Kolkata ever became urbanized, the Bidyadhari spill basin was already an ecosystem in its own right. It is true that as the Bidyadhari progressively silted up and failed to bring in as much saltwater as before to feed the *bheris* or fish ponds in the beginning of the twentieth century, the salinity of the *bheris* declined while non saline waste water started flowing into the Bidyadhari spill basin from the city of Kolkata since the 1880s. This induced a transformation in the pisciculture of the region; from the 1930s, the fisheries in the area receiving the wastewater influx started becoming sewage-fed. Consequently, the nature of the fish population in the *bheris* also changed, even while the world of flora too transformed in this part of the Bidyadhari wetland.[30] But the question that environmental scientists urgently need to answer is whether this transformation has made the sewage-fed zone an independent and autonomous ecosystem obliterating the ecosystemic integrity of the wider Bidyadhari spill basin as the official literature implies. Our fieldwork suggests that the sewage-fed area has transformed, no doubt, but the transformation is from a saline water to a brackish water system. The fish population has definitely transformed but not the entire world of aquatic and amphibian species which have retained a remarkable continuity and identity with the pre-existing system and the wider Bidyadhari wetlands. As the soil of the entire Bidyadhari wetlands still retains considerable salinity, the flora, despite transformation in the sewage-fed area, displays remarkable streaks of continuity and identity as is patently evident in the massive proliferation of brackish-water-fed bullrush and elephant grass all over the Bidyadhari country, whether outside the sewage-fed zone or inside. This prompts us to suggest that the governmental discourse is mechanically closed to the idea that every ecosystem is from its inception complex and includes zonal variations and yet get defined in a holistic sense. Thus, the sewage-fed zone is a distinctive part even within what holistically remains a ecosystem – the Bidyadhari wetlands.

The West Bengal Government's cartographical configuration of the EKW – the supposed 'peri-urban fringe' – reinforces the impression that the official representation is lopsided. Mouzas like Nonadanga, Madurdaha in Tiljala Police Station, Kalikapur in Kasba Police Station, Chak Ganiagachha, Barakhola, Kendua, Rajapur and Bademasur in East Jadavpur police stations were still very much part of the concerned wetlands ecosystem in 1990s and, spatially speaking, were on the immediate periphery of the urban built space, being situated within one kilometre of the Eastern Metroplitan Bypass – the highway that has acted as the communication spur enabling the eastward expansion of Kolkata into the wetlands since the beginning of the 1990s. Yet in the official map of the EKW, published in the middle of the 1990s,[31] these places were not included. One cannot help feeling that there were considerations other than ecological in drawing up the map in this way – considerations that this chapter will subsequently figure out.

What emerges from the foregoing discussion is that the government's techno-centric, Kolkata-centric imagining[32] – whether textual or cartographic – of the wetlands to the east of the city has the effect of erasing the long-term historical perspective in which an ecosystem needs to be understood in order to be conserved. It is in the appropriate historical perspective that question needs to be raised whether the inflow of waste water from Kolkata (then Calcutta) since the late nineteenth century and its utilization by farms and fish-ponds since as late as the 1930s constitute the only crucial signature on the biogeochemical cycles that cumulatively constitute these wetlands, or it historically interacts with other signatures accumulated over centuries.

Whereas the channelling of the city's sewage into the wetlands occurred as late as the last quarter of the nineteenth century, the region as an agglomeration of saltwater lakes – the 'Great Salt Lake(s)' as the officials of the British East India Company named it – dated back to approximately the sixteenth century and had come to be constituted as a low-lying spill basin of a tidal river system dominated by Bidyadahari. The vast expanse of this marshy terrain was determined by the long and circuitous course of the Bidyadhari. The river, as surveyors found in the late nineteenth and early twentieth centuries began as a tidal drainage channel, by the name of Nona Gang, a little south-east of Dogachia, which lies between the rivers Sunti and the Padma. The river then flows past Jessore Road and Barasat-Basirhat rail tract. Just south of this railway tract, the Harua Gang meets the Nona on the right and the combined stream is known as the Bidyadhari, which is now in a heavily silted condition. The Harua itself serves as a drainage outlet of the extensive swamps to the east of the Dhapa-bil around Rajarhat-Bishnupur (22'37' N and 88'30' E). Further south (about 20 km), Bidyadhari receives the Bhangar Kata Khal (which drains the Salt Water Lakes of east Calcutta and is itself linked with the Krishnapur Canal, Circular Canal and the New Cut Canal) on the right bank and the Kulti (or Chaumuha Gang) on the left bank. Below this confluence, the Bidyadhari flows south as the tidal Kumarjol Gang. There is another branch of the Bidyadhari to the south of Bamanghata (88'29'E and 22'31' N) into which the Central Salt Water Lake Channel, in its turn, is emptied.[33] It flows south-east, receiving the Tolly's Nullah from the east and giving off the tidal Piali Nadi flowing south from its right bank before reaching Port Canning where it receives the other branch, i.e. Kumarjol Gang referred earlier. This south-flowing united stream joins the Matla estuary which also receives Piali and flows into the Bay. It is this circuitous route which determines why such far flung areas as outlined in the very introduction of this essay are included in the 'Bidyadhari country' – the spill-basin of the Bidyadhari. The salinity of the ground water of this extensive region and the saline to saline-alkaline nature of the soil of the region also derives largely from the once-lively tidal action of the Bidyadhari.[34] The nature biota, too, derives from the way in which the tidal action has shaped the soil, water and atmosphere in the region. However, in order to comprehensively understand the complexity of the ecosystem of the Bidyadhari country, we need to situate the environmental signature of the Bidyadhari within context of the gamut of pre-existing biogeochemical signatures on a terrain that still bears the palaeographic, stratigraphic and hydrological signatures of developments from at least the Quaternary period to the Recent.[35] Thus, it is an extremely longue dureè history of the earth system of this region in its dynamic evolution, dialectically situated within the wider dynamics of the Ganges Brahmaputa delta, and not merely the short history of sewage-fed agriculture and pisciculture that determines the nature and expanse of the Bidyadhari wetlands. It is precisely this history that the governmental discourse of the last two decades silences.

Consequently, the integral relation between this terrain and the Sundarbans, too, is completely elided in the discourse; and yet for long, before the emergence of Kolkata as a city, the Bidyadhari wetlands were very closely integrated with the Sundarbans, with which it exists in a continuum, not merely geological but also biological.[36] The official discourse in recent years has gone completely silent about the ways in which the signature of this kindred relationship is still evident in the geosphere, biosphere and hydrosphere of the wetlands. The fauna, particularly the bird and reptile population of the Bidyadhari country and the Sundarbans proper are very similar.[37] The case of flora is a significant pointer to the integral relationship with the Sundarbans. During the time of Lord Clive, the swamps to the east of the then Calcutta was covered with Sundarbans jungle, infested with alligators, wild boars and even tigers.[38] Thus, the wetlands were very much a part of the Sundarbans as late as the early British period.[39] This is confirmed by the fact that in devising land settlement, the British excluded almost the entire terrain of the Bidyadhari wetlands from the purview of the Permanent Settlement (devised for the rest of Bengal) and developed instead a settlement that they applied alike to the reclaimed areas of the Sundarbans proper and the reclaimed areas of Bidyadhari country – the *patitabadi taluk* lease system. It is worth recollecting that the East India Company, on getting the zamindari of the 24 Parganas in 1757, found the Bidyadhari wetlands not only depopulated (presumably as a consequence of raids by Arakanese and Portuguese pirates) but also under low but dense forest cover. This should be appreciated in conjunction with the information that as late as the second half of the eighteenth century, mangrove swamps extended to almost the neighbourhood of Sealdah.[40] The rest of the dense undergrowth in this spill basin comprised reeds, elephant grass and bulrushes of the *hogla*, *nal*, *pati* variety – species that still grow fast and thick in the Bidyadhari country wherever urban infrastructure and concrete have not smothered them.[41] More than a century later, a map of the Presidency Division appended to W.W. Hunter's *Statistical Account of Bengal*, Vol. 1, Part 1, published in 1875 – when Sundarbans had receded from the immediate vicinity of the then Calcutta – much of Haroa, Rajarhat, Bhangar, Sonarpur and of course, Canning were still shown under forest cover.[42] That the environment of the Bidyadhari country is congenial to the lesser mangroves is further borne out by the presence of a massive cluster of *genwa* trees – a lesser mangrove – in Anandapur in the eastern part of the Kasba Police Station as late as the early 1990s.[43] Sporadic samples of this species are still to be found in Madurdaha, Chak Kalar Khal mouzas and even within the EKW,[44] which the government does not care to see in relation to the Sundarbans. With environmental sustainability depending in both micro-climatic and macro-climatic sense on these crucial wetlands, the government's silence about this region being a crucially interlocked natural annexe of the Sundarbans is not merely unfortunate but pernicious. We strongly argue that what is being sought to be represented under the epithet 'peri-urban' as the annexe of the city of Kolkata, is more patently 'peri-Sundarbans' – if we are allowed to coin the term – and needs to be conserved as such from the aggressive agenda of 'development by urbanization'.

The long-settled inhabitants of the wetlands, with an intimate everyday knowledge of the terrain and an age-old relationship between their life and livelihoods, on the one hand, and the wetlands, on the other, perceive this spill basin as '*jalajami anchal*' or '*bada anchal*' (wetlands region). They tell us that the *doba* (bogs or small swamps) and the paddy fields in the neighbourhood that are being rampantly acquired by the 'promoters' on the ground that they are 'not *bheris* and, therefore, not wetlands' are actually veritable parts of the *jalajami* (wetlands). Even if the bogs and small ponds that dots the region are not *bheris*, they, too, sustain pisciculture, albeit of the poor man; after all, during the period from August to October, the region remains totally water-logged for months together. The rice cultivation takes place in this marshy terrain only in winter. The local people take great care to emphasize that the *bheris* (water bodies usually bigger than five cottahs in size), *bils* (ponds), *dobas* (bogs or swamps), the (winter) paddy fields, the intervening beds of vegetable cultivation and the numerous canals that criss-cross the entire region cumulatively sustain the varied world of *badar prani* (fauna of the wetlands) which they lament are fast disappearing since the inauguration of the EM Bypass.[45] The locals also keenly feel the integral relation between the Sundarbans and the Bidyadhari country. It is very significant that Utpalendu Mondal, a bureaucrat and litterateur hailing from the Sundarbans, describes the entire stretch of Bidyadhari "flowing through Deganga, Haroa, Rajarhat, Bhangar and Sonarpur to meet the Matla in Canning" as a river of the Sundarbans.[46]

'We can Manage the Environment!'

An interesting development to have reinforced the government's failure to arrest the decimation of the wetlands is a change since the 1990s in the ethos of governance from administration to management. In an age of corporate capitalism, managerialism is being projected as a more cost conscious, efficient and effective paradigm of rendering public service that also supposedly ensures greater democracy, impartiality and public accountability governance. But, what is there on the flip side of this managerialism in the case of the environmental governance of the wetlands ecosystem of the Bidyadhari spill basin is pertinent to explore. With the formation of Wetlands Management Authority, created in 2004 by the West Bengal Government, an ethos of ad hoc management has taken the front seat, relegating to the background whatever concern for long-term planning the government had in the past. The recent fascination with managerialism is starkly evident in the names of new-fangled agencies of wetlands governance and the recent literature on the concerned ecosystem – the East Kolkata Wetlands Management Authority or such reports by the IWMED as "Management of Urban and Peri-Urban Wetlands: A Rapid Appraisal Programme for Fragile Areas".[47] It is, indeed in sync with this management-centric ethos that the concerned authorities are keen to represent the wetlands in terms of very short-term and recent features that make the wetlands ecosystem look conveniently simple and neatly manageable. This imagined simplicity and manageability might give the state the space to sustain an official propaganda that though the ecosystem is fragile and development by urbanization somehow inevitable, the committees, authorities and boards instituted by the state can 'manage' the 'fragility'. This chapter will subsequently demonstrate that this oversimplification and spatial contraction of the wetlands picture is only facilitating massive encroachment, particularly on the wetlands area outside the waste recycling zone and the public unconcern about it.

From this managerial perspective – a stance of conviction that everything including anthropogenic imbalances in natural systems can be technologically fixed – the scientists' perspective so crucial for knowing and sustaining the complex dynamics of an ecosystem is not deemed necessary, as is evident from the nature of the committee formed for East Kolkata Wetlands Management Authority.[48] It is almost entirely bureaucratic, neither academic nor democratic. No elected functionary of any such mechanism has been accorded a place. The executive body of the management authority has no environmentalist of national or international eminence as member, and the expert committees envisaged in its constitution are given a purely advisory status.[49] Evidently analysis and planning have been effectively marginalized to the point of redundancy. Treating the wetlands less as a complex ecosystem to be holistically understood and nurtured, and more as an immediate problem to be 'managed' has come to characterize West Bengal's environmental governance, especially since the turn of the twentieth century.

Calcutta Metropolitan Planning Organization's Basic Development Plan of 1966, too, prescribed that the city should not grow eastwards. This verdict was again reiterated for pertinent geohydrological and environmental reasons by the Calcutta Metropolitan Development Authority's "Plan for Metropolitan Development, 1990-2005" (1990). Voicing its concern about "private land transaction and development activity in the area" leading to "indiscriminate encroachment on the green areas, wetland and water bodies" CMDA plan asserted, "The direction of [urban] development should be reoriented to restore it to north and west."[50] It should be admitted that this environmental injunction on eastward urban expansion was violated in the beginning of the 1960s by the then chief minister of West Bengal, Bidhan Chandra Roy, when he founded Salt Lake (later named Bidhan Nagar after Bidhan Chandra Roy) as a satellite township using up a quarter of the then existing wetlands to the east of Kolkata. However, Roy's apologists can say that environment and ecology had not become factors to be reckoned with by the agencies of governance, and Roy in building this township, moreover, was trying to solve the problem of refugee influx from East Pakistan rather than further the market in real estate.[51] But in the new millennium, that too with a dedicated Wetlands Authority, one would have expected a strict implementation of imperative of reorienting urban development away from wetlands ecosystem in the east. Instead, however, urbanization towards the east and south-east has been tremendously reinforced during the last few years with polluting marble companies, outlets of retail giants, skyscrapers and realtor-led middle-class housing, profusely erupting immediately adjacent to the wetlands, without maintaining the buffer zone necessary for saving a fragile ecosystem from urban encroachment.

It is significant that the Calcutta Metropolitan Planning Organization's Basic Development Plan of 1966 prescribed that the city should not grow eastwards. This verdict was again reiterated for pertinent geohydrological and environmental reasons by the Calcutta Metropolitan Development Authority's "Plan for Metropolitan Development, 1990–2005" (1990). Voicing its concern about 'private land transaction and development activity in the area' leading to "indiscriminate encroachment on the green areas, wetland and water bodies", the CMDA plan asserted, "The direction of [urban] development should be reoriented to restore it to north and west."[52] But in the new millennium, that too with a dedicated Wetlands Authority in place, one would have expected a strict implementation of the imperative of reorienting urban development away from wetlands ecosystem in the east. Instead, urbanization towards the east and south-east has been tremendously reinforced directly exposing this fragile ecosystem to a typically urban biosphere, atmosphere and groundwater depletion.

Significantly, long before a management-oriented perspective had come to dominate governance in West Bengal, the Town and Country Planning Act of 1979, even without using words like ecosystem had advocated safeguards for the protection of the entire wetlands and had insisted on a buffer zone between the wetlands and the city.[53] The January 2008 declaration by the state government that it will tolerate no further encroachment on the wetlands was evidently and admittedly taken with view to conserving the wetlands and its biodiversity in the face of environmental degradation and global warming. Yet, nothing was done to revoke the recent sanction given by the Kolkata Municipal Corporation to the project of a 45-storey apartment complex (Bengal NRI Complex) adjacent to the existing wetlands, indeed on what was until recently very much a part of the wetlands stretch outside the boundaries of the EKW. What is significant is that the developer of the apartment complex, Bengal NRI Complex Limited, is a joint sector company with six representatives of the state government on the board of directors. The project manager's press statement takes care to confidently assert that 'they had kept in mind [read managed] the ecological aspects'. The developer guarantees that 'eco-friendly innovations' shall be a major hallmark of the project, but never mentions the likely effect of the project on the wetlands barely half a kilometre away. This seems to stem from complacency that Madurdaha, the mouza where the building is coming up, is not within the East Kolkata Wetlands as the official map delineates it. Of course, this official EKW map, as we have already indicated, is a truncated representation of the wetlands and Madurdaha was, indeed, until very recently, a part of the deltaic wetlands.[54] But even if it were not, the very presence of a giant skyscraper with its predictably huge vehicular population and its massive air-conditioning arrangements is itself untenable on the immediate boundaries of Bhagabanpur, Goalpota and other places very much within the EKW and still abounding in immensely productive *bheris* and paddy fields (of winter rice). The government, imbued with present-day capitalism's management *mantra* probably expects to 'manage' the earth system – the complex interlocking of the geosphere, hydrosphere, atmosphere and biosphere[55] – by making it obey human-made, cartographical boundaries and keep carbon monoxide stalled at the boundary between the EKW and its immediate neighbourhood! This is obviously an outcome of the West Bengal Government not caring to have on the concerned 'management authority' any internationally or nationally acclaimed environmental scientist who could have acquainted the bureaucrats with the fundamentals of earth system science, the most recent revolution in the earth science that helps generate a comprehensive understanding of global warming and climate change.[56] Even more glaringly, the Bhaba Atomic Research Centre has been given land in Chak Garia, itself a part of the Bidyadhari wetlands only recently converted from swamps and paddy field to urban housing area, adjacent to the *Khudirabad* area of the EKW, to conduct underground nuclear test aimed at path-breaking advances in nuclear medicine.

Governance, Globalization and Goons

A probe narrowly focused on the domain and departments of governance, however, cannot comprehensively explain why the encroachment on the wetlands is proving to be unstoppable. Indeed, however, critical the tools of analysis we use, governance cannot be critiqued self-referentially; governance has to be situated in relation to relevant or connected developments in society, outside the immediate domain of governance. Our attempt to probe the role of governance in the wetlands question, thus, took us unavoidably to the field – to the wetlands itself, to the scene of 'development' along and near the EM Bypass, to the actual sites where land-grabbing has now become an art of muscle, terror and subterfuge. Indeed, we have seen in the wetlands how governance as we idealize it has gone by default or has been 'allowed' to go by default by the powers that be. Maybe, this is the way in which the neo-liberal dictum, 'that government is best which governs the least' manifests itself under conditions of globalization in the countries of the global south, particularly where corporate capital plays a predatory role in relation to land and other natural resources! Given the economic dynamics of the time, the local bases of power have come to imbricate developments which ultimately derive from global developments in the world of capitalism to cumulatively devour the wetlands into a projected mega-urban space. How the will of the powers that be at the local level (which prominently includes the local committees of the party in power in West Bengal)[57] uses the party channel to influence the administration to make governance inoperative so that the 'promoter' can silently have land/water-body alienated from the peasant and/or fishermen is an interesting study.

It should not be missed that from the last decade of the twentieth century and particularly during the first decade of the twenty-first, even while the rhetoric of wetlands conservation came to be habitually reiterated in the corridors of governance, West Bengal government started displaying an increasing eagerness to court FDI and generally resonate to the forces of capitalist globalization, arguing that there was no alternative to compromising with the neo-liberal paradigm of development in a post-Washington-Consensus world. In this environment, the recently constructed EM Bypass came to be regarded as an ideal lifeline for a projected mega-urbanization on either side of it. This was a time when the vast wetlands close to the Bypass had started being eyed by a whole range of vested interests from real estate agents to suppliers of building materials to various kinds of brokers and land mafia. With the ruling party in West Bengal promising to stay in power for much longer with an assured mass base, these vested interests climbed on to the party bandwagon generating at the local level a burgeoning nexus between the party and the 'promoters'.[58] It is in this context that we shall try to understand those extra-governmental pulls and pressures that determine the 'development'-friendly governance of the wetlands. Indeed, this attention to the forces of globalization, on the one hand, and the dynamics of local power at the most micro-level (where local 'promoter'-mafia-party nexus works out its own permutations and combinations) helps us see how certain 'lapses' and coordination 'failures' in governance are, indeed, acts of commission rather than of omission, or to be more exact, how apparent omissions conceal a politics of commission.

Let us raise certain questions which apparently defy explanation and in any case do not seem to be interconnected. Our effort here will be to show how these apparently incoherent bits do, indeed, fit into a jigsaw puzzle, the complete canvas of which is a weave of global capitalism and local eddies of power and interest, both imbricating the domain of environmental governance and frustrating all possibilities of the remaining wetlands to the east of Kolkata from being saved from encroachment by the various agencies of 'development'. Let us outline the apparently unconnected questions. Why, for example, does the end of the 1980s and beginning of the 1990s, when the so-called Washington Consensus came to cast a far-reaching shadow on 'development' in the global South,[59] stand out as the period when a no-holds-barred urban development at the cost of wetlands conservation came to be officially inaugurated?[60] Why has there been such a confusing variety of map on the wetlands and why, despite the Calcutta High Court Green Bench castigating the government for its inability to supply precise maps, no definitive map – whether of the deltaic wetlands as a whole or of the EKW – was prepared until 2006, by which time thousands of acres of wetlands had been lost to mindless urbanization? Is there, then, some method in this cartographic madness as it were and, does anybody benefit from this confusion? Why, despite the obvious existence of the same wetlands ecosystem outside and all around the EKW, is there a great effort on the part of the government to pass the EKW off as the entire stretch of wetlands to the east of Kolkata? Does this misrepresentation benefit specific interest groups? If so, why exactly is the government playing a second fiddle to these interests? Was the formation of the Wetlands Management Authority necessary to serve these interest groups; otherwise why, after the Town and Country Planning had already brought out the existence of deltaic wetlands beyond the waste recycling zone and had suggested a comprehensive legal protection for the wetlands as a whole, a specially empowered authority like the EKWMA is trying to single out only the waste recycling zone for protection? Does all this have any common denominator with all the upcoming rural roads in the wetlands under the *Pradhan Mantri Gram Sadak Yojna* linking the wetlands villages, not with one another, but with the EM Bypass, the spur of post-liberalization urbanization in Kolkata.

It is important, therefore, to understand the post-globalization, post liberalization conjuncture in its implications for the *jalajami anchal*. The conjuncture has two levels of significance for 'development by urbanization' in the area. One is the government's new-fangled courtship with FDI as such. This has entailed granting prime locations to transnational investors in IT, infrastructure development or wholesale trade. The other is the creation of an urban atmosphere attractive to corporate capital in general. The second also involves giving special privileges to 'investment by the NRI', which itself is a post-liberalization concept. With the EM Bypass already inaugurated and augmented with arterial connectivity with Kolkata's administrative, business and cultural hubs, the wetlands to the immediate east of the Bypass (and sometimes also to the immediate west of it) appeared to the government as the best bait of a location to woo investors and infrastructure developers with. Understandably, the period since the end of the 1980s, particularly from the 1990s, has seen a dramatic spurt of an urbanity of an 'international' kind.[61] The story of the tide of capitalist globalization reaching the *jalajami anchal* around the once tidally active Vidyadhari started with not merely the construction of super luxury hotels in the wetlands just outside the waste recycling zone, i.e. in the buffer zone between the city and the EKW, but really with the mulling of the idea to set up a World Trade Center in the same area in the late 1980s. Later, of course, Salt Lake has been extended (in its Sector Five avatar) at the cost of the wetlands and a plush IT hub created typically in an age of outsourcing. Metro Cash and Carry, as we have already mentioned, has been given a prime location in the buffer zone at the cost of (winter) paddy fields and the livelihood of more than twenty peasant families. With even more severe implications for the already emaciated wetlands, a MOU was signed in 2006 between the West Bengal government and the Indonesia-based Salim-Ciputra group regarding the proposed Eastern Link Highway, an 85 km, four lane expressway from Barasat, headquarters of North 24-Parganas district to Raichak in South 24-Parganas. Even though the government is not divulging the exact route, with its fixed termination points and its remarkable width, this expressway virtually has no geographical option but to run through the *jalajami anchal* to the east of Kolkata.[62] The question of the expressway will be discussed in detail later in this chapter.

At a more general and ramified level, the impact of globalization and liberalization has snowballed into a multi-layered eastward expansion of Kolkata into the wetlands. At one end of the spectrum is the government-led development by urbanization, mainly in the form of land grants to corporate-managed civic amenities (from education to health to joint sector housing). It is in this context that we situate the way in which even while the green bench of the Calcutta High Court was sitting in judgement on the Public vs State of West Bengal case, regarding encroachment on the wetlands, the government began making haste as allegedly an investment of four billion rupees was at stake.[63] While a vast stretch to the immediate east of the EM Bypass (very much a part of the *jalajami anchal* and representing the green buffer zone essential for the ecological survival of the EKW) from Madurdaha in the north to Panchpota in the South has been generally earmarked by the state government as the site for an expansive hub of technological education,[64] the Mukundapur area has now been specifically earmarked for a health city. Interestingly, at a time, when the state-run health system, the only recourse available to the indigent masses, is being allowed to languish, at a time when the performance state-run education has been very poorly rated nationally, all educational institutions and hospitals which are being granted land by the state in this area are funded by private capital and cater to the social bracket from the middle class upwards. Our visit to the *mouzas* of Barakhola and Mukundapur, adjacent to the Eastern Bypass (close to the junction of the Bypass and the widening Anwar Shah Road connector) has interesting revelations to hold forth.[65] Our peek into the space enclosed for Shri Sikshayatan in Barakhola, revealed a swamp full of the typical wetlands flora of these deltaic wetlands – water hyacinths, bull-rush and elephant grass. Adjacent to this, is an upcoming concrete structure being constructed for the AMRI group of hospitals. The security personnel guarding the site – two local youths – readily volunteered the information that the site of construction was 'nothing but *jalajami*', albeit under winter paddy cultivation 'until the other day'. About 30 yards away from the site to the east, there is still a big water body where fishermen are still doing piscicultrure, surrounded by upcoming concrete structures and besieged with great apprehension of losing this accustomed livelihood any day to the 'cause' of 'development by urbanization'.

However, in the *jalajami anchal,* traditionally known for its 'land wars', the consequences of globalization and privatization has come to interpenetrate with the structures of power – albeit changing – at the very local level, i.e. at the level of the village. Most cultivators and/or fishermen do not have deeds of ownership because the land in this area, originally reclaimed from forests – this being once a part of the coastal mangrove forests – was settled by the English East India Company with the leaders of the original clearers as lessees.[66] In the case of the *bheris* (big water bodies where fish is cultivated), too, the deed is still in the possession of the *bheri* lessee. It is in this context that even up to the 1970s, these 'zamindars',[67] whether as the lessees of cultivable land or owners of *bheris,* lorded over their respective properties and sought to extend them at the cost of other lessees with the help of their bands of retainers. There was an old conflict, especially between the farm 'zamindars' and fishery 'zamindars' and their respective mafia.[68] Land grabbing was widespread in the area in the 1960s and many open questions of landownership have not been permanently settled since.[69] In the early 1980s, however, the party in power in West Bengal since 1977 occupied these 'zamindari' areas, with the result that most *bheri* owners became absentees in the wetlands, virtually creating the space for de facto occupancy rights for the peasants, fishermen and persons doubling up as both.[70]

However, with the EM Bypass constructed and the commercial potential of the area adjacent to the Bypass sky-rocketing, real estate agents, both home-grown and from areas outside, besieged the wetlands, with their respective mafia connections. And this was also the juncture when the role of the ruling party started transforming in relation to the peasants and fishermen, who were the occupational anchors of the wetlands ecology. Dembowski's study, in referring to an incident in the wetlands in 1991, clearly alludes to the emerging alignment between the ruling party, the 'promoter' and the mafia. We suggest that in a quest for perennial electoral success, the party – by then in power for three consecutive terms – discerned the new emerging power in the wetlands and aligned with it, while the real estate agents realized the efficacy of being patronized by a party with an evidently burgeoning mass base and power of persuasion. In the meantime, economic liberalization had been inaugurated and development by urbanization had come to be vigorously pursued, creating opportunities for various kinds of 'promoters', big and small, global and local; niche markets were created for all of them in a cumulative atmosphere of rampant, unplanned and uncontrolled urbanization. The consequence for the wetlands' peasants and fishermen has been ironic, however; the same party which had empowered them in the beginning of the 1980s was now acting on behalf of the real estate agents, persuading or pressurizing the peasants and/or fishermen to sell off their occupancy right in land and/or water bodies on the ground that they had no registered position in the land. Numerous interviewees, whether peasants or fishermen or peasant-fishermen, have recounted to us the ways in which local committees of the party have cited this absence of title deeds as a 'handicap' and advised them to 'get whatever they could out of immediate sales, before it was too late'. Again, the small swamps, which were commons that the (winter) paddy cultivators used during monsoon for cultivating fish on a small scale,[71] have come to be treated as no-man's land by the agents of urbanization and promptly occupied by the promoter-politician nexus. It becomes understandable, therefore, why the rhetoric of environmental governance in the state so carefully elides the question of landownership in the wetlands even though the environmental sustainability of the region (maybe of the whole planet) demands that this anomalous land situation be immediately addressed and the peasants' and fishermen's occupancy right over the land and water bodies be somehow protected. It seems to be equally clear why a land use map, so crucial for the protection of this peculiar ecosystem is yet to be prepared. Evidently, there are interests that benefit from environmental governance being thus pursued in isolation from the land question.

Keeping this context in mind, the question of maps can provide a very pertinent entry into the politics of wetlands governance. No wonder, the same interests that sustain the inertia regarding the preparation of a land use map also sustains a cartographic confusion regarding the boundaries of the deltaic wetlands to the east of Kolkata. Ever since the 1990s, as encroachment came to besiege the wetlands and litigations erupted, the map became a bone of contention and issue that vexed the judges if only because no official map of the wetlands was available and the otherwise available maps were discordant. It is significant that even in 2006, no definitive map of the wetlands was published. This raises questions as to whether the government for some reason feels constrained to sustain nebulosity of boundaries. In 1992, Justice Banerjee of Calcutta High Court while sitting in judgement on the PUBLIC vs State of West Bengal case complained about the 'sketchy and incorrect maps' supplied to him by the government.[72] Dembowsky in his pioneering study of public interest litigations in relation to the wetlands discerns beneath this apparent inability of the government to supply maps, a veritable unwillingness to do so.[73] We seek to develop upon Dembowski's suspicion in the light of our own research.

It will be helpful in this connection to identify the areas that the 'promoters' and urban developers would like to see excluded from the area covered by the Calcutta High Court's 1992 ban on changing the character of the land (wetlands). One is Rajarhat which was earmarked by the government for mega-urbanization in the early 1990s. Significantly, the area so earmarked happened to be the recharge belt for many of the deltaic wetland rivers and its urbanization was bound to create a barrier for the overland flow and the flow from the northern upgrade, inducing rain water influx into both Bangladesh and core Kolkata.[74] Even in the beginning of the 1980s, extensive swamps existed to the east of the Dhapa-*bil* or the Dhupi-*bil* around Rajarhat-Bishnupur;[75] Rajarhat-Bishnupur particularly typified the depressed land to the east of Kolkata that was still the most important of the depressed tracts between each set of two rivers – tidal in character – that mark deltaic Bengal, with its innumerable marshes and *khals* (canals/palaeo-channels).[76] The other areas to be excluded were the completed/projected townships and cooperative housing enclaves in the *jalajami anchal* on either side of the Bypass, e.g., Baishnabghata-Patuli Township, Panchasayar (lit. the vicinity of the five lakes),

Survey Park and so on, apart from the sites for completed/projected health city, private hospitals, private educational institutions, shopping malls and so on. Indeed, given the rising market price of land on either side of the EM bypass, the powers that be would obviously want to have the 'wetlands' character of the entire stretch silenced in public discourse. This intended silencing and its related strategies constitute a veritable cartographical politics, which, in turn, ties up with other elisions and deletions elsewhere in official records. Thus, even while the West Bengal government has steadily superseded all other maps of the wetlands with Ghosh's map of the EKW as if the EKW were the 'authentic' wetlands, the list of wetlands water bodies within the Kolkata Municipal Corporation area prepared by the KMC now has, for some reason, an entire column deleted. One researcher suspects, on the basis of her fieldwork in the concerned CMC wards in the easternmost parts of the city – where water bodies do not exist any longer[77] – that this deletion is deliberate, aimed at generating the idea that this area was never a part of the wetlands. [78] In reality, many segments of the areas recently added to the jurisdiction of the KMC on the eastern side of the city were, until very recently, integral parts of the wetlands ecosystem.

Pieced together in this way the jigsaw of wetlands governance helps us discern an integral relation between this cartographical politics and an apparently well-meaning Act passed in 2006. The East Kolkata Wetlands (Conservation and Management) Act 2006, aimed at making a precise demarcation of the limits of the East Kolkata Wetlands, preparing and maintaining a map and a land schedule showing the boundaries of the area, the plot numbers of the land comprised in the wetlands, the actual land use of each plot (i.e. fishery, paddy land, etc.), formulating policy and legislation as deemed necessary for promoting their wise use, and preparing a management action plan for the East Kolkata Wetlands area, consistent with the stipulations of the Ramsar Convention. It is highly significant that the 1992 High Court Order and even the Town and Country Planning Act of 1979 had already provided safeguards for the protection of the entire wetlands and a buffer zone between it and the city.[79] What greater safeguards the 2006 Act came to provide is the question. The answer is none, as the Committee constituted under the Act is bureaucratic, undemocratic and devoid of any compulsory representation from the environmental scientist community.[80] A careful reading of the Act, however, reveals the real significance. It is through this Act that the EKW map came to be officially foregrounded as the only officially sanctioned wetlands map, and an exclusive focus on the Ramsar site of sewage-fed fisheries came to be institutionalized and normalized, silencing, for all official purposes, the existence, a large segment of the same ecosystem spilling over beyond the boundaries of the Ramsar site.[81] But what is even more disturbing is the realization that this Act is aimed at relaxing even the protection granted to the Ramsar site. The Act virtually undoes the High Court ban on any change in the character or the mode of use of land within the EKW, by providing legalized space for application for such change and empowering the Collector to permit such change if s/he deems fit in the light of the existing statutes.[82] It is very significant that such an Act was passed at a time when the Eastern Link Highway was being projected and the administration knew, in its heart of hearts, that the expressway has no option but to run through the EKW.[83]

The politics of maps and Acts may be read in conjunction with the politics of road construction. Despite the Central government's sanction of a huge amount of money for the construction of rural roads under the Prime Minister's Rural Road Scheme, the state of West Bengal has not been able to achieve more than 48 per cent of its stipulated target of a total of 3265 km projected for the state for the year 2007-08.[84] In this scenario, it is very interesting that this scheme has been energetically applied, however, to the rural *panchayats*, to the immediate east of Kolkata. This flurry of (rural) road-building activity, inconsistent with the sluggishness elsewhere in the state, becomes explicable, however, when we register the way in which the new (rural) roads in this area connect not so much the villages with one another in the rural interior of the wetlands,[85] but the villages, almost invariably, with the EM Bypass, giving the real estate agents the opportunity to utilize this newfangled road connectivity and exploit the green expanse of the wetlands interior for real estate business.

It would be befitting to end this chapter with an account of our fieldwork in the police stations of Rajarhat and Bhangor.[86] This is the area in the *jalajami anchal* (in North and South 24-Parganas respectively) where, under the supervision of the West Bengal Housing Infrastructure Development Corporation (HIDCO), the land reclamation area officially sanctioned for the New Town surreptitiously spills over into an extra of 3075 hectares, never officially sanctioned for the New Town,[87] and ultimately reaches out towards the extensive areas in which registration of land transfer, mortgage, etc., had recently been declared 'opposed to state policy' under the notification number 1568-F.T. [of the Finance (Revenue) Department of West Bengal] dated 11 September 2006 in the perceptible trail of the MOU regarding the Eastern Link Highway.[88] Confirming popular perceptions and fear of the 'promoter'-mafia combine, my vehicle came to be searched and I came to be interrogated threadbare as an 'outsider' about my reasons for coming to the area and 'loitering about'; my interrogators were motorcyclists menacingly doing their rounds in what appeared to be a huge simulated desert all around the Bagjola Canal. The inhabitants – peasants and fishermen – told me that the area that now appeared to be a desert stretching right up to the horizon had been full of marshes and paddy fields and beds of mustard and vegetable cultivation just a month or two back; water bodies were being frenziedly filled up and even big water bodies were taking a week to fill up, with fillers working round the clock. Maybe, this desertification was aimed at claiming that this terrain was not wetlands anyway and, therefore, justified in being developed as an 'international city' or a state of the art autobahn. But, a careful observation would reveal that in order to simulate this desertification, a silting Bagjola Canal had been cleverly helped to its demise at its eastern end through the construction of earthen dykes in its bed, over which truckloads of rubbish was being transported from one side to another; the locks for controlling canal-water discharge into the (former) paddy fields and bheris had been jammed. One could also detect, in the beds being filled up, scattered pieces of pipe – carefully broken, it seemed – that it had once carried the canal-water for the irrigation of the agricultural land on either side. I was reminded that despite all the governmental rhetoric about wetlands conservation, the much-needed step of desiltation of the numerous canals and palaeochannels in these deltaic wetlands had never been systematically implemented. The motorcyclists, menacingly keeping a watch on me and simultaneously supervising the filling-up operations in the surreal desertscape (simulated under the aegis of HIDCO) reminded me of media reports of alleged collaboration between HIDCO and the Gour-Ruis Syndicate,[89] which doubles up as (rubbish) supplier-fillers and mafia in the Rajarhat area. The syndicate headed by Gour Mondal and Ruis Naskar is said to be patronized by the West Bengal Housing and Public Health Engineering minister.[90]

And this, brings us back a full circle from the domain of power at the local level and the role of the party in relation to this power base to the domain of governance. The desertification of the wetlands in Rajarhat and Bhangor, aimed at erasing all traces of the wetlands topography from the sites of the intended New Town extension and the proposed Eastern Link Highway, is being executed under the aegis of HIDCO, one of those recently formed bodies, which bear the mark of corporatization of governance in West Bengal. Neo-liberal ideas of governance advocate such corporatization as a means to undoing red tape and ensuring efficient governance. The question is whether, in the case of the wetlands, this claim is actually borne out. It may be recalled in this connection that not all scholars have lauded the corporatization of governance; critical scholars have pointed out how the very structure of corporatized governance embodies the risk of a decline in accountability to the public.[91] The corporation being at one or more removes from the electorate and being often protected against the right to information, the possibility for such a system being undemocratic, unresponsive and opaque can be high, indeed. In the present case, therefore, we are not surprised to find that the Comptroller and Auditor General of India indicted HIDCO for shoddy work, sans proper project reports and annual plans and sans coordination between land acquisition and development. More seriously, it has been indicted for not fixing fair and reasonable market price for the land acquired.[92] Again at a press conference on 29 May 2008 at the Writers' Building, a minister of West Bengal government, too, alleged that HIDCO was involved in profiteering in Rajarhat.[93] While the Division Bench of the Calcutta High Court had ordered (on 13 February 2007) the work of filling up of the Dhupi-*bil* in Rajarhat to stop, Pradyot K. Biswas, the managing director of HIDCO publicly declared in May 2007 that he has not heard of any such order and, therefore, has not stalled the work.[94] It is locally alleged that the Gour-Ruis Syndicate controls the contracts that HIDCO makes with local 'promoters'.[95] It is often claimed that the corporatization of governance can be made accountable through close monitoring and vigil.[96] But even if such ministerial vigil were conscientiously forthcoming in West Bengal, the case is, the wetlands is delightfully conducive to the Corporation's collusion with all kinds of vested interests. The area, where the desertification is being done in the heart of the wetlands is conveniently hidden from the public gaze. Moreover, care seems to have been taken to make the desertification site as inaccessible as possible through poorest possible maintenance of roads and the terrorizing ways of the mafia. Thus, HIDCO seems to be taking advantage of the lack of public knowledge about the wetlands and the secluded nature of the area to conduct a desertification, practically hidden from the public eye. What we got to observe during our fieldwork, thus, seems to be a concerted act of subterfuge. First, the notification stalling registration of sale was served in area in keeping with, as we sense, the requirements of the Salim-Ciputra project. Then, in order to bypass the environmentalists' criticism of the apprehended encroachment on the wetlands, even before formal acquisition, the land was 'bought' from peasants by local agents with the predictable assistance of the mafia, and was finally converted into a barren 'desert' for the public to see at a more convenient time.

Notes

1. See, for example, Renu Khator, Environment, Development and Politics in India, University Press of America, New York and London, 1991.
2. Selections from the Records of Bengal Government, 1865–1904, p. 4, cites Captain Alexander Hamilton's impression of the Salt Lakes in 1706. Also see Jamini Mhan Ghosh, 'Reclamation of Salt Lakes: Dr. Roy's Dream', in Calcutta Municipal gazette, vol. 81, 1954-65, p. 148, for q relevant quotation from the journal of the ship H.M.S. which anchored at the port of Calcutta in 1748. Also see, John H. Grose, Voyage to the East Indies, vol. 2, 1772, p. quoted in Haraprasad Chattopadhyay, From Marsh to Township East of Calcutta: A Tale of Salt Water Lake and Salt Lake Township, Calcutta, K.P. Bagchi and Company, p. 8.
3. Government of Bengal, *Rivers of the Bengal Delta: Lectures Delivered by S.C. Majumdar*, Calcutta, 1941, pp. 87-94; Chattopadhyay, From Marsh to Township, pp. 2-3.
4. Subrata Sinha, 'Whither Kolkata's Deltaic Wetlands?', The Contemporary Manager, p. 59. Subrata Sinha is a former deputy director general of the Geological Survey Of India. The present author has immensely benefitted from academic discussions with him about the concerned wetlands.
5. Subrata Sinha, 'Whither Kolkata's Deltaic Wetlands?', The Contemporary Manager, p. 59.
6. Subrata Sinha, 'Whither Kolkata's Deltaic Wetlands?', The Contemporary Manager, p. 59.
7. Subrata Sinha, former Deputy Director General, Geological Survey of India, as interviewed by the author on 27 February 2008.
8. Subrata Sinha, 'Kolkata Calling for Life', in *Sahara Time*, 8 October 2005.
9. The Ramsar Convention – officially, The Convention on Wetlands of International Importance especially as Waterfowl Habitat (1971) – is an intergovernmental treaty covering all aspects of all aspects of wetlands conservation and wise use, recognizing wetlands ecosystems as extremely crucial to biodiversity conservation. See Dhrubajyoti Ghosh, p. 7.
10. Subrata Sinha as interviewed by the author on 27 February 2008.

11. *Ibid.*
12. Subrata Sinha, 'Kolkata Calling for Life', in *Sahara Time*, 8 October 2005.
13. Institute of Wetland Management and Ecological Design, *Preliminary Study on Biodiversity of Sewage-fed Fisheries of East Kolkata Wetland Ecosystem*, http://www.docudesk.com, p. 5,
14. Hans Dembowski, *Taking the State to Court: Public Interest Litigation and the Public Sphere in Metropolitan India*, 2001, Asia House online version, p. 83.
15. At the end of the 1980s and beginning of the 1990s, it was a handful of environment bureaucrats who, unable to protest against the government themselves, took the remarkable initiative of motivating, briefing, and mobilizing NGOs and others agents in civil society against what they perceived as the government's deviation from the cause of environmental protection of the wetlands. See, Dembowski, p.
16. *Ibid.*, pp. 84, 99. 'West Bengal's bureaucracy is not adequately organized to deal with the delicate needs of these environmentally fragile ... urban fringes and adjoining areas', as Debowski observes.
17. *Ibid.*, p. 85.
18. *Ibid.*, pp. 86-87.
19. For such allegations in court, see Dembowski, pp.102-135.
20. Institute of Wetland Management and Ecological Design, *Preliminary Study on Biodiversity of Sewage-fed Fisheries of East Kolkata Wetland Ecosystem*, http://www.docudesk.com.
21. I found it out while conversing with Ashok Nath Basu, the chairperson of the WBPCB in early September 2008.
22. Institute of Wetland Management and Ecological Design, *Preliminary Study on Biodiversity of Sewage-fed Fisheries of East Kolkata Wetland Ecosystem*, http://www.docudesk.com, p. 6.
23. The technology of using recycling sewage through natural processes of purification and then feeding the fish population in *bheris* on it was initiated in 1929 by an enterprising fishery owner. But the system really proliferated with the completion of the B.N. Dey's drainage outfall scheme, carrying wastewater from Calcutta to Kulti and inter alia supplying wastewater to the fish ponds by gravity. See Dhrubajyoti Ghosh, p. 48-49.
24. Germán Adell, *Literature Review Theories and Models of the Peri-Urban Interface: A Changing Conceptual Landscape*, Peri-urban Research Project Team, Development Planning Unit, University College London, 1999, p. 1.

25. *Ibid.*
26. Institute of Wetland Management and Ecological Design, *Preliminary Study on Biodiversity of Sewage-fed Fisheries of East Kolkata Wetland Ecosystem*, http://www.docudesk.com, p. 6.
27. Subrata Sinha, the geologist and environmentalist, confirms this.
28. It is ironic that Dhrubajyoti Ghosh, the bureaucrat who passionately crusaded from behind the scenes for the preservation of the wetlands and sensitized civil society about its uniqueness, himself contributed to this Kolkata-centric perspective in his own way. His formative influence on the governmental discourse on EKW and its character as a supposedly isolable ecosystem derives from Ghosh being simultaneously a bureaucrat and a person who began systematic research on the concerned wetlands in the 1980s on behalf of the state government.
29. The practice of sewage-fed fishery effectively began in the 1940s.
30. Haraprasad Chattopadhyay, pp. 56-61.
31. Dhrubajyoti Ghosh, Participatory Management in Waste Water Treatment and Reuse in West Bengal, UWEP occasional paper, Nieuwehaven, July 1996, p. 6. This map is an official version of the map of the sewage recycling zone prepared in 1985 as the first of its kind by Dhrubajyoti Ghosh. But interested parties in government have projected that map as representing the whole of the deltaic wetlands to the east of Kolkata.
32. The techno-centric understanding of the wetlands as a site characterized by the technology of waste recycling was the brainchild of Dhrubajyoti Ghosh. Ghosh, who was a civil engineer to begin with. He was understandably fascinated by the way in which the wetlands fisherfolk had innovated a pisciculture based on the technique of sewage recycling (in the *bheris*), which also inexpensively served to recycle Kolkata's sewage, the management of which would have otherwise become an immense technological and financial problem for the city. Though Ghosh was equally fascinated by the environment-friendly – natural, as he called it – character of the technique, we have to admit that his techno-centric vision precluded a more holistic appreciation of the complexity of the Bidyadhari wetlands. The exclusive focus on sewage recycling automatically narrowed down in Ghosh's imagination (and in the imagination of everyone influenced by his definition) the expanse of the wetlands, which in reality was a much bigger area than simply the sewage recycling zone.
33. The West Bengal District Gazetteers: 24-Parganas, Calcutta, 1994, p. 21.
34. *Ibid.*

35. *Ibid.*, pp. 26-27.

36. Indeed, these wetlands were very much a part of the Sundarbans even as late as the early British period. See, *West Bengal District Gazetteers, 24-Parganas*, 1994, p. 21. Again, at least, two species of mangrove, known as *genwa* and *keora* in the vernacular, was quite common in these wetlands, even fifty years back, as numerous interviews conducted by the present author among the old inhabitants of the wetlands explicitly reveals. Those referring to the wetlands by the token of Calcutta's urbanity and the supposedly surrogate existence of the wetlands as the fringe should be made aware (by using botanical history) that even as late as the second half of the eighteenth century, mangrove swamps extended to almost the neighbourhood of Sealdah, one of Calcutta's rail termini from the second half of the nineteenth century. See Samaren Roy, *Calcutta: Society and Change, 1690-1990*, iUniverse, 2005, pp. 8, 19, 26. Entally, a locality close to Sealdah derives its name from *hental* (hatal pneumatophores) which grew there.

37. L.S.S. O'Malley, *Bengal District Gazetteers: 24-Parganas*, Calcutta, 1994, pp. 22–31.

38. Suresh Chandra Ghosh, .*The Social Condition of the British Community in Bengal: 1757-1800*, 1970, p. 150, quoted in Haraprasad Chattopadhyay, From Marsh to Township: East of Calcutta, p. 7.

39. See, *West Bengal District Gazetteers, 24-Parganas*, 1994, p. 21.

40. Samaren Roy, *Calcutta: Society and Change, 1690–1990*, iUniverse, 2005, pp. 8, 19 and 26.

41. L.S.S. O'Malley the pervasive undergrowth of bullrushes, large sedges and other marsh species in his gazetteers, published in 1914. O'Malley, *Bengal District Gazetteers: 24-Parganas*, p. 22.

42. See the map in W.W. Hunter, *Statistical Account of Bengal, vol. 1, part 1: Statistical Account of the District of 24-Parganas* (1875), Calcutta, 1998.

43. Interview of Radahrani Hati (96) of Anandapur dated 3 March 2008.

44. We have seen and photographed these specimens during our field trips in the Madurdaha, Chak Kalar Khal, Chowbaga and Kheyadaha monzas.

45. These self-perceptions of the old inhabitants of the wetlands is gleaned from our extensive and intensive ethnohistorical fieldwork done in the region over the period of the last two years. This account of the disappearance, specie by specie, is confirmed by NGOs like Prakriti Samsad as also by reports prepared by IWMED.

46. Utpalendu Mondal, 'Sundarbaner Andha Nadir Kathakata' in Nimnagangeya Sundarban Sanskriti Patra, (River Special, number 1), vol. 7, June 2006, pp. 67-69.

47. IWMED,. 1988.
48. For the composition of the committee, see http://webenvironment/nic.in/html_files/mgnt_east_kolkata_wetlands.htm.
49. Subrata Sinha, 'Whither Kolkata's Deltaic Wetlands?', *The Contemporary Manager*, p. 61.
50. CMDA, 'Plan for Metropolitan Development 1990-2015' quoted in Hans Dembowski, *Taking the State to Court: Public Interest Litigation and the Public Sphere in Metropolitan India*, 2001, Asia House online version, p. 91.
51. Chattopadhyay, *From March to Township*, p. 86.
52. CMDA, 'Plan for Metropolitan Development 1990-2015' quoted in Dembowski, *Taking the State to Court*, p. 91.
53. See the West Bengal Town and Country Planning Act, 1979.
54. That Madurdaha was not merely a part of the wetlands but had even big bheris in its jurisdiction is borne out by scholarly accounts. See the list of bheries in Haraprasad Chattopadhyay, *From Marsh to Township East of Calcutta: A Tale of Salt Water Lake and Salt Lake Township*, Calcutta, K.P. Bagchi and Company, 1990, pp. 62-69.
55. Michael C. Jacobson et al., *Earth System Science from Biochemical Cycles to Global Change*, San Diego, 2000, pp. 3-4.
56. Claude Allegre and Vincent Courtillot, 'Revolution in the Earth Sciences', *Philosophical Transactions: Biological Sciences*, vol. 354, no. 1392 (December 29, 1999), p. 1917.
57. West Bengal represents an unique case in post-1947 India in the sense that the same political coalition has been ruling the state for thirty-one years by now since the state assembly elections of 1977. Though technically, it is a ruling coalition, the present author chooses to use the term ruling party as the Communist Party of India (Marxist) or the CPIM is by far the most powerful and, therefore, undoubtedly the dominant partner in the coalition. By calling the CPIM the ruling party we also reflect a hugely overwhelming popular perception shared by the supporters and the detractors of the party alike.
58. The term 'promoters' is a contemporary popular usage in West Bengal that refers to a whole range of agencies from upmarket realtors to civil contactors to small property developers to land mafia.
59. John Williamson, 'What Washington Means by Policy Reform', in John Williamson (ed.), *Latin American Readjustment: How Much has Happened*, Washington, Institute for International Economics 1989; Nancy Birdsall and Augusto de la Torre, *Washington Contentious: Economic Policies for Social Equity in Latin America* (Carnegie

Endowment for International Peace and Inter-American Dialogue, 2001); Pedro-Pablo Kuczynski and John Williamson (eds), *After the Washington Consensu*, Institute for International Economics, 2003.

60. The proposal for an extension of Kolkata's satellite township, Salt Lake, towards Rajarhat-Goplapur, very much a part of the *jalajami anchal* was mooted in the end of the 1980s. See, Aditi Nath Sarkar, 'The East Calcutta Wetlands', in Sukanta Chaudhuri (ed.), *Calcutta: The Living City, vol. II*, Calcutta, Oxford University Press, 1990, p. 175.

61. Since the inauguration of the New Town at Rajarhat and particularly since the return of the ruling party to power for the seventh consecutive term in office, the official rhetoric of development by urbanization is constantly referring to 'Kolkata, the international city'. Indeed the word 'international city has come into official currency with especially with the government signing a much hyped deal, billed the 'New Kolkata International Development Project' with the Salim-Ciputra Group of Indonesia in July 2006 for investments up to `20,000 crore in infrastructure development. See Maureen Nadini Mitra, 'Wetlands Wasted: West Bengal Threatening Unique Ecosystem' in *Down to Earth*, 15 September 2006, p. 7.

62. For critiques of this proposed project, see Subrata Sinha, 'Kolkata Calling for Life' in *Sahara Time*, 8 October 2005, p. 20; Maureen Nadini Mitra, 'Wetlands Wasted: West Bengal Threatening Unique Ecosystem' in *Down to Earth*, 15 September 2006, pp. 7-9. Mitra writes, 'Government officials say that the actual route of the highway has not been mapped yet, but ecologists familiar with ecology of the area say it is unlikely such a road can be built without cutting through the East Kolkata wetlands – a protected Ramsar site'.

63. *The Statesman*, 3 March 1992.

64. Private engineering colleges are literally mushrooming in the buffer zone and sometimes even encroaching on the EKW.

65. We did our fieldwork in Mukundapur-Barakhola in September 2008.

66. These eastern parts of the Alipur Sadar sub-division, like the sub-divisions of the Diamond Harbour, Basirhat and the eastern parts of Bararsat sub-division, 'had from the beginning of the British periods, a land tenurial system very different from what [the Permanent Settlement] prevailed in the rest of Bengal.' With the aim of extracting land revenue from these 'Sundarban areas', the British sought to have the jungle cleared and people settled on the land. For this purpose, they created a system of lessees and sub-lessees among the class of leading clearers. See, Government of West Bengal, *West Bengal District Gazetteers: 24-Parganas*, Calcutta, 1991, pp. 124-5.

67. These long-term lessees are locally referred to as zamindars.
68. Dembowski, p. 97.
69. Dembowski, p. 97.
70. The fishermen even came to form their cooperatives with support from the ruling party.
71. Our ethnographic studies in the area have yielded this picture of *dobas* being used as commons.
72. The Statesman, 13 March 1992 and 7 April 1992; *The Telegraph*, 13 March 1992.
73. Dembowski, Taking the State to Court, p. 106.
74. Subrata Sinha, 'Whither Kolkata's Deltaic Wetlands?' *Contemporary Manager*, Year and Date, pp. 59-62
75. West Bengal District Gazetteers, 24-Parganas, 1994, p. 21. Though the gazetteer was ultimately published in 1994, the data that went into the making of the volume had been collected by the beginning of the 1980s.
76. *West Bengal District Gazetteers, 24-Parganas*, 1994, p. 23.
77. Her study of topo-sheets in a chronological order reveal that numerous water bodies had been there in the earlier decades.
78. Kamalini Dasgupta, 'Encroachment of Water Bodies in East Calcutta: Causes and Consequences', in *Innovations in Geography*, 1998, pp. 191-4.
79. Sinha,
80. We have discussed this earlier in the chapter.
81. For a copy of the Act, see Government of West Bengal, *The Kolkata Gazette, Extraordinary*, 11 October 2006.
82. *Ibid.*
83. The understanding with the Salim-Ciputra Group regarding the proposed expressway has been shelved in the aftermath of the West Bengal panchayat elections in which the ruling *party* has suffered significant and unprecedented setbacks. However, the project has not been abandoned as a couple of ministers have publicly declared.
84. See Dainik Statesman, 28 August 2008.
85. Such interconnectivity of the villages was badly needed for social and economic reasons, now that the numerous canals in the wetlands, once used for inter-village transportation, have fallen into disuse as a result of accumulated silt that the administration has not cared to dredge.
86. We did our fieldwork in this area in May-June 2007.

87. For a detailed reportage of the illegal reclamation under the stewardship of HIDCO, defying High Court orders, see *Dainik Statesman*, 11 May 2007.

88. For a copy of the notification, see Government of West Bengal, *The Kolkata Gazette*, Extraordinary, 11 October 2006.

89. See, for example, Dainik Statesman, 30 May 2007. Regarding a detailed account of the connection between the ruling party, the promoters and the goons see Debashis Bhattacharyya, 'The Real Estate of Things', in *The Telegraph*, 7 November 2004.

90. *Ibid.*; Dainik Statesman, 11 May 2007.

91. Richard Mulgan, 'Contracting Out and Accountability, Graduate Public Policy Program', Australian National University, Discussion Paper 51, May 1997.

92. CAG, India, 'Performance Reviews Relating to Government Companies', in the *Audit Report (Commercial) for the Year Ending 31 March 2007*, pp. 17-92.

93. See Dainik Statesman, 30 May 2008.

94. See Dainik Statesman, 11 May 2007.

95. *Ibid.*

96. Richard Mulgan, Contracting Out and Accountability, Graduate Public Policy Program, Australian National University, Discussion Paper 51, May 1997.

12

Biofuel Policy Process in India: Context, Actors and Discourses[1]

Shailesh Nagar

Introduction

The current world economy runs on fossil fuels. This is especially true for the transport sector that accounts for around 20 per cent of the total world delivered energy consumption and is dependent on petroleum fuels for 98 per cent of its energy requirement (EIA[a], 2007). With the emergence of China and India as new growth centres in the world, scrambling for fossil fuels has become intense[2] (IEA, 2007). An emphasis on energy security has also led to the quest for alternative sources of energy that can replace petroleum dependence. Biofuels are one such alternative that has been emphasized by various countries and international institutions as fuels for the future.

Biofuels are any fuel that is derived from biological sources. Wood, charcoal, dung and plant-based oils (used as fuel) are some examples of conventional biofuels. However, recent emphasis has been on plant-based oils that can be used to supplement petroleum fuels. Such biofuels can be categorized into two types, bioethanol and biodiesel, depending on whether it is a supplement of petrol or diesel respectively. Further, based on the feedstock from which biofuels are extracted, biofuels are categorized as first generation (if the feedstock is edible in nature), second generation (if the feedstock is non-edible) and third generation (if the source of oil is whole plant material or micro-organism like algae).

Biofuels in the conventional sense have always been an important source of energy. Even in the present times, almost half of the world's population, especially in the rural areas, depend on biofuels to provide cooking energy[3] (Johansson et al., 1993).

However, the new biofuels (bioethanol and biodiesel) have lately gained importance due to various economic, geo-political and environmental reasons.

This chapter attempts to provide an insight into the Biofuel policy process in the Indian context. The chapter first presents a theoretical framework of policy process and its relation to governance to be used in the discussion section. In later sections, the chapter discusses the role of context and different actors, their positions and influence that they may have on the policy process. The role of various actors, viz., state, private sector and civil society has been analyzed. The discussion section then attempts to analyze the emergence of Biofuel policy through theoretical lens.

Background

At the global level, the European Union (EU) and the United States of America (USA) are the major geographical drivers of biofuels. Whereas USA is more keen on bioethanol, EU strategy is focused primarily on biodiesel. EU has further proposed to source most of its biofuel requirement from developing countries (CEC, 2007).

An emphasis on biofuels as an alternative energy source has been an issue of concern lately. These concerns are related to the impact of biofuel not only on the food security (Ziegler, 2008) but also on the environment and socio-economy (CEC, 2006).

However, as of now, the biofuel policy process around the world does not seem to be affected by these concerns. For example, EU is continuing with its biofuel policy but with stricter criteria for sustainable biofuel production (CEC, 2008). India, on the other hand, sees its biofuel programme to be sustainable because of the programme's dependence on non-edible feedstock, which is supposed to be derived from wasteland and thus does not entail diversion of farmland or food crops (Chauhan, 2008).

In India, Planning Commission's 'Vision 2020' report called for plantation of non-edible oil yielding plants on large areas of waste and degraded lands in the country (Gupta, 2002). Taking a cue from the report, the Indian government decided to blend 5 per cent ethanol in petrol in selected states and announced a biodiesel purchase policy in 2005[4] (MoPNG 2004, 2005). Various state governments drafted policies and had setup institutions for promoting biofuels in their respective states. The states have also formed rules for allocation of wastelands to various entities for the plantation of biodiesel crops. Encouraged by the government's actions and sensing opportunities in the upcoming sector, various companies have proposed large investments to set up biodiesel production facilities.

In a country where land is a precious and contested resource, biofuel is considered a win-win situation by some actors as biofuel plantations on the wasteland would not only lead to energy security but would also provide livelihoods to the rural communities. However, a few academic as well as empirical studies and experiences of several Non Government Organizations (NGO) about the so-called wastelands and the dependence of communities on these resources provide a different set of context and discourse (Shiva and Sankar, 2008; Negi et al., 2006). Moreover, the media and some international organizations have lately been critical of the impacts of biofuel.

Though the term 'biofuel' pertains to ethanol as well biodiesel, it is mainly biodiesel production in India that is surrounded by concerns and controversies. While, it would be desirable to look at the comprehensive biofuel issue including ethanol; in this study, the term biofuel refers to biodiesel unless specified otherwise.

Governance and Policy Process

The concept of governance is not new and broadly implies the process of decision making and the process of implementation. Though initially, the concept of governance was applied only as political governance at national level, currently corporate governance, international governance and local governance are also different ways in which the concept is perceived. During the period from 1950s to 1970s, the theory of political governance was '*concerned with policy development and policy implementation, and it adopted a top down, or legislator's, perspective*' (Maryntz, 2003, 27). The first expansion of this view of governance included '*the structure and behavioural dispositions of the object of political control*' and '*recognised that governability varies considerably between policy fields (or sectors)*' (ibid, 29). This led to improved understanding of the conditions of policy effectiveness. The second expansion was a result of evolving understanding which undermined the basic assumption that the state is the control centre of society. Two separate strands of discussions evolved as a result of this understanding which included market principles and horizontal self-organization as alternatives to hierarchical political control (ibid.).

Although the concept of governance has expanded over a period of time, it still retains the original core which is related to policy making and its implementation. Thus, policy process is seen as a sub-set and first part of the governance process.

Theories of the Policy Process

The whole process of policy making is more discursive than linear and involves a multitude of variables that define and in turn get influenced by the policy process (Sabatier, 1999; Kingdon, 2003; Radaelli, 1995). In simple terms, a policy process is defined as consisting of various stages. Essentially, these can be divided into agenda setting, issue formulation, discussion and policy formulation, implementation and evaluation (see Brewer and deLeon, 1983). Various authors (see Lindblom, 1993; Sabatier, 1999) criticize such a 'stages approach' for its simplistic description and implied assumption that policy making is a systematic and rational process. Instead, policy process has been described as a 'primeval soup' "with action occurring fitfully as problems become matched with policy ideas considered to be in the political interests of a working majority of the partisans with influence over a policy domain" (Kingdon, 1984 cited in Lindblom, 1993, 10).

Policy process involves various actors, networks, their interactions and their knowledge, communication of knowledge and politics; and thus needs to be seen through 'multiple lenses' for a holistic understanding of it (Sabatier, 1999). Various theoretical frameworks have evolved that focus on different variables in the policy process. For example 'institutional rational choice frameworks' looks at 'how institutional rules alter the behaviour of intendedly rational individuals motivated by material self-interest'. 'Multiple-streams framework' focuses on "policy process as three streams [problems, policy and politics] of actors and processes...which operate independently of each other, except when a 'window of opportunity' permits policy entrepreneurs to couple the various streams" (Sabatier, 1999, 8-9). Sabatier analyzes a wide range of theoretical frameworks for analysis of the policy process and suggests that understanding the policy process requires attention to the policy debates and the role such debates play in the overall process. According to him, debate not only involves scientific knowledge but also deeply held values, interests, money and coercion. He further suggests that knowledge is not only used for generating and advancing an idea in the policy making process but also, sometimes, evidences are misrepresented to undermine the opponent's position or advance one's own ideas.

Argumentative Approach to Policy Analysis

The argumentative approach focuses on argumentation in policy analysis. Arguments are needed not only to clarify positions with respect to an issue but also to bring other people to a particular position (Majone, 1989). Majone further argues that in the process of argumentation, rationalizations are given by various actors who seek to justify the policy by appealing to the "public interest and the intellectual merits of the case" (*ibid.*, 2). For Majone "[a]rgumentation is the key process through which citizens and policymakers arrive at moral judgements and policy choices" (*ibid.*, 2).

Hajer sees the challenge to argumentative analysis as finding "ways of combining the analysis of the discursive production of reality with the analysis of the (extradiscursive) social practices from which social constructs emerge and in which the actors that make these statements engage" (Hajer, 1993, 45). Thus, it is not only important to look at the arguments that various actors provide but also the context in which these arguments are embedded.

Concepts of Policy Process as a Discourse

"Discourse as a term has many meanings and is used in various ways by different theorists (Mills, 1997). Discourse can be defined as 'ensemble of ideas, concepts and categorizations that are produced, reproduced, and transformed in a particular set of practices and through which meaning is given to physical and social realities" (Hajer, 1995, 44).

Hajer's concept of discourse coalition is important in the sense of identifying similar set of discourses that stakeholders, having interest in a particular issue, engage in. Such coalitions present a particular view of the constructed reality. Conflict or struggle among such coalitions to dominate the discursive space is seen as the main aspect of the policy process. In fact, discourse coalitions emerge because various actors would struggle to create 'discursive hegemony' (Hajer, 1995, 65). Hajer points to two main conditions that a discourse coalition needs to fulfil to dominate the policy process, viz., the successful use of rhetoric to dominate the discursive space and second, ideas of the dominant discourse to come in institutional practice (Hajer, 1993, 48). These are termed as discourse structuration and discourse institutionalization respectively. Discourse structuration happens "when a discourse starts to dominate the way a society conceptualizes the world" (*ibid.*, 46). Hajer further suggests that social constructs also do not 'free float' but can be tied to some institutions and actors. When a discourse becomes successful it takes the form of an institution and this process can be termed as discourse institutionalization (*ibid.*).

Using Policy Theory for Studying Biofuel Policy Process

Identifying factors that influence the emergence of a shift in policy is a difficult task. Further, as Schmidt and Radaelli (undated) argue, "in looking for causal influence, discourse can never be *the* factor that explains policy change, or *the* cause. Leaving aside the question of whether any one factor can be *the* cause – we believe none can be". Therefore, besides taking an actor oriented approach to analyze interests, positions and arguments in the following sections, the concepts of policy process as discourse are used in the discussion section. However, a systematic use of constructivist approach to policy analysis would involve the method of discourse analysis, which is not employed in this chapter due to the lack of primary data. But these concepts are used in discussion to look at the results of the analysis from a theoretical perspective.

Biofuel Policy Context in India

Energy Economic Context

Demand for petroleum fuel constitutes 40 per cent of the total energy requirement in India, and India is projected to be the third largest net importer of oil in the world (EIA[b], 2007; IEA, 2007). There is an increasing gap in production and consumption of crude oil in India (see Figure 1) costing the country '1972.77 billion as import bill in 2005-06.[6]

Transport sector is the second largest consumer of petroleum oil in India and is slated to grow at the fastest rate as compared to other economic sectors (IEA, 2007). Moreover, petroleum oil provides 95 per cent of transportation fuel.[7] With the exception of biofuels and Compressed Natural Gas, there are no alternative fuels for use by the transport sector at present.

To reduce the environmental impact due to growth in the transport sector, Auto

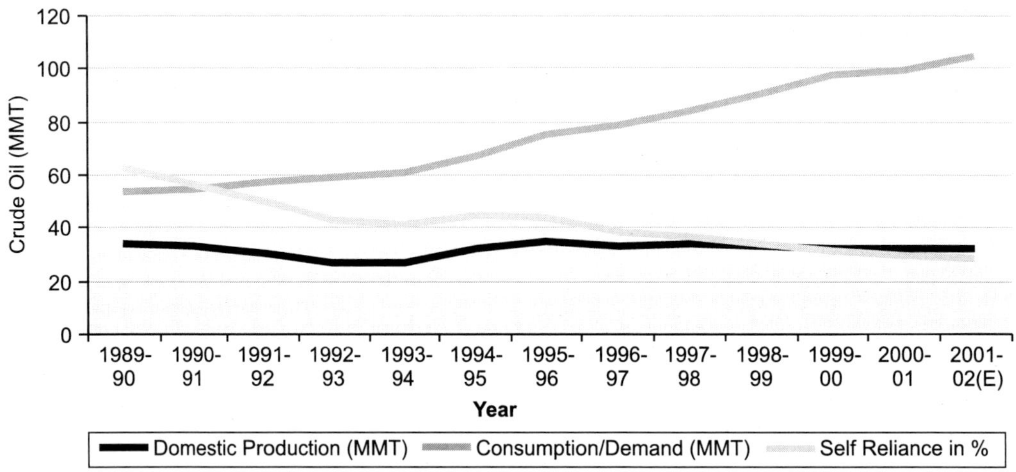

Fig. 1: Crude Oil Demand, Production and Self-Reliance in India

Source: indiastat.[5]

policy of the Government of India (GoI) stipulates emission norms for vehicles. The new vehicles, under the policy, are expected to comply with Bharat III stage norms by 2010. Blending of biofuel is expected to reduce the emission in the transport sector. Further, India is also signatory to Kyoto protocol but not bound by emission reduction target. However, it can benefit from the Clean Development Mechanism under the protocol.[8]

The rural energy scenario is also pertinent for biofuel policy context in India. Around 72 per cent of the population in India still lives in rural areas. Seventy-seven per cent household in rural areas and 23 per cent in urban areas still depend on firewood and dung for fuel (Shrivastava and Mathur, 2007). Biomass sources like wood, chips and dung cakes, contribute around 30 per cent of the total primary energy consumed in the country (Gokhale, 2006). Village common lands, wastelands and forestland constitute a major source of this biomass.

Ecological Degradation and Wasteland

Land resource in India is under tremendous human and livestock pressure as it supports around 16 per cent of the world's human and 20 per cent of livestock population on a mere 2.5 per cent of the world's geographical area (GoI, 2001). A large part of this land area is also designated as wasteland, which is around 55 mha.[9] Nevertheless, wastelands are not barren areas devoid of vegetation but are degraded common lands that are used by a large number of rural communities for their livelihoods (see Box 1).

BOX 1: Wasteland

Wastelands is a medieval English term used in a legal sense to refer to land that was unoccupied, undeveloped or uncultivated. As a result, the land could not be the source of any tax or other revenue to its owner. The term was similarly applied to property that had been allowed to deteriorate, or had even been purposely damaged, so that its value (whether in terms of selling price or rentability) decreased. Unfortunately the term wastelands continued to be used effectively in British India and subsequently in Independent India to denote lands, which were 'unoccupied' or 'undeveloped' and could be conveniently diverted to various development or plantation schemes. Many of these lands were actually grazing lands used by the village poor, the landless or migratory pastoral herding communities but seldom have these 'grazing' needs been carefully considered in 'wasteland development' programmes.

Source: Ramdas and Ghatge (2006).

Besides wastelands, India has 19.39 per cent of its land area under the forest land category. Around 41 per cent of forest cover of the country has already been degraded (MoEF, 2006). More than 95 per cent of India's forest is under state ownership. However, communities have been using forest resources for various purposes like grazing, collection of wood and non-wood forest products, timber, medicinal plants, etc. It is these wastelands and degraded forestlands that are proposed to be used for the cultivation of biofuel feedstock (MoEF, 2006).

Rural Livelihood Context

Large majority of the rural population in India is dependent on agriculture and animal husbandry for their livelihoods. Agriculture sector (including Animal Husbandry) provides livelihood to nearly 60 per cent of the population (GoI[a], 2007). Figure 2 shows the growth in livestock in India over the last 50 years. The total contribution of livestock sector to the Gross Domestic Product (GDP) was 4.70 per cent in 2004-05 (GoI[b], 2007).

Further, it is mostly the poor that are dependent on the livestock in India. This is evident from the Planning Commission's statement:

> [t]he ownership of the livestock is more evenly distributed with landless labourers and marginal farmers owning bulk of livestock. The progress in the sector results in balanced development of the rural economy particularly in reducing the poverty amongst the weaker sections (GoI[b], 2007).

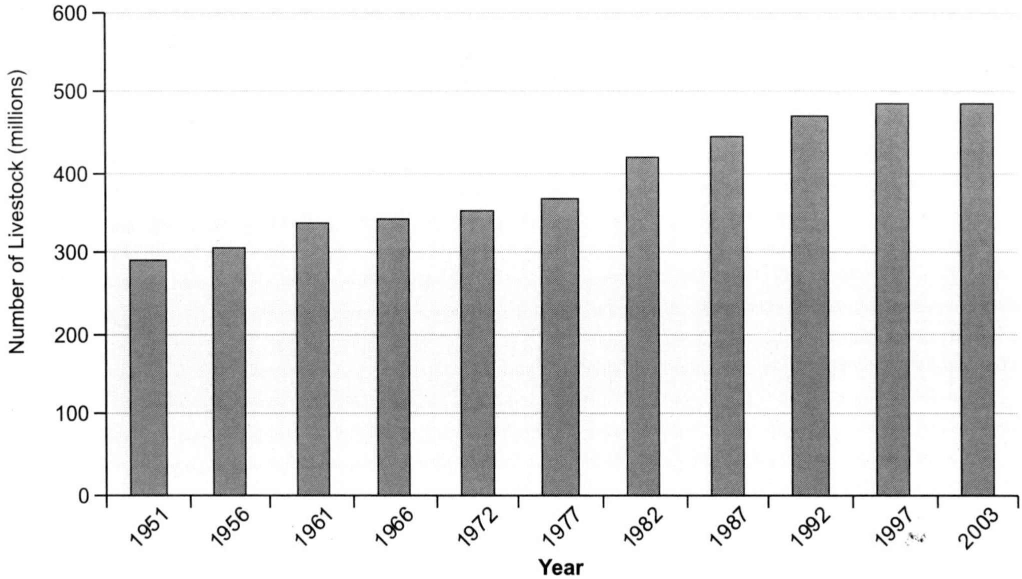

Fig. 2: Growth of Livestock in India

Source: National Dairy Development Board.[10]

Table 1: Grazing Resources in India (2000-2001)

Resources	Area (million ha.)	Percentage of Total Geographical Area
Forests	69.41	22.70
Permanent pastures, grazing lands	10.90	3.60
Cultivable wasteland	13.66	4.50
Fallow land	24.99	8.10
Fallow land other than current fallows	10.19	3.30
Barren uncultivable wastelands	19.26	6.30
Total common property resources other than forests	54.01	17.70
Livestock units/ha. of common property resource	6.07	

Source: GoI[b], 2007.

A significant part of the feedstock for the livestock comes from forest and non-forest lands including wastelands (GoI[b], 2007). Table 1 provides a list of grazing resources and respective land area in India. Although most of these lands are under the state ownership, at the ground level these are managed as public or common lands. Stressing on the development of Common Property Resources (CPR) and wastelands for livestock development, the expert committee on animal husbandry in its report to Planning Commission noted that:

> The Common Property Resources (CPR)... constitute the most important input for livestock production and subsistence for the poor. These are under depletion and degeneration affecting the livelihood security of the poor (GoI[b], 2007, 124).

Thus, we see that the context for emergence of biofuel policy in India projects a very complex picture. While on the one hand, India's growing economy is leading to rising oil import bill, on the other hand, majority of India's rural population subsist on the fuels that are derived from biomass, which in turn comes mainly from forest and non-forest common lands. International and national policy scenarios provide an opportunity for initiating programmes for alternative energy and regeneration of degraded lands. There is also the problem of addressing the issue of land degradation related to a large livestock population, especially as a large number of people are dependent for their livelihoods on the same degraded lands or the so called 'wastelands'.

State and the Biofuel Discourse

Planning Commission

An analysis of the Planning Commission[11] reports from 2002 onwards on the issue of biofuels is provided in Table 2. The period in which the biofuel agenda surfaces in the policy circles is the Tenth Plan period of 2002-07. However, the tenth Five-Year Plan (FYP) document does not carry any reference to biodiesel but mentions the decision to introduce mandatory blending of ethanol with petrol in a phased manner in the country (GoI, 2002). It was the Vision 2020 report of the Planning Commission released in December 2002 that can be considered as the harbinger of biofuel programme and policy in India. The report links the development of biofuel with agriculture and suggests that:

> [a]doption of an agriculture-based energy policy...could generate millions of additional on-farm jobs and lucrative alternative markets for farm produce, while reducing the country's dependence on imported fuels (Gupta, 2002, 5).

In the report, the wastelands were not only seen in terms of providing feedstock for production of biodiesel but also various other products for the benefit of rural community.

> Afforestation of India's vast expanse of wastelands and depleted forest areas for production of wood pulp, timber, fuel, fodder, biomass power, edible and fuel soil [sic], fuel, herbs and medicinal plants for exports can create millions of jobs, while reversing environmental degradation and supporting industrial development (Gupta, 2002, 39).

Further, the report envisioned the use of wastelands for biofuel production in two ways. First, for the generation of feedstock to be used for a national network of

Table 2: Planning Commission Documents and Reports

Documents	Date	Proposed Biofuel Development
10th Five Year Plan	2002	No mention of development of biofuel except ethanol blending
Report of the Committee on India: Vision 2020	December 2002	Mentions biofuel development but more stress on use of wasteland for decentralized biomass production for rural electrification
Report on the development of biofuel	April 2003	Main document providing direction for development of biofuel mainly for substitution of petroleum fuels in transport sector (although it mentions use of biofuel for energy provision in rural areas)
Mid-term appraisal of 10th FYP	2005	The approach paper to mid-term appraisal cites land rights as the main issue in development of wasteland for biofuel but mid-term appraisal does not mention that. It also does not recommend anything with regards to biofuel.
Report of the expert committee on Integrated Energy Policy	August 2006	Calls for an integrated mission on bio-energy having objectives of biodiesel from non-edible oil, ethanol from cellulose and energy plantations
Report on new and renewable energy for the 11th plan	December 2006	The target period for 10 per cent substitution of biofuel increases to 2032.
Approach paper to 11th FYP	December 2006	Calls for an integrated view of energy policy involving different sectors. Recognizes that development of wastelands may be causing a conflict with pastoral livelihoods.

Source: Self.

small, decentralized biomass power plants and second, for cultivation of Jatropha to be used as a feedstock for production of biodiesel. In fact, it places more stress on the decentralized power and diversion of more wasteland for producing power than biodiesel through cultivation of Jatropha.

While the idea of biofuel as a substitute of petroleum fuels and use of wastelands for its production started on a low-key note, it gained prominence in the report on development of biofuels (see Table 3 for assessment of wasteland requirement in the report on biofuel development). However, not much progress was made at the ground level till the mid-term of the tenth FYP when Ministry of Petroleum and Natural Gas (MoPNG) announced biodiesel purchase policy in October 2005. But there were also indications of government's awareness of the complexity surrounding wastelands as the approach paper to the mid-term review mentioned land rights as the main issue in development of wasteland.

Table 3: Diesel and Biodiesel Demand, Area Required under Jatropha for Different Blending Rates

Year	Diesel Demand (Mt)	Bio-Diesel @ 5% Mt	Area for 5% Blending (Mha)	Bio-Diesel @ 10% Mt	Area for 10% Mha	Bio-Diesel @ 20% Mt	Area for 20% Mha
2001-02	39.81	1.99	N.A.	3.98	N.A.	7.96	N.A.
2006-07	52.33	2.62	2.19	5.23	4.38	10.47	8.76
2011-12	66.90	3.35	2.79	6.69	5.58	13.38	11.19

Source: Tewari (2003).

Subsequent documents of the Planning Commission are not very enthusiastic about the development of biofuel in the sense that these documents neither provide further plans nor mention the progress made. On the contrary, approach paper to Eleventh FYP, in fact, problematizes the biofuel issue

> Biodiesel (Jatropha) planting is being promoted through state agencies without seeing all the consequences such as blocking the migration routes of animals and encroaching upon herd-passing pathways. It is vital to ensure that the commons are protected (GoI, 2006).

Central Government

Though the issue of development of biofuel started in 2003, it was only in July

2006 that various ministries and departments were given specific responsibilities through a government notification for developing biofuel programme (PIB 2007). At present, various ministries of the central government are involved in the biofuel programme. Prominent among these are Ministry of New and Renewable Energy (MoNRE), Ministry of Agriculture (MoA), MoPNG, Ministry of Rural Development (MoRD) and Ministry of Science and Technology (MoST).

These ministries have different roles, interests and stakes in biofuel development. Similar to the case of Planning Commission, all these central Ministries also started with both the options in biofuel end use, i.e. biofuel as transportation fuel and biofuel as decentralized energy source. However, the 'Mission document on decentralized energy' suggests that though many states have demarcated land for cultivating biofuel crops, the issue of biomass as a source of energy has lacked attention (Gokhale, 2006).

An analysis of press releases of various ministries on the issue of biofuels reveals that the position of all the ministries is similar on biofuel development, i.e. they all promote biofuels. During initial years, there was no differentiation between using agriculture land or wastelands for production of biofuel. The Minister of Agriculture in fact emphasized the need for making biofuel cultivation economically viable for farmers as an alternative crop (PIB, 2006). Even the Planning Commission's approach paper to Eleventh FYP mentions development of biofuel as a strategy for increasing agricultural output (GoI, 2006).

Except for a couple of questions in the Lok Sabha (lower house of the Indian Parliament) on the negative impacts of biofuels, proceedings of Lok Sabha and press releases from different ministries and Prime Minister's Office (PMO) largely convey a pro-biofuel agenda of the government. However, a shift in the statements is observed from March 2008 onwards, starting from the Prime Minister's (PM) criticism of the US policy of using food crop for production of biofuel. Later, MoA also expressed its concern on rising food prices due to biofuel development. However, the government remains enthusiastic about development of biofuel as is evident from this recent statement from the Minister of Science and Technology:

> we have the ability to completely rewrite the geopolitics of oil if we ensure that the efficiency of transportation in the country – specifically diesel transportation is improved and biodiesel substitution takes place on a war footing (PIB 2008).

State Governments

Nineteen states are at present involved in the biofuel programme in India[12] (Lok Sabha 2007). Several states like Chhattisgarh, Andhra Pradesh and Rajasthan have taken lead in pushing biofuel programmes in their states in terms of creating institutions for promoting the programme, allocating land for generating feedstock and linking the plantation programme with various schemes. The states have also come out with various models for biofuel programme, which mostly fall in the category of Public Private partnership. However, there is no information on how successful these programmes and plantations have been and how much biofuel is available from these efforts at present.

Objectives Behind the State Programmes

The reason for the states to go ahead with the programme without a clear national policy is given in the statement of Chhattisgarh Biofuel Development Authority (CBDA) executive director:

> we have launched our Jatropha plantation programme taking a cue from the Planning Commission's document, National Mission on Biodiesel. We are aware that the GoM [Group of Ministers] on bio-fuels is deliberating the issue. The broad policy of the central government has already been enunciated in the Planning Commission document (Sharma, 2008).

Almost all the state governments are involved in the biofuel programme with the following objectives (except for Gujarat state):

1. Utilizing wasteland
2. Generating Rural Employment
3. Working towards energy security in the country

Whereas all the other states follow the rhetoric of Central Government in using wasteland for energy security and rural prosperity, policy in Gujarat clearly sees a need to bring large areas of wasteland under use by granting lease to big companies or expert farmers. All the states stress on the involvement of private players in development of biofuel programme. Some states like Chhattisgarh and Uttarakhand are already providing subsidies, tax and excise exemption to the companies.

Allocation of Land

At present, the states of Chhattisgarh, Andhra Pradesh, Gujarat, Rajasthan, Madhya

Pradesh, Uttarakhand and Orissa have a clear policy on leasing out wasteland for cultivation of biofuel crop. Despite the fact that Chhattisgarh has one of the lowest area of wasteland available, the state is a leader in promotion of biofuel plantations with 154,000 hectares of plantations done on wastelands till 2007.[13] However, it is not clear whether the wastelands have been leased or not. Rajasthan state has identified wastelands in various districts and has started plantation of Jatropha on these areas and degraded forest areas. Andhra Pradesh government has also demarcated some areas for operation by different private companies. Besides wasteland, degraded forest land is also targeted for plantation of Jatropha in various states (SPWD 2006).

State Institutions for Biofuel Development

Various institutions have been formed to promote biofuel development in the states. Either the biofuel promotion agenda has been linked to already existing departments (as in Rajasthan and Andhra Pradesh, where the responsibility has been given to District Poverty Initiative Programme and Rain Shadow Area Development Authority respectively), or new organizations have been created with the task of promoting of biofuel in the state (e.g. in Chhattisgarh and Uttarakhand).

In terms of institutional set up, Chhattisgarh and Uttarakhand are the leading states in India for biofuel. CBDA was formed in January 2005 with the objective of promoting biofuel industry and programme in the Chhattisgarh state. Uttarakhand Biofuel Board, which is the main agency in the state of Uttarakhand for promotion of biofuels, has been formed with a partnership between state government, Forest Development Corporation (FDC) and entrepreneurs. In this business model, FDC will undertake plantations on Van Panchayat lands[14] and provide certainty of raw material supply to entrepreneurs who purchase the feedstock and produce biodiesel. However, the purpose and where the produced biofuel will be sold by the entrepreneur is still uncertain, as is evident from an entrepreneur's statement:

> I'm not going to sell to the oil companies because they pay just ₹ 26.50 a litre. I'm going to sell it to a whole range of other industries that can use it for their machines (Civil Society News, 2007).

Thus, at the national level, the biofuel development programme in terms of institutionalization in India does not seem to have progressed much. Though the national policy has been recently announced, Planning Commission, which initiated the idea, has cautioned about its impact on the pastoral livelihoods.

In terms of the states, whereas a few states have taken lead in biofuel programmes, many are yet to come out with clear policies on the issue of biofuel. Overall however, it can be said that all the states are positive on the development of biofuels and have initiated programmes for facilitating the production of biofuels.

Private Sector and the Biofuel Discourse

The biofuel industry in India is still in its incubation phase and is behind its European counterparts (see Figure 3). This section discusses interests and issues of this fledgling industry.

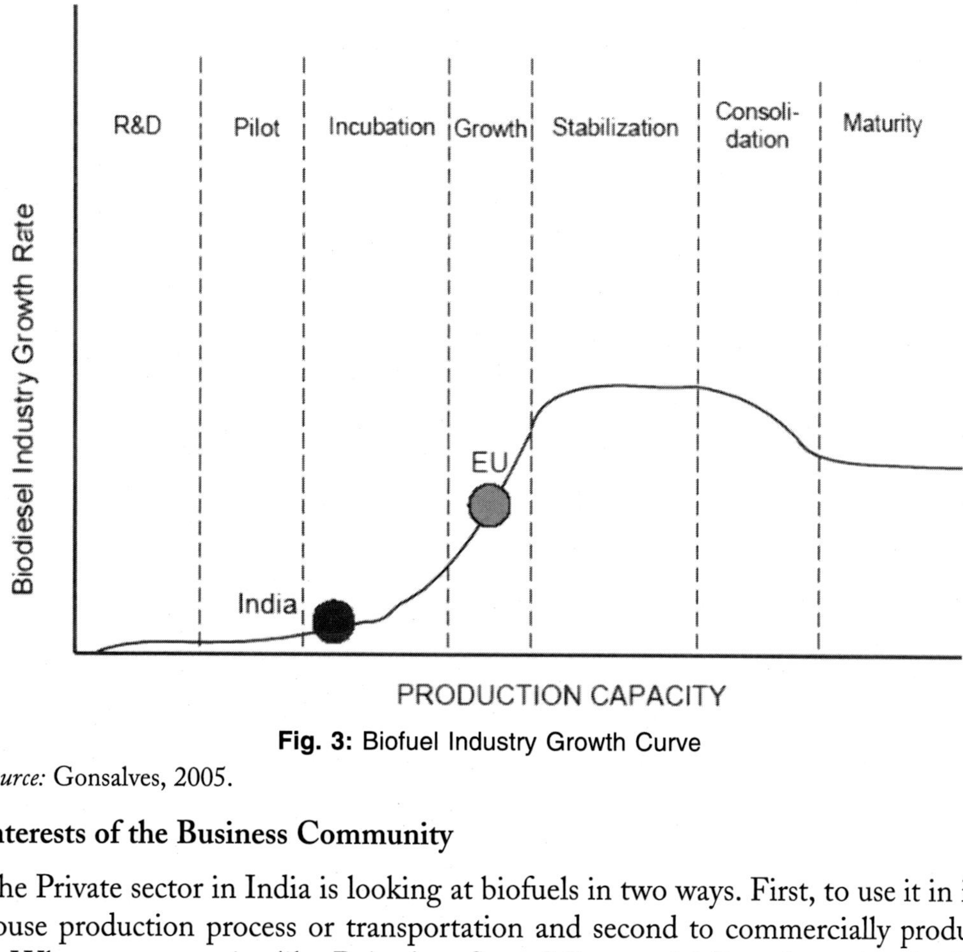

Fig. 3: Biofuel Industry Growth Curve

Source: Gonsalves, 2005.

Interests of the Business Community

The Private sector in India is looking at biofuels in two ways. First, to use it in in-house production process or transportation and second to commercially produce it. Whereas companies like Rajasthan State Mines and Minerals are involved in in-house use of biodiesel, D1-Mohan and Reliance have plans or are already producing it commercially. Further, there has been collaboration between Indian companies and mostly European companies in producing feedstock, biodiesel as well as its marketing. This arrangement might also be evolving to cater not only to the domestic market in India but European markets as well.

For making investments in the upcoming industry, as their counterparts in Europe, the Indian industry also requires an assurance from the government about the sustainability of the biofuel industry in terms of a coherent government policy. Many industrial houses are in fact waiting for announcement of such a policy before they enter into the sector (Frost and Sullivan, 2006).

As an infant industry, biofuel companies are also seeking incentives, viz., income tax, excise and sales tax exemptions, etc., from the central and state governments so that the cost of production could be minimized. This has been granted to a certain extent as some industries have got land from the government and subsidies are provided to the farmers for planting fuel crops. Further, there are tax incentives and excise cuts from the government as is evident from the statement in the annual report of Southern Online Biotechnologies, which says that:

> [t]he policy...[should be] encouraging the production and usage of Biodiesel. Several financial incentives such as reimbursement of stamp duty, exemptions in sales and income taxes, rebates on power, subsidy on cleaner production measures, quality certification, etc., are available (SOBL, 2007, 19).

The government in the 2007-08 budget has provided a pass-through status to biofuel projects set up by industry.[15] Excise duty is not levied on biodiesel and in the 2009-10 budget, the customs duty has also been reduced from 7.5 per cent to 2.5 per cent.[16] However, Kojima and Johnson (2005) argue that these protection measures need to be temporary in nature otherwise inefficient allocation of resource may result.

Ensuring availability of feedstock is one of the main factors in developing biofuel industry. Though various state governments have come out with wasteland allocation orders, there seems to be less enthusiasm in industry to take these lands. This is evident from the fact that some big industries like Reliance, Mission Biofuels and D1 have gone for contract farming instead of large-scale plantations[17] on degraded lands themselves.

Sufficient feedstock does not seem to be available as yet from domestic sources for production of biodiesel and the industry is banking on the maturity of domestic feedstock crop. Meanwhile, various companies have established their refineries for production of biodiesel. At present, these companies are importing feedstock from East Asia in terms of palm oil, fat and used oil, etc. But to protect the domestic biofuel plantation industry, MoNRE has sought the Cabinet's approval for imposing duties and taxes on imported biofuels.[18] This will be done in consultation with the finance ministry and agriculture ministry. Nonetheless, the industry is banking on maturity of the domestic feedstock crop.

Issues in the Biofuel Industry

There are two main issues related to the private sector with regards to the production of biofuel in India. They are diversion of farmland for growing fuel crop and export of biodiesel from India.

Although the government's rhetoric is that no agriculture land or food crop will be diverted for production of biofuel, the business strategy of industry seems to rely on productive farmland. This goes against the sustainability argument, frequently given in favour of the biofuels in India. In a workshop on biofuel in 2006, a representative of Reliance Life Sciences said:

> [the] research of reliance shows that Jatropha will not come in a big way from Reliance's own land or from those of high end farmers. Typically 25–30 per cent land is fallow, which all said and done will be the major source of Jatropha. Apart from that, 5–10 per cent of the land of small farmers will have to be targeted...the idea is to offer partnerships in terms of local organizations/farmer producer organizations (SPWD, 2006).

There is a possibility that oil seeds and other food grains may also be used for biofuel production in India. This is evident from a news report in which the Minister of Agriculture said that India has to go for importing food grains because the existing food grain and oil seeds were being diverted for biofuel production (Chaudhary, 2007). The Minister of Agriculture, in response to a question in Parliament, also conveyed the possibility of diversion of food grains for industrial use.[19] Further, feedstock from other countries that is coming from agriculture lands is being used for biofuel production in India.[20] In fact, organizations like United Nations Industrial Development Organization (UNIDO) are encouraging Indian companies to undertake plantations of fuel crops in African countries (ET, 2007). However, as the Frost and Sullivan (2007) report suggests, the import of feedstock may be a stopgap arrangement till the domestic biofuel crops start production.

Export of Biodiesel

Some companies like Naturol and Southern Online Biofuels in India have been set up as Export Oriented Units. What this means is that the biofuel that is produced by the company will be sold in the export market. While the companies mention on their websites that domestic markets would also be catered to, if the price of biodiesel is more in the European market, the units will be more interested in exporting. This is evident from Naturol website, which states that:

> [h]igh quality raw material (Crude Palm & Soya Oils) are available from Indonesia, Malaysia and South America and Naturol's structuring as an Export Oriented Unit enables tax efficient import of the raw materials... [e]xports are contemplated to Europe in view of significant market scope and better value for the end product. Confirmed arrangements are already in place for sale of 100 per cent of the output.[21]

There are also European biofuel companies that are eyeing Indian biofuel market. 'India is a rather new thing for us but we can buy Jetropha Curcas from India to begin with', said Osmo Kammonen, senior vice-president, communications, Neste Oil.[22] According to Abhishek Maharishi, CEO, Centre for Jatropha Promotion and Biodiesel, Rajasthan, if the Indian government implements its policy on jatropha cultivation in right earnest the country could be a leading exporter.[23]

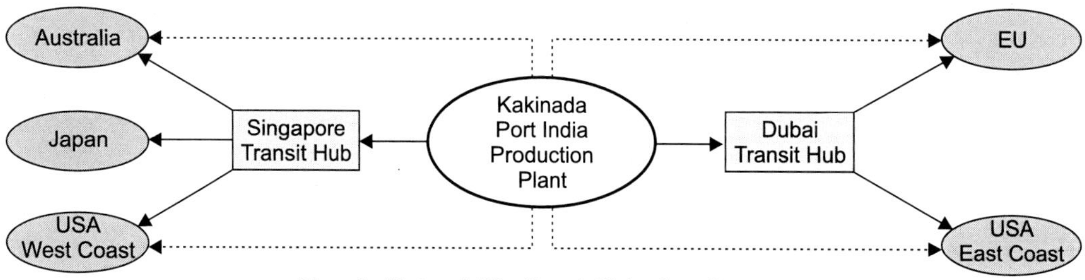

Fig. 4: Naturol Biodiesel Shipping Routes

Source: Naturol Website.[24]

Moreover, most of these production facilities are based in the eastern coast port of Kakinada to reduce the cost of transportation for import of feedstock from East

Asia and export of the produced biodiesel to the markets in Australia, Japan, US and EU (see Figure 4). The fact that produced biofuel may be exported to markets outside India to fetch a better price goes completely against the government's plan to ensure energy security.

Civil Society in the Biofuel Discourse

NGOs and the Discourses

There are two sets of positions and discourses within the Non-Government Organization (NGOs), pro-biofuel and anti-biofuel. Both the positions, actors involved and arguments are analysed in this section.

Pro-biofuel

Biofuel for Commercial Purpose

A number of NGOs are involved in facilitating the production and sale of biofuel crop from farm areas. The nature of involvement is mostly in using their association with rural households and their groups in facilitating the extension of material and knowledge required for production of biofuel feedstock, mostly Jatropha. Most of these NGOs are using institutional forms of cooperatives and producer companies to organize farmers into producing and selling biofuel crops to the companies for production of biodiesel to be supplemented in petroleum fuel (see Box 2).

Biofuel for Rural Electrification

There are a small number of NGOs that are involved in using biofuel as means for rural electrification in remote villages. NGOs like Winrock in Jharkhand, IRADE in Haryana and Gram Vikas in Orissa are involved in providing electricity in remote villages through biofuel run generators.

Arguments for Biofuel

Pro-biofuel NGOs believe in the same arguments of win-win situation, sustainable development and rural prosperity that government and industries are providing. This is not only true for NGOs that are promoting biofuels for use as commercial commodity but also those NGOs that are promoting it as fuel for electricity generation. For example, Winrock's pro-biofuel argument is based on efficient use and development of wasteland, contribution of the project to national and local energy security and stimulating local economy.

Box 2: Cases of Pro biofuel NGOs

Biofuel for Commercial Purpose

Dhan Foundation, through its supported producer Company KTL has tied up with Mission Biofuels company to utilize its network of 20,000 Self Help Groups for contract farming of over 25,000 acres of land in eight districts of state of Tamil Nadu (MBIL 2006). It is envisaged that this arrangement will benefit below poverty line families also which account for half of the 400,000 families associated with. KTL's responsibility in this endeavour is to organize farmers to undertake this activity whereas Mission Biofuel would be responsible for developing planting material and providing quality Jatropha curcas seedlings to farmers. Mission Biofuel company would also provide micro credit facilities to farmers to meet the cost of farming biofuel crop. KTL would benefit in terms of service charges and incentives on productivity. On the other hand, any benefit arising from carbon trading would be accrued to Mission Biofuel.

Biofuel for Rural Electrification

Winrock, an NGO, is implementing ProBIOS project aimed at facilitating Government Officials and other stakeholders through strategic capacity building and appropriate technology partnership with European Union (Winrock 2006). Winrock is also involved in the project of rural electrification from the produced biofuel in Chhattisgarh. Through the success of the project, Winrock attempts to influence government's policy for improving rural India's access to clean and affordable energy. Although Winrock accepts the current attention given to blending of biodiesel, it urges for also looking at other uses of biodiesel. Winrock seems to be in favour of biofuel however their objective or end use of biofuel is rural electrification rather than diesel substitution in transportation. However, the NGOs promoting biofuel for rural electrification justify using wasteland for the production.

Anti-biofuel

Failure of Earlier Programmes

Organizations taking the anti-biofuel position view the whole biofuel programme as a repeat of earlier failed programme of promotion of Eucalyptus on government and private land. As a consequence, their argument is:

> the projections do not take into consideration various environmental, economic and social aspects, which have direct impact on the suitability of the crop as a commercial product or cultivation for cash income superseding existing land use (Negi et al., 2006).

Issue of Wasteland and Livelihoods

The issue of wastelands is the most important argument raised by the anti-biofuel organizations. The argument is that wastelands are usually the common property resource of the village on which the small, marginal and landless as well as livestock rearing communities depend and thus biofuel production on these lands marginalizes these communities and threatens their livelihood security. The argument is based on the studies carried out by academicians like N.S. Jodha and others on the contribution of common lands to the rural livelihoods especially in the dry land regions of India. Further, it is argued that though the lease of land is given for a particular period, it seldom happens that it is cancelled and the land is given back to the village community (Negi et al., 2006). Moreover, the mechanism involved in identifying wasteland is not a transparent one and can be influenced by the companies. Negi et al. (2006) argue that whether it is a farmland or common land, food security is an issue with the growing of biofuel.

> When agricultural lands are diverted from food crops to biodiesel crops, there is scarcity of food. When common lands are diverted to Jatropha from fodder, there is less food for animals and the livestock economy is undermined. Less animals means less dairy products which directly affects the nutritional security of the people especially the children. Less animals also means less organic manure which undermines food security by robbing soils of vital organic matter needed for renewal of soil fertility.

Although there are projections of generation of millions of man days from biofuel industry, the opportunity cost of shifting land use has not been calculated (Shiva and Sankar, 2008). Further as Shiva and Sankar argue, land grabbing by private companies in collusion with the state is happening in the name of biofuel programme.

> Land is being acquired in many parts for India to fuel the cars of the rich… land grab for biofuels has emerged as a threat for the agrarian and livestock economy in many states in India. It is also threatening the decentralized democracy of the country, which has made local communities, the competent bodies to make decisions on natural resources…[t]his kind of land grab will totally pauperize our peasantry and destroy their livelihood (Shiva and Sankar, 2008).

Other Arguments

It is also argued that the scientific basis for a viable yield of biodiesel from plants is doubtful and there is a high probability that biodiesel produced will be marketed to European markets and thus will not lead to energy security of the country (Negi et al., 2006).

Academia

Status of Biofuel Research

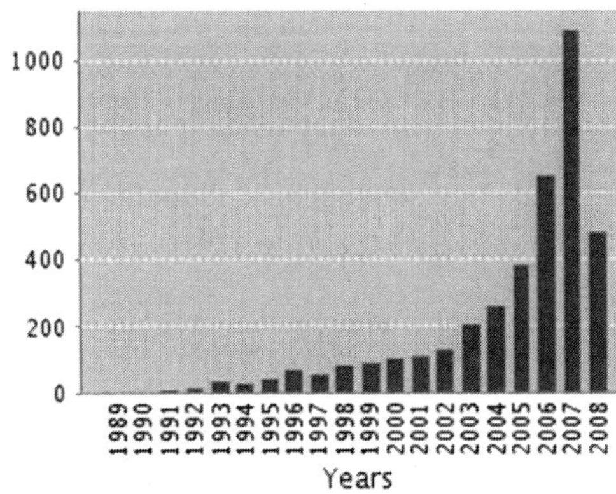

Fig. 5: Science Citation Index

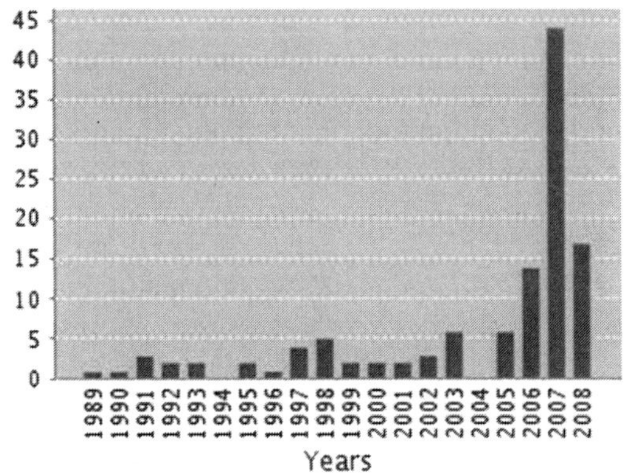

Fig. 6: Social Science Citation Index

Source: ISI Web of Knowledge.[25]

Biofuel is an intensely debated issue mostly at the international level. In India, the research on the biofuel issue is almost non-existent, especially in the social sciences. Figures 5 and 6 depict the number of articles published about biofuels in scientific and social science journals respectively and suggest that in the international academic circles, it is the scientific aspect of biofuel that is being researched most than the social science aspect of the biofuel. Moreover, it is also clear from these figures that the interest in the biofuel issue is also of recent origin.

Further, whatever findings are available in the social sciences, they tend to be non specific to the context and equivocal and uncertain about the environmental, social and economic impacts. There have also been instances of scientific studies that showed biofuels in a positive light and influenced policy but were in fact based on wrong or 'bad' science. Pimentel and Patzek mentions that a 'review of the reports that indicate that corn ethanol production provides a positive return indicates that many inputs were omitted... [which mislead] policy makers and the public' (Pimentel and Patzek, 2005, 65).

Science of Biofuels

Although there is plethora of studies on the positive environmental benefits of biofuels, considerable doubt has been expressed about these benefits, especially in terms of CO_2 emission reduction and impact on virtual water flows (Fargione et al., 2008; Peters and Thielman, 2007; Achten et al., undated; Hughes et al., 2007).

Although some studies suggest that second-generation biofuel like Jatropha are better because they can grow on less fertile soil without requiring much water (see Openshaw, 2000), others like Russi (2007) argue that biofuels may not provide the environmental benefits that it envisages. This is due to a need for intensive cultivation and thus increasing use of fertilizers, pesticide and machinery especially on poor quality lands. Quoting various authors, Russi also argues that Energy Return on Investment[26] of biofuels is low and therefore the claim that it provides energy security may not hold ground (*ibid.*).

Research on Socio-economic Aspects

As with the scientific research on energy and environmental benefits, socio-economic research is also not certain about the benefits of biofuels. At the macro level, some studies point to the unintended effect of biofuel promotion. For example, production costs of biofuels are still higher than those of fossil fuels and therefore governments need to come out with promotion measures such as tax exemptions or blending quotas (Kher, 2005).

There has also been concern regarding the livelihood objectives of the biofuel programme. Rajagopal (2007) argues that there are diverse needs of the rural poor from the wastelands that are unlikely to be fulfilled by Jatropha plantations and shifting land use may lead to potential conflicts at the micro level.

Research Institutions

Various Universities in India like the Tamil Nadu Agriculture University in the state of Tamil Nadu and Maharana Pratap University of Agricuture and Technology in Rajasthan are undertaking research on biofuel development. Such programmes in the universities are primarily funded by the Indian Council for Agricultural Research as well as industry in which the industry will fund the research and would benefit from the research outputs. Though a fair arrangement, it has come into question following a case involving biopiracy by D1 plc, a multinational biofuel company.[27]

Various other institutions like ICRISAT and TERI are also involved in research on biofuel crops and its promotion. These institutions again get their funding either from the government or from other organizations whose mandate is to promote biofuels (see Box 3). Whereas the position of these institutions is pro biofuel due to the funding that is received, the recent debate of food vs fuel seems to affect their discourse as well. This is evident from the cautious approach sought by the Director General of TERI in relation to biofuel development:

> We should be very, very careful about coming up with biofuel solutions that have a major impact on the production of food grains and may have an implication for overall food security (Reuters, 2008).

Box 3: Cases of Research Institutions

International Crops Research Institute for the Semi-Arid Tropics (ICRISAT)

Funded by IFAD to the tune of US $1.5 million, ICRISAT has been involved in researching on a crop Sweet Sorghum, which they term as smart crop as it can produce ethanol from the juice of its stalk and seeds can be eaten. ICRISAT believes that food security and biofuels can coexist (ICRISAT 2008). ICRISAT is also in collaboration with various industries for commercialization of the smart biofuel crop. ICRISATs research also has strong partnership with the government as well. Government's funding to ICRISAT has increased from US$ 400,000 in 2005 to US$ 1.4 million in 2006. ICRISAT is also leading a consortium of partners for developing sweet sorghum as a source of biofuel under the National Agricultural Innovation Programme of the Government of India. ICRISAT's emphasis on sweet sorghum counters the global debate against biofuels, which are said to be taking away food crop agricultural lands for growing biofuel crops. Highlighting this position, Director General of ICRISAT said, 'We develop systems that increase the incomes of the poor, not those that trade off biofuels against food and feed security or the environment' (ICRISAT, 2008).

The Energy and Resources Institute (TERI)

TERI is involved in research and undertakes projects in the area of energy and natural resources. TERI has considerable influence on the policy especially after its Director General became Chairman of the IPCC and shared Nobel Peace Prize in 2007 on behalf of IPCC with Al Gore. TERI is involved in a $9.4 million Project Green with BP International Limited to plant 8000 hectares of land in the state of Andhra Pradesh with Jatropha for production of biodiesel. TERI has also drafted a detailed project report for use of wasteland for biodiesel production, which is under the consideration of the Ministry of Agriculture.

Media

A newspaper, Hindustan Times was reviewed as a representative of media for news on biofuel from January 2002 to May 2008.[28] As seen in Figure 7, a content analysis of the media items on biofuel reveals that there has been significant coverage about biofuels in 2007 and 2008. This trend is similar to the trend shown in the academia. While it was the pro-biofuel news that was dominating the coverage till 2007, in 2008, there were more news items about anti-biofuel. Anti-biofuel news items are largely international in nature and pertain to the food price rise and its link with the diversion of food crops for producing biofuels, especially in the US. The issue of food price rise started in late 2007 and has dominated the biofuel agenda in the media since then. The issue of wasteland and pastoralist livelihoods finds mention only once in June 2007. In fact, out of nineteen news items that convey the anti-biofuel view, only two are not related to food price rise.

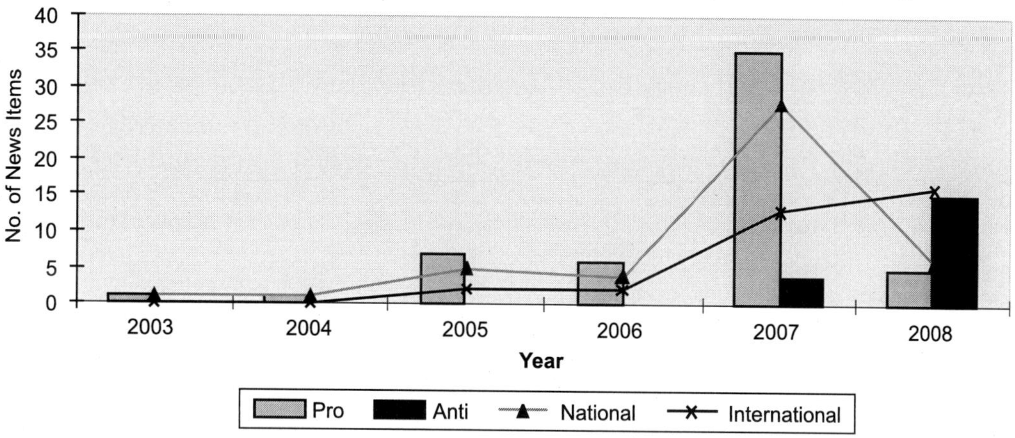

Fig. 7: Position and Nature of the Media Items on Biofuels

Source: Own calculations.

Thus, it is obvious that media has largely been positive about the biofuel issue till 2007, which is when the issue of food price rise and its link with biofuel became prominent. The issues raised by some NGOs and academia, which seem to be more relevant to the national context do not find space in the media. This points to the weakness or powerlessness of the anti-biofuel discourse in the country. However, another anti-biofuel discourse, that of food vs fuel, which is international in character and origin, has been able to get more attention in the media signifying its power.

Thus, from the nature of research that is being pursued in biofuels, it is obvious that the approach for biofuel development is more techno-centric and focuses on technical aspects of producing biofuel rather than its impact on socio-economy especially livelihoods. Also, such technocratic approaches only look at energy demand and supply options and reduce environmental concerns to a secondary level which leads to failure of the biomass programmes based on such approaches (Cadenas and Cabezudo, 1998).

NGOs as well as the Research community (both physical and social science) are divided in their opinion with regards to benefits of large-scale plantation and use of biofuels, especially in the developing countries.

Though most of the universities and research institutions are positive about the development of biofuels, issues related to knowledge transfer and biopiracy need to be addressed. Moreover, because of the issue of food vs. fuel, research institutions have become cautious about the development of biofuels.

Media's position was positive till 2007 when the issue of food price rise became the dominant one and biofuels were criticized. However, this criticism was international in nature and issues raised by anti-biofuel actors within India still remain largely unrecognized.

Discussion

An analysis of the context and actors involved and their viewpoints suggests the presence of two sets of discourses, pro-biofuel and anti-biofuel (see Table 4). 'Anti-biofuel' discourse does not mean that the discourse and actors are completely against the development of biofuel, but it is against the dominant view of seeing biofuel only in terms of its blending with petroleum fuels and import substitution. The Anti-biofuel discourse is also critical of the role and interests of various actors involved in the promotion of biofuels.

Discourse Coalitions, Hegemony and Discursive Shift in the Biofuel Issue

In the biofuel issue, there are two sets of coalitions that have emerged and which are formed around pro and anti-biofuel discourses. Whereas the pro biofuel discourse can be associated mainly with the State and Private Sector, the anti-biofuel discourse has a few NGOs and a section of Academia as actors. These actors employ specific sets of arguments to push forward their agenda in the policy environment.

Table 4: A Description of Factors in Favour and Against the Biofuel

Factors/Discourses	Pro	Against
Context	Increasing fossil fuel requirement, increasing import bill, land degradation, need (non-obligatory) to reduce Green House Gas emissions	Rural use of biomass, option of developing decentralized energy systems, wasteland catering to livestock economy
Actors	Central Government, State Governments, Industry, NGOs, Academia, Research Institutions	NGOs, Academia
Arguments	• Energy security • Rural prosperity • Environmental benefit	• Land grabbing by industries • Adverse impact on pastoral livelihoods • Environment and energy benefits of biofuels debatable

Pro biofuel discourse has been able to exert hegemony over anti-biofuel discourses, which is evident from the institutionalization that has happened at the state level and the non-recognition of anti-biofuel discourse by the central government. This discursive hegemony is evident in the push for biofuel programme that various state governments have provided. This push has been in terms of state governments coming out with orders for allocating lands to industries for biofuel production and creating institutions in the state for promotion of biofuel programme. CBDA in Chhattisgarh and Uttarakhand Biofuel Board in Uttarakhand are examples of such discourse institutionalization. These bodies are involved in promotion of biofuel production and industry in their respective states. Such an institutionalization projects the inherent power of pro-biofuel discourse.

However, at the central level, the pro biofuel discourse has shifted slightly towards approaching the issue in a cautious way. The shift is visible in the statement of the Planning Commission, which was the initiator of the pro biofuel discourse. The central government has also raised concerns about the impact of biofuel on food security and food prices. While, a shift in the position of Planning Commission seems to have been caused by recognition of adverse impact of biofuel programme on pastoral livelihoods, which is a national issue and directly relevant to the biofuel programme, the central government's concern relates to the more general global concern over food vs. fuel issue.

Conclusion

This chapter sets out to look at the factors and discourses, which affect the formulation of a national policy on biofuels in India. The preceding sections have presented the discourses around the issue of biofuels as expressed by three sets of actors, viz., the government (central and states), the private sector and civil society (NGOs, academia and media).

In conclusion, it can be said that policies are influenced by discourses depending on how powerful these are, not only in terms of what the discourses are conveying but also the context and issues these are talking about. This seems to be the case for biofuel policy in India. As shown by the above analysis, various contextual factors, actors and discourses seem to be influencing the emergence of biofuel policy in India. It has been shown that though the issue of biofuel is around seven years old, the national policy on biofuel only recently was approved only recently. However, various states have already initiated programmes for allocating wastelands for biofuel plantations and created institutions with the responsibility of promotion of biofuels. In doing this, the states and industries as well as a few NGOs and research institutions are following a pro biofuel discourse with a particular contextual view. At present, as shown by the above analysis, it is the pro biofuel discourse that is dominating the policy arena. The Indian anti-biofuel discourse, which has a different view of the context and which suggests that the interest of actors, especially industry may be against the objectives of the programme, does not seem to affect the dominant discourse.

Though Indian anti-biofuel discourse lacks power, it is the global food vs. fuel discourse that has caused some concern in the policy arena. The food vs. fuel discourse has been widely discussed in the political circles and the media in EU and elsewhere in the world. Various UN agencies have also joined in criticizing the role of biofuels in food shortage and price rise, which has made the food vs. fuel discourse powerful. Food security being a strategic, moral and political issue, the Indian government was reluctant to come out with a national policy on biofuels, which inevitably involved the issue of land use change, especially wastelands. This issue was also problematic because the Left parties, on whose support the previous central government was formed, were against the leasing of wasteland to the private sector. These factors may have provided some advantage to the anti-biofuel discourse, and it can be concluded that the anti-biofuel discourse is lately beginning to gain ground in India. But for the time being, the pro-biofuel discourse seems to be the dominant one.

On the theoretical ground, it can be said that though it would require further research, this chapter also points to different scenarios that might emerge with regards to biofuel in India. The issue of fuel price rise and import dependency has led central government to come out with a national biofuel policy, which encourages the development of biofuel industry in India. However, the objective of reducing import of petroleum fuel will not be achieved if the industries continue exporting biodiesel to lucrative markets in Europe. Banning the export of biofuel may be one of the alternatives that the Indian government has, but this will have to be pursued in conjunction with providing other incentives to the industry and raising the support price of biodiesel so that the fledgling biofuel industry can become viable. However, in all these cases, the issue of land use is central. Whereas shifting wastelands for biofuel production would have its impact on the pastoral livelihoods, using agriculture land would be detrimental to food security. Thus, it can be concluded that if the Indian government decides to go ahead with biofuels it will have to confront the issue of land use change, whether it pertains to wastelands or agriculture land.

References

[1] Achten W., Mathijs E., Verchot L., Singh V.P. and Muys B. (undated), Bio-diesel from Jatropha: The Life-Cycle Perspective, Online source [http://www.biw.kuleuven.be/lbh/lbnl/forecoman/pdf/Abstracts/Achten/Achten%20abstract%20poster%20gotheborg.pdf] accessed on 26/05/08.

[2] Brewer G. and deLeon P. (1983), *The Foundations of Policy Analysis*, Monterey.

[3] Cadenas A. and Cabezudo S. (1998), Biofuels as Sustainable Technologies: Perspectives for Less Developed Countries, *Technological Forecasting and Social Change*, 58, 83-103.

[4] CEC (Commission of the European Communities) (2006), An EU Strategy for Biofuel, Communication from the Commission, SEC (2006), 142.

[5] CEC (Commission of the European Communities) (2007), Biofuel Progress Report: Report on the Progress Made in the Use of Biofuels and Other Renewable Fuels in the Member States of the European Union, Communication from the Commission to the Council and the European Parliament, Brussels. Online source [ec.europa.eu/

energy/energy_policy/doc/07_biofuels_progress_report_en.pdf], accessed on 28/04/07.

[6] CEC (Commission of the European Communities) (2008), Statement of Energy Commissioner Andris Piebalgs in Response to the Biofuels Report of the House of Commons. Online source, [http://europa.eu/rapid/pressReleasesAction.do?reference =IP/08/64&format=PDF&aged=1&language=EN&guiLanguage=en] accessed on 13/05/2008.

[7] Chaudhary G. (2007), Govt to Go Slow on Wheat Imports, *Hindustan Times*. Online source [http://www.hindustantimes.com/News-feed/Business/] accessed on 06/05/08.

[8] Chauhan C. (2008), Learn about Biofuels from Us: India to US, *Hindustan Times*. Online source accessed on 06/05/08.

[9] Chopra K. (2001), Wasteland and Common Property Land Resources, *Seminar*, 499.

[10] Civil Society News (2007), Biofuels are for Bharat. Online source [http://civilsocietyonline.com] accessed on 19/05/08.

[11] ET (2007), India should Tap Biofuel Sources in Africa, *Economic Times*. Online source [http://economictimes.indiatimes.com/articleshow/2275307.cms], accessed on 05/05/08.

[12] EIA[a] (Energy Information Administration) (2007), International Energy Outlook: 2007, Office of Integrated Analysis and Forecasting, U.S. Department of Energy. Online Source [www.eia.doe.gov/oiaf/ieo/index.html] accessed on 28/04/08.

[13] EIA[b] (2007), Country Analysis Briefs: India, Department of Energy, USA. Online source [http://www.eia.doe.gov/cabs/India/pdf.pdf] accessed on 15/05/08.

[14] Fargione J., Hill J., Tilman D., Polasky S. and Hawthorne P. (2008), Land Clearing and the Biofuel Carbon Debt, *Sciencexpress*, 4. Online source retrieved on 06/05/08.

[15] Frost and Sullivan (2007), Strategic Analysis of the Indian Biofuels Market. Online source [http://www.frost.com/prod/servlet/report-analyst.pag?repid=P12C-01-00-00-00] accessed on 01/05/2008.

[16] GoI (2001), The State of Environment – India 2001.

[17] GoI (2002), Tenth Five Year Plan, Planning Commission, India.

[18] GoI (2006), Towards Faster and More Inclusive Growth: An Approach to the 11th Five Year Plan (2007–2012), Planning Commission, Delhi.

[19] GoI[a] (2007), Towards Faster and More Inclusive Growth: An Approach to the 11th Five Year Plan (2007–2012), Planning Commission, Delhi.

[20] GoI[b] (2007), Report of the Working Group on Animal Husbandry and Dairying for the Eleventh Five Year Plan (2007–2012), Planning Commission, Delhi.

[21] Gokhale A.M. (2006), Mission Document in Evolution: National Mission on Decentralized Biomass Energy for Villages and Industries.

[22] Gonsalves J.B. (2005), An Assessment of the Biofuels Industry in India, UNCTAD.

[23] Gupta S.P. (2002), Report of the Committee on India Vision 2020, Planning Commission, Government of India.

[24] Hajer M. (1993), 'Discourse Coalitions and the Institutionalization of Practice: The Case of Acid Rain in Britain', in Fischer F. and Forester J. (eds.), *The Argumentative Turn in Policy Analysis and Planning*, London, UCL Press.

[25] Hajer M. (1995), *The Politics of Environmental Discourse: Ecological Modernization and the Policy Process*, Oxford, Clarendon Press.

[26] Hughes S., Partzsch L. and Gaskell J. (2007), The Development of Biofuels within the Context of the Global Water Crisis, *Sustainable Development Law and Policy*, 58, 58-62.

[27] IEA (International Energy Agency) (2007), World Energy Outlook 2007: China and India Insights. Online source accessed on 28/04/08.

[28] Johansson T.B., Kelly H., Reddy A.K.N. and Williams R.H. (1993), *Renewable Energy: Sources for Fuels and Electricity*, London, Earthscan.

[29] Kher R. (2005), Biofuels: The Way Ahead, *Economic and Political Weekly*, 40 (51).

[30] Kingdon J.W. (2003), *Agendas, Alternatives and public policies*, Longman.

[31] Kojima M. and Johnson T. (2005), Potential for Biofuels for Transport in Developing Countries, Energy Sector Management Assistance Programme, The World Bank Group, Washington.

[32] Lindblom C.E. (1993), *The Policy-Making Process*, Prentice-Hall.

[33] Lok Sabha (2007), Lok Sabha no. 14, Supplementary Question No. 223 dated 30/11/07, GoI.

[34] Majone G. (1989), *Evidence, Argument and Persuasion in the Policy Process*, London, Yale University Press.

[35] MBIL (2006), Mission Biofuels Increases Foothold in Upstream Feedstock Business, Press Release by Mission Biofuels India Limited.

[36] Mills S. (1997), *Discourse*, London, Routledge.

[37] MoEF (Ministry of Environment and Forests) (2006), Report of the National Forest Commission, Government of India.

[38] MoPNG (2004), Gazette Notification on Blending of Ethanol in Petrol, Government of India. Online source [http://petroleum.nic.in/gaznew.pdf] accessed on 13/05/08.

[39] MoPNG (2005), Biodiesel Purchase Policy, Government of India. Online source [http://petroleum.nic.in/Bio-Diesel.pdf] accessed on 25/04/08.

[40] Negi K.and Komal J.K. (2005), Report on Promotion of Biofuel in India: Issues and Prospect, SPWD, New Delhi.

[41] Openshaw K. (2000), A Review of Jatropha Curcas: An Oil Plant of Unfulfilled Promise, *Biomass and Bioenergy*, 19, 1-15.

[42] Peters J. and Thielmann S. (2008), Promoting Biofuels: Implications for Developing Countries, *Energy Policy*, 36, 1538-1544.

[43] Pimentel, D. and Patzek T.K. (2005), Ethanol Production Using Corn, Switchgrass, and Wood; Biodiesel Production using Soybean and Sunflower, *Natural Resources Research*, 14 (1), 65-76.

[44] PIB (Press Information Bureau) (2006), Centre to Launch Special Mission for Biofuel Crops: Shri Pawar, GoI. Online resource [http://pib.nic.in/release/release.asp?relid=20142] accessed on 12/05/08.

[45] PIB (2007), Immense Potential for Public-Private Partnership, NRI Role in Agriculture, GoI.

[46] PIB (2008), India and EU to Strengthen Co-operation in Renewable Energy Research, GoI.

[47] Radaelli C.M. (1995), The Role of Knowledge in the Policy Process, *Journal of European Public Policy,* 2(2), 159–83.

[48] Rajagopal D. (2007), Rethinking Current Strategies for Biofuel Production in India, paper presented at the International Conference on Linkages in Water and Energy in Developing Countries.

[49] Ramdas S.R. and Ghotge N.S. (2006), India's Livestock Economy, *Seminar*, 564.

[50] Mayntz R. (2003), 'New Challenges to Governance Theory' in Henrik P. Bang (ed.), *Governance as Social and Political Communication*, Manchester University Press.

[51] Reuters (2008), UN's Pachauri Urges Caution in Biofuel Use. Online source [http://uk.reuters.com/article/oilRpt/idUKL2654981020080326], retrieved on 26/05/08.

[52] Russi D. (2007), Biofuels: Solution for Energy Crisis, *Economic and Political Weekly*, 42(19).

[53] Sabatier P. (ed.) (1999), *Theories of the Policy Process*, Westview Press.

[54] Schmidt V.A. and Radaelli C. (undated), Opening the Black Box: Europeanisation, Discourse, and Policy Change, Introduction for a Symposium Issue of West European Politics.

[55] Scoones I. (2006), *Science, Agriculture and the Politics of Policy: The Case of Biotechnology*, Orient Longman.

[56] Sharma A.K. (2008), Even as GoM Deliberates, Some States Kick-off Biofuel Schemes, *The Financial Express*, published on 25/02/08. Online source [http://www.financialexpress.com/news/Even-as-GoM-deliberates-some-states-kick-off-biofuel-schemes/276702/0] accessed on 19/05/08.

[57] Shiva V. and Sankar M. (2008), Biofuel Hoax: Jatropha and Land Grab, Navdanya.

[58] Shrivastava L. and Mathur R. (2007), India's Energy Security: Briefing Paper – Dialogue on Globalization, Friedrich Ebert Stiftung. Online source [http://library.fes.de/pdf-files/iez/global/04809.pdf] accessed on 17/05/08.

[59] SPWD (2006), Proceedings of the Workshop on 'Biofuels the Issues Involved, Specific Implications for Wastelands and Livelihoods'.

[60] SOBL (2007), Annual Report 2006-07, Southern Online Biotechnologies Limited.

[61] Tewari D.N. (2003), Report of the Committee on Development of Biofuel, Planning Commission, GoI.

[62] Winrock (2006), Biofuel India: Sustainable Fuel for the Energy and Transport Sector, *Newsletter*, Vol. IV, Issue IV.

[63] Ziegler J. (2008), Promotion and Protection of All Human Rights, Civil, Political, Economic, Social and Cultural Rights, including the Right to Development, Report of the Special Rapporteur on the Right to Food, United Nations General Assembly. Online source accessed on 13/05/08.

Notes

1. The chapter was written in 2008 when the Biofuel Policy was yet to be announced. The National Biofuel Policy which was announced in December 2010 which is not much different from the draft policy on which this chapter is based. The salient features of the National Biofuel Policy are:
    - Setting up of a National Biofuel Coordination Committee under prime minister for broader policy perspective

- Setting up of a Biofuel Steering Committee under the cabinet secretary to oversee implementation of policy
- Biodiesel production to be encouraged from non-edible oil seeds in waste, degraded, marginal land
- An indicative target of 20 per cent blending of bio-fuels in diesel and petrol by 2017
- Minimum support price to be announced for farmers producing non-edible oil seeds
- Financial incentives for second generation biofuels, including a national biofuel fund

2. China and India are expected to experience the fastest expansion in transportation sector energy use in the world (EIAa, 2007).
3. In India almost 70 per cent of the population lives in rural areas and consume 30 per cent of the total primary energy, which is largely derived from fuelwood, chips and dung cakes (Gokhale, 2006).
4. The Indian Government declared a Biofuel Purchase Policy in 2005 whereas a comprehensive biofuel policy that sets the direction in which the sector is to move and incentives and structures to facilitate is still pending.
5. *Source:* www.indiastat.com accessed on 13/05/08.
6. *Source:* http://petroleum.nic.in/petstat.pdf accessed on 20/05/08.
7. In 1996-97 Transport sector's share in final energy consumption in India was 22.3 per cent (Source: www.indiastat.com accessed on 15/05/08.
8. The Clean Development Mechanism (CDM), allows a country with an emission-reduction or emission-limitation commitment under the Kyoto Protocol to implement an emission-reduction project in developing countries. Such projects can earn saleable certified emission reduction (CER) credits, each equivalent to one tonne of CO_2, which can be counted towards meeting Kyoto targets. The developed country can benefit in terms of meeting their emission reduction targets, whereas developing country like India can benefit from the technology and project funds that are channelized. (*Source:* http://unfccc.int/kyoto_protocol/mechanisms/clean_development_mechanism/items/2718.php accessed on 23/05/08.)
9. Different sources give different areas of wasteland. For example, National Wasteland Development Board (NWDB) gives the figure of 129.57 mha with non-forest wasteland being 93.69 mha. Department of Land Resources (DoLR) estimates based on National Remote Sensing Agency (NRSA) data suggest that the wasteland area is around 55.27 mha in 2003. Such a huge difference in the estimation of wasteland

is attributed to different methods of data collection. Whereas NWDB's method was based on the reclassification of the standard land use data, DoLR estimates were based on remote sensing techniques (Chopra, 2001).

10. *Source:* http://www.nddb.org/statistics/population_india_species.html accessed on 28/05/08.
11. Planning Commission is the central level body formed in 1950 for formulating plans for the most effective and balanced utilization of resources and determining priorities. The commission works out sectoral targets and provides promotional stimulus to the economy to grow in the desired direction in the form of five year plans which are informed by various studies conducted or supported by the commission. (*Source:* http://planningcommission.nic.in/aboutus/history/func.htm accessed on 05/05/08.)
12. *Source:* http://164.100.24.208/lsq14/quest.asp?qref=56641 accessed on 13/05/2008. India has 28 States and 7 Union Territories.
13. *Source:* www.cbdacg.com/cbda.htm accessed on 12/05/08.
14. Van Panchayats are Local Forest Councils, which have the rights over development and use of forest land around their village for forestry purposes. Van Panchayats is a unique institution in Uttarakhand recognized by the constitution of India.
15. A pass-through status means that no income tax or no dividend distribution tax is levied. http://www.thehindubusinessline.com/2007/05/05/stories/2007050505331000.htm
16. *Source:* http://indiabudget.nic.in/ub2009-10/bs/speecha.htm accessed on 23/09/2010.
17. Though the companies mention their plans for large-scale plantation, no data is available on the scale of plantation undertaken except contract farming. Moreover, it is the government departments and NGOs that are involved in plantations on degraded lands. It may be that companies may also attempt to procure feedstock from government agencies, producer companies, village cooperatives or other groups or traders.
18. *Source:* http://www.hindustantimes.com/Search/Search1.aspx?q=bio-fuel&f=1%2f1%2f2006&t=4%2f30%2f2008
19. *Source:* http://164.100.24.208/lsq14/quest.asp?qref=31517 accessed on 05/05/08.
20. *Source:* http://www.biodieselnow.com/forums/t/18578.aspx accessed on 20/05/08.
21. *Source:* http://www.naturol-bio.com/inside/projects_bm.php accessed on 11/05/08.
22. *Source:* http://www.hindustantimes.com/StoryPage/StoryPage.aspx?id=5e52552c-f73a-473d-ba0d-4b9654cb1844 accessed on 11/05/08.

23. *Source:* http://www.hindustantimes.com/StoryPage/StoryPage.aspx?id=5e52552c-f73a-473d-ba0d-4b9654cb1844 accessed on 11/05/08.
24. *Source:* http://www.naturol-bio.com/inside/nbsr.php accessed on 11/05/08.
25. A query about biofuel on the ISI Web of Knowledge Science Index resulted in 3918 records as on 9 May 2008 whereas the same query on Social Science index resulted for only 120 records. Search on (biofuel OR biofuels OR bio-fuel OR bio-fuels OR biodiesel) in Web of Science All Years Science Citation Index, Social Science Citation Index and Arts and Humanities Citation Index.
26. EROI = Energy output/(indirect + direct energy input).
27. D1 hired head of Department of Forestry of the University, who was also responsible for projects on developing high yielding variety of Jatropha. Soon after he left the university and joined D1 as technical director, theft of germplasm was reported by the university. The germplasm was later found in the house of the accused and a case was filed. *Source:* http://www.downtoearth.org.in/full6.asp?foldername=20060228&filename=news&sec_id=4&sid=13 accessed on 23/05/08.
28. Selection of Hindustan Times was done on the basis that it is the largest selling single edition English language daily newspaper in India. The website of the newspaper was searched for news items related to biofuel (biofuel or biofuels or bio-fuel or bio-fuels or biodiesel or biodiesel). A total of 70 items were found relevant and were analysed.

SECTION 3

Methods and Tools

13

Self-discipline as a Regulatory Instrument for Environmental Governance (EG) and Gandhian Approach

Nimisha Shukla

The issue of Environmental Governance has become one of the greatly debated one, since the current economic thinking has not resolved it in a sustainable manner. The mainstream economics, i.e. neoclassical economics has been advocating market and thereby price system for efficient allocation of a resource. But in certain cases, especially in case of natural resources, market does not provide all the solutions to the issue of governance. The other approach is Institutional approach that emphasizes on the role of institutions for environmental governance. The limitations of these approaches have made a case for alternative approaches. The chapter tries to analyse the Gandhian approach as one such approach as an alternative to existing approaches to environmental governance leading towards sustainable development.

Environmental Governance

Environmental governance means rules, processes and behaviour that affect the way powers are exercised in the field of environmental policies, particularly as regards to openness, participation, accountability, effectiveness and coherence. The characteristics of EG can be summerized as under:

- Multilevel interactions among, but not limited to, state, market and civil society that interact with one another in formal or informal ways.

- Formulation and implementation of policies in response to environmental related demands and inputs in the society.
- Bounded by rules, procedures and widely accepted behaviour.
- Objective is to attain environmentally sustainable development.

What is the state of EG today? In spite of global environmental treaties, it is generally poor from local to national to international levels. The important factors responsible for not so good environmental governance are:

- Dealing with natural resources locally, i.e. decentralization of power has not become reality.
- Trans-boundary issues to manage ecosystem across national borders.
- Lack of transparency regarding environmental laws and regulations and half-hearted implementation.
- Failure in implementation of participatory approach in identifying and incorporating public opinion while developing environmental projects and policies.
- Lack of integration between environmental thinking in mainstream economic and development decisions regarding trade and finance.
- Ad hocism and lack of coordination in environmental agreements.
- Inadequate global environmental governance to face pollution and resource challenges.
- Fragmentation of responsibilities, funding, priorities, roles, actors, and geographic locales leads to responses that are less coherent, effective, and systematic than needed.

The issues regarding environment and its governance for sustainable development are as under:

- Preservation and Conservation of Environmental Resources
- Valuation of Environmental Damages
- Inclusion of Environmental Cost in Natural Resource Accounting
- Trade and Environment
- Climate Change
- Property Rights
- Degradation of Natural Resources

The current urgency of discussion on governance has its origin in the fact that our traditional institutions, i.e. market and state have kept pace neither with the changing world around us nor with the expectations of citizens. To design a system that is agile enough to address evolving needs and relevant enough to be viewed as legitimate in the eyes of the world's citizens, thoughtful analysis is necessary.

Economic Theories on Environmental Issues

The process of liberalization, privatization and globalization of the economies of different nations started in the last decade of the twentieth century. The neoclassical economics is centred on market and its transactions. The price mechanism is supreme and all activities are reduced in transaction form. If environmental and social activities fail to be reduced in the transaction form, which generally is the case, they are ignored in the market model.

Neoclassical economics has recognized this limitation of the market mechanism. The development of Environmental Economics was the result of this failure. Economic theories of environmental issues fall under the following categories:

Market Specific Issues

The neoclassical economic theory assumes perfectly competitive market, lack of transaction cost and well-defined property rights. In the real world, the competitive conditions vary and generally one finds the oligopolistic market structure. Neo-classical economists argue that since in oligopolistic market, the total production in the economy is less than in perfectly competitive market, natural resources would be saved. In reality, each firm would like to grab large market share that leads to overexploitation of natural resources.

Public Good Character

A pure public good is characterized by non-rivalry and non-excludability. The problem of Free Riding is common in such cases. Similar is the case for Common Property Resource. A resource is said to be in common domain if it possesses the characteristic of non-excludability. The Tragedy of Commons (Hardin, 1967) arises in case of such good.

Externality

The damage that occurs from negative externality will translate into efficiency loss and it misallocates resources. Since environmental economics, by internalizing externality, treats pollution as a bad and uses the existing framework for analysis, it once again fails to include all non-economic characteristics.

Market Failures

Market failure is a situation when market prices fail to reflect the true cost of a commodity or a service. In case of non-measurable benefits from environment like bequest or existence value or non-utilitarian benefits like aesthetic beauty, market does not give the right signal. In some cases, market does not even exist for the resource in question.

Environmental Governance in Neoclassical Economics

In neoclassical economics, environmental policy measures deal with the environment by analysing the threats of scarcity and pollution. The methods developed are: optimizing in case of natural resources and assigning property rights on pollution in order to incorporate them in price system and in decision process. The pure market solutions to environmental governance are price rationing and quantity rationing. "They affect costs and benefits of alternative actions open to economic agents, and thereby influence the behaviour of decision makers in such a way that the alternatives are chosen that lead to an environmentally more desirable situation than in the absence of the instrument" (Singh, 2009). In either case, it is assumed that through adjustments in market, the social optimum level of pollution can be achieved. There is a gradual tilt in favour of MBIs (Shankar, 2001). Tintenberg (1997) has also supported the economic incentive approach to achieve environmental goals more flexibly and at a lower cost than traditional regulatory approach.

- Environmental charges are widely used instrument for environment and natural resource policy. A pure environmental charge is Pigovian charge where the marginal social cost of pollution equals the marginal damage to pollution. Some of the examples are emission charges, fuel taxes and congestion charges.
- Tradable permits can be considered as the principle alternative to taxes as an efficient mechanism for pollution like individual transferable quotas in fisheries and tradable energy certificates for energy production.
- Under a deposit-refund scheme the purchaser of a product pays a deposit on the container or the product. The key feature to this approach is that it provides

an incentive for the consumer to return the waste and it has no negative budgetary impact on the public sector.

- Liability law requires someone who causes an injurious outcome to pay for the clean-up and to compensate those who were injured by the action. By forcing the party that caused the damage to bear all of the costs of that damage, liability law removes the externality and the biased decision making that results from it.
- Setting standards is another instrument to EG. It is also known as CAC policy where the authority decides ambient/emission/technology standards for pollution control and the firm failing to achieve is fined.

Neoclassical environmental economics aims at getting price rights, assuming that better information on external cost would lead to more efficient use of scarce environmental resources. It presents an upper limit on society's ability to solve the environmental problems by the strict coercion to enforce environmental regulations, as Hardin (1968) had suggested. Shankar (2001) has given a detailed description, preconditions and evaluation of the economic instruments. He has compared various instruments of governance. Instrument choice becomes an important issue especially in developing countries as political will is not strong enough to implement them which would be reflected in ineffectiveness of the instruments. Sterner (2003) has given an exhaustive outline in this regard. Keeping in view the welfare maximization perspective of neoclassical economics, choice has to be made among alternative policy measures. With the assumption of full information, any of the instruments could be used equally effectively to internalize the externality. In the absence of the assumption, the efficacy of the instruments differs.

Environmental Governance in Institutional Economics

The other school of thought in economics is the institutional thought. Environmental governance is best understood in institutional economics as the establishment, reaffirmation or change of institutions to resolve conflicts over environmental resources. It has been found that institutional measures to govern environment take long time to have the desirable impact. They can be termed as 'preventive measures' (Singh, 2009). It also explains that the choice of these institutions is a matter of social justice rather than of efficiency.

Institutions are defined as systems of rights, rules and decision-making processes.

According to the traditional institutional thought, the causes and consequences of prevalent economical structures are organizations, institutions, preferences, values, etc. Role played by institutions in causing and solving the problems arise from human-environment interactions can be reflected by the resource allocation decisions, division of labour and remunerations to the factors of production. The social and economic life needs to be understood within the ecological system. Ecological Economics deals with the two-way links between ecological and economic systems. The three roles played by environment for the economy are important to understand the resilience capacity of an ecosystem and also the tolerance of economy to ecological changes. The theory of co-evolution includes the natural and the societal worlds to evolve in synergy. It has been developed within ecological economics and founded on evolutionary economics that focuses on changes in history, society, ethics and technology and their impact on institutions over time. Among them, technological changes are very important as they influence the resource use significantly, hence economy-ecology relationship. In fact, all the systems are interrelated with each other.

Institutions influence social practice, assign role to the participants and govern interactions among them through property regimes. Environmental and resource regimes can be considered as special kind of regimes. Olson's Theory of Collective Action (1971) states that 'Unless the number of individuals in a group is quite small, or unless there is coercion or some other special devise to make individuals act in their common interest, rational, self-interested individuals will not act to achieve their common or group interests.' According to him, despite the free riding problem, voluntary groups can provide collective goods in a wide variety of areas including education, labour unions, and natural resources (Singh, 1994). The governance issue in Institutional Economics has explained by Ostrom in a detailed manner. According to Lyon (2006), Ostrom has laid down the foundation for a theory of environmental governance by combining theory, experiments and field research. The case of Common Property Resources like irrigation, fisheries and pastures is well discussed by her. The theoretical foundation is provided by the Game Theory where rules of the games are decided and observed by the group. The pessimism of Hardin in the Tragedy of the Commons is replaced by Ostrom's designing principles where she lays down a set of rules for a successful irrigation management. Her solution includes elements like bounded rationality, altruism and social capital. Communities have shown in the past and increasingly today that they can collaborate for long-term resource management. The term social capital captures the idea that social bonds and norms are critical for sustainability. Where social capital is high in formalized groups, people have the confidence to invest in collective activities, knowing that others will do so too. Successful governance, in Institutional Economics, needs a number of conditions to be satisfied. They are as follows. Information provision, conflict resolution, rule compliance, provision of infrastructure and readiness to accept the change. Young (1997) notes that a complete understanding of forms and functions of the local-level institutions is necessary to effectively implement the environmental governance policies because the compatibility of top-down and bottom-up institutional arrangements are necessary. Her designing principles can be summarized as clearly defined group boundaries; rules governing the use of collective goods to be matched to local needs and conditions; most individuals affected by these rules to participate in modifying the rules; right of community members to devise their own rules to be respected by external authorities; existence of a system for monitoring member's behaviour; graduated system of sanctions; access to low-cost conflict resolution mechanisms for Community members and multiple layers of nested enterprises (www.cooperationcommons.com/node/361, retrieved on 21/10/2010). Besides Ostrom's pioneering work in CPRs, a number of scholars have worked for CPR regimes like Jodha (1982, 1985, 1996), Bromley, Berkes, Gibbs (Berkes, 1989), Singh and Shishodia (2007) and Pastakia (2008).

Thus, the issue of environmental governance is handled differently by the neoclassical economists and the ecological economists. The difference between the two schools can be seen in terms of nature of sustainability. Neoclassical economists relate weak sustainability with purely economic growth and support constantly incremental economic growth measured in increasing Gross Domestic Product (GDP). However, increasing GDP does not necessarily mean increase in social welfare. Institutional economists, on the other hand, have accepted the importance of strong sustainability where stock of natural capital is to be maintained and kept intact over the years. The strong sustainability argument is concerned with inter and intra generational justice. By discarding the consumer sovereignty and individual rationality assumptions, it tries to internalize the environmental values into decision-making process of individual and firm, thereby examining the rise of environmental concern in society.

The neoclassical economists take the route of economic assessment and valuation of natural resources and the possible solutions to rationalize the human ecology interface. However, it fails to determine the critical minimum safe standards and the policies for its governance. Institutional economics finds the solution by change in institutions, social relations and understanding of natural system for which the approach needs development of necessary regulating instruments, judiciary and other institutions to transform human behaviour from anthropocentric to ecocentric, hence the issue of governance cannot be understood only in economic terms.

It should be interesting to note that the neoclassical solutions are more or less relaxed to the pollution issue. The institutional approach is more concerned with the management of natural resources. It tries to establish such institutions that can manage the scarce and degrading resource sustainably. Both the approaches seem to have concern for the poor and marginalized section of the society. The inter-generational equity argument of sustainable development supports the programme for poverty removal and livelihoods guarantee for disadvantaged section of the society. But in neither approach, individual behaviour is questioned. In this context, it is important to understand the behaviour of individual and its consequences on the environment and environmental governance.

Gandhian Approach to Environmental Governance

It is recognized by many scholars (Swinton and Roberto, 2003; Ravnborg, 2003) that since the rich tend to exploit the nature substantially, their actions have to be governed. The taste and preferences of a rich consumer will have to be reformed and limits to his wants will have to be introduced in the society in order to contain the perpetually increasing consumption of material goods and services. In this era of science and technology, the scope for luxury expansion is enormous. The normative issue of ethics is absent in this analysis. To curtail the consumption, tastes and preferences of the consumer need to be changed in such a manner that he not only limits his demand for material goods, but also limited goods in limited quantity and gets maximum satisfaction. The aspiration to reach the living standards of the rich of the developed nations by world population is an impossible task, as the world has a limited stock of natural resources. Does any alternative exist for sustainable development through individual demand regulation? The answer lies in disciplining an individual regarding his wants.

Gandhi had argued that the world has enough to satisfy everybody's need, but not for even one person's greed. Gandhi's approach to individual behaviour was based on the ethical premises. He thought and introduced the idea of regulating the human action by influencing human nature at the beginning of the development process itself. It should be interesting to understand the human nature in Gandhian thought. Gandhi's man is not economic, but is moral. The distinction between need and want is also important in Gandhian approach. The satisfaction of need is a necessary condition for a human being to be alive and to perform to her *dharma*, but it is not sufficient. These needs are very few and limited in range and number. They require categories of goods and not specific products. These needs are basic wants. The wants are not essential for human well-being and tend to change with time and are conspicuous in nature. The ultimate goal of man in Gandhian thought is quest for Truth that Gandhi called the God. His idea of human nature consists of 'need to perfect oneself through love and social action' (Lutz, 1985). The by-product of which would not be self-interest, but self-suffering and sacrifice. Gandhi believed that "Progress towards *Swaraj* will be in exact proportion to the increase in the number of workers who will dare to sacrifice their all for the cause of the poor" (ed. Kher, 1976). The two central pillars of Gandhian thought, viz., Truth and Ahimsa determine the nature of human. The truly rational human being would not be guided by the purely economic considerations, but by the conscience or inner voice. "He will not fill his house with unnecessary furniture and will use the minimum of clothes that are necessary" (Selected Works of Mahatma Gandhi, vol. 4, 1968, p. 459). This is the key to moral growth and self-actualization. He has said, "by economic progress, I mean material progress without limit and by real progress we mean moral progress, which again is the same thing as progress of the permanent element in us" (Collected Works, 2000, p. 274). Gandhi's idea of human nature has its origin in Ruskin's 'Unto This Last' that suggests that 'socially meaningful individual action cannot be deduced from utilitarian principles and balances of expediency, but by balance of justice' (Lutz, 1985).

Gandhian doctrine of non-possession also helps one to understand individual self-discipline. It was one of the key ekadash *Vrats* (eleven vows) that Gandhi had proposed for individual self-development. Possession implies provision for future. He says, 'God never stores for morrow'. "The rich have superfluous store of things which they do not need, which are therefore neglected and wasted; while millions are starved to death for want of sustenance" (Gandhi, 2005). He has also written, 'this principle is really a part of non-stealing. Just as one does not deceive, so one must not possess anything which one does not really need. … In observing this principle, one is led to progressive simplification of one's life" (as quoted in Haq, 1995). This positive doctrine implies that individual should limit her needs and spend the rest for the welfare of others. Sethi (1978) puts it as "Gandhi's call for cutting down demands and his principle of non-possession were designed both to crest a quick rate of growth and full-employment, less on the basis of individual profit incentives and more on the basis of joint efforts and community advantage". Gandhi had suggested a consumption pattern and behaviour for the affording classes that was to be moderated by ascetic and paternalistic values. Raval (1971) has termed this as the 'Gandhi Effect'.

Gandhi's concern about the type of economic development model that would lead to sustainable development was thus relevant then and relevant now. Gandhi had anticipated the consequences of western type of industrialization even in the 1930s when the population was around 350 million. In the September 14, 1934 issue of *Harijan* he wrote, "we can never industrialize India, unless of course, we reduce our population from 350 million to 35 million or hit upon markets wider than our own and dependent on us." The Gandhian model would result into reduction in income and wealth disparities in desirably non-violent manner. In this model, non-possession and non-stealing play an important role. Diwan (1995) defines non-possession as possession by all. It also implies voluntary poverty that can be achieved by institutional arrangements. It is based on the principle of equality, i.e. exploitationless non-violent sustainable society. The high rate of savings, resulting from limited consumption, would translate into high investment and high output. With limits to private wants, public consumption would increase. Ultimately, it would create a society where there is 'private poverty and public affluence'. Diwan and Gidwani make several points of distinction between neoclassical concept of consumption and Gandhian concept. The neoclassical basic propositions are limited resources and insatiable wants; maximization of utility as ultimate goal; budget constrained consumption; independent individual utility functions; waste of resources and only economic considerations acting as deterrent for individual growth. Gandhian moral human being refutes all these propositions. For Gandhi, resources are adequate to satisfy basic needs of all; satisfaction of needs as the basic objective; need-centred consumption; interdependent individual utility functions and relative independent and self-sufficient economy to lead to better individual growth.

Dasgupta (1996) has introduced ethical preference to explain the Gandhian concept of Imitating Wants. It is individual preference that is "modified by reflection, corrected by knowledge and experience and regulated by ethical principle". Multiplying daily wants makes an individual 'erosive of contentment, personal autonomy, self-respect and peace of mind'. For Gandhi, contentment was happiness. It should be very clear at this point that Gandhi was never in favour of a poor to be content by his poverty. He emphasized on every human being's right to live. In Young India, he wrote "every one must have balanced diet, decent house to live in, facilities for education of one's children and adequate relief."

The road to self-discipline goes via Gandhi. Gandhi had shown a way for individual welfare maximization by changing the very definition of welfare. Self-regulation is both incentive in form of self-improvement and punishment against greed and having more and more by creating externality. It would also address the issue of efficiency and intra generational equity. Gandhi believed that as man does not have control over the future consequences of his actions, he should control his present actions (Iyengar, 2008). Hence, he was in favour of determining a set of feasible actions rather than analysing and trying to predict about the consequences that were uncertain and perhaps often unpredictable. He rediscovered and devised a set of individual action that he called *yam-niyam.* Yam-niyam, in Indian culture, is a set of rules that an individual should pursue for the betterment of present life and *moksha* (salvation). Gandhi renames them as *Ekadash Vrats*, i.e. eleven vows. They are truth, non-violence, chastity, control of the palate, non-stealing, non-possession, fearlessness, removal of untouchability, bread labour, respect to all religions and swadeshi. These vows regulate individual behaviour, making her self-disciplined and thereby helping immensely in individual self-improvement. If one thinks them in the context of environmental governance, they help in limiting individual desire for using more and more goods and services, thereby restricting the demand for consumption and saving the scarce natural resources. It should be interesting to understand that a self-disciplined individual in a society would lead to sustainable development path more effectively than the society imposing discipline on the individuals. Similar to mainstream economics, Gandhian economic thought also places individual to the centre stage, but the difference is fundamental. The Gandhian individual would, by her voluntary actions, lead to a better environmental governance than the coercive powers used by any institution.

The production side in Gandhian approach is equally important. Gandhi believes not in mass production but production by masses. He advocated and promoted the decentralized production system. Gandhiji had visualized the tendency of Western civilization that made economic transactions complicated and then used technology to simplify them. In 'Hind Swaraj', he had made the mention of this tendency and expressed his strong rejection of such a civilization. He believed that the village level self-sufficiency could be achieved by providing maximum opportunities to simple techniques of production at the local level. His preference for simple system in place of complicated system is expressed in his views regarding excessive the use of machine that displaces labour. His Swadeshi argument, in this context, is: "A Votary of Swadeshi will carefully study his environment, and try to help his neighbour wherever possible, by giving preference to local manufacturers, even if they are of an inferior grade or dearer in price than things manufactured elsewhere. It is sinful for me to eat American wheat and let my neighbour, the grain dealer, starve for want of customers." His emphasis on Khadi and other cottage industries follows the same line of argument. Decentralised production is preferred not only because it generates opportunities of employment and provides livelihood support to masses, but also as it generates less externality in terms of non-economic costs. The production process is less resource-energy intensive and creates less waste than the modern mechanized production process. In other words, it is non-violent, non-exploitative system of production. For a labour surplus country like India, Gandhian decentralization production process seems more relevant and sustainable.

The other Gandhian concept related to production side is of Trusteeship. In agriculture, indigenous system of natural resource management with traditions and techniques was recognized by Gandhi, and Vinoba implemented it through Bhoodan and Gramdan movements. These movements aimed to establish that the land was to be managed mainly in common property regime where privatization for access, use and development was to be allowed with commonly agreed restrictions. They were "so original in its conception, so novel in methods, and so revolutionary as to its objectives that special efforts has to be made to understand it and to place it into proper perspective" (Gadgil as quoted by Joshi, 1975, p. 89). As against, Green Revolution Technology (GRT), with intensive use of agro-mechanical and biochemical technologies, was successful in increasing production of certain crops in specific areas, but it had also resulted into serious environmental problems and in some places irreversible damage to the ecology. The introduction of Genetically Modified (GM) technology is not without dangers. The increase in number of farmers' suicide is the phenomenon observed in the last few years. Nearly

70 per cent in rural areas still rely on agriculture and other land-based activities for their survival and development. The Bhoodan/Gramdan approach would develop people's institutions and redefine property rights to manage land resource in villages. Hence, it is relevant even today.

In the industrial sector, trusteeship is reflected in the payment made to labour. Gandhi prescribed labour intensive technology with respectable wage rate to labour by which he/she can have a decent standard of living. The trustee would keep in mind not the marginal product of labour alone, but the societal marginal product which would be inherently higher than the former. The positive externality generated in the process would be beneficial to the society as a whole. The approach was reflected during the mill labourers' strike at Ahmedabad during 1918. In the environmental context, it would not produce environmental bads, but would be sustainable in nature.

Among Gandhian successors like J.C. Kumarappa, Narahari Parikh and Kishorlal Mashruwala, J.C. Kumarappa has been the most prominent speaker as far as environment is concerned. Although, environmental issues were not so serious as they are today, he wrote 'Economy of Permanence' (reprint-2007) where he talked about five kinds of society: Parasitic Society that destroys the source of its benefit (robber murdering a child for ornaments), Predatory Society that reflects benefit without contribution (pickpocket), Society of Enterprise where benefit and contribution are correlated with a readiness to take risk (agriculturist), Society of Gregation where benefit accrues to the group rather than an individual (member of local council) and Society of Service where contribution is made without any regard to any benefit received by the worker (relief worker). Individual following Gandhian principles would definitely belong to the Society of Service.

If one examines the environmental issues faced by India; the solution may lie in Gandhian approach. The approach inherently includes the governance aspect. Decentralised production system with critical minimum assistance from machine (capital) would generate less externality and less wastage. A Swadeshi minded individual with control over wants would not demand more than justified and would save the natural resources and energy in the world. The lifestyle of an individual following *ekadash vrats* would be sustainable from the societal point of view. A self-disciplined individual behaviour is the key to betterment of society and environment. It creates conducive social environment for effective environmental governance. A non-violent society where non-possession and non-stealing exist along with voluntary poverty and practise over palate would be a sustainable society. Environmental governance is all about influencing individual behaviour in a predictable manner so that the society could achieve sustainable development. It tries to control individual actions so that the consequences and outcomes of these actions can also be controlled. Gandhi, by his *ekadash vrats*, had prescribed to control individual action. In other words, he wanted to change the lifestyle of individual. As Iyengar (2004) has rightly put it "It is in this context that lifestyle will have to be necessarily brought on the agenda of sustainable development debate." There is a need to address this issue in new light and the Gandhian approach may be one of the sustainable solutions.

References

[1] Beckerman, W., 1998. "Economic Growth and the Environment: Whose Growth? Whose Environment?" *World Development*, Vol. 20, No. 1.

[2] Berkes, Fikret, 1989. "*Common Property Resources: Ecology and Community-based Sustainable Development*", Belhaven Press.

[3] Boulding, K., 1992. "The Economics of Coming Spaceship Earth", in Markandeya Anil and Richardson Julie (eds.), *The Earthscan Reader in Environmental Economics,* Earthscan Publications Ltd., London.

[4] Coase, R., 1960. 'The Problem of Social Cost', *Journal of Law and Economics*, 3.

[5] Dasgupta, Ajit K., 1996. *Gandhi's Economic Thought*, Routledge, London.

[6] Diwan, Romesh and Lutz Mark (eds.), 1985. *Essays in Gandhian Economics*, Gandhi Peace Foundation, New Delhi.

[7] Diwan, Romesh and Sushila Gidwani, 1985. "Elements in Gandhian Economics", in Diwan, Romesh and Lutz Mark (eds.), *Essays in Gandhian Economics*, Gandhi Peace Foundation, New Delhi.

[8] Gandhi, M.K., 1976. *Social Service, Work and Reform*, (ed.) V.B. Kher, Navjivan Publishing House, Ahmedabad.

[9] Gandhi, M.K., 2005. Reprint 'From Yervada Mandir', Translated from original Gujarati '*Mangal Prabhat*' by Valji Govindji Desai. Navjivan Publishing House, Ahmadabad, November.

[10] Huq, A.M., 1985. "The Doctrine of International Trade: A Gandhian Perspective", in Diwan Romesh and Lutz Mark (eds.), *Essays in Gandhian Economics*, Gandhi Peace Foundation, New Delhi.

[11] Hardin, G., 1968. 'The Tragedy of Commons", *Science*, 162.

[12] Iyengar, Sudarshan, 2008. "Gandhi's Economic Thought and Modern Economic Development: Some Reflections", R.S. Bhatt Memorial Lecture, Bhavnagar University, Bhavnagar.

[13] Iyengar, Sudarshan, 2004. "Sustainable Development and Indian Economy: Some Reflections", E.F. Schumacher Memorial Lecture delivered at the Nagpur University on February 5, 2005.

[14] Jodha, N.S., 1996. "Property Rights and Development', in Susan S. Hanna, Carl Folke and Karl-Goran Maler (eds), *Rights to Nature*, Island Press, Washington D.C.

[15] Jodha, N.S., 1985. "Market Forces and Erosion of Common Property Resources" in Agriculture Markets in Semi-Arid Tropics, Proceedings of an International Workshop, October 24–28, 1983, *International Crop Research Institute for Semi-Arid Tropics*, Patancheru, Andhra Pradesh.

[16] Jodha, N.S., 1882. "The Role of Administration in Desertification: Land Tenure as a Factor in Historical Ecology of Western Rajasthan" in Brian Spooner and H.S.. Mann (eds), *Diversification in Development: Dry land Ecology and Social Perspective*, Academic press, London.

[17] Joshi, P.C., 1975. *Land Reforms in India: Trends and Perspectives*, Institute of Economic Growth, Delhi.

[18] Kumarappa, J.C, 2007 (reprint). *Economy of Permanence*. Magan Sangrahalaya Samiti, Wardha, Maharashtra.

[19] Lyon, Thomas, 2006. Environmental Governance: An Economic Perspective. Working paper. University of Michigan.

[20] Olson, Mancur, 1971. "*The Logic of Collective Action: Public Goods and the Theory of Groups*", Harvard University Press.

[21] Ostrom, Ellinor, 1990. "*Governing the Commons: The Evolution of Institutions for Collective Action*", Cambridge University Press.

[22] Paalova, Jouni and W. Neil Adger, 2006. "New Institutional Economics and the Environment: Conceptual Foundations and Policy Implications", Working Paper EDM 02-06. Centre for Social and Economic Research on Global Environment, University of East Anglia, UK.

[23] Pastakia, Astad, 2008. *Locked Horns: Conflicts and their Resolutions in Community based Natural Resource Management*, Books for Change, Karnataka.

[24] Pigou, A. C., 1932. *The Economics of Welfare*. MacMillan, London.

[25] Raval, M.N., 1971. "Contentment and Containment of Wants – A Suggested

Interpretation", in Raval M.N. et.al. (eds), *Gandhiji's Economic Thought and its Relevance at Present*, South Gujarat University, Surat.

[26] Ravnborg Helle Munk, 2003. "Poverty and Environmental Degradation in the Nicaraguan Hillsides", in *World Development*, Vol. 31, No. 11, pp. 1933–1946.

[27] Sankar, Ulaganathan (ed.), 2001. *Environmental Economics: Reader in Economics*. Oxford University Press, New Delhi.

[28] Sethi, J.D., 1978. *Gandhi Today*, Vikas Publishing House Pvt. Ltd., New Delhi.

[29] Singh, Katar, 1994. *Managing Common Pool Resources: Principles and Case Studies*, Oxford University Press, India.

[30] Singh, Katar, 2009. "Environmental Degradation and Measures for its Mitigation", *Indian Journal of Agricultural Economics*, Vol. 64, No. 1 (January-March 2009).

[31] Singh, Katar and and Anil Shishodia, 2007. *Environmental Economics: Theory and Applications*, Sage Publications Private Limited, New Delhi.

[32] Sterner, Thomas, 2003. *Policy Instruments for Environmental and Natural Resource management*, The World Bank, Washington, DC, USA.

[33] Swinton Scott M. and Quiroz Roberto, 2003. "Is Poverty to Blame for Soil, Pasture and Forest Degradation in Peru's Altiplano", in *World Development*, Vol. 31, No. 11, pp. 1903–19.

[34] Tintenberg, T.H., 1997. 'Economic Instruments for Environmental Regulation' in Anil Markandeya and Richardson Julie (eds), 1992. *The Earthscan Reader in Environmental Economics*, Earthscan Publications Ltd., London.

[35] Young, O.R. and Others, 2008. *Institutions and Environmental Change*, MIT Press, Cambridge, London.

14

Forest Certification: A Voluntary Instrument for Environmental Governance

Karin Kaechele, Peter May, Eeva Primmer and Grit Ludwig

Certification of Forestry Practice

Conformity of Production Practices with Certification Criteria

Certification is a procedure by which a third party gives written assurance that a product, process or service conforms with certain standards. It is also a guarantee of origin that is used to orient the consumer in product choice, with some form of added value, usually derived from environmental integrity and/or social fairness. Often, certification schemes are considered non-state and market driven but typically they involve public sector actors and assume conformance with state regulation. The degree to which certification reflects autonomy and external verification varies. According to Conroy (2007), certification processes may be classified into three distinct stages, characterizing different degrees of autonomy in verification and monitoring:

(i) Codes of conduct or declarations of good intentions adopted unilaterally on the part of companies, known as "*First party certification*". These have the advantage to call attention to the consumer regarding the form of production (socio-environmental footprint of the purchase), and not only what is being produced (price, quality). However, these instruments carry the risk of being used inappropriately as certificates or testaments of sustainability simply to avert criticism. Due to their unilateral character, these instruments offer limited credibility on their own and are mere expressions of the adopting organizations' willingness to enter a market and compete on the grounds of social acceptability and environmental integrity.

(ii) Initiatives of business groups and associations in an activity adopting defined labels and certificates. This type of initiative has been called "Second party certification" since it includes the intervention of another actor, an association, besides the company itself. The certification schemes advocated by some states and groups of states can be considered to fall under this category, as the state is somewhat external to the certified producing companies (Cashore, 2005). It similarly allows the consumer to focus attention on aspects of production or on how internal corporate operations are conducted. Because they are verified by an actor external to the company, these certifications have a bit more credibility, but this depends on the credibility of the independence of the external actor with respect to the specific company under review.

(iii) "Multi-stakeholder" initiatives, also called "Third party certification" are inspired by the "stakeholders" theory enunciated by Freeman (1984).[1] An important characteristic in this approach is that the "third party" is a non-state private regulator (Cashore, 2005). This approach seeks to manage social and environmental responsibility in response to concerns expressed by numerous interested or associated parties. It assumes that the company needs to invest in engagement with its "stakeholders" not only for ethical reasons but also to access and maintain a position in the market, achieve and maintain reputation and improve competitiveness. From this perspective, a company worthy of a certificate is one that is attentive to its stakeholders' concerns. Thus, this third category of certification instruments presents a completely different way of dealing with environmental responsibility, in which dialogue and interactions with and among stakeholders are of paramount importance. Certification thus challenges the traditional state-centred idea of regulation, as it shifts control and power from the public sector to the auditing third party and to final consumers. In doing so, it establishes a basis for consumer confidence, expressed in legitimation of third-party labeling.

Initiatives Toward Forest Certification Around the World

The movement in favour of forest certification began at the end of the 1980s, with commercial boycotts by consumers in Northern countries against logging of tropical timbers originating from deforestation. In this context, European and North American tropical wood consumers, concerned with their long-term business prospects formed an alliance for protection of tropical forests – the *Woodworker's Alliance for Rainforest Protection* (WARP), and published a "Good Wood List" in an effort to protect wood suppliers derived from "good management". In 1993, representatives of NGOs, suppliers and buyers of wood met in Toronto, initiating a process that led to the creation of the "Forest Stewardship Council" (FSC). In response to the lack of criteria to define what constituted good forest management practice, three international chambers, representing commercial, social and environmental concerns instituted 10 principles and a rigorous body of subsidiary norms (Azevedo-Ramos et al., 2006).

The FSC gained popularity also among northern timber producing and processing actors and states, partly spurred by the general trend of searching for forms of governance alternative to state control in both North America and Europe (Rametsteiner and Simula, 2003; Cashore, 2003). In some cases, the evolution of the FSC stimulated fierce dialogue between different forestry regimes and sustainability standard controlling systems, with forest industries and timber producers dominantly favouring national certification schemes at the outset (Cashore, 2003). With further legitimacy pressure from markets and environmental NGOs, many northern timber processing and consuming countries dependent on international markets eventually also adopted the FSC system (Cashore, 2003; Gulbrandsen, 2004). In countries such as the USA, Finland and Norway, where landownership was predominantly small-scale and the forest sector was relatively powerful, the national certification systems maintained their position of dominance over the FSC.

The European national forest certification schemes are grouped under the Pan-European Forest Certification (PEFC) scheme, which functions as a rather open umbrella, but which is internationally powerful due to its large geographical coverage. Clearly, throughout the disputes, the FSC has remained popular among environmental NGOs, and has continued to attract companies and regimes that are most sensitive to market and social legitimacy pressures.

Internationally, voluntary forest certification has evolved since its inception in the 1980s, and now embraces a range of systems in operation which are in competition. Among these, the principal labels include:

- **Forest Stewardship Council** – FSC, is an international non-governmental organization, founded in 1993, which accredits certifiers throughout the world, guaranteeing the certified parties obey strict quality norms. Certifiers undertake a methodology based on the FSC Principles and Criteria (P&C; see listing in Annex), adapting themselves to the reality of each region or production system. The FSC has decentralized into a number of national or regional initiatives, which have developed their own respective P&C, adapted to local technical conditions, forest resources and legal context.
- **Programme for the Endorsement of Forest Certification Schemes – PEFC** (originally Pan European Forest Certification). The PEFC Council was created in June 1999, also of voluntary nature, based on its own criteria defined in the Helsinki and Lisbon Conferences of 1993 and 1998, respectively, on European Forest Protection. A primordial objective of this system is the recognition of different systems operating in the European Community. However, PEFC schemes embrace those adopted in other regions as well. For example, the Brazilian Cerflor system (see below) has received provisional recognition by PEFC.
- **A Range of Diverse National Systems** (Sweden, Finland, Norway, Germany, the UK, United States, Canada, South Africa, Indonesia, Malaysia, New Zealand, Chile, Austria, Ghana, Belgium and others).
- In Brazil, the **Cerflor** system – the Brazilian Programme for Forest Certification, was conceived by the Brazilian Silvicultural Society (SBS) in 1996, though it only began to operate nearly a decade later. Cerflor was created in partnership with sectoral associations, research and training institutions, NGOs and with the support of several government agencies, including the national standards institute. It differs from the Brazilian FSC standard in some respects, having somewhat more relaxed criteria for social concerns. However, Cerflor enjoys considerable credibility in part due to its PEFC recognition.

According to Purbawiyatna & Simula (2008: 10) "almost two-thirds (65%) of the world's certified forests (in 22 countries) carry a PEFC certificate, while the FSC's share is 28 per cent (in 78 countries); the remaining forests are certified solely under national systems. Most of the certified forests in the tropics are FSC-certified." The FSC had more than triple the number of products under chain-of-custody certification in 2007 as compared to PEFC certifiers.

Approximately, eight per cent of the global forest area has been certified under a variety of schemes (FAO, 2010) cited in ETFRN (2010). One recent estimate suggests that approximately one quarter of global industrial round wood now comes from certified forests. Most of these advances have occurred outside the tropics: less than two per cent of the forest area in African, Asian and tropical American forests are certified. Most certified forests (82%) are large and managed by the private sector (ETFRN, 2010).

The Forest Certification Process

Certification is a voluntary process through which a forestry enterprise is evaluated by an independent organization – the certifier – permitting that the firm's compliance with environmental, economic and social concerns is verified in accordance with the P&C of the particular certification system being applied.

The process can be broken down into its principal stages:

- **Initial contact** – The forestry operation enters into contact with the certifier.
- **Evaluation** – A general analysis of management, documentation and field appraisal. Its objective is to prepare the operation to receive certification. In this phase, public consultations may be arranged, so as to obtain feedback from stakeholders.
- **Adaptation** – After evaluation, the forestry operation should adapt non-conforming practices if these appear.
- **Certification of operation** – The forestry operation receives the certification. In this stage, the certifier prepares and makes available a public summary.
- **Annual monitoring** – After certification, the operation is monitored at least once each year to maintain the certification.

Actors Involved in Forest Certification Processes

Usually, the actors involved in certification processes represent timber producers, civil society organizations, researchers, industries and, to varying degrees and with varying roles, also government authorities. When there is a community forest management plan, the local government is involved. The graph below shows how the actors are distributed within two distinct types of forest certification applied in Brazil: FSC and Cerflor. In general, the objective of the group is to develop P&C that fit each region for native forest management or forest plantations. Public consultation and the involvement of local communities are also part of the process of certification.

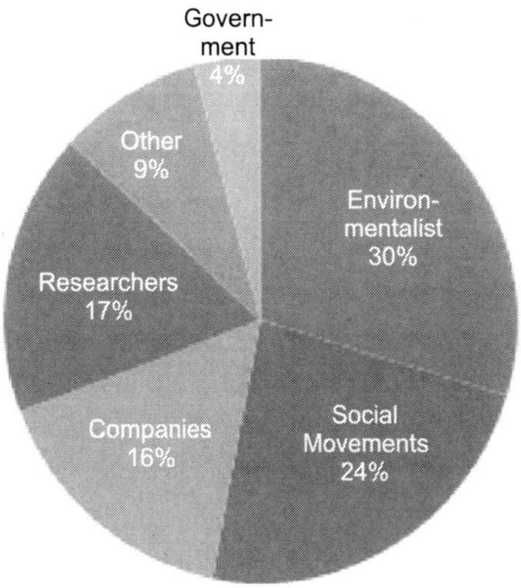

Fig. 1: Actors Involved in FSC Certification

Source: Adapted from Greenpeace (2002).

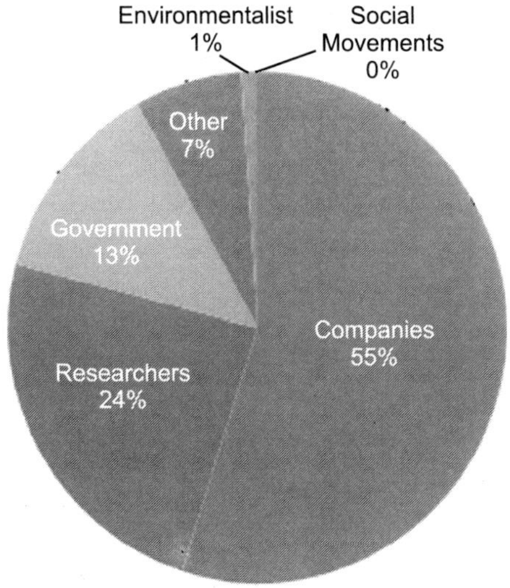

Fig. 2: Actors Involved in Cerflor Certification

Source: Adapted from Greenpeace (2002).

As is clear from the graph presented, the FSC process seeks to attain a balanced representation among social actors, with the exception of government, while CERFLOR is heavily weighted toward corporate actors, researchers and government, with little or no representation of environmental or social civil society organizations. This pattern has been found to be typical in comparative research across many regimes where FSC competes with local schemes (Cashore, 2005).

Baseline

The certification process is generally progressive. The forest enterprises at first meet basic requirements and over time, improve performances based on the auditor's recommendations.

Certification is also an adaptive and gradual process that permits certain flexibility of rules and criteria. As an example, FSC cites its adoption of the SLIMF (Small and Low Intensity Managed Forests) procedures for progressive adaptation to general P&C. The simplified SLIMF audit procedures can be used in enterprises, such as communities, small farmers and businesses that manage small areas or low intensity forests. It can also be applied to non-timber forest enterprises, provided they are not based on plantations. Using the SLIMF method, the audit process simplification reduces costs and time needed for evaluation. In this type of technical evaluation, although the same FSC standards and rules are applied, the simplification in the process enables small producers to participate in certification appropriate to their scale and special needs.

Monitoring, Reporting and Verification (MRV)

Verification is a key tool of socio-environmental responsibility initiatives; verification involves checking compliance of procedures with criteria. It covers inspections and tests performed at different points of the production chain or on the whole process.

The strictness of the verification phase ensures credibility of the initiative; the agency in charge of this should be independent with no financial and corporate ties to the initiative. Thus, the agency's independence ensures autonomy and impartiality of the verification process.

The transparency of verification is crucial. The information available should include: the methodology used, the points checked as well as the positive and negative results of implementation procedures and criteria.

Finally, a socially responsible verification should feature a conflict resolution mechanism that makes it possible for the players, regardless of whether or not they participate in the initiative, to denounce actions not complying with their commitment.

Performance of Certification in Environmental Governance

Effectiveness for Biodiversity Conservation and the Provision of Ecosystem Service

Forest certification should assure that the timber used in a given product originates from forests managed and processed in accordance with sustainability principles in a fashion that is simultaneously ecologically sound, socially just and economically viable. Additionally, conformance with standing legal codes is a universal certification requirement. In this way, certification entails both public and private regulation characteristics (Potoski, 2004; Cashore, 2005).

Effectiveness in forest certification refers to the amount of native forest that is managed and not clearcut or the proportion of forest managed according to sustainability criteria, but also refers to how local actors are engaged in the forest management enterprise.

Some authors (Gullison, 2003; Price, 2003; Brotto, 2010; Imaflora, 2009) agree that certification has helped to improve management practices and to conserve forest biodiversity within certified forests in the tropics as well as in other regions where state governance of forest management has faced challenges (Rametsteiner and Simula, 2003; Cashore, 2005; Keskitalo, 2009). However, the true extent of conservation benefits remains unknown due to a lack of rigorous and independent information. Many agree that certification is not equivalent to full conservation and point at the limitations of certification in reducing deforestation rates. Some examples of biodiversity assessment on forest certification are described below:

In 2009, Imaflora, the Institute for Forest and Agricultural Management and Certification, a SmartWood certifier based in Brazil conducted a study of the impact of FSC in a planted forest in southern Brazil and an extractive community in Acre, which revealed that FSC Forest certification resulted in positive impacts regarding the environmental aspects assessed, such as natural resource conservation, forest management, and its contribution towards the conservation of flora and fauna and the water resources of natural ecological systems.

In its evaluation in Acre extractive communities where forest management is performed, positive impacts were found to have resulted from FSC certification actions. The survey found that the use of fire for clearing planted areas is a common practice in all Extractive Settlements areas studied. However, the findings indicated that slash and burn clearing is less harmful in the certified communities than in the non-certified ones due to the forest care requirements of the certification method. Hunting is widespread both in certified and non-certified areas however, with respect to the care taken during this practice, the survey found a significant difference between the certified and non-certified groups: of the certified areas, 87 per cent reported the use of measures for protecting wild animals, compared with only 44 per cent of the non-certified groups. The measures cited by the certified communities were hunting only when food is needed and using no dogs in hunting. Beyond these measures, they also reported the use of some others, such as hunting season calendars, not killing animals, nursing their young and preserving trees that provide food for such animals (Imaflora, 2008).

When analyzing planted forests in southern Brazil, natural resource conservation was assessed by the following actions of the enterprises sampled: environmental licensing, legal reserve[2] registration, control of invasive species in Permanent Protection Areas (APP), reforestation with native species and studies of fauna and flora. Furthermore, Imaflora investigated signs of forest conversion in the enterprise (replacement of forest fragments for agricultural, livestock, forestry, etc.) and the proportion of native forest remaining on the property. Impacts of FSC certification on natural resource conservation in the enterprise studies were evident. The certified enterprises control weeds in APP, initiate and maintain fauna and flora studies and do not carry out any forest conversion aside from that necessary to observe effects in a control site.

Due to the constant changes in legislation, the certified enterprises presented mechanisms for monitoring the environmental legislation and securing or being in the process of obtaining environmental licenses and legal reserve registrations. Imaflora also examined evidence of riparian forest uses in APPs, as well as care in the forest management in the surrounding areas. According to the enterprise representative's testimony, there was certification impact on the different treatment given to the management of the areas close to APPs: sensitive natural area delineation, pre- and post-harvest evaluation in the buffer areas, targeting the harvest, and identification of trees for bird conservation.

The impact generated by the certification actions in extractive communities is low (Imaflora, 2008; Imaflora, 2009; TEEBa, 2010). However, there is little quantitative evidence regarding the long-term impacts of certification on biodiversity and the environment. FSC certification positively impacts forest planning and inventorying, silviculture, biodiversity protection, and monitoring and compliance.

In a recent publication organized by ETFRN (2010), biodiversity benefits from forest certification are explored. Below some examples are cited from this recent survey.

Price (2010) describes research conducted in Bolivia and in the Brazilian Atlantic forest evaluating the impact of certification on those forests. Price concluded that the rate of forest loss in the FSC-certified forests was lower than that observed in some of the country's national protected areas. He pointed out that one reason for this is that FSC standards require compliance with legislation. This compliance, along with the remaining rigorous requirements of the FSC standards are more effective in conserving these native ecosystem remnants than the delimitation of protected area status, since often such delimitation only creates 'paper parks'.

Brotto (2010) assessed certification's effectiveness on biodiversity conservation in the Peruvian Amazon, and the economic results arising from such certification. A relationship is drawn between certification and pressures for conversion of native forest into pasture or agriculture land. Since such pressures are high, the opportunity cost to maintain a forest is also high, while the cost for certification is double than that of the opportunity cost of retiring land from agriculture. The authors conclude that where a REDD+ project is associated with forest certification, the impact on biodiversity conservation was higher because landowners received a premium on their products.

Gullison (2003), in assessing the overall international experience with FSC considers that certification can contribute to biodiversity conservation, but that the incentives offered by certification are insufficient to prevent deforestation, and the volume of certified forest products currently on the market is too small to significantly reduce logging pressure on High Conservation Value Forest (HCVF). He adds that FSC made great contributions to protection of native forests in temperate countries but in tropical forests, very little progress has been made. He concludes stating that industrial logging can produce direct benefits such as avoiding deforestation or improving the value of managed forests, and also indirect effects such as providing alternative timber supplies to those from HCVF.

Economic and Social Impacts

In general, the most beneficial impacts found with regard to forest certification were economic and social in character, while the most negative refer to certification cost. Although global demand is growing for certified tropical timbers and other forest products, the intensity of investment, continued difficulties in licensing and transport, unclear land tenure as well as conflict with competing land uses at the frontier, imply that the overall effect of certification has not been to dramatically enhance sustainability at a sectoral level, especially in the Brazilian Amazon. Nevertheless, embarking on a certification strategy in most cases can consolidate the bargaining position of certified timber enterprises with their buyers, as well as providing potential economic advantages (May, 2005).

In general, forest management activities are costly in terms of financial and operational aspects and require those involved in the extraction sites to have high technical capacity in terms of forest inventory, cutting techniques, harvesting and skidding. For this reason, community forest management often must rely on external agencies and the effectiveness of forest management is limited. The cost of FSC certification is seen as exorbitant (50,000–150,000 USD depending on enterprise scale), which is especially problematic in developing economies (Schepers, 2010). In general, certification can place insurmountable requirements and costs on communities and small-scale actors, and therefore increases the relative power of large-scale operators (Klooster, 2005). With regard to the direct costs that result from forest management certification, there is evidence that certification in the tropics is more costly than in temperate or boreal forests for two reasons: First, non-tropical forests are less complex and thus require lower auditing time and preparation, and second, temperate and boreal forests often already have some well-established management procedures in place. Consequently, raising management standards to the required level is less costly. Investors from industrialized countries are usually accustomed to a dense and strict regulatory environment and hence it may be easier for them to comply with rigorous certification criteria (Pattberg, 2005). Considerable cost differences for certification between developed and developing countries have been identified by Gullison (2003): certification costs for large forestry companies in the United States or Poland stand at US$ 0.02 to 0.03 per cubic meter, compared to US$ 0.26 to 1.10 in tropical countries and over US$ 4.00 for small-scale producers in Latin America. With only 6-8 per cent of global timber production entering international trade and environmentally sensitive markets only existing in Europe and North America, producers from developing countries have significantly less access to premium markets. As a consequence, timber imports from industrial countries increasingly originate from industrialized countries (Chan, 2008; Pattberg, 2005). In sum, certification tends to have the effect of systematically privileging northern companies in contrast to small-scale forest managers in developing countries and emerging economies.

In FSC certification, most of the time, there is no premium or final price differentiation upon timber sales, but it is observable that certified timber is more easily accepted by the market. In some cases, there is a premium, for instance, in the case of FSC certification in communities in Tanzania, where certification enables the communities to earn more than US$ 19 per log, compared to a previous US$ 0.08 (FSC 2010). Central to the Tanzanian project's success is consumer demand for sustainably harvested timber (particularly in the international market), an important driver for future community wood production in the country.

Other surveys of changes encountered in certified areas have concentrated on the economic aspects of national markets, such as studies focused on Bolivia, Malaysia and the USA. On the whole, in such countries, certification has promoted better access to the market and higher prices, especially for the most processed hardwoods (Kollert and Lagan, 2006; Newsom et al., 2006; Nebel et al., 2005).

In the northern hemisphere, the FSC is perceived as more ambitious in terms of environmental and social requirements than the national or supplier driven certification systems (Rametsteiner, 2003; Gulbrandsen, 2004; Cashore, 2005; Keskitalo et al., 2009). The pressure for developing more ecologically integrative and socially sensitive practices is more explicit in the more externally and internationally audited FSC system. In countries like Russia, requirements for conservation are significantly higher and more explicit in the FSC, whereas in the Nordic countries and the USA, the conflict between the FSC and other systems centres more on who has authority than the level of conservation.

In general, the most positive aspects found were economic and social, while the most negative refer to the certification process and its cost.

Institutional Context and Requirements

It was observed that some institutions influence the success of certification in terms of biodiversity conservation both in the national and international certification systems. Two categories can be mentioned: (a) formal institutional requirements; (b) cultural and social requirements. The following formal requirements support certification:

- effective formal institutional infrastructure and forest legislation;
- effective laws on property or land rights;
- institutional framework or governing structure that permits the distribution of benefits in case of community involvement;
- verification for certifying timber quantity and certification of local impact and, if possible, biodiversity conservation analysis.

Case studies have shown that forest certification has been most successful in states which have a conducive forest governance framework which guarantees the enforcement of forest laws; and provide land tenure security (Ebeling, 2009), (Gueneau, 2008). Therefore, it was found that at present, there are few developing countries where forest certification is likely to achieve widespread success (Ebeling, 2009). Actually, this may be one reason for the fact, that currently 87.75 per cent of FSC-certified forests are situated in the temperate and boreal zone and only 12.75 per cent in the tropics and subtropics (FSC, 2010). Tropical countries often lack the infrastructure to facilitate certification and without the assistance of states, incentives to join a private regulatory system may be too weak (Pattberg, 2005). On the other hand, certification is not in a position to effectively compensate for the shortcomings of public action. If illegal harvesters cannot be excluded from the resource, the incentive for legal harvesters to harvest at a sustainable rate is reduced, if not entirely eliminated (Shepers, 2010). Another aspect is that a large part of the interventions in forests occurs outside the market economy or within informal economic systems. This applies for instance for fuelwood collection. A large amount of wood is produced and consumed in developing countries; a high percentage of this is used for energy consumption (FAO, 2010). Therefore, forest certification is not able to address all aspects of forest protection (Gueneau, 2008).

Nevertheless, certification has indirectly contributed to defining sustainable forest management standards by helping to reach an agreement on the definition of the good practices that are introduced into national legislation (Gueneau, 2008; TEEBb, 2010).

The cultural, social and economic requirements are related to consumer maturity including considerations on sustainability and even the level of the country's economic development in consumer decisions. Vallejo and Hauselmann (2000) point out the importance of consumer activists who can promote forest management and certification. "Consumer organizations can play an important role in initiating and advocating change in consumption patterns, and have the means to provide consumers with information that allows them to make informed choices. Consumer organizations can play a role – and have the skills to do so – in encouraging governments and industry to adopt policies and methods that will promote sustainable consumption" (Vallejo and Hauselmann, 2000: 27). If governments, e.g. German (German Government, 2007) lead the way in adopting national procurement policies to purchase only certified forest products for construction purposes, they could give an example and accelerate a change in consumer behaviour (Shepers, 2010).

The Role of Forest Certification in a Policy Mix

As we have seen above, the participation of the State is important to ensuring the efficiency and effectiveness of the certification process. Conditions for a contribution of forest certification to biodiversity conservation include a conducive forest governance framework and a certain level of land tenure security in the forest country. Certification needs the coercive power of governments to clamp down on illegal trading of forestry products (Shepers, 2010). The rise of certification systems has generated new challenges and opportunities for conventional state regulation as well as interaction between private and public regulation. These have, at best, produced more credible and effective governance structures, while they run a risk of mere legitimizing of existing practices (Potoski, 2004; Cashore, 2005; Keskitalo, 2009; Bartley, 2010). At worst, certification can actively compete with state regulation, undermining both standard setting apparatus. The presence of multiple norms within a given country or region (e.g., FSC and Cerflor in Brazil) may lead to confusion on the part of the consumers, while it can also undermine compliance with the more rigorous standards. On the other hand, it is not always desirable to enforce the most rigorous standards where it is important to show progress toward incorporation of a larger proportion of forests under certification norms. Adaptive and gradual adoption starting with less rigorous criteria, such as those adopted in the SLIMF system, enhance the prospects of system expansion.

Perhaps the most promising development that the certification schemes can provide for a policy mix, is the pressure to consider different governance and control systems simultaneously and hence, to allow interaction across public and private boundaries. According to WWF (2010), certification alone cannot solve the challenges of sustainable forest management, stating: "[Certification] is a tool which works. It is time for governments and international institutions that aim to promote more sustainable management of tropical forests to make more and better use of it" (WWF, 2010: 30). It is up to all the stakeholders to ensure that the tool is properly and effectively used in conjunction with other complementary tools and policies such as government regulation and consumer awareness.

References

[1] Azevedo-Ramos C.; Carvalho Jr., O. and Amaral, B. (2006), Short-term Effects of Reduced-Impact Logging on Eastern Amazon Fauna, *Forest Ecology and Management*, 232, 26–35.

[2] Bartley, Tim (2010), Certification as a Mode of Social Regulation, *Jerusalem Papers on Regulation & Governance,* Working paper no. 8.

[3] Bodet, K. Lamarche (2007), La responsabilité sociale des entreprises comme innovation institutionelle: Une lecture regulationniste. Revue de la régulation: Capitalisme, Institutions, *Pouvoirs* 1, 19. http://regulation.revues.org/index1283.html

[4] Brotto, Lucio (2010), Biodiversity in the Peruvian Amazon. *ETFRN News* 51, 112-118.

[5] Cashore, B., Auld., G. and Newsom, D. (2003), Forest Certification (eco-labeling) Programs and their Policymaking Authority: Explaining Divergence among North American and European Case Studies, *Forest Policy and Economics* 5, 225–247.

[6] Cashore, B., G. van Kooten, C., Vertinsky, I., Aulda, G. and Affolderbach, J. (2005), Private or Self-regulation? A Comparative Study of Forest Certification Choices in Canada, the United States and Germany. *Forest Policy and Economics* 7, 53–69.

[7] Chan, S. and Pattberg, P.H. (2008), Private Rule-Making and the Politics of Accountability: Analyzing Global Forest Governance, *Global Environmental Politics* 8, 103-121.

[8] Conroy, M. (2007), *Branded! How Certification Revolution is Transforming Global Corporations,* Gabriola Island, BC, Canada. New Society Publishers.

[9] Ebeling, J. and YasuÉ, M. (2009), The Effectiveness of Market-based Conservation in the Tropics: Forest Certification in Ecuador and Bolivia. *Journal of Environmental Management* 90, 1145-1153.

[10] ETFRN, European Tropical Forest Research Network (2010), Biodiversity Conservation in Certified Forests. *ETFRN Newsletter* 51, September, p. 228, Wageningen, The Netherlands.

[11] FAO (2010), Global Forest Resources Assessment, *FAO Forestry Paper* 163.

[12] Freeman, R.E. (1984), *Strategic Management: A Stakeholder Approach*, Pitman, Boston.

[13] FSC, Forest Stewardship Council (2010), *Global FSC Certificates: Type and Distribution.* http://www.fsc.org/fileadmin/web-data/public/document_center/powerpoints_graphs/facts_figures/Global-FSC-Certificates-2010-08-16-EN.pdf

[14] German Government (2007), *Gemeinsamer erlass zur beschaffung von holzprodukten*

(joint order on the procurement of wood products), http://www.verwaltungsvorschriften-im-internet.de/bsvwvbund_17012007_NII5421040.htm

[15] Greenpeace (2002). Certificação Florestal: CERFLOR Empresas e governo têm credibilidade para realizar certificação florestal? http://www.greenpeace.org/brasil/PageFiles/4081/certificacao_florestal_20021220.pdf.

[16] GUÉNÉAU, S. and Tozzi, P. (2008), Towards the Privatization of Global Forest Governance?, *International Forestry Review*, 10: 550-562.

[17] Gulbrandsen, L.H. (2004), Overlapping Public and Private Governance: Can Forest Certification Fill the Gaps in the Global Forest Regime? *Global Environmental Politics* 4, 75-99.

[18] Gullison, R.E. (2003), Does Forest Certification Conserve Biodiversity? *Oryx* 37(2), 153–165.

[19] Imaflora (2008), *Impacto da certificação florestal FSC em comunidades agroextrativistas do acre* in Imaflora, ed. Imaflora, USP, Entropix, Piracicaba, SP.

[20] Imaflora (2009), *E certificar, faz diferença? Estudo de avaliação de impacto da certificação FSC/RAS*, Imaflora, Piracicaba.

[21] Keskitalo, E.C.H., C. Sandström, M. Tysiachniouk and J. Johansson (2009), Local Consequences of Applying International norms: Differences in the Application of Forest Certification in Northern Sweden, Northern Finland, and North-west Russia. *Ecology and Society* 14(2): 1.

[22] Klooster, D. (2005), Environmental Certification of Forests: The Evolution of Environmental Governance in a Commodity Network, *Journal of Rural Studies* 21, 403–417.

[23] Kollert, W. and Lagan, P. (2006), Do Certified Tropical Logs Fetch a Market Premium? A Comparative Price Analysis from Sabah, Malasya. *Forest Policy and economics*, n. 9: 862–868.

[24] May, P.H. (2005), Forest Certification in Brazil. In: Cashore, B. et al., *Confronting Sustainability: Forest Certification in Developing and Transitioning Countries*. Yale University School of Environmental Studies and Forestry, pp. 337–362.

[25] Nebel, G., Quevedo, Lincoln, Jacobsen, J.B. and Helles, F. (2005), Development and Economics Significance of Forest Certification: The Case of FSC in Bolivia. *Forest Policy and Economics* 7(2): 175-186.

[26] Newsom, D., Bahn, V. and Cashore, B. (2006), Does Forest Certification Matter? An Analysis of Operation-level Changes Required during SmartWood Certification Process in the United States. *Forest Policy and Economics* 9(3): 197-208.

[27] Pattberg, P.H. (2005), The Forest Stewardship Council: Risk and Potential of Privat Forest Governance, *Journal of Environment and Development* 3, pp. 356-374.

[28] Potoski, M. and Prakash, A. (2004), Regulatory Convergence in Non-governmental Regimes? Cross-national Adoption of ISO 14001 Certifications. *The Journal of Politics* 66(3): 885-905.

[29] Price, F. (2010), The Nature Conservancy and Tropical Forest Certification, *ETFRN News* 51: 105-111.

[30] Purbawiyatna, A. and Simula, M. (2008), Developing Forest Certification; Towards Increasing the Comparability and Acceptance of Forest Certification Systems. International Tropical Timber Organization (ITTO) – *ITTO Technical Series* 29: 10.

[31] Rametsteiner, E. and Simula, M. (2003), Forest Certification—An Instrument to Promote Sustainable Forest Management?, *Journal of Environmental Management* 67, 87–98.

[32] Samuelson, J. (2008), Green Stakeholders: Pesky Activists or Productive Allies? *Harvard Business Review.* http://www.hbrgreen.org/2008/03/green_stakeholders_pesky_activ.html

[33] Schepers, D.H. (2010). Challenges to Legitimacy at the Forest Stewardship Council. *Journal of Business Ethics*, p. 279-290.

[34] TEEBa (2010). D2 chapter 9. http://www.teebweb.org/

[35] TEEBb (2010). D1 chapter 5. http://www.teebweb.org/

[36] Vallejo, N. and Hauselmann, P. (2000). Institutional Requirements for Forest Certification – A Manual for Stakeholders, Working Paper.

[37] WWF (2010). *Certification and Roundtables: Do They Work? WWF Review of Multi-stakeholder Sustainability Initiatives*, WWF UK, London, UK.

Notes

1. Stakeholders are those groups that affect and/or are affected by the organization and its activities. These can include, but are not limited to: landowners, administrators, functionaries and labor unions, clients, associates, business partners, suppliers, competitors, government and regulatory agencies, the electorate, non-governmental organizations/non-profits, pressure groups and opinion leaders, and local and international communities. In fact, the definition of the stakeholders' boundaries becomes a determining factor (Bodet & Lamarche, 2007). As J. Samuelson recalls: "...and if you discern who your stakeholders are, it is very likely that they will do this for you..." (Samuelson, 2008).

2. Legal reserve is the share of native vegetation rural properties in Brazil area required to preserve as part of the "social function" of property, in accordance with the national Forest Code. In the Mata Atlantica rainforest and in the savanna this share is 20 per cent. In the Amazon biome, if the property is located in the forest this percentage is 80 per cent and in the savanna 35 per cent. The Forest Code is currently the object of efforts to undermine its protection of remaining private forestlands by rural landowners.

This study was supported by European Union funded project "Assessing the role of economic instruments in policy mixes for biodiversity conservation and ecosystem services provision" (POLICYMIX; Project No: 244065).

ANNEX 1

FSC Certification Principles

In the case of FSC, accredited institutions adopt the ten principles that should be applied to the forest management operation. They are:

1. *Compliance with FSC Law and Principles:* The forest management should respect all laws applicable in the country where it operates, international treaties, agreements signed by the country and compliance with all FSC P&C;
2. *Responsibilities and Rights of Ownership and Land Use:* The rights of ownership, long term land use and forest resources should be clearly defined, documented and legally established;
3. *Rights of Indigenous Peoples:* The rights and costumes of indigenous people to own, use and manage their land, territories and resources shall be recognized and respected;
4. *Community Relations and Worker Rights:* The forest management activities shall maintain or enhance the long-term social and economic welfare of forest workers and local communities;
5. *Benefits from the Forest:* The forest management operations shall encourage the efficient use of multiple forestry products and services to ensure the economic feasibility and a wide range of environmental and social benefits;
6. *Environmental Impacts:* Forest management shall conserve ecological diversity and its associated values, water resources, soil, fragile and singular ecosystems, landscape and thus, maintain the ecological functions and forest integrity;
7. *Management Plan:* The management plan, appropriate to the proposed operational scale and intensity, shall be written, implemented and updated. The long term objectives of forest management and the way to attain them shall be clearly defined;
8. *Monitoring and Evaluation:* The monitoring shall be conducted as per scale and intensity of Forest management to assess forest conditions, forest product yields, custody chain, management activities and social and environmental impacts;

9. *Maintenance of High Value Conservation Forest:* The management of high conservation value forest shall preserve or enhance the attributes which define such forests. Decisions related to high conservation value forest shall be always considered with precaution;
10. *Plantations:* The plantation shall be planned and managed according to the P&C numbers 1 to 10. Taking into account that plantations can provide a wide range of social and economic benefits and contribute to meet the requirements for global forest products, it is recommended that they contemplate management, reduce pressures and promote the restoration and conservation of natural forests.

Source: FSC.

15

Pollution Control and Welfare in General Equilibrium: Is there a Tradeoff between Tax and Standard?

Kausik Gupta

Introduction

Today, there is no controversy on the view that environmental pollution all over the world has reached an alarming level and immediate steps should be taken by all nations to save the global economy from its harmful effects. Economic activity affects the environment in diverse ways. Land and water are adversely affected when materials and energy are drawn from them for performing economic activities like production and consumption. Discharge of wastes from industry and domestic living pollutes the economy badly. The issue of pollution control has gained importance due to increasing concern among the environmentalists, academicians and policy makers regarding the state of natural environment and conservation of natural resources in developing countries.

The "Environmental Kuznets Curve" gives the most likely relation between the environment and economic development. It states that there exists an inverted U-shaped relationship between per capita income and environmental degradation. In case of developing countries, it has been found that the peak of this curve is reached at a relatively high level of per capita income. There can be various reasons for this, and one of these can be the existence of a large informal sector causing huge environmental pollution.[1] In the developing countries, informal sector constitutes a large part of the manufacturing and service sector. This sector provides a major part of employment in most developing countries. Empirical evidence suggests that most of the informal sector units produce intermediate inputs for the formal manufacturing sector on a subcontracting basis, and this sector is a major source of environmental pollution.

Another important issue that needs to be mentioned in connection with pollution control is transfer of environmentally sound technology (EST hereafter) from developed to developing countries. EST is also referred to as *'green technology'* or *'green capital'* in the environmental economics literature. One of the most important aspects of liberalization is the inflow of foreign capital to developing countries in the form of foreign direct investment (FDI). As a result of FDI, residents of the host country come into contact with foreign entrepreneurs who possess superior technical skills and know how. These new ideas lead to transfer of technology from the foreigners to the residents of the host country and it takes place through observation discussion and training. This transmission can be considered as a spillover or external effect on the host country.[2] So, technology transfer in developing countries takes place mainly through FDI. Empirical investigations in this area by Mansfield (1961, 1968) also support the validity of this hypothesis.

In the trade-environment literature, it has been argued, following the 'industrial flight' and 'pollution haven' hypotheses that trade liberalization leads to FDI in pollution-intensive industries in the developing countries. However, empirical studies by Duerksen and Leonard (1980), Pearson (1987) and Leonard (1988) show that there is no evidence of widespread relocation of industries to pollution haven.

The question that arises here is why the issue of pollution control is so important in the context of the globalization for most of the developing economies. Perrings, Bhargava and Gupta (1995) have tried to answer this question with special reference to a developing country like India. They have shown that much industrial growth in the developing countries is due to employment, investment and value added by informal sector [or more broadly the small scale enterprises (SMEs)] in environmentally damaging activities like chemicals, textiles, leather and fur products, food processing, non-ferrous metal work, charcoal and fuel wood supply. It is difficult to get data on how far the informal sector is responsible for this pollution as against the large firms. However, it can be argued that as the informal sector firms have limited access to EST and as they use backward technology, these firms are responsible for a major share of pollutants. The formal sector firms in developing countries actually subcontract the informal sector firms to undertake a number of tasks and processes that are "dirty" from the environment point of view.

Hence, we can argue that it is mainly due to the existence of informal sector firms in developing countries, domestic pollution control measures fail to restrict pollution in developing countries. It also explains the fact as to why pollution level is so high in developing countries despite an insignificant share of FDI in polluting activities of these countries. In fact, following Findlay's (1978) 'contagion hypothesis', we find that FDI leads to technology transfer and it includes transfer of EST.

The present chapter attempts to throw theoretically some light on the debate related to tax versus standard in the context of environmental pollution control in a developing economy. It is based on a three-sector general equilibrium framework for a small open economy where the issue of green capital has been brought explicitly. The motivation behind this study originates from the fact that this issue is particularly important from the point of view of policy making in the context of a developing economy and almost all the theoretical works on this subject focus on partial equilibrium framework. In fact, there is absence of any work, at the theoretical level, that considers the debate between pollution tax and standard using a general equilibrium framework. Such a framework not only helps us to understand the inter-sectoral linkages that we find in a developing economy but also helps us to examine whether there actually exists any tradeoff between pollution tax and standard in a developing economy. Though our model has been constructed at a general level, such a framework can easily be used for a developing economy like India.

The framework is based on a small open economy type general equilibrium structure that has been used by various authors to analyze trade and environmental issues [For example, Chichilnisky (1994), Copeland and Taylor (1994, 1995), etc.] Various authors to link informal sector with environmental pollution have also used this framework. [See for example, the works by Gupta (2002a, 2002b), Chaudhuri and Gupta (2004), Chaudhuri (2005), Basu (2006), etc.]. The present model considers a structure where the issue of pollution control tax as well as environmental standard has been considered without compartmentalizing the economy into formal and informal sectors. Moreover, the study brings the concept of green capital explicitly at the static level.

Some of the recent research studies on water pollution abatement in India have found that the pollution tax on industrial water use should be several times higher than the current rate of water cess to realize the prescribed water quality standard. Gupta, Murty and Pandey (1989) have estimated the cost of water treatment for the paper and pulp industry, oil refineries, chemicals and sugar. Mehta, Mundle and Sankar (1993) have also carried out one study for estimating the marginal cost of abatement. Again Murty, James and Mishra (1999) have conducted a study that estimated a kind of pollution tax for the manufacturing industry for realizing a specified standard. But all these empirical studies are based on partial equilibrium analysis, theoretically whose validity depends on various restrictive conditions. The present chapter thus can be considered as an important contribution in the context of the theoretical literature on pollution control. Not only does it take into account various inter-sectoral linkages in the context of pollution control by using a general equilibrium framework, but it also helps us to draw the welfare implications of pollution control for a developing economy.

The basic idea behind the chapter can be explained as follows. We consider a three-sector general equilibrium model. We assume that environmental pollution occurs through the production of goods of the polluting manufacturing sector using traditional capital. This sector is required to pay pollution emission tax. There is also a certain maximum allowable level of pollution decided by the pollution regulatory authority. Pollution coefficient is assumed to be an increasing function of maximum allowable pollution. We have tried to show that even if the maximum allowable level of pollution is reduced, the polluting sector may produce adverse effects on the actual environmental pollution level of the economy. However, we find that pollution control in the form of increase in the rate of emission tax on the polluting sector is unambiguously successful in reducing pollution generated from the sector. Apart from this, it is also shown that pollution control in the form of reduction in maximum allowable pollution improves welfare under some sufficient condition although it leads to an increase in urban unemployment. However, pollution control in the form of increase in emission tax reduces both urban unemployment and welfare of the economy under some sufficient conditions. Thus, our study shows in the context of a general equilibrium structure that an increase in environmental tax is preferred compared to an improvement in environmental standard under reasonable conditions.

The plan of the chapter is as follows. First section specifies the basic model. Next section examines the impact of pollution control, and makes a comparison between the effectiveness of tax and standard. The next section is an extension of the model with unemployment. The concluding remarks are made in the last section.

The Model

We consider a small open economy with three sectors: the agricultural sector (x), the polluting manufacturing sector (y) and the non-polluting manufacturing sector (z). Thus, both sectors x and z are assumed to be non-polluting sectors within the economy. The small open economy assumption implies that the economy is a price taker in the international market so that the product prices are fixed. Production function in each sector exhibits constant returns to scale, variable coefficient technology and diminishing marginal productivity to the variable factors. Sectors 'x' and 'y' use traditional capital, K_t, which is perfectly mobile between these two sectors. Sector 'z' uses sophisticated, sector-specific green capital K_g, which implies the use of EST. Labour is mobile among the three sectors. Sectors 'y' and 'z' employ labour at the contractual (fixed) wage rate $\bar{w}$. The other sector (that is sector 'x') is the residual sector. It employs the remaining workers at the competitive (flexible) wage w. Thus, there is full employment of labour. The product of the agricultural sector is considered as a numeraire and its price has been set equal to unity. Sector x produces exportable product, whereas sectors y and z are the import-competing sectors. These types of assumptions are widely used in the literature on general equilibrium theory of international trade as we find in various extensions of Jones' (1965, 1971) type structure. The present model is also an extension of Jones' (1965, 1971) type structure.

The following symbols will be used in the formal presentation of the model:

a_{Li} = Labour-output ratio in the i-th sector, i = x, y, z
a_{Ki} = Capital-output ratio in the i-th sector, i = x, y, z
P_i = Price of the product of the i-th sector, i = x, y, z
w = Competitive equilibrium wage of sector 'x'
$\bar{w}$ = Contractual fixed wage rate of sectors 'y' and 'z'
X = Level of output of sector 'x'
Y = Level of output of sector 'y'
Z = Level of output of sector 'z'

r = Rate of return on traditional capital
R = Rate of return on green capital
L = Labour endowment
K_t = Traditional capital stock
K_g = Stock of green capital
α = Emission coefficient of sector 'y'
β = Emission tax rate
Ω = Maximum allowable pollution (in terms of per unit of output of sector 'y')

Competitive equilibrium conditions are given as follows:

$$wa_{Lx}(w/r) + ra_{Kx}w/r) = 1 \quad (1)$$

$$\bar{w}a_{Ly}(\bar{w}/r) + ra_{Ky}(\bar{w}/r) + \beta\alpha(\Omega) = P_y \quad (2)$$

$$\bar{w}a_{Lz}(\bar{w}/R) + Ra_{Kz}(\bar{w}/R) = P_z \quad (3)$$

In equation (2) $\alpha' > 0$ implying that a reduction in maximum allowable pollution leads to less per unit emission from the polluting sector.

Mobility of traditional capital between sectors 'x' and 'y' is given by

$$a_{Ky}(\bar{w}/r)Y + a_{Kx}(w/r)X = K_T \quad (4)$$

Sector specificity of green capital is given by

$$a_{Kz}(\bar{w}/R)Z = K_G(\Omega) \quad (5)$$

where $K_G' < 0$.

The reason behind the sign of K_G' is that when there is an improvement in environmental standard in the form of reduction in maximum allowable pollution, we find that the suppliers of green capital are more motivated to supply environmentally sound sophisticated capital. This is because as a result of a reduction in Ω, it is expected that there will be an increase in the use of green capital.

Mobility of labour among the three sectors is given by,

$$a_{Ly}(\bar{w}/r)Y + a_{Lz}(\bar{w}/R)Z + a_{Lx}(w/r)X = L \quad (6)$$

From equation (3) we can determine R as $\bar{w}$ and P_z are given. From equation (2), given P_y and Ω, we can determine r. Putting the value of r in equation (1) we can determine the value of w. Hence, the input-output ratios are known. Equation (5) can be used to determine Z. Finally from equations (4) and (6), we can determine

Y and X. In this model, R is determined independently of Ω. Thus, a_{KZ} (and also a_{LZ}) remains unchanged due to any change in Ω.

The Comparative Static Exercises

We would like to examine the impact of a reduction in maximum allowable pollution on the economy's level of environmental pollution and welfare. We consider that in an attempt to improve environmental standard, government adopts strict environmental regulation policy by reducing maximum allowable pollution expressed in terms of reduction in Ω.

A reduction in Ω leads to adoption of EST and this leads to an increase in the supply of green capital K_G. From equation (5), we see that this change implies an increase in Z as a_{KZ} remains unchanged. Again, there is no change in a_{LZ} due to reduction in Ω, implying an increase in a_{LZ} Z due to reduction in Ω. Thus ($L-a_{LZ}Z$) falls. This leads to a fall in the effective supply of labour for sectors 'x' and 'y'. This, we call effect 1 of a reduction in Ω. We can refer to it as the *Primary Rybczynski type effect.*

Again, we see that a reduction in Ω leads to a reduction in $\alpha(\Omega)$. As a consequence of this, effective price of sector 'y', i.e. $[P_y - \beta\ \alpha(\Omega)] = P_y^*$ increases. From equation (2), it can be said that this increase in P_y^* with given $\bar{w}$, leads to an increase in r. From equation (1), we again find that this increase in r reduces w, given that the price of the product of sector 'x' is unity. Thus, we find that there are reduction in the levels of a_{KY} and a_{KX} implying reduction in demand for traditional capital at initial levels of Y and X and increase in the levels of a_{LY} and a_{LX} implying increase in demand for labour at initial levels of Y and X. It actually implies that there is an increase in effective supply of traditional capital and a reduction in effective supply of labour. This is our effect 2. We can refer to it as *Secondary Rybczynski type effect.* The ultimate effect is the combination of *Primary Rybczynski type effect* and *Secondary Rybczynski type effect.* We refer to this as the *Rybczynski type effect.* Given the assumption that sector 'y' is more capital-intensive than sector 'x', we find that an increase in effective supply of capital and reduction in effective supply of labour causes the capital-intensive sector to expand (i.e. Y increases) and the labour-intensive sector to contract (i.e. X falls).

Total emission of pollutants in the economy is the emission from the polluting sector, i.e. $E = \alpha Y$.

$$\begin{aligned} dE/d\Omega &= \alpha'Y + \alpha(dY/d\Omega) \\ &= \alpha Y\,[(\alpha'/\alpha) + (1/Y)(dY/d\Omega)] \\ &= (\alpha Y/\Omega)\,[(\alpha'\Omega/\alpha) + (\Omega/Y)(dY/d\Omega)] \\ &= (\alpha Y/\Omega)[e_{\alpha,\Omega} + e_{Y,\Omega}] \end{aligned} \tag{7}$$

where $e_{\alpha,\Omega} > 0$ is the elasticity of the emission coefficient with respect to Ω and $e_{Y,\Omega} < 0$ is the elasticity of output of the polluting sector with respect to Ω.

So, we find that $dE/d\Omega < 0$ if and only if $|e_{Y,\Omega}| > |e_{\alpha,\Omega}|$.

Proposition 1: *Pollution control in the form of reduction in maximum allowable pollution in a small open economy may increase the emission of pollutants from the polluting manufacturing sector. In fact, under the condition $|e_{Y,\Omega}| > |e_{\alpha,\Omega}|$, a reduction in maximum allowable pollution leads to an increase in emission of pollutants in such an economy.*

Now, we examine the impact of an increase in emission tax rate β on the pollution level.

An increase in β leads to a reduction in the effective price of Y, i.e. a reduction in the level of $[P_Y - \beta\alpha(\Omega)] = P_Y^*$. Given , from equation (1) we find that reduction in P_Y^* causes a fall in r. Again, given the price of the product of the agricultural sector, from equation (1) we find that a fall in r causes a rise in w. So, an increase in β causes both $(\bar{w}/r)$ and (w/r) to rise, though it causes no change in $(\bar{w}/R)$. It causes both a_{KY} and a_{KX} to increase on one hand and a_{LY} along with a_{LX} to fall on the other. However, as there are no changes in the level of $(\bar{w}/R)$ we find that an increase in β causes no change in the levels of a_{KZ} and a_{LZ}. Increase in the levels of a_{KY} and a_{KX} means that there is a rise in the demand for traditional capital, for initial of X and Y, and therefore a fall in the effective supply of K_T. Again, reduction in the levels of a_{LY} and a_{LX} means there is a reduction in the demand for labour, for initial of X, Y and Z (and also for given a_{LZ}). It means an increase in the effective supply of labour available for sectors 'x' and 'y'. It is to be noted that as Z remains unchanged due to an increase in β, the demand for labour in sector z also remains unchanged due to an increase in β. Hence, the ultimate outcome is the operation of a *'Secondary Rybczynski type effect'*. Increase in effective supply of labour and reduction in effective supply of capital causes the capital-intensive sector 'y' to contract and the labour-intensive sector 'x' to expand. In other words, Y falls and X increases due to an increase in β.

Thus, the effect on total emission of pollutants from the polluting sector is given by

$$(dE/d\ \beta) = \alpha\ (dY/\ d\ \beta) \tag{8}$$

As $(dY/d\ \beta) < 0$, we can conclude unambiguously $(dE/d\ \beta) < 0$. In other words, an increase in emission tax rate reduces the level of emission of pollutants in the economy. We summarize our results in the form of the following proposition.

Proposition 2: *Pollution control in the form of an increase in the rate of emission tax on the polluting manufacturing sector in a small open economy is successful in reducing the pollution generated from this sector as well in reducing the total pollution of such an economy.*

On the basis of the above discussion, we may conclude that an improvement in environmental standard is not successful in reducing the pollution whereas an increase in emission tax rate reduces unambiguously the level of pollution in the context of our general equilibrium framework.

Next, we would study the impact of a change in maximum allowable pollution on social welfare. We consider a quasi-concave social utility function, u, which depends on consumption demand of the three final goods, (D_X, D_Y and X_Z) and the level of emission E. It is also assumed that an increase in the level of pollution causes a negative externality on social welfare.

Thus,
$$u = u\ (D_X, D_Y, X_Z, E) \tag{9}$$

Here, $u_x > 0$, $u_y > 0$, $u_z > 0$ and $u_E < 0$.

Considering $dV = (d\ u/u_x)$ as a measure of change in welfare measured in units of the product of sector 'x' we can write

$$dV = d\ D_X + P_Y d\ D_Y + P_Z d\ D_Z - \rho dE \tag{10}$$

where $(u_E/u_x) = -\rho$, (given $\rho > 0$); ρ is the real social cost per unit of pollution.

The budget constraint facing the economy (the trade balance condition) is given by

$$D_X + P_Y D_Y + P_Z D_Z = X + P_Y Y + P_Z Z \tag{11}$$

or
$$D_X + P_Y D_Y + P_Z D_Z = wL + (\bar{w} - w)(a_{LY} Y + a_{LZ} Z) + rK_T + RK_G\ (\Omega) + \beta E \tag{12}$$

In equation (12), we assume that the tax revenue βE is distributed in a lump sum manner among the capitalists and the workers.

Taking the total differential of equation (12) and using equation (10), we can write after some algebraic manipulation the following equation:

$$dV + \rho dE = Ldw + (\bar{w} - w)\ (a_{LY}dY + Yda_{LY} + a_{LZ}\ dZ) - (a_{LY}Y + a_{LZ}Z)\ dw + K_T dr + RK_G'\ d\Omega + \beta dE$$

or $$V\hat{V} = w\hat{w}[L - (a_{LY}Y + a_{LZ}Z)] + (\bar{w} - w)L\ [\lambda_{LY}\hat{Y} + \lambda_{LY}\sigma_Y\ \theta_{KY}\ \hat{r} + \lambda_{LZ}\hat{Z}] + rK_T\hat{r} + \Omega RK_G'\hat{\Omega} + E(\beta - \rho)\hat{E} \quad (13)$$

where θ_{ij} is the share of ith input (in value terms) in the product of the jth sector (in value terms), σ_Y is the elasticity of factor substitution in the 'y' sector, λ_{ij} is the share of ith factor (in physical terms) in the jth sector in the total factor endowment of that sector.

From equation (1) using the envelope condition, we get

$$\hat{w} = -(\theta_{KX} / \theta_{LX})\hat{r} \quad (14)$$

Again from equation (2) using the envelope condition, we get

$$\hat{r} = -(\varepsilon_1 / \theta_{KY}) \quad (15)$$

where $\varepsilon_1 = \pi\varepsilon$, $\pi = (\beta\alpha/P_y)$ is the share of emission tax (for unit level of output)in the price of the product of the polluting sector and $\varepsilon = \alpha'\ (\Omega/\alpha)$ is the elasticity of emission coefficient with respect to maximum allowable pollution. As $\varepsilon > 0$ and $\pi > 0$, we have $\varepsilon_1 > 0$.

Finally, from equation (5), we get

$$\hat{Z} = e_{KG\Omega}\hat{\Omega} \quad (16)$$

where $e_{KG\Omega} = (\Omega K_G'/K_G) < 0$ is the elasticity of green capital with respect to maximum allowable pollution.

Using equations (14), (15) and (16) and after some algebraic manipulations we can rewrite equation (13) as:

$$V(\hat{V} / \hat{\Omega}) = (\varepsilon_1 r / \theta_{KY})(a_{KX}X - K_T) + (\bar{w} - w)L[\lambda_{LY}(\hat{Y} / \hat{\Omega}) + \lambda_{LY}\sigma_Y\ \theta_{KY}(\hat{r} / \hat{\Omega}) + \lambda_{LZ}\varepsilon_{KG,\Omega}] + \Omega R'_{KG} + E(\beta - \rho)(\hat{E} / \hat{\Omega}) \quad (17)$$

Change in welfare can be shown as the sum total of four effects, viz., factor-income effect given by $[(\varepsilon_1 r/\theta_{KY})(a_{KX}X - K_T)]$, labour reallocation effect given by

$(\bar{w} - w)L[\lambda_{LY}(\hat{Y}/\hat{\Omega}) + \lambda_{LY}\sigma_Y\theta_{KY}(\hat{r}/\hat{\Omega}) + \lambda_{LZ}e_{KG,\Omega}]$, green capital effect given by $\Omega R'_{KG}$ and emission effect given by $E(\beta - \rho)(\hat{E}/\hat{\Omega})$. As we find $a_{KX}X < K_T$, $e_{KG,\Omega} < 0$ and both $(\hat{Y}/\hat{\Omega})$ and $(\hat{r}/\hat{\Omega})$ are negative we conclude that the factor-income effect, labour reallocation effect and the green capital effect are negative. Here, only the sign of emission effect is indeterminate. We know that $(\hat{E}/\hat{\Omega}) < 0$ if $|e_{Y,\Omega}| > |e_{\alpha,\Omega}|$. Thus if $\beta > \rho$, emission effect is negative so that a reduction in maximum allowable pollution increases welfare.

We now consider the expression for change in welfare as a result of an increase in emission tax rate. We follow the same procedure as that of the earlier case where we have considered the impact of reduction in maximum allowable pollution on social welfare and after some simplification we can write equation (12) as

$$V(\hat{V}/\hat{\beta}) = (\hat{r}/\hat{\beta})r[K_T - a_{KX}X] + L(\bar{w} - w)[\lambda_{LY}(\hat{Y}/\hat{\beta}) + \lambda_{LY}\sigma_Y\theta_{KY}(\hat{r}/\hat{\beta})] + \alpha Y(\beta - \rho)[(\beta/(\beta - \rho)) + (\hat{Y}/\hat{\beta})] \quad (18)$$

Therefore, change in welfare is the sum total of factor income effect, labour reallocation effect and emission effect.

Once again, the sign of emission effect is indeterminate. Other two effects are negative. Under the sufficient condition $\beta > \rho$ and $|(\hat{Y}/\hat{\beta})| > [\beta/(\beta - \rho)]$, we find that emission effect is negative so that an increase in emission tax rate reduces welfare.

Proposition 3: *Pollution control in the form of a reduction in maximum allowable pollution improves welfare whereas pollution control in the form of increase in emission tax rate reduces welfare under some reasonable sufficient conditions.*

Extensions of the Model

Suppose we assume that the two manufacturing sectors (polluting and non-polluting) are located in the urban area and the agricultural sector is located in the rural area. As in the basic model, the manufacturing (urban) wage rate is assumed to be fixed at a level, $\bar{w}$, much higher than the agricultural (rural) wage rate, w. We consider Harris-Todaro (1970) type of migration mechanism from the rural area to the urban area. So equation (19) is added to our basic model that we refer to as the migration-equilibrium condition and write it as follows:

$$\bar{w} = (1 + \mu)w \tag{19}$$

μ is the urban unemployment rate [$\mu = (U/(a_{Ly}Y + a_{Lz}Z))$, where U is the level of urban unemployment].

The allocation of labour force among various sectors is modified as follows:

$$[a_{Ly}(\bar{w}/r)\, Y + a_{Lz}(\bar{w}/R)\, Z](1 + \mu) + a_{Lx}(w/r)X = L \tag{6'}$$

The working of the extended model is similar to that of the basic model. In the extended model, μ is determined from equation (19).

We also modify the capital-intensity condition of the basic model as follows:

$$(a_{Ky}/a_{Ly}(1 + \mu)) > (a_{Kx}/a_{Lx})$$

It implies that sector 'y' is more capital-intensive than sector 'x' in 'employment-adjusted terms'.[3] It is to be noted that $(a_{Ky}/a_{Ly}\,(1 + \mu)) > (a_{Kx}/a_{Lx}) \Rightarrow (a_{Ky}/a_{Ly}) > (a_{Kx}/a_{Lx})$.

The major results of the model remain unaltered even when the model is extended with unemployment. We have only the additional effect on urban unemployment as a result of changes in pollution control instruments.

A reduction in maximum allowable pollution reduces w. It implies an increase in the urban unemployment rate,m, from equation (19). Again, reduction in Ω raises 'r'. From Section 3, we have found that a reduction in Ω increases the values of both Y and Z. Even in the presence of urban unemployment, this result is valid and we are not repeating the explanations behind the results here. As $\bar{w}$ is given, we find that $(\bar{w}/r)$ falls implying an increase in $a_{Ly}(\bar{w}/r)$ causing an increase in $a_{Ly}Y$. It is to be noted that though $a_{Lz}(\bar{w}/R)$ is independent of changes in Ω, a reduction in Ω causes an increase in Z so that $a_{Lz}Z$ increases. Increase in urban unemployment rate, μ, along with increase in urban employment, $(a_{Ly}Y + a_{Lz}Z)$, causes increase in the level of urban unemployment $U = \mu(a_{Ly}Y + a_{Lz}Z)$.

In case of an increase in emission tax rate, we find that the opposite things happen. Increase in b raises w, reduces r, reduces μ, reduces Y (causes no change in the levels of a_{Lz} and Z) and also reduces $a_{Ly.}$ Thus, the level of urban unemployment falls as a result of increase in β.

Proposition 4: *Pollution control in the form of a reduction in maximum allowable pollution increases the level of urban unemployment whereas pollution control in the form of increase in emission tax rate reduces the level of urban unemployment.*

The welfare implications are similar to those of the earlier model. The only difference is that here we have an additional unemployment effect. So to get the same welfare implications, we need to modify the sufficient conditions marginally.

Conclusion

In the present chapter we thus find that the effects of pollution control creates a bunch of tradeoff in front of the policy makers. To be more specific, first, we consider the effects of pollution control in the form of reduction in maximum allowable pollution. Such a measure may increase pollution generated from the polluting sector. In fact, it increases pollution under some reasonable conditions. Apart from this, such a measure improves welfare under some sufficient conditions. Finally, if Harris-Todaro (1970) type urban unemployment is introduced in this model, we find that such a measure increases urban unemployment. Next, we consider the effects of pollution control in the form of increase in emission tax. Such a measure reduces pollution generated from the polluting sector though it reduces welfare under some sufficient conditions. However, increase in emission tax reduces urban unemployment. So, from the point of view of pollution control, increase in emission tax is better compared to reduction in maximum allowable pollution as a pollution control measure. Interestingly, if the objective of the policy makers is to improve, social welfare reduction in maximum allowable pollution appears to be a better measure compared to increase in emission tax rate. Finally, from the point of view of reduction in urban unemployment, increase in emission tax rate is a superior measure compared to reduction in maximum allowable pollution. Thus, there is a trade off in front of the policy makers between tax and standard from the point of view of reducing pollution and improving social welfare on one hand and from the point of view of reducing urban unemployment and improving social welfare on the other.

References

[1] Basu, T. (2006), "Some Theoretical Aspects of Informal Sector in a Developing Economy", Unpublished PhD Dissertation, Department of Economics, The University of Burdwan, West Bengal, India.

[2] Chaudhuri, S. (2005), "Pollution and Welfare in the Presence of Informal Sector: Is There Any Trade off?", *Keio Economic Studies* (forthcoming).

[3] Chaudhuri, S. and Gupta, K. (2004), "Inflow of Foreign Capital, Environmental Pollution and Welfare in the Presence of an Informal Sector". *Paper presented in the 3rd Indian Statistical Institute Conference of Economic Research Unit*, January 2004.

[4] Chichilinsky, G. (1994), "North-South Trade and the Global Environment", *The American Economic Review*, 84(4): 851-874.

[5] Copeland, B.R. and Taylor, M.S. (1995), "Trade and Transboundary Pollution", *The American Economic Review*, 85(4): 716-737.

[6] Copeland, B.R. and Taylor, M.S. (1994), "North-South Trade and the Environment", *The American Economic Review*, 109: 755-787.

[7] Duerksen, C. and. Leonard, H.J. (1980), "Environmental Regulations and Location of Industries: an International Perspective", *Columbia Journal of World Business (Summer)*, 15: 52-68.

[8] Findlay, R. (1978), "Relative Backwardness, Direct Foreign Investment and the Transfer of Technology: A Simple Dynamic Model", *Quarterly Journal of Economics*, 92: 1-16.

[9] Gupta, D.B., Murty, M.N. and Pandey, R. (1989), "Water Conservation and Pollution Abatement in Indian Industry: A Study of Water Tariff", National Institute of Public Finance and Policy, New Delhi.

[10] Gupta, K. (2002a), "The Urban Informal Sector and Environmental Pollution: A Theoretical Analysis", Working Paper No. 02-006, Centre for Environment and Development Economics (CEDE), Environment Department, University of York, UK.

[11] Gupta, K. (2002b), "A Theoretical Understanding of the Issues of Environmental Pollution and Expansion of Urban Informal Sector in a Developing Economy", *Unpublished Post-Doctoral Report*, University of York, UK.

[12] Harris, J.R. and Todaro M.P. (1970), "Migration, Unemployment and Development: A Two-Sector Analysis", *American Economic Review,* 60: 126-142.

[13] Jones, R.W. (1965), "The Structure of Simple General Equilibrium Models", *Journal of Political Economy,* 73: 557-552.

[14] Jones, R.W. (1971), "A Three Factor Model in Theory, Trade and History", in J. Bhagwati, R.W. Jones , R. Mundell and Vanek (eds), *Trade, Balance of Payments and Growth,* Chapter 1, North Holland, Amsterdam.

[15] Koizumi, T. and Kopecky, K.J. (1977), "Economic Growth, Capital Movements and the International Transfer of Technical Knowledge", *Journal of International Economics*, 7: 45-65.

[16] Leonard, J. (1988), *Pollution and Struggle for the World Product,* New York: Cambridge University Press.

[17] Mansfield, E.M. (1961), "Technical Change and the Rate of Imitation", *Econometrica,* 29: 741-766.

[18] Mansfield, E.M. (1968), *Industrial Research and Technological Innovation,* New York, Norton.

[19] Mehta, S., Mundle, S. and Sankar, U. (1993), "Incentives and Regulations for Pollution Abatement with an Application to Waste Water Treatment", National Institute of Public Finance and Policy, New Delhi.

[20] Murty, M.N., James, A.J. and Misra, S. (1999), *"Economics of Water Pollution: The Indian Experience",* Oxford University Press, New Delhi.

[21] Pearson, C. (1987), *Multinational Corporations, Environment and the Third World,* Durham: Duke University Press.

[22] Perrings, C., Bhargava, S. and Gupta, J. (1995), "The Transfer of Environmentally Sound Technology to Small and Medium Scale Enterprises in Developing Countries: A Survey of the Issues". Paper prepared for UNCTAD, Geneva.

Notes

1. See for example the works of Gupta (2002a, 2002b), Chaudhuri and Gupta (2004), Chaudhuri (2005), Basu (2006), etc.
2. See Koizumi and Kopecky (1977) for details. Findlay (1978) has also used this "contagion hypothesis" in his theoretical analysis of technology transfer and relative backwardness.
3. See Khan (1982) for details.

16

Dynamics of Land Use Changes and Forest Degradation in a Himalayan Watershed: An Application of Bio-economic Modelling

Rakesh Kumar Sharma, Prem Lall Sankhayan and Ranveer Singh

Introduction

Increasing population pressures and inappropriate environmental and developmental policies in the mountainous regions like Himachal Pradesh are deteriorating the sustainability of natural resources. Decline in dense forest by 10 per cent in Himachal Pradesh in the recent past has become a cause of concern for the policy makers as well as for the environmentalists (FSI, 2003). While total biomass productivity exceeds human and animal consumption by a wide margin, there is a progressive loss in forest cover (Moench and Bandyopadhyay, 1986). Simultaneously, changing land use and cropping patterns together with integration of commercial horticultural crops are leading to new farming systems (Sharma et al., 2007; Singh, 1999). The growing area under horticultural cash crops over the last few years has put increased pressure on forest resources through land clearing, and declining agricultural residues and its increasing demand. The loss of forest and its impact on the environment and sustainable land use cannot be ignored, and requires immediate attention by policy makers. The situation in Himachal Pradesh represents a complex and dynamic involving interaction of biophysical and socio-economic factors requiring a multidisciplinary approach to analyze it, rather than following a simplistic single disciplinary approach.

A useful interface between human behaviour and biophysical processes, especially in terms of resource extraction and stock changes are best captured with the bio-economic models (Holden and Shiferaw, 2004; Sankhayan et al., 2003). This approach incorporates economic and ecological factors and appears to be more realistic at a micro watershed level due to relatively homogeneous conditions. However, the modelling of factors determining ecological and economic value may result in conceptual and methodological problems (Chopra and Adhikari, 2004). This study presents such an effort at a micro watershed level in the western Himalayan state of Himachal Pradesh. The main objective of the study is to maximize discounted gross margins from all activities over the model horizon with income or profit serving as a proxy for the utility to the people of watershed. It also analyzes the effects of alternate policy scenarios on land use changes and forest degradation and the economic well-being of local communities. This knowledge is useful in identifying suitable policy options for the abatement of ongoing degradation processes and ensures the sustainability of natural resources in the region.

Study Area

Chabri micro watershed is situated in the Solan district of the State of Himachal Pradesh and falls in the wet-temperate forest zone (GOHP, 2002). This zone constitutes about 31 per cent of the state's forest cover (GOHP, 2007). The entire state constitutes a major natural watershed in the north Indian region encompassing watersheds of four major tributaries of Indus, namely, Chenab, Ravi, Beas and Sutlej, and that of Yamuna. The micro watershed under study is a catchment area of Chabri, a rivulet that drains into Ashwani, a tributary of Yamuna. It is a small mountainous, oval-shaped valley with steep slopes, typical of the landscape pattern in the mid hill zone of the state. Due to differences of moisture availability, the northern slopes of the watershed are densely forested, while the southern slopes have mainly grasslands, mixed with patches of forest and scrub. Altitude of the watershed ranges from 1600 m to 1950 m a.s.l. and the average temperature vary from −4°C (in winter) to 28°C (in summer) during the year. The average annual rainfall was 596 mm and snowfall was 65 cm during the period 1993-2003 (GOHP,

2005). The watershed, measures about 896 hectares, encompasses nine villages with total of 102 households having human population of 703. Out of the total watershed land area, about 68 hectares are under cultivation (Table 1).

Table 1: Area under Different Land Use Categories in the Watershed

Sl. No.	Land Use Type	Abbreviation Used	Area (ha)	Percentage of Total Land Area
1	Total cultivated land area in rainy season	CULT_K	68.14	7.6
2	(i) Irrigated cultivated land area in winter season	CULTI_R	31.44	3.5
	(ii) Unirrigated cultivated land area in winter season	CULTU_R	36.70	4.1
3	Land under orchards	ORCH	7.08	0.8
4	Culturable wasteland	CULTW	15.00	1.7
5	Fallow land	FALLOW	2.78	0.3
6	Pastures and grassland	PASTGZ	257.00	28.7
7	Protected forests	PFOREST	302.00	33.7
8	Reserve forests	RFOREST	220.00	24.6
9	Land under non-agricultural uses	NAGRIU	24.00	2.7
10	Total for the watershed (2 to 9)		896.00	100.0

Cultivation of field and horticultural crops, livestock rearing and forest product extraction in the watershed is quite similar to the other regions of the state. The farm size is rather small with 46 per cent of the households owning less than one hectare land. Of the total cultivated area, 54 per cent is rain fed and 46 per cent has year round irrigation facilities. There are two distinct cropping seasons, namely, the rainy season (*kharif*) and winter season (*rabi*). The most widely cultivated crops during the *kharif* season are maize, tomato and capsicum as against wheat and barley during the *rabi* season (Table 2). Beans, potato, ginger and cabbage are also grown on some land area mainly as cash crops. While the vegetable crops on non-irrigated land are grown only in the *kharif* season, these crops are grown in both the seasons on irrigated land. Cultivation of flowers, such as, carnation, gladiolus, chrysanthemum and lily, have become very popular in the recent past, which presently occupies about 8.19 hectares of the land. The flower growing activities are not only more profitable, but also ensure better utilization of household labour through well-distributed operations throughout the year. Farm households also

Table 2: Cropping Pattern in Watershed (area in hectares)

Crop Growing Season	Crop	Crop Growing Months	Area Under Crops			
			Irrigated	Un-irrigated	Total	Percentage of Total Cropped Area
Rainy	Maize	July-October	13.20	14.98	28.18	22.0
	Pulses	July-October	1.80	0.64	2.44	1.9
	Ginger	July-October	0.28	0	0.28	0.2
	Capsicum	July-October	6.48	0	6.48	5.1
	Tomato	July-October	6.02	0	6.02	4.7
	Beans	July-October	3.40	2.08	5.48	4.3
	Potato	July-October	1.64	0	1.64	1.3
	Cabbage	July-October	0.16	0	0.16	0.1
	Miscl./*Kharif* fallow	July-October	3.00	6.27	9.27	7.2
	Total Rainy season		35.98	23.97	59.95	
Winter	Wheat	Nov-June	3.56	6.29	9.85	7.7
	Barley	Nov-June	4.24	6.52	10.76	8.4
	Garlic	Nov-June	0.92	0	0.92	0.7
	Ginger	March-June	0.37	0	0.37	0.3
	Mustard	Nov-June	0.04	0.12	0.16	0.1
	Tomato	March-June	5.22	0	5.22	4.1
	Capsicum	March-June	5.20	0	5.20	4.1
	Peas	Nov-June	2.36	0	2.36	1.8
	Potato	March-June	0.68	0	0.68	0.5
	Cabbage	March-June	0.04	0	0.04	0.0
	Miscl./*Rabi* fallow	Nov-June	0.62	23.77	24.39	19.0
	Total Winter crops		23.25	36.70	59.95	
Annual	Gladiolus	July-June	3.04	0	3.04	2.4
	Carnation	July-June	3.08	0	3.08	2.4
	Chrysanthemum	July-June	1.72	0	1.72	1.3
	Lily	July-June	0.35	0	0.35	0.3
	Total Flowers		8.19	0	8.19	

grow several other crops for self-consumption but only on a very small and negligible proportion of land area that could not be accounted for in this study.

Methodology

Non-linear Bio-economic Model

To analyze the relatively complex systems of large number of interacting economic and biophysical variables, a dynamic non-linear programming bio-economic model has been built. Data used in the model on land, labour, capital, factor and product prices and other parameters for various activities are obtained from farm household surveys. The model considers optimization of agent's (watershed in this case) objective function, incorporated as discounted gross margins subject to a set of constraints, such as, land area according to quality, seasonal labour requirements and capital availability.

The general algebraic modelling system (GAMS) (Brooke et al., 1998) has been used with MINOS solver and the model is run for a time horizon of 20 years, i.e. 2007 to 2026.

The aggregate utility (Ut) at time t for the watershed is expressed by following equations:

$$U_t = \sum_{i}^{u} \sum_{j=1}^{s} (a_{ijt} y_{ijt}^{ca}) + \sum_{i=u+1}^{v} (a_{it} y_{it}^{la}) + \sum_{i=v+1}^{w} (a_{it} y_{it}^{fa}) \quad t = 1, 2, \ldots, T$$

where, $a_{ijt} = (p_{it} q_{ijt}) - \sum_{r=1}^{m} (c_{rijt} x_{rijt})$

$$a_{it} = (p_{it} q_{it}) - \sum_{r=1}^{m} (c_{rit} x_{rit})$$

The abbreviations used in the above equations are as follows:

y_{ijt}^{ca} = level of ith crop activity (i = 1, 2, 3, …, u) grown in j^{th} category of land (j = 1, 2, 3, …, s) unit during the tth year (t = 1, 2, 3, …, T).

y_{it}^{la} = level of ith livestock and livestock product activity ($i = u + 1, u + 2, u + 3, \ldots, v$) during t^{th} year.

y_{it}^{fa} = level of ith forest activity ($i = v + 1, v + 2, v + 3, \ldots, w$).

a_{ijt} = is the per unit gross margins from i^{th} crop activity grown in j^{th} land category during the tth year.

a_{it} = is the per unit gross margins from i^{th} activity other than crop activity during the tth year.

q_{ijt} = yield of the ith crop grown in j^{th} land category during t^{th} year.

q_{it} = yield of the ith non-crop activity during the tth year.

c_{rijt} = cost of rth resource used on i^{th} crop in j^{th} land category during year t.

c_{rit} = cost of rth resource used on i^{th} non-crop activity during year t.

x_{rijt} = the quantity of rth resource used per unit of the associated crop activity.

x_{rit} = the quantity of rth resource used per unit of the associated non-crop activity.

p_{it} = per unit prices of products.

Model considers the maximization of net present value of aggregate utility at watershed level as denoted by the following equation.

$$\text{Maximize } \sum_{t=1}^{T} 1/(1+\partial)^t U_t$$

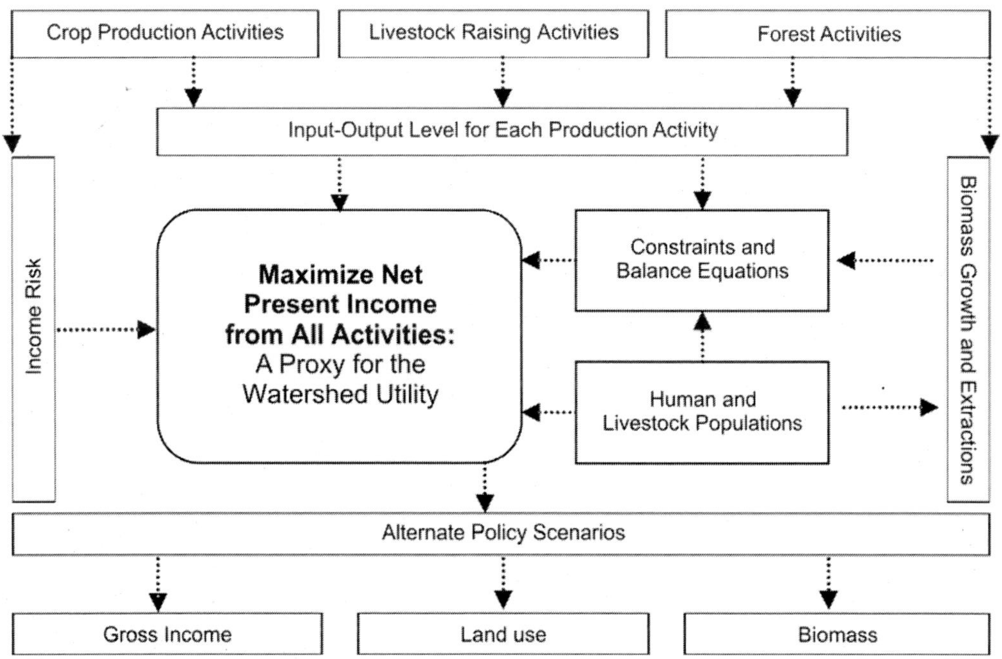

Fig. 1: Analytical Framework of the Bio-economic Model

where, ∂ is the annual per cent discount rate. Based on average annual inflation rate during the past one decade, it is taken as 5 per cent per annum in this study, to convert the stream of gross margins over the model horizon into present value equivalent.

Variance-covariance matrix has been incorporated in the model as used by Hazell (Hazell, 1971). It is derived from the yield and price data of crops over the last five years. This makes the risk equation quadratic and the dynamic model non-linear. Like the income/gross margins, the variance has also been discounted in the model. Whereas discounting of income helps in analyzing the present value of the future income, the discounted variance in income over time brings us closer to reality by assuming that the risks in gross returns become less important in the distant future. Analytical framework of the bio-economic model is explained in the flow diagram presented in Figure 1.

Activities Used in the Model

Crop, livestock and forest activities have been included in the model. Relatively, minor crops are not considered for modelling purposes. Thus, crops that are grown on at least half hectare of land area are included in the model. The model also makes a provision for the labour hiring for all activities during each of the 12 months.

Constraints in the Model

Constraints for land were incorporated according to crop growing seasons, i.e. *kharif* and *rabi* by different land use types, such as irrigated and non irrigated land. Because of incorporation of crop activities by crop growing seasons in the model, land availability constraints are used within homogenous land units accordingly. Labour availability constraints (man-days equivalent) are considered according to months. The labour availability increases with growth of population over the model horizon. This can be supplemented through labour hiring. Based on the observations related to interest on borrowed capital and expenditure levels of the farmers in the watershed, only 15 per cent of the annual gross margins during the tth year are assumed to be available for working capital during the $t + 1$ year. In this study, the concept of gross margins is simply used for giving a useful indication of the production and economic efficiency of crop activity per hectare of land. Higher extent of fixed costs in the new agricultural ventures and dependence on bank finances make the gross margins a better index of income.

Biomass Growth

A logistic growth model which explicitly incorporates carrying capacity (Renshaw, 1991) has been considered in the following biomass growth equation.

$$B_{t+1,j} = e^{(\rho - \lambda)} B_{t,j} / [1 + B_{t,j} (e^{(\rho - \lambda)} - 1)/K_j]$$

where, B = total above-ground biomass, ρ = intrinsic growth rate of biomass, λ = loss due to miscellaneous factors such as decay, fire, illegal felling, etc., and K = carrying capacity of land. The subscripts t and j represent time period and land use category.

Total biomass extraction (TBX) is represented by the following equation:

$$TBX_t = \sum_b E_{b,t} * P_t$$

where, E is the per capita consumption of biomass, t is time period, and b represents biomass type, classified as fuel wood, fodder, timber and other uses. Due to the sufficient grasslands in the watershed, crossbred livestock are preferably served with grasses and compounded feed purchased from the market. It is due to this reason that the equal consumption requirements of both types of livestock have been assumed in this study.

Human and livestock population growth in the model is expressed by the following equation:

$$P_{t+1} = P_t * (1 + \delta)$$

where, P_t is the total population (human/livestock) in the watershed during year t and δ is its corresponding average annual per cent growth rate.

Parameters Used in the Model

Parameter values used in the model are either derived from the survey data or assumed. Though the assumptions have been made under the guidance of available studies and localized approximation, their limitation on policy guidance cannot be ruled out. Table 3 presents the values of some of important parameters used in the model.

Table 3: Values of Some Important Parameters Used in the Base Scenario

Sl. No.	Parameter	Unit	Value of Parameter
1	Households in the watershed	Number	102
2	Size of household – average	Number	6.89
3	Workers per household – average	Number	2.65
4	Growth rate of population	% per annum	1.60
5	Livestock in the watershed	Number	471
6	Growth rate of livestock	% per annum	1.04
7	LPG connections in the watershed	Number	31
8	LPG cylinders consumption by each connection	Number	4
9	Cost of using one LPG cylinder	Rupees	314
10	Discount rate	% per annum	5
11	Fuel wood equivalent of one LPG cylinder	Tonnes	0.23
12	Proportion of gross margins ploughed back into business	%	15
13	Growth rate of tree biomass	% per annum	1.01
14	Periodic loss of tree biomass through decay, fire, etc.	% per annum	0.51
15	Initial tree biomass density by land units	Tonnes^{-ha}	CULTI_R =2.82, CULTU_R=10.70, ORCH=4.56, FALLOW=13.16, PFOREST=728.27, PASTGZ=8.40
16	Annual use of tree biomass	Tonnes	F_LEAVES=121; F_WOOD=549; TIMBER=141

Note: Abbreviations for land use units are the same as given in Table 1.

Model Scenarios and Calibrations

Total variance in income (VIT) and gross margins from current/existing level of crop, livestock and forest activity has been calculated. The VIT so calculated, represents current income risk and has been set as a bound in the base scenario (BASE), so that the income optimization is done within the current level of risk. Such an assumption is made to compare the existing plan with the optimized

BASE as both represent the same level of VIT. The other scenarios however represent true optimizing plans with no limits of VIT. A brief explanation of these scenarios has been presented in the Table 4.

Table 4: Brief Description of Model Scenarios

Sl. No.	Abbreviation for Scenario	Meaning	A Brief Explanation of the Scenario	Objective
1	BASE	Business as usual	Business as usual depicting current state	Income optimization with current level of VIT
2	HULPG	Higher use of LPG gas	LPG connections and annual usage increase by 5 per cent every year	Income optimization
3	SCBRD	Substitution of crossbred livestock	Crossbred livestock grows by 2.08 per cent per annum and local breeds are reduced by 2.87 per cent per annum so that the total number at the end of model horizon remains same as exists at present.	Income optimization
4	HEMIG	Higher emigration	Emigration out of watershed increases by 2 per cent per annum	Income optimization

The survey data have provided some initial model parameters with respect to cropping pattern and biomass stock. The model was then run under different scenarios over a period of 20 years, i.e. from 2007 to 2026. For the model time horizon, the basis for the biomass calibration was the past and future perceptions of the people and foresters in the watershed, along with researchers' field observations and overall trends at the state level. The scenario analysis was carried out to examine the relative significance of available policy options on the outputs of model.

Method for Biomass Estimation

The allometric equation developed by a study in the adjoining Himalayan region of Nepal (Sharma and Pukkala, 1990) has been used to estimate forest biomass.

$$\ln v = a + b * \ln (d) + c * \ln (h)$$

where, ln is natural log, v is stem over bark volume in m^3, d is diameter in cm, h is height in meters, and a, b, c are the parameters for the dominant species in the watershed.

To get the stem biomass (*SB*), over bark volume (v) of each tree obtained from the above relation is multiplied by the species specific wood density (*WD*).

$$SB = v * WD$$

Wood densities for each species (air dried and with 12–15 per cent moisture content) and stem to branch and stem to foliage biomass ratios for different species were obtained in published sources (HMG, 1988; Jenkins et al., 2005; Luna, 1996; Sharma and Pukkala, 1990; WAC, 2006). More details about sample plots, tree species and their wood density sources are available in Sharma et al. (2008).

Data Collection

A household survey was done to obtain the data relating to crop, livestock and forest activities in the watershed. Whereas, the data on agricultural and livestock activities pertain to the year 2005-06, the data relating to tree biomass is based on survey undertaken in April/May, 2006. All the 102 households in the nine villages of the watershed were interviewed for obtaining the information relating to demography, land holdings, livestock, cropping pattern, input-output of crops and forest related activities. Since extractions from the forests are illegal, the figures given by the inhabitants are most likely to underestimate the total forest biomass usage. Tree biomass from reserved forests was not included in the model as the use of this forest by the local people is negligible due to severe restrictions, greater distance from village habitations and relatively lesser availability of fodder trees.

Seventy plots in the six dominant land use categories were selected to obtain tree biomass data. Plot size ranges between 100 m^2 to 10000 m^2. The number of plots was proportional to land area under specific land use categories. To increase the normality of the field data, however, the plot area was increased for land use categories with smaller proportions of the total land area (Squiers & Wistendahl, 1976). To encompass the range of topographic conditions and spatial distribution in regard to human settlements, the location of plots was chosen first by the stratified sampling method and then within each strata by judgement sampling which is a non probability sampling method based on the researcher's own judgements about the representative population (Kothari, 1990). Due to highly heterogeneous landscapes of mountainous regions, this type of selection of plots was highly essential in order to avoid under or over estimation of biomass of the entire watershed. In every plot, plant diameter at breast height (dbh), i.e. 1.37 meters from ground level, was measured with a diameter tape (FSI, 2002). Tree height was measured by using a clinometer. All trees with a diameter at breast height (DBH) greater than 5 cm, identified to species and their abundance were counted within each sample plot. Data on yield and prices of crops for the last five years were obtained from the Department of Land Records, State Department of Agriculture, H.P. and from a related study conducted by Agro-Economic Research Centre, Shimla (Singh et al., 2006).

Results

The results of this study have been analyzed with respect to biomass requirements, growth of biomass stock, cropping pattern and incomes of households under alternate policy options as reflected through different model scenarios.

Biomass Requirements of Human Population

The tree biomass requirements of the human population are observed to increase constantly over the model horizon in the BASE (Fig. 2). An increase in LPG use over the years will lower the pressure on forest biomass as brought out by the

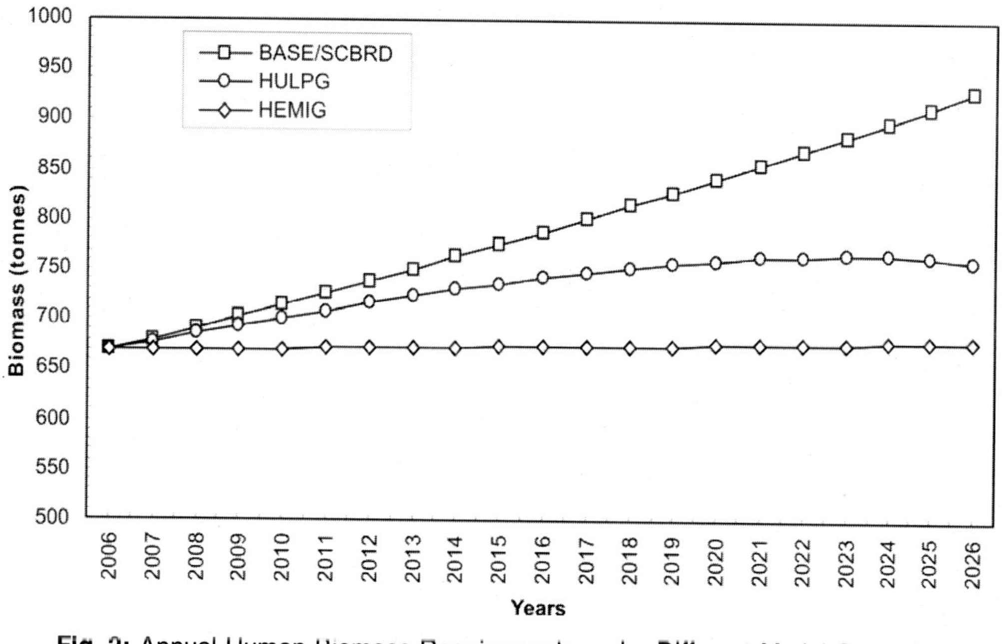

Fig. 2: Annual Human Biomass Requirements under Different Model Scenarios

HULPG as a result of substitution of fuel wood by LPG. Biomass requirements in HULPG increase at a diminishing rate and start to decline near the end of model horizon. SCBRD does not have any relevance to human requirements of biomass and is, therefore, identical to the base model scenario. With higher emigration out of watershed as reflected in HEMIG, the total human biomass requirements remain almost constant over the entire model horizon. Thus, the impact of population growth rate on increasing biomass requirements as reflected in the base scenario is negated by the increased emigration of people to towns and cities in search of better employment opportunities.

Biomass Requirements of Livestock

Fodder leaves, especially those of oak trees (*Quercus leucotricophora)* are required mainly during the dry season, when other sources are rather scarce. Only SCBRD has relevance for assessing tree biomass requirements of livestock over the years (Fig. 3). HULPG and HEMIG will be identical to BASE as they do not influence livestock requirements. Whereas, in the BASE livestock requirements of biomass increase over the years with growing number of livestock, in SCBRD, substitution of crossbred livestock from local breeds decreases biomass requirements initially

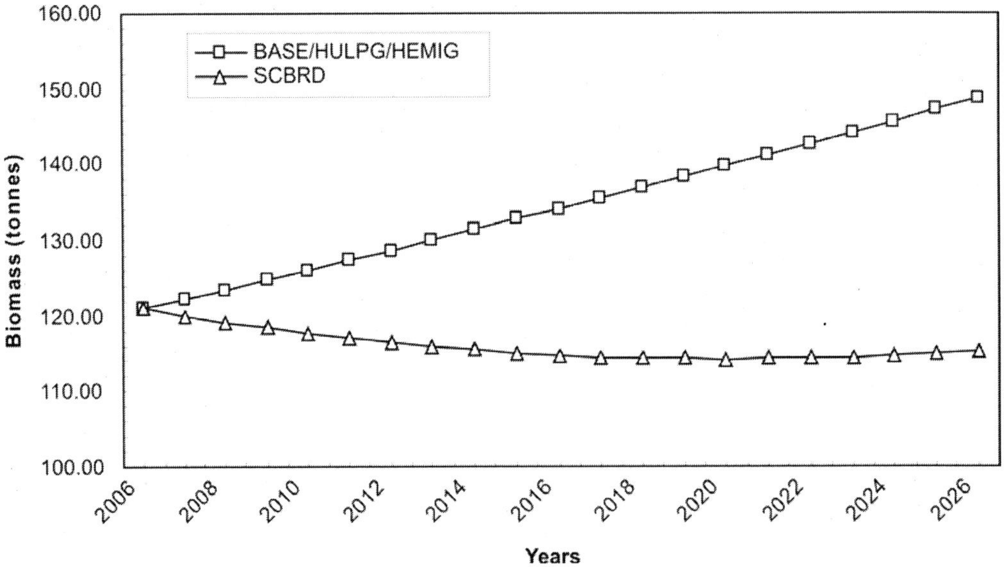

Fig. 3: Biomass Requirement of Livestock in Scenario 3 Compared with the Base Scenario

and maintains them at a constant level. The main reason for such a trend is the greater decline in local breeds as a result of substitution by relatively fewer crossbred animals.

Total Biomass Extractions in Different Model Scenarios

Tree biomass extractions to meet the fodder, fuel wood, timber and miscellaneous requirements in watershed are the highest in the BASE when compared to other model scenarios (Fig. 4). Relative significance of different policy options in lowering the biomass extractions and pressure on forest resources is highlighted by the three alternate policy scenarios representing lower extraction levels. Biomass extractions remain not only at the lowest level but also almost constant over the entire model horizon in HEMIG. HULPG results in lower biomass extractions over the years when compared to BASE. After showing an increase in the first half of model horizon, biomass extractions in HULPG remains more or less constant during the later years. This decline in biomass extractions is due to substitution of LPG for fuel wood. In SCBRD, biomass extraction increases over the entire model horizon, though remaining slightly lower than that of the BASE throughout.

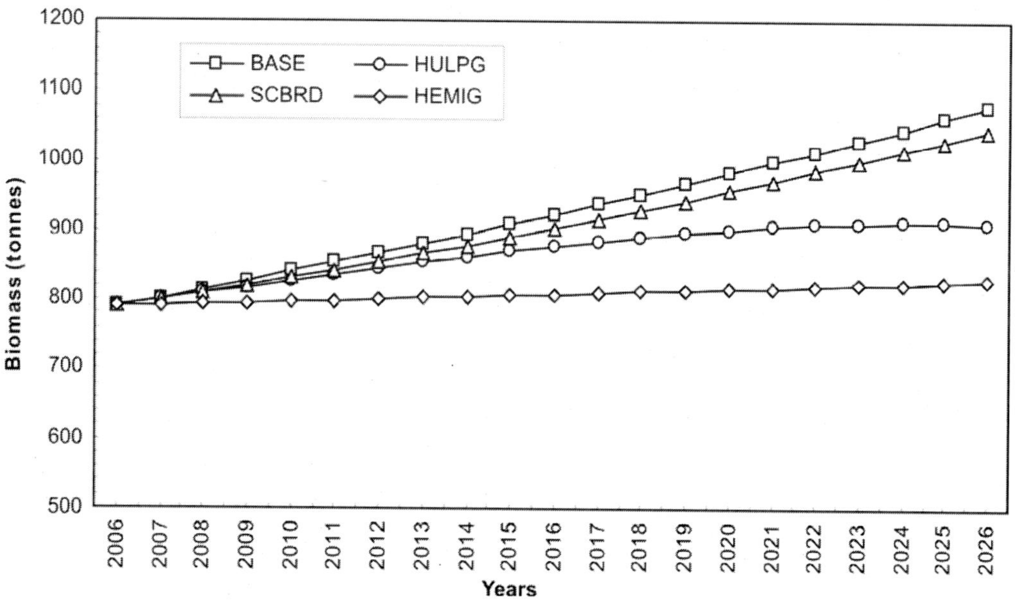

Fig. 4: Total Tree Biomass Extracted under Different Model Scenarios

Growth of Biomass Stock

In the BASE, there is a slight increase of biomass stock in the beginning of the model horizon that tapers off at a later stage (Fig. 5). Biomass production in the watershed may be sustainable in the short run but growing human requirements are reflected by projections of continuous decline in tree biomass in the BASE. SCBRD shows some improvements in tree biomass stock over BASE, but it fails to sustain at the current level. The highest growth in biomass stock is recorded in HEMIG due to higher emigration rate and the resulting reduced requirements of fuel wood and timber. HULPG also shows desirable growth of biomass over the entire model horizon. The situation could be further improved with popularizing the use of improved energy sources, such as, biogas, electricity and solar energy.

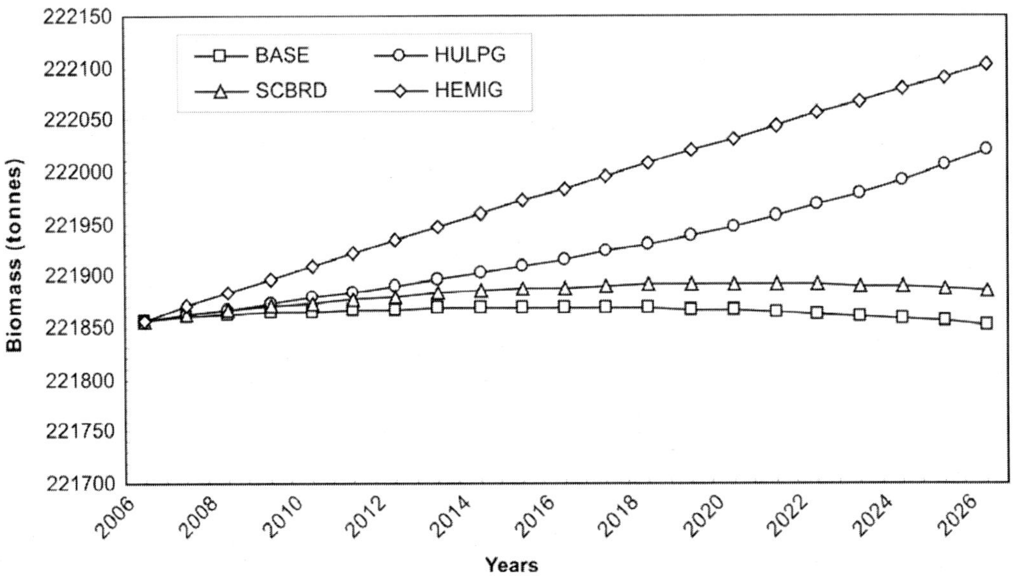

Fig. 5: Growth of Stock of Tree Biomass under Alternate Model Scenarios

Cropping Pattern

There is not much variation in cropping pattern in alternate scenarios if compared to the BASE. This is due to the very nature of alternate policy scenarios that have been primarily built for biomass production. Maximization of TDGM (total discounted gross margins) raises the watershed income to 593,691 thousand rupees in BASE, which is nearly double than the existing cropping plan. Whereas, capsicum, beans and tomato are grown in the *kharif* season, peas and wheat are grown in *rabi* season on irrigated and non irrigated land respectively (Fig. 6).

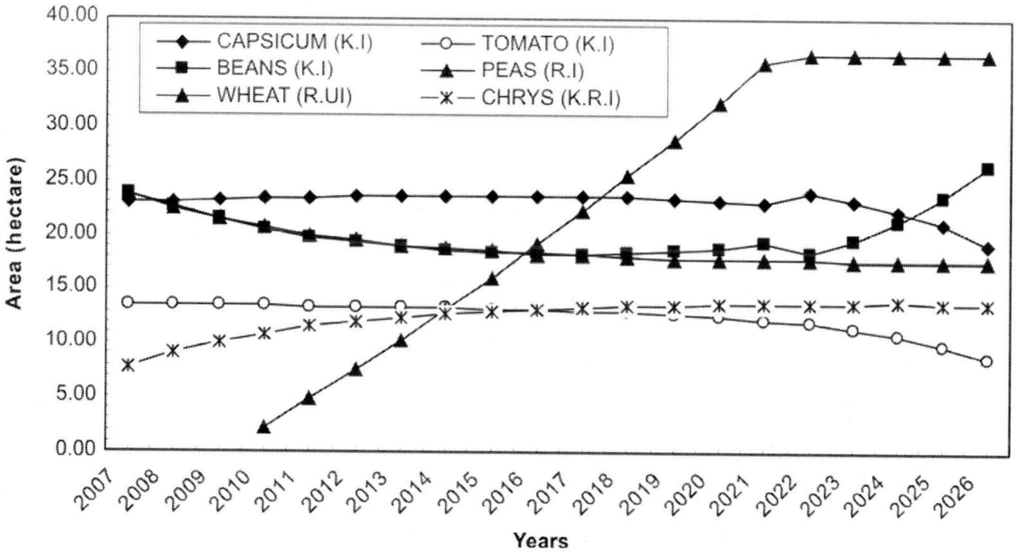

Fig. 6: Dynamics of Cropping Pattern in the Base Scenario

As an annual crop, chrysanthemum occupies the land in both the seasons. By comparing BASE to the existing plan, it is observed that the farmers are more considerate to risk rather than profits as they diversify agriculture by cultivating several crops with low risk level than only a few crops that maximize the income. However, crops such as maize and barley, which are dominant crops in the watershed, are missing in the optimum plans due to less gross margins or model constraints.

Household Income and Input Requirements

The four optimum plans have the potential to increase the income by more than 77 per cent when compared to the current level of TDGM of 3,24,248 thousand rupees. Even in the BASE which also considers the current level of risk, income can be raised by 83 per cent. Net present value of the total gross margins in each of the alternative model scenarios is presented in Table 5.

An increase in emigration rate lowers the watershed income by causing labour scarcity that has to be compensated for by hiring labour from outside the watershed

Table 5: Changes in Income (total discounted gross margins) and Other Parameters in Different Model Scenarios

Sl. No.	Model Scenario	TDGM (₹ '000)	Capital Requirements (₹ '000)	Labour Hiring Requirements (Man Days)
1	BASE	5,93,691	1,39,880	251
2	HULPG	5,74,369	1,34,743	690
3	SCBRD	5,93,788	1,39,907	242
4	HEMIG	5,80,931	1,36,526	6,935

and thus raising input costs. It is observed that there is a little scope of supplementing farm income by remittances received from the emigrants from the watershed due to the high expenditure requirements in the towns and cities. Whereas the increased use of LPG has a favourable effect on biomass growth, the burden of extra costs for the purchase of LPG will lower the watershed income. The substitution of crossbred livestock for local breeds helps in raising the income of people.

From the current requirement of 83,625 thousand rupees, capital requirements exceeds above 1,30,000 thousand rupees in each scenario. Capital requirements move in a similar direction as TDGM in each model scenario. The capital availability constraint is one of the major reasons for such a trend. Though the substitution of crossbred livestock requires less labour than the base level, higher use of LPG will require more labour during the entire model horizon. Though the higher use of LPG will result in labour savings from the forest activity and increased cost of LPG but the alterations in the optimum crop plan will raise the labour use and reduce capital requirements when compared to the BASE which represent a plan with fixed VIT at current level. All optimum plans except HEMIG however use less labour than the current level of 769 man days.

Discussion

Cultivation of crops contributes the largest component of farmers' income in the watershed. Therefore, this activity uses bulk of the available labour and capital resources. Despite the fact that in a hill farming system, livestock and forest activities contribute little to total income, they command a special significance due to the interdependence of different components within the farming system (Tulachan and Neupane, 1999). Traditional practices based on the principle of self-sufficiency, and religious and cultural traditions further strengthen these mixed agricultural systems. Higher profits from cash crops like flowers and off-season vegetables, distant markets and poor marketing infrastructure discourage the commercial rearing of livestock.

Livestock rearing is an integral part of the hill farming system for meeting the requirements of milk, farm yard manure and bullock draft power. The contribution of livestock activity to the total income in the watershed is however too small. Livestock rearing has become more important in recent years with the substitution of improved livestock for local breeds. Since the forests are government owned and there are several restrictions on forest product extraction, forest contribution to watershed income is also negligible. Traditional dependence on forest products for miscellaneous needs, however, means that forest product extraction plays an important role in the Himalayan farming systems (Gouri et al., 2004).

Comparison of the existing cropping pattern with the optimum crop plan infers that the farmers are more sensitive to risk rather than profits. This tendency is explained by the diversification of agriculture by cultivating several crops with low risk level than the crops that maximize the income only. Cultivation of traditional crops, such as, maize and barley, is still carried out by the people in Himalayan region despite low economic viability. Capital availability is a major constraint in agriculture, especially for newly introduced horticultural crops that require large investments. In addition to the personal savings, which are dependent on annual expenditure level, the capital formation requires an efficient banking network and good enterprise in villages. The labour requirements are likely to increase substantially with the emerging cropping patterns (Chand, 1997). Increasing emigration will further aggravate the labour shortage (Sharma, 2005). Labour scarcity will pose a serious problem to the farmers, especially in the context of specialized cultivation of flowers and vegetables.

The inhabitants of the watershed perceive a definite decline in the tree biomass density over last twenty years despite high biomass density in the forest as a whole (Sharma et al., 2008). Forest fire, illegal felling, unscientific lopping, decay, and climate change, are some of the important factors which have been attributed to the ongoing forest degradation. If these factors are not managed properly, they can result in reduced forest cover even as overall biomass productivity exceeds demand (Moench & Bandyopadhyay, 1986). Biomass accumulation is also being reduced by changing environmental conditions, irrespective of the current density (Monte-Luna et al., 2004). Changes due to anthropogenic pressures have adversely affected the carrying capacity of land (Ehrlich et al., 1989). In view of the absence of precise estimates of the main affecting parameters, i.e. loss due to miscellaneous factors such as decay, fire, illegal felling, etc., and carrying capacity of land, these predictions can at best be taken only as indicative of the system behaviour under different model scenarios. This should be helpful in providing useful directions for devising appropriate policies for steering biomass growth in the desired direction.

The watershed is located in a forest region with easy access and abundance of useful tree biomass, therefore, the per capita fuel wood consumption is found to be relatively higher (3.56 kg/day) than the average of forested districts (1.70 kg/day) in Himachal Pradesh (Rai and Chakarabarti, 1996). With improvement in transportation and other infrastructure combined with economic development in the area, several households have started using LPG as a substitute for the fuel wood (Sharma et al., 2007). However, the traditional stoves and fuel wood are still preferred due to economic reasons (Kanagawa and Nakata, 2007) for cooking, water heating, space heating, lighting, livestock rearing, etc. Among various activities, cooking requires relatively more energy (Pohekar et al., 2005). Modern cooking fuels can provide significant health, productivity and environmental benefits (Heltberg, 2004). But without income generation, which is reflected by opportunity cost, rural households do not adopt improved energy sources (Kanagawa & Nakata, 2007). Since, placing the burden of better forest growth entirely on local populations is not likely to be accepted, or successful, compensating subsidies for LPG is a popular policy option. The subsidies in the urban areas can be withdrawn and the saved amount could be used for the bioenergy programmes that will improve the quality of life in rural areas and reduce the pressure on forests (Ravindranath and Hall, 1995). Increased availability of LPG may prove a better alternative than the subsidies due to weak cross-price elasticities among alternate sources of fuel (Gupta and Kohlin, 2006). As the purchasing power is the only criterion for selection of a cooking device (Pohekar et al., 2005), increasing local income in rural watersheds is critical to promote the adoption of efficient energy sources. The vegetative biomass requirements of improved breeds of livestock are higher due to higher consumption requirements and practice of stall-feeding (Singh et al., 2005). But, due to the sufficient grasslands in the watershed, crossbred livestock are preferably served with grasses and compounded feed purchased from the market.

Conclusion

The entire state of Himachal Pradesh has seen a rapid change in cropping pattern over the last few years. Cultivation of cash crops of vegetables and flowers, especially in the controlled conditions of poly-houses is becoming a popular trend. Irrigation facilities and easy availability of capital are the major constraints in the adoption of these crops. Therefore, more direct policy efforts by the government are needed for removing these bottlenecks. Knowledge dissemination regarding the costs, returns, risks and cultivation methods of these new crops must be provided at the farm level to encourage more people to start such ventures. Due to the high risk level attached to these profitable crops, efforts must be made to develop local market yards, better road network and easy credit facilities. Such efforts will encourage the farmers to substitute profitable cash crops for the traditional crops, thereby increasing self-employment, incomes and level of living in villages. The rearing of improved livestock is becoming popular, but due to distant markets and lack of proper marketing infrastructure, commercial rearing is still not possible. Livestock products continue to be used for self-consumption only in rural areas. Policies that strengthen the dairy industry together with better marketing infrastructure can encourage the commercial rearing of livestock.

Contribution of the watershed forests towards favourable agro-climatic conditions and better recharging of irrigation sources is an important source for prosperity. Such benefits are however difficult to estimate in monetary terms. The impact of forests on sustainability of farming system is very substantial in the Himalayan regions. Despite the effective governmental efforts to protect the forest land area, declining forest density is an indication of the ineffectiveness of current policies to control periodic losses due to decay, development, fire and illegal activities. While efforts like tree planting and removal of decaying trees will augment the regeneration process, strict control of forest fires and illegal/unscientific extraction of timber and forest products will help in containing periodic losses.

Though the demand for woody biomass has a relatively lesser role in forest degradation in this region, efforts to promote improved cooking stoves, LPG, biogas and pressure cookers together with substitution of fewer crossbred livestock to local livestock are likely to be successful policy options for lowering fuel wood and fodder demand. Government must ensure a regular supply of LPG in the forested regions of the Himalayas. It will not only save wastage of biomass energy on cooking but will also be labour saving, especially in the wake of new agricultural ventures demanding more labour. The price subsidy to at least new and small users will also help in this regard. Since the forests possess a macro-environmental importance, the central government must compensate states to preserve forest resources. States can easily identify the households in such regions through its vast administrative network.

Better educational facilities with more emphasis on vocational training will provide better employment opportunities in the urban areas. It will help in increasing the emigration from rural areas, thereby lowering the forest biomass demand.

The results of this study have more relevance to the regions with similar agro-climatic and forest conditions. It will also have a wider implication to the whole Himalayan region with respect to changing activities and the optimum resource usage. More efforts for the studies adopting a system approach at micro watershed scale will be highly useful for devising region specific policies and will serve a better alternative to the generalized macro analysis.

Acknowledgement

Authors gratefully acknowledge the financial support for this work from the Norwegian University of Life Sciences, Aas, Norway and the Integrated Institute of Himalayan Studies, Shimla. Travel grant by the UGC to first author for presenting this article in the Tenth Biennial Conference of ISEE at Nairobi is gratefully acknowledged.

References

[1] Brooke, A., Kendrick, D., Meeraus, A. and Raman, R. (1998). *GAMS User's Guide,* Washington DC, USA: GAMS Development Corporation.

[2] Chand, R. (1997). *Agricultural Diversification and Development of Mountain Regions – With Special Reference to Himachal Pradesh,* New Delhi: M.D. Publications.

[3] Chopra, K. and Adhikari, S.K. (2004). "Environment Development Linkages: Modelling a Wetland System for Ecological and Economic Value", *Environment and Development Economics* 9(1), pp. 19-45.

[4] Ehrlich, P.R., Daily, G.C., Ehrlich, A.H., Matson, P. and Vitousek, P. (1989). "Global Change and Carrying Capacity: Implications for Life on Earth", in DeFries, R.S. and Malone, T.F. (eds.), *Global Change and Our Common Future,* Washington D.C.: The National Academies Press, pp. 19-28.

[5] FSI (2002). *The Manual of Instructions for Field Inventory*, Forest Survey of India, Dehradun.

[6] FSI (2003). *State of Forest Report 2003*, Dehradun, India: Forest Survey of India.

[7] GOHP (2002). *Himachal Pradesh Development Report*, Shimla: Government of Himachal Pradesh.

[8] GOHP (2005). *Management Plan of Chail Wildlife Sanctuary, Plan Period 1999–2000 to 2008-09*, Shimla: H.P. Forest Department, Govt. of Himachal Pradesh.

[9] GOHP (2007). *Himachal Forests: Forest Cover by Different Forest Types*, http://hpforest.nic.in/frst2.htm (accessed 9 July 2007).

[10] Gouri, Mudgal, S., Morrison, E. and Mayers, J. (2004). *Policy Influences on Forest-based Livelihoods in Himachal Pradesh, India*, London: International Institute for Environment and Development.

[11] Gupta, G. and Kohlin, G. (2006). "Preferences for Domestic Fuel: Analysis with Socio-economic Factors and Rankings in Kolkata, India", *Ecological Economics* 57(1), pp. 107-121.

[12] Hazell, P.B.R. (1971). "A Linear Alternative to Quadratic and Semivariance Programming for Farm Planning under Uncertainty", *American Journal of Agricultural Economics* 53(1), pp. 53-62.

[13] Heltberg, R. (2004). "Fuel Switching: Evidence from Eight Developing Countries", *Energy Economics* 26(5), pp. 869-887.

[14] HMG (1988). *Master Plan for the Forestry Sector Nepal: Forest Resources Information Status and Development Plan*, Kathmandu, Nepal: His Majesty's Govt. of Nepal (HMG) Ministry of Soil and Conservation.

[15] Holden, S.T. and Shiferaw, B. (2004). "Land Degradation, Drought and Food Security in a Less-favoured Area in the Ethiopian Highlands: A Bio-economic Model with Market Imperfections. *Agricultural Economics* 30(1), pp. 31-49.

[16] Jenkins, J.C., Chojancky, D.C., Heath, L.S. and Birdsey, R.A. (2005). *Comprehensive Database of Diameter-Based Biomass Regressions for North American Tree Species*, Baltimore, MD: Third USDA Symposium on Greenhouse Gases and Carbon Sequestration in Agriculture and Forestry.

[17] Kanagawa, M. and Nakata, T. (2007). "Analysis of the Energy Access Improvement and its Socio-economic Impacts in Rural Areas of Developing Countries", *Ecological Economics* 62(2), pp. 319-329.

[18] Kothari, C.R. (1990). *Research Methodology: Methods and Techniques*, New Delhi: Wishwa Prakashan.

[19] Luna, R.K. (1996). *Plantation Trees*, Dehradun, India: International Book Distributors.

[20] Moench, M. and Bandyopadhyay, J. (1986). "People Forest Interaction: A Neglected Parameter in Himalayan Forest Management", *Mountain Research and Development* 6, pp. 3-16.

[21] Monte-Luna, P.D., Brook, B.W., Zetina-Rejón, M.J. and Cruz-Escalona, V.H. (2004). "The Carrying Capacity of Ecosystems", *Global Ecology and Biogeography* 13(6), pp. 485-495.

[22] Pohekar, S.D., Kumar, D. and Ramachandran, M. (2005). "Dissemination of Cooking Energy Alternatives in India – A Review", *Renewable and Sustainable Energy Reviews* 9(4), pp. 379-393.

[23] Rai, S.N. and Chakarabarti, S.K. (1996). *Demand and Supply of Fuel Wood, Timber and Fodder in India*, Dehradun: Forest Survey of India.

[24] Ravindranath, N.H. and Hall, D.O. (1995). *Biomass, Energy, and Environment: A Developing Country Perspective from India*, London: Oxford University Press.

[25] Renshaw, E. (1991). *Modelling Biological Populations in Space and Time*, Cambridge: Cambridge University Press.

[26] Sankhayan, P.L., Gurung, N., Sitaula, B.K. and Hofstad, O. (2003). "Bio-economic modelling of Land Use and Forest Degradation at Watershed Level in Nepal", *Agriculture, Ecosystems & Environment* 94(1), pp. 105-116.

[27] Sharma, E.R. and Pukkala, T. (1990). *Volume Equations and Biomass Prediction of Forest Trees of Nepal*, Kathmandu, Nepal: Publication No. 47(1), Ministry of Forests and Soil Conservation, Forest Survey and Statistics Division.

[28] Sharma, L.R. (2005). *Quality of Life in the Himalayan Region*, New Delhi: Indus Publishing Company.

[29] Sharma, R.K., Sankhayan, P.L. and Hofstad, O. (2008). "Forest Biomass Density, Utilization and Production Dynamics in a Western Himalayan Watershed", *Journal of Forestry Research* 19(3), pp. 171-180.

[30] Sharma, R.K., Sankhayan, P.L., Hofstad, O. and Singh, R. (2007). "Land Use Changes in the Western Himalayan Region – A Study at Watershed Level in the State of Himachal Pradesh, India", *International Journal of Ecology and Environmental Sciences* 33(2-3), pp. 197-206.

[31] Singh, R., Vaidya, C.S. and Karol, A. (2006). *Likely Demand of Vegetables of Himachal Pradesh in the Neighbouring Consuming States During Next Ten Years*, Shimla: Agro-Economic Research Centre.

[32] Singh, R., Karol, A. and Singh, P. (2005). *Livestock-Crop Production Systems-Analysis for Sustainable Production*, Shimla: Agro-Economic Research Centre, H.P. University.

[33] Singh, R.B. (1999). "Land Use Change, Diversification of Agriculture and Agroforestry in North-West India", in Haque, T. (ed.), *Land Use Planning in India*, New Delhi: NCAEPR, pp. 122-130.

[34] Squiers, E.R. and Wistendahl, W.A. (1976). "Sample Unit Selection for Studies of Herbaceous Oldfield Vegetation", *Ohio Journal of Science* 76(4), pp. 185-188.

[35] Tulachan, P.M. and Neupane, A. (1999). *Livestock in Mixed Farming Systems of the Hindukush-Himalayas. Trends and Sustainability*, Kathmandu, Nepal: International Centre for Integrated Mountain Development.

[36] WAC (2006). Wood Density Database. http://www.worldagroforestry.org/Sea/Products/AFDbases/WD/index.htm (accessed 7 September 2006).

17

An Investigation into the Relationship between Fish Biodiversity and Profit Maximization

Anita Chattopadhyay Gupta

Introduction

The sustainable use of fish resources is central to fisheries management, given the long-term importance of the fisheries sector in terms of nutrition and employment. However, today's major concern centres around the unsustainable levels of species exploitation with unbridled fish-catch practices leading to the depletion of fish stocks, reduction in diversity and disruption of the ecological equilibrium. A re-analysis of the FAO Catches Statistics (Pauly et al., 1998) reveals progressive 'fishing down' of food chains as fishing effort responds to depletion of original target stocks, where one species is exploited more than another. As a result, their relative abundance changes, as has been witnessed in the North Atlantic (Sherman, 1990). This is referred to, in the literature as 'fishing down the food web'. Virtually, all commercially valuable marine populations are now overexploited. Overexploitation diminishes species population and reduces economic return. As the most valuable species are overfished, they are quickly replaced by catches of less desirable ones. It is seen that a large share of today's global catch consists of previously unused, less valuable species. This type of phenomenon has been identified as 'fishing down the value chain' (Kasulo and Perrings, 2001) in the literature. 'Fishing down the food web' implies a shift from long-lived, high trophic level fish towards short-lived, low-trophic level fish species whereas 'fishing down the value chain' a shift from high economically valued species to low economically valued species measured in terms of market prices.[1] Whatever be the fishing sequence, it will have an impact on fish biodiversity with a change in composition and relative abundance of harvested species. So, a desire to increase profits may hamper economic biodiversity conservation and thereby affect the value of the fishery.[2]

This linkage between fish biodiversity and profitability creates an important entry point of research in this chapter. This chapter looks into the loss of fish biodiversity due to excessive exploitation of the species and its consequent impact on the profitability of fishery. The study focuses on the Digha fishery in West Bengal on the eastern marine coast of India on the Bay of Bengal. It is pertinent to mention here that the sustainability issue of the fisheries sector, in isolation, has been dealt in some empirical works pertaining to Digha fishery and they are essentially biological and static in nature (Central Marine Fisheries Research Institute, 1984; Guha et al., 1994; Das et al., 1996; Das et al., 2000; Dhar, 2004; Jana, 2004). The issue of investigating any relationship between biodiversity and profitability has largely been neglected in the literature for this particular location. Further, a void exists in the literature in terms of bio-economic modelling of the fishery in a dynamic profit-maximization set-up. Also the question of biodiversity needs to be addressed in the light of various reports[3] of the marine fisheries of West Bengal.

In an attempt to bridge these gaps in the literature, this chapter reports on the dynamics of the profit-maximizing regime and estimates the dynamic maximum economic yield and net present-value of fishery profit that is maximized here. At a broader academic level, this chapter attempts to contribute to the base of literature that has entailed the shift in paradigm in the way research is being conducted at the socio-ecological-economic interface of human endeavour: from a "segmented-specialisation approach" to "collective integration approach". It is a shift from traditional research based on case studies in an isolated way to an integrated wider perspective of case study on both bio-economic aspects along with sustainable regional development along with issues relating to environmental governance.

There are two important parts in this chapter: the theoretical framework, and an empirical validation. The theoretical aspect has been modelled in an extension of the aggregated Gordon-Schaefer standard fisheries model. A sensitivity analysis has been conducted with respect to small perturbation in discount rate to examine the impact of changes in the value of discount rate on profit under different biodiversity scenarios. In the end, wc examine whether economic biodiversity conservation are in conflict with profitability of the fishery.

Section 2 of this chapter relates the reader to the study site. Section 3 focuses on the importance of biodiversity and its ecological and economic aspects. Section 4 presents data analysis and socioeconomic aspects of Digha fishery. This section analyses the economic condition of the fishermen and provides a background for their strive to catch high-valued species. The theoretical framework, modelling and results of model estimation have been presented in Section 5. Optimum values of the variables under profit-maximizing regime have been derived in Section 6. Section 7 reports results of sensitivity analysis. Section 8 consists of the concluding remarks.

The Study Area

Our study area is part of the coastal area of West Bengal. The total coastal area of West Bengal stretches between the mouths of rivers Herobhanga or Harinbhanga on the Indo-Bangladesh border in the east and Subanarekha in the west, the total length of which is about 220 kms. Quite naturally, fishing activities in this zone provide economic sustenance and a source of livelihood to a cross-section of people who, in turn, support the flourishing trade in this lower Ganga deltaic region. The coastline of West Bengal spreads over two maritime districts – 24 Parganas (South) and East Midnapore. There are 13 marine fish landing centres in 24 Parganas and 27 in East Midnapore. The Contai coastal belt under the district of East Midnapore is considered to be highly potential in respect of marine fisheries activities. The coastline stretches from Digha under Ramnagar-I Block to Talpati Ghat under Khesuri-II Block and is about 60 km. in length. Digha is situated close to the Gangetic mouth on the east of India at lat. 21°36'N. and long. 87°30'E. It is located in the West Midnapore district of the State of West Bengal of Eastern India and lies in the southern-most part of the state on the bank of Bay of Bengal. With the introduction of diesel using powerboats, deep-sea fishing and mechanization in fishing is taking an upturn. It has been observed in Digha coastal areas that total marine fish landing mainly consists of sardine, hilsa, coila, pomphret, croakers, Bombay duck, catfish, ribbon fish, shark, shankar, prawn, etc. Thus, a total 37 varieties of fish are found here. These varieties have been divided into five groups considering their importance from the viewpoint of their demand and price.[4] Among them, the contribution of hilsa in total catch per trip was found to be maximum in Digha. It was followed by two types of pomfret: Chinese and Silver pomfret being one variety and the other being Black pomfret. So, we see from the collected data that mainly four varieties of marine fish dominate the Digha fishing industry in terms of both prices and quantity. They are Hilsa, Chinese and Silver Pomfret, Black Pomfret and Prawn. More than 50 per cent of the total value of catch was contributed by these four species. Individual contributions of other 33 species in terms of value are not very significant. Also, these other 33 varieties of fish such as (in local vocabulary) *sardine, mackreal, chela, para* and *American bhetki* have a very low price range in the market. These have been grouped under the heading 'others'. The Digha Fishermen and Trader's Association regulates fishing activities in that area and acts as a profit-maximizing unit within a larger competitive fish market.

Importance of Biodiversity

The importance of biodiversity[5] had long been recognized by ecologists and environmentalists. But the main focus came into being with the initiation of the Convention on Biological Diversity in 1992 (UNCED, 1992). The emphasis was on conserving biodiversity to achieve the sustainable use of its components and therefore to secure the fair and equitable sharing of the resources which that biodiversity represents. Our study relates to that area of the Convention that emphasizes on "... marine and other aquatic ecosystems, and the ecological complexes of which they are part..." and the value that they represent.

Conservation of biodiversity[6] is important in environmental management programmes (Turner and Gardner, 1991; Reid and Miller, 1989). Measuring biodiversity is one of the central issues in ecology because of its importance in devising conservation strategies. However, incorporation of biodiversity in a fisheries model is a difficult task. This difficulty arises from the lack of a single practical operational definition and measurement of biodiversity. A simple measure in the literature of ecology used for quantifying fish diversity is to count the number of species in the habitat or community. This measure is considered to be too simplistic and so other indices measuring biodiversity based both on number and abundance of species have been identified. The idea of species diversity has two distinct concepts: species richness and abundance. Species richness is the number of species in a community, while abundance explains the relative proportion of each species in the community. The Shannon index[7] is a very well-known example of the richness index group. An important example of dominance index is the Simpson's index.[8]

The main difference between the above two type of indices is that species richness indices are weighted more towards uncommon species while dominance indices are weighted more towards the abundant species. The question now is one of selecting the most appropriate method of measuring diversity.[9] The choice of the index should depend on the component of diversity being measured. If the main concern is on rare species, then richness-based species should be used. But if the major interest lies in the abundance of the commonest species, then dominance indices are preferred. In our case of Digha fishery, data on catch per species will be used to compute the level of biodiversity. Here, dominance indices is the most appropriate measure as catch data change shows changes in the abundance of dominant species. In order to apply the Simpson index to the case of fisheries, the unit of measurement must be changed from individuals in a sample population to biomass in the total catch (Goda and Matsuoka, 1986). So, the Simpson index (henceforth called the unweighted or ecological Simpson's index) can be expressed as:

$$D_t = \sum_{i=1}^{s} (Y_{it} / Y_t)^2$$

where Y_{it} is the catch of the ith species harvested in period t, Y_t is the total catch in period t and s is the number of species harvested in period t. The use of this estimate enables us to identify an empirical relation between the diversity index and total catch. These diversity indices are basically ecological in nature as they emphasize on ecological differences among species that comprise a community or habitat.

Heywood (1995) reports about the growing perception among both ecologists and economists that the importance of biodiversity lies first and foremost in its role in the production of goods and services that are useful for human welfare, i.e. in its social-economic importance. An individual harvested species is valued for specific properties that make it useful in either production or consumption. The biodiversity that supports such species derives its value from this. Any measure of diversity should accordingly reflect this (Perrings, 2000; Heywood, 1995). Ecological and economic values are not necessarily the same. It does not follow that if biodiversity is important to the functioning of some ecological system then it will automatically be valuable for society. Nor does it follow that a species that is rare will be economically scarce and hence valuable. So, there is no necessary correspondence between ecological biodiversity measures and economic value of biodiversity. Systems with a high biodiversity value by any of the standard indices may or may not have high economic value. So, to reflect the socio-economic value of diversity, the ecological diversity measures need to be modified (Kasulo and Perrings, 2001). In fisheries, as most of the species caught are marketed, an economic value of a species can be approximated by using market prices (Hanemann, 1988). The rationale for social-economic valuation of biodiversity lies in the fact that the signals generated by the market system, i.e. prices lead to excessive rates of biodiversity loss (Heywood, 1995). Market prices influence the exploitation of a fishery and hence the level and direction of effort. Targeting of effort towards particular species leads to elimination of highly valued species, and to a reduction in biodiversity and productivity (Barbier et al., 1994). To capture the economic value of species, the Simpson's biodiversity index is modified such that it uses market values of species caught rather than the total amount of species caught. Now, the actual amount of the species will be weighted by price. Therefore, the Simpson's index becomes (henceforth called the weighted or economic Simpson's index):

$$B = \sum_{i=1}^{s} (P_i Y_i / TR)^2$$

where B is the economic biodiversity index, P_i is the per unit price of species i, and TR is the total revenue. When all the species have the same market value, the solution for economic biodiversity index is the same as the ecological biodiversity index. When the community is dominated by species of high market value, economic biodiversity index will be greater than an ecological biodiversity index of the same community and vice versa.

Ecologically, it is acknowledged that when the major concern is about the uniqueness of species, then each type of species should have equal inherent value. However, when economic considerations are taken into account, then different species are assumed to have different values. Biodiversity may take on different values depending on people's perception of the economic or ecological importance of species diversity to human welfare (Barbier et al., 1994). In our study, following the work by Kasulo and Perrings (2001), biodiversity is weighted by its economic significance. This is important because it reflects the value of biodiversity to humans. Thus, more weight is given to species with higher market values.

Data Analysis

Data for this study has been collected from the Digha Fishermen and Fish Traders' Association[10] in Digha covering the period 1993-94 to 2002-03. Catch is measured as kilogram of fish landed and effort is represented by fishing months.[11] Digha fishery, in recent years, has seen a shift in fish species harvested towards catches of fish species of very low local value (ranging between Indian ₹ 4–35 per kg) consisting of sardine, chela and kaante which we have clubbed under the heading 'others'. This transition in fish catch from high valued to low valued species points to the role of the market and the effects of economic forces in loss of biodiversity. The decline in the dominance of hilsa in total catch reflects not only a decline in the trophic level of fishes but can also be associated with its economic value. The total landing of hilsa has declined to 1 per cent in 2002-03 whereas its contribution was 34 per cent in 1993-94. In contrast, the total landing of the species such as *sardine*, *chhela* and *kaante* has increased from 43 per cent in 1993-94 to 75 per cent in 2002-03. It is interesting to note in this context that hilsa, which is a very popular traditional fish, has a high average price of ₹ 73.18 per kg while *chhela*, *sardine* and *kaante* are valued at very low average prices of ₹ 9.77 per kg. The market price in this case reflects people's preference and is one of the reasons for the overexploitation of hilsa. So, not only is there a shift in relative dominance of fish species in total catch, it also reflects an exploitation from valuable to less valuable species. A comparative analysis of the unweighted and weighted Simpson indices is carried out by using the data on catch per species for the fishery of Digha. The Simpson economic biodiversity is constructed by weighting the simple ecological Simpson's index by average prices so as to capture fluctuations in value. It will capture any shift that may occur in fish value resulting from the over-exploitation of high-valued species. Data shows that in a comparison between the Simpson unweighted and weighted indices, we find the value of the weighted index is lower than that of the unweighted index. It is because of the differences in the value of the species caught that the differences in the two indices occur. The lower values of the weighted indices in comparison with the unweighted index reflects that on average, catches are dominated by less valuable species. If catches had been dominated by valuable species, price weighting would increase their dominance even further and the weighted indices would have higher values than unweighted indices (Kasulo and Perrings, 2001).

The socio-economic impact of loss of fish biodiversity when associated with a shift from high valued to low valued species is generally negative. Most of the fishermen operating in Digha coastal area are socio-economically backward with average literacy rate, given by census 1991, at only 30.68 per cent. According to the Digha Development Authority, there are 600 countryboat owners, 100 motorboat owners and 400 trawler owners operating in the fishery. The average family size in Digha is 4.74 persons/family (census 1991). The marine fishermen in Digha are mostly local people with negligible proportion of migrants, about 4 per cent. With respect to land holding, average land per fisherman is very small. The primary reason behind this is that they find fishing business more profitable than cultivation. They work full time in fishing and do not have practically any other source of income. The shift in fish catch from high-valued to low-valued species means lower profits for the fishing vessel owners and hence crew labourers hired on per trip basis run the risk of losing their jobs. The trawler owners invest large amount of capital on boat and net while the countryboat owners, having non-mechanized boats, invests the least. Since these fishermen have poor economic background, they mostly have to borrow mainly from cooperative banks and private sources such as moneylenders called the Aratdars and Mahajans. A loss in fish diversity (reflected through fall in value of catch) will reduce profits and will mean an additional pressure in repayment and a subsequent debt trap for them. On the other hand, the crew labourers running the risk of unemployment and having no alternative source of income becomes worse off. In a survey conducted on Digha marine fishermen, Guha and Neogy (1996) has found that lower income group of fishermen spend approximately 60 per cent of their monthly expenditure on food while higher income group spends 52 per cent on an average on food items. So it is the crew labourer fishermen who are likely to be hit hardest by the decline in fish diversity.

Modelling Biodiversity

The most marked effect of biodiversity loss occurs on the productivity of the resource. The effects of changes in fish diversity on fish productivity is observed in terms of the benefits of biodiversity in maintaining the aquatic ecosystems which produce the fish resources that are used for human consumption (Barbier et al., 1994). Fisheries bear the effect of biodiversity loss through declining biological and economic productivity and a diminished range of harvested species. The biodiversity variable can be introduced in the Gordon-Schaefer model through the production function that specifies a relationship between fish biodiversity as an input and fish catch as an output.

We now consider the following notations to specify our model

Y = fish catch
X = fish stock
E =fishing effort
r = intrinsic growth rate
q = catchability coefficient
K = environmental carrying capacity of fish stock
D = ecological biodiversity index
B = economic biodiversity index
p = average price
c = average cost
δ = discount rate
$\dot{X}$ = net growth in fish stock
U = catch per unit adjusted effort (Y/DE),

In the standard model, we have the expression for time rate of change in the stock of fish biomass as

$\dot{X} = rX(1 - X/K) - qXE$ and at steady state
$= 0 \Rightarrow rX\,(1 - X/K) = qXE$
or $X = K\,(1 - q/rE)$

The Gordon-Schaefer production function is

$$Y = qXE$$

On substituting the value of X in the above equation, we have

$$Y/E = qK - q^2(K/r)E.$$

The effect of species diversity on fish productivity can be captured through an additional term in the fisheries production function (Kasulo and Perrings, 2001). Thus, we have

$$Y = qDEX \tag{1}$$

where D is the ecological biodiversity index constructed on the basis of Simpson's index.

Again, we have $$Y = qBEX \tag{2}$$

where B is the economic biodiversity index constructed by weighting the Simpson's index with market prices of the species.[12]

The growth functions become

$$\dot{X} = rX(1 - [X/K]) - qDEX \tag{3}$$

and $$\dot{X} = rX(1 - [X/K]) - qBEX \tag{4}$$

The sustainable yield functions become

$$Y = qDEX = qDEK(1 - qDE/r) \tag{5}$$

and $$Y = qBEX = qBEK(1 - qBE/r) \tag{6}$$

Therefore, $$(Y/DE) = qK(1 - qDE/r) = qK - q^2K/r.DE \tag{7}$$

$$(Y/BE) = qK(1 - qBE/r) = qK - q^2K/r.BE \tag{8}$$

Equations (7) and (8) relates catch per unit of adjusted effort to adjusted effort[13] where effort is adjusted with ecological biodiversity index, D in the former equation and with economic biodiversity index, B, the latter.

Alternatively, we can write the sustainable yield function as

$$(Y/AE) = qK(1 - qAE/r) = qK - q^2K/r.AE$$

and $$Y = qKAE - q^2K/r.(AE)^2$$

where AE is the adjusted effort adjusted with the inclusion of biodiversity indices.

Differentiating sustainable yield function with respect to AE and setting that equal to zero, we have

$$\partial Y/\partial AE = qK(1 - 2qAE/r) = 0$$

or $$AE_{msy} = r/2q \tag{9}$$

For estimation purposes, we have followed the approach of Schnute (1977) where both types of biodiversity indices are introduced. It defines a population growth function in terms of U, i.e. catch per unit adjusted effort (Y/DE), where adjustment of effort is made on the basis of ecological biodiversity index, D. Therefore,

$$\dot{U} = rU(1 - U/qK) - qDEU \tag{10}$$

Equation (10) has been obtained by considering $Y/DE = U$ and by using the

Gordon-Schaefer production function so that $Y = qDEX$ implies $Y/DE = qX = U$ or $X = U/q$.

Dividing both sides of Equation (10) by U, we have

$$(\dot{U}/U) = r - qDE - (r/qK)U$$

or

$$1/U.(dU/dt) = r - qDE - (r/qK)U.$$

The equation can be framed after time averaging and thereby smoothing out the data as

$$\ln X_t^* = r - qE_t^* - (r/qK)\ U_t^* \qquad (11)$$

where $X_t^* = U_t^*/U_{t-1}^*$; $E_t^* = (E_{t-1} + E_t)/2$; $U_t^* = (U_{t-1} + U_t)/2$; $E_t^* = E_t D_t$ and $U_t^* = Y_t/(E_t D_t)$, D_t being the ecological biodiversity index constructed earlier.

The modified biodiversity-incorporated Schnute equation, where the effort is adjusted on the basis of the economic biodiversity index, is

$$\ln X_t^* = r - qE_t^* - (r/qK)\ U_t^* \qquad (12)$$

where $X_t^* = U_t^*/U_{t-1}^*$; $E_t^* = (E_{t-1} + E_t)/2$; $U_t^* = (U_{t-1} + U_t)/2$; $E_t^* = E_t B_t$ and $U_t^* = Y_t/(E_t B_t)$, B_t being the economic biodiversity index constructed earlier.

Alternatively, in general terms, we can write

$$\ln X_t^* = r - qE_t^* - (r/qK)U_t^* \qquad (13)$$

where $X_t^* = U_t^*/U_{t-1}^*$; $E_t^* = (E_{t-1} + E_t)/2$; $U_t^* = (U_{t-1} + U_t)/2$; $E_t^* = E_t A_t$ and $U_t^* = Y_t/(E_t A_t)$, where A is the vector of biodiversity indices where $A = D$ or B as the case may be.

Our analysis uses the Schnute model, first including ecological biodiversity measure in equation (11) and the economic biodiversity measure in equation (12). The regression analysis is based on time series data where the time period is from 1993-94 to 2002-03 (i.e. the number of observations is 10). Table 1 shows the results of regression.[14]

The R^2 and $\bar{R}^2$ statistics indicate an improvement with inclusion of economic biodiversity as against ecological biodiversity index indicating the importance of the role of markets affecting fish harvested via price signals. The difference between the two models basically lies with the presence or absence of the economic forces that are at play. The model with unweighted (ecological) biodiversity index expresses

Table 1: Regression Results of the Schnute Models (equation 13) in its Modified Forms (1) with Introduction of Ecological Biodiversity Index (2) with Introduction of Economic Biodiversity Index

Equation of Schnute Model	Constant	Coefficient of E_t^*	Coefficient of U_t^*	R^2 Statistic	$\bar{R}^2$ Statistic
with inclusion of ecological biodiversity index	1.10174 (4.52187)	–0.0003181 (–3.56027)	–0.00260084 (–2.6065)	0.643079	0.5538487
with inclusion of economic biodiversity index	1.29711 (5.88448)	–0.0002845 (–4.67727)	–0.0026378 (–3.39413)	0.732351	0.665439

(t-values are given in the parentheses, level of significance measured at 5 per cent)

Notes: 1. $E_t^* = (E'_{t-1} + E'_t)/2$, $E'_t = E_t D_t$ and $U_t^* = (U_{t-1} + U_t)/2$, $U_t = (Y_t / E_t D_t)$

2. Dependent variable: X_t^*, where $X_t^* = U_t^* / U_{t-1}^*$

a sort of subsistence fishery, which is harvested for self-consumption and not marketed. With the opening of a market, some species of fish are more in demand due to their high value and there is pressure on these species. So, the model with weighted (economic) biodiversity index acts like a commercial fishery where high-valued fish is harvested for profit making. The incentive to increase profit with the development of a larger market acts as a strong force to reduce biodiversity. In Digha, the fish harvested is not only sold locally but also has a large regional and export market and so fishing gears are adjusted accordingly. Here, it is found that market plays a strong role in the harvest from the fishery. The weighted biodiversity index integrates the economic and biological differences of the fish species and therefore reflects more accurately on the bioeconomics of the fishery. So, the Schnute model incorporated with economic biodiversity index helps sufficiently to explain the effects of economic biodiversity on fish harvest. Therefore, the use of the model with economic biodiversity index is more apt here as a management tool to sustain fisheries and in the process help conserve fish biodiversity.

Optimum Values of the Variables

The model with the economic biodiversity index registered a better performance. It can be seen that an improvement occurred after the introduction of a weighted economic biodiversity index and now the model explains that about 73 per cent of the variation in fish biomass, which is a good fit for the regression line. Since it helps to explain a large proportion of the variation in fish biomass, this equation will be used for our subsequent analysis. However, it is to be mentioned in this connection that Digha Estuary has faced over the years increasing problems of water pollution which affects its fish harvest. This is mainly due to the fact that Digha, with its vibrant tourism industry, has attained considerable urbanization since last twenty years. This has caused large-scale discharge of sewage to the estuary. The study by Roy (2004) has shown that Digha daily produces over 3.2 million litres of sewage. The discharge of sewage from hotels drains through canals, which ends in the estuary. Weather here is represented by level of pollutants washed into the estuary. The amount of rainfall in Midnapore district is used as a rough indicator of the level of water pollution. An ideal measure of water quality should have been the concentration of nutrients and suspended particles in the water layer of the estuary. Alternatively, the level of chlorophyll should have been a better indicator of pollution than the amount of rainfall. But such detailed information is not available on a long-term basis. However, it has been observed that annual yield of sediments and nutrients deposited in the estuary are dependent on the amount of rainfall in the coastal area.[15] Hence, in our estimation of the regression equation (12) in the presence of economic biodiversity we have incorporated an additional environmental quality variable rainfall (W) and we specify it as follows:[16]

$$\ln X_t^* = r - qE_t^* - (r/qK)U_t - reW_t^* \tag{12a}$$

where $X_t^* = U_t^*/U_{t-1}^*$; $E_t^* = (E_{t-1} + E_t)/2$; $U_t^* = (\mathrm{U}_{t-1} + U_t)/2$; $E_t^* = E_tB_t$ and $U_t^* = Y_t/(E_tB_t)$, B_t and e is the impact of W on net rate of growth of fish stock.

We have re-estimated the modified Schnute equation in the presence of economic biodiversity index and environmental quality variable as shown by equation (12a) and the results are stated in the form of Table 2:

Table 2: Regression Result of the Schnute Model (with introduction of environmental quality variable and economic biodiversity index)

Equation	Constant	Coefficient of BE or E^*	Coefficient of U or U^*	Coefficient of W or W^*	R^2 Statistic	$\bar{R}^2$ Statistic
Modified Schnute model	1.527634 (2.00819)	–0.000019 (–3.29691)	–0.0294984 (–2.94028)	–0.0004943 (–1.26947)	0.896241	0.851772

(t-values are given in the parentheses)

One can now estimate the optimum values of the variables in the presence of economic biodiversity. The values of the parameters have been calculated and using these values the optimum value of the variables have been calculated. These estimated optimal values are actually the base values of or model. From Table 2 we find that the weather variable is insignificant at 5 per cent level of significance, though it is significant at the 10 per cent level. So, we have used the revised estimates of the parameters when the weather variable is included. However, for the theoretical specification of our dynamic analysis we have ignored the weather variable as its elimination will not significantly hamper our basic conclusion. This is mainly due to the fact that in this chapter we want to focus on biodiversity issues rather than on water pollution issues. From our estimates in Table 2 we find that the intrinsic growth rate, r = 1.15 (dmnl/year) is the intercept value[17] of the regression of the modified equation (12a). The value of catchability coefficient, q = 0.000019 (1/fishing hours) is the value of the coefficient of the effort function of the regression of the modified equation (12a). The environmental carrying capacity of fish stock, K = 2725631.8 kg is found by using the value of the coefficient of the catch per unit effort function and then plugging in the values of r and q. Average weighted economic biodiversity index B = 0.3946 dmnl is the average of the economic biodiversity indices constructed for the period under study. Average price which is the aggregative average of the prices of all fish species under our consideration during the time period of our study is P = ₹ 43.637616 (kg/year). Average cost, c, is the total cost incurred by fishermen calculated on the basis of their wages both for labour in boats and trawlers and its value is ₹46.65569/fishing hour. Discount rate, δ is approximated by the current market rate of interest at 0.11 (dmnl/year). It is only the discount rate that is calibrated and not estimated.

The economic biodiversity index that has been considered in our regression procedure is actually the average of the economic biodiversity indices constructed over the time horizon of our study period of ten years, 1993-94 to 2002-03. A comparative analysis of the unweighted and weighted Simpson's indices has been carried out by using the data on catch per species for the Digha *Mohona* (Estuary) fishery. The Simpson's economic biodiversity is constructed by weighting the simple ecological Simpson's index by average prices so as to capture fluctuations in value. It will capture any shift that may occur in fish value resulting from the over-exploitation of high-valued species. It is seen that the value of the weighted index is lower than that of the unweighted index. It is because of the differences in the value of the species caught that the differences in the two indices occur. The lower values of the weighted indices in comparison with the unweighted index reflects that on an average, catches are dominated by less valuable species. If catches had been dominated by valuable species, price weighting would increase their dominance even further and the weighted indices will have higher values than unweighted indices (Kasulo and Perrings, 2001). It suggests a decline in economic biodiversity associated with a shift in fish catch from high-valued to low-valued species. In the context of this empirical validity generated through the data obtained from the Digha Fisheries Association, we have compared three different biodiversity scenarios, reflecting 'fishing down the value chain' that is occurring in the fishery in Digha: one, a scenario where the fishery has a wide range of different valued fish species, i.e. high level of economic diversity (past situation), another being the average level of economic biodiversity in the fishery (current situation) and the third, a scenario where the fishery has fish species mostly of similar values, i.e. low level of economic diversity (projected future situation). Generally, the value of B ranges from 1 for the lowest diversity (where the fishery is dominated by species of the same value) to 1/s, where s is the number of species, giving a high level of fish diversity (where fishes have a wide range of differentiated market values).

The values of the variables in case of the dynamic model have been calculated for the profit-maximizing regime. The need for deducing the values of the variables under the dynamic model become important since to judge the sustenance of the fishing industry, static rent maximization is not optimal if the objective is to maximize present value of profit.

These values are tabulated under three alternative biodiversity scenarios of the fishery. Since in Digha fishery, the Digha Fishermen and Traders' Association regulates the local fishing activities and acts as a competitive profit-maximizing unit in the larger regional fish market, we have ultimately focused on the dynamics of the profit-maximizing regime and used it for our sensitivity analysis.

Dynamic Analysis of the Optimal or Profit-Maximizing Regime

In the dynamic framework, fishers seek to maximize the present value of profits over a time horizon 0 to T subject to the constraint of net growth of fish stock. The problem can be stated as

$$\text{Max. } \pi = \sum_{t=0}^{T} (pY_t - C_t)\rho^t$$

where ρ = 1/1 + δ, and δ is the rate of discount. Here ρ is the discounting factor, subject to

$$X_{t+1} - X_t = rX_t(1 - X_t/K) - Y_t$$

where
$$Y_t = qX_t B\, E_t \text{ and } C_t = cE_t \qquad (14)$$

We can rewrite the problem as

$$\text{Max.} \sum_{t=0}^{T} (pqX_t BE_t - cE_t)\rho^t$$

subject to
$$X_{t+1} - X_t = rX_t\,(1 - X_t/K) - qX_t\, BE_t \qquad (15)$$

The current value Hamiltonian, H_c, for this problem is

$$H_c = (pqX_t\, BE_t - cE_t) + \rho\nu_{t+1}\,(rX_t\,(1 - X_t/K) - qX_t\, BE_t) \qquad (16)$$

where ρ (the co-state variable) is the current value shadow price associated with a change in the fish stock, E_t is the control variable and X_t is the state variable. The first-order necessary conditions for a maximum are

$$\partial H_c/\partial E_t = 0 \qquad (17)$$

$$\rho\nu_{t+1} - \nu_t = -\partial H_c/\partial X_t \qquad (18)$$

and
$$X_{t+1} - X_t = \partial H_c/\partial \rho\nu_{t+1} \qquad (19)$$

Equations (17) and (18) give

$$(pqX_t\, B - c) - \rho\nu_{t+1}\, qX_t B = 0$$

$$\rho\nu_{t+1} = p - (c/qX_t)$$

and
$$\nu_{t+1} = (1 + \partial)[p - (c/qX_t B)] \qquad (20)$$

Equation (18) gives

$$\rho\nu_{t+1} - \nu_t = -\,pqE_t - \rho\nu_{t+1}\, r\{1 - (2X_t/K)\} + \rho\nu_{t+1}\, qBE_t \qquad (21)$$

Steady-state implies that $\nu_{t+1} = \nu_t = \nu^*$ and $X_{t+1} = X_t = X^*$. So, equation (21) becomes

$$\nu^*(\rho - 1) = qBE_t\,(\rho\nu^* - p) - \rho\nu^* r\{1 - (2X_t/K)\}. \qquad (22)$$

Putting ρ = 1/(1 + δ) and using equation (20) (after putting $\nu_{t+1} = \nu^*$), we get

$$BE_t = (1/cq)\,(pqBX_t - c)\,[\delta - r\{1 - (X_t/K)\}]. \qquad (23)$$

Again, equation (21) at steady-state gives

$$BE_t = (r/q)\{1 - (X_t/K)\}. \tag{24}$$

Comparing (23) and (24) and by letting $\Omega = c/Bpq$, we get

$$X^*_{dyn.} = \tfrac{1}{4}\,[\{\Omega + K(1 - \delta/r\} + \sqrt{[\{\Omega + K(1 - \delta/r)\}^2 + 8K\Omega(\delta/r)]}. \tag{25}$$

Once $X^*_{dyn.}$ is known, we can determine the optimum levels of effort and catch as

$$E^*_{dyn.} = (r/q)\{1 - (X^*_{dyn.}/K)\}/B \tag{26}$$

$$Y^*_{dyn.} = qX^*_{dyn.}\,BE^*_{dyn.} \tag{27}$$

Hence, the optimum level of *NPV* of profit is

$$NPV^*_{dyn.} = \sum_{t=0}^{T}(pY^*_{dyn.} - cE^*_{dyn.})\,(1/1+\delta)^t \tag{28}$$

Here $X^*_{dyn.}$, $Y^*_{dyn.}$, $E^*_{dyn.}$ and $NPV^*_{dyn.}$ are respectively the optimal values of fish stock, harvest, effort and net present value of profit.

The optimal values of the variables in the dynamic framework have been calculated. The results are shown in Table 3.

Table 3: Dynamic Competitive Profit-Maximizing Values of the Variables under Three Alternative Economic Biodiversity Scenarios

	Profit-Maximizing Solution (Dynamic Framework)			
Alternative Scenarios of Economic Diversity of the Fishery	**Stock (kg)**	**Harvest (kg/year)**	**Effort (fishing hours/year)**	**PV of Profit (₹)**
Situation 1: High economic biodiversity	14,03,567.7	79,312.17	14,870.40	9,74,557.84
Situation 2: Average economic biodiversity	13,34,194.2	1,26,329.54	12,629.75	17,33,954.10
Situation 3: Low economic biodiversity	12,91,007.7	1,52,923.61	6,234.36	22,47,745.50

From Table 3, we find that with progressively lower levels of biodiversity, stock size and effort decreases while fish harvest rises. This is evident when we look at Situation 1 (catch: 2,64,913.46 kg/year; effort: 12,903.42 fishing hours/year) and compare it with Situation 2 (catch: 2,70,780.52 kg/year; effort: 6,618.47 fishing hours/year) and Situation 3 (catch: 2,77,360.45 kg/year; effort: 2,638.39 fishing hours/year). We also observe NPV of profit to increase with lower diversity (an increase from ₹39,91,152.55/year in Situation 1 to ₹40,16,415.89/year in Situation 2 and a further rise to ₹41,13,563.35/year in Situation 3). So, economic diversity reduction is associated with a rising level of NPV of profit masking the existence of the potential threat of a loss of the valuable fish species in the fishery.

Sensitivity Analysis

Pertubations in Discount Rate

Now let us consider the impact of changes in some parameters on the optimal values of the variables under the profit-maximizing regime. We consider first, *ceteris paribus*, the impact of perturbations in the discount rate, δ, (base δ = 0.11) on the optimal values of the variables. The optimal values of the variables given in Table 3 are considered as the base values in our sensitivity analysis. Since the discount rate, approximated by the market rate of interest, represents the opportunity cost of investing in the fishery vis-à-vis other allied industries, we have considered a range here from 0.9 to 0.13 between which the market rate of interest has varied over the last 10 years (as reported from Reports of Currency and Finance of the RBI). The results of such perturbations are presented in Table 3.

From Tables 4 and 5, we find that higher discount rates result in lower optimum values for the stock variable and higher optimum values for both catch and effort. So we find that with discount rate fall (increase), there is an increase (decrease) in stock level of fish biomass but a fall (increase) in fish harvest. This result is in accordance with Conrad and Clark (1994). But, even though there is an increase in optimal harvest from 1,26,329.54 kg/year to 1,32,094.55 kg/year and further to 1,37,769.96 kg/year with a rise in δ (for example, a rise in discount rate from 0.11 to 0.12 and further to 0.13), net present value of profit declines. NPV of profit decreases from the base value of ₹17,33,954.10/year to ₹16,55,341.10 and even further to 15,78,135.60/year as δ increases from 0.12 to 0.13. The reason may be that the cost involved in effort needed for harvest more than offsets the revenue since we observe that this rise in fish harvest is associated only with increasing effort levels. With increase in discount rate, the optimum level of effort also increases from 12,629.752 hours (when δ = 0.11) to 13,296.049 hours (when δ =

Table 4: Impact of Perturbations of the Discount rate, δ, on the Optimal Values

Value of δ	Stock (kg)	Harvest (kg/year)	Effort (fishing hours/year)	NPV of Profit (₹/year)
0.09	13,52,365.00	1,14,526.31	11,295.37	18,87,813.70
0.10	13,43,234.10	1,20,503.01	11,965.62	18,10,318.90
0.12	13,25,109.00	1,32,094.55	13,296.04	16,55,341.10
0.13	13,16,023.60	1,37,769.11	13,962.96	15,78,135.60

Reference/Base values: Discount rate = 0.11, Stock = 13,34,194.2 kg, Harvest = 1,26,329.54 kg/year, Effort = 12,629.752 fishing hours/year and NPV of profit = ₹ 17,33,954.1/year.

Table 5: Impact of Perturbations of the Discount Rate on NPV of Profit

Change of Discount Rate	NPV of Discounted Profit (₹/year)	Change with Regard to Reference/Base Value (%)
0.09	18,87,813.70	+ 8.87
0.10	18,10,318.90	+ 4.40
0.12	16,55,341.10	− 4.53
0.13	15,78,135.60	− 8.98

0.12) and even further to 13,962.96 hours (when δ = 0.13). The positive relation between fish harvest and effort at each level of discount rate when associated with declining values of optimum NPV of profit implies that the rise in revenue from higher level of harvest is here associated with relatively increasing costs due to rising levels of effort.

This analysis was done on the basis of an average level of fish economic biodiversity currently existing in Digha *Mohona* (Estuary) fishery. When economic biodiversity considerations are brought in the fishing process, it is seen that it has a considerable impact on profit maximization of the fishery. In the past years, Digha *Mohona* (Estuary) fishery was composed of a much higher range of economically valued fish species. Our intention is to note how the gradual erosion of fish economic biodiversity affects the optimal values of the fishery under different discount rates. Here, we have first looked at the actual level of economic fish biodiversity currently prevalent in the Digha *Mohona* (Estuary). Next, we have contrasted this against two alternative economic biodiversity scenarios – (1) a situation where there are a high number of differentiated priced fish species (past case), and (2) a situation where all fish species have the same marketed value (projected case).

Table 6 shows two alternative scenarios which are distinct from the one currently prevalent in Digha *Mohona* (Estuary) fishery. In the first case, we have a large market for expensive species, and so there is an additional pressure of exploitation on them. In the second case, fish species are all of equal value and so here, the fishery is mostly of the subsistence type exploited solely for food which may be true in the future considering the current trend of exploitation. As discount rate increases (decreases), fish stock steadily declines (rises) but fish harvest and fishing effort rises (fall) under both the scenarios.

Table 6: Impact of Perturbations in the Discount rate, δ (base value: δ = 0.11), on Optimal Values of Stock, Harvest, Effort and NPV of Profit under Two Alternative Scenarios: (1) High Economic Diversity, and (2) Low Economic Diversity in the Fishery Model

Value of δ	Case 1 (high economic biodiversity)			Case 2 (low economic biodiversity)		
	Stock (kg)	Harvest (kg/year)	Effort (fishing hours/year)	Stock (kg)	Harvest (kg/year)	Effort (fishing hours/year)
0.09	14,21,747.30	66,115.30	12,237.59	13,09,187.00	1,41,978.91	5,707.79
0.10	14,12,662.00	72,755.83	13,553.32	13,00,101.70	1,47,494.14	5,970.95
0.11	14,03,567.70	79,312.17	14,870.40	12,91,007.40	1,52,923.61	6,234.36
0.12	13,94,491.60	85,764.57	16,184.84	12,81,931.80	1,58,251.40	6,497.24
0.13	13,85,406.30	92,132.77	17,500.61	12,72,842.10	1,63,496.51	6,760.52

We find that in the first case, as discount rate increases, fish harvest increases from 79,312.17 kg/year (δ = 0.11; the base case), to 85,764.57 kg/year (δ = 0.12) and further to 92,132.77 kg/year (δ = 0.13). Correspondingly, the fishing effort also increases from 14,870.40 fishing hours/year (δ = 0.11; the base case) to 16,184.84 fishing hours/year (δ = 0.12) and further to 17,500.61 (δ = 0.13) fishing hours/year. Similarly, it can be seen that as discount rate rises from the base value of 0.11 to 0.12 and further to 0.13, fish harvest rises from 79,312.17 kg/year (δ = 0.11; the base case) to 72,755.83 kg/year (δ = 0.10) and further to 66,115.50 kg/year (δ = 0.09) corresponding to falling effort from 6,234.24 fishing hours/year (δ = 0.11) to 13,553.32 fishing hours/year (δ = 0.10) and further to 12,237.59 fishing hours/year (δ = 0.09) in the first situation. But fish stock falls with increasing discount rate (δ = 0.11, optimal stock = 14,03,567.70 kg; δ = 0.12, optimal stock = 13,94,491.60 kg and at δ = 0.13, optimal stock = 13,85,406.30 kg).

In the second case, we find that with an increase in discount rate from base case

(δ = 0.11) to δ = 0.12 and later to δ = 0.13, optimal harvest rises from 1,52,923.61 kg/year (δ = 0.11) to 1,58,251.40 kg/year (δ = 0.12) and further to 1,63,496.51 kg/year (δ = 0.13). Similarly, optimal effort increases with increase in discount rate (at δ = 0.11, optimal effort = 6,234.36 fishing hours/year; and at δ = 0.12, optimal effort = 6,497.24 fishing hours/year; and at δ = 0.13, optimal effort = 6,760.52 fishing hours/year). But as also in the first case, stock falls with increasing discount rate (at δ = 0.11, optimal stock = 12,91,007.40 kg and at δ = 0.12, optimal stock = 12,81,931.80 kg and at δ = 0.13, optimal stock = 12,72,842.10 kg). With a fall in discount rate from the base level (δ = 0.11), both fish harvest and fishing effort falls (at δ = 0.11, fish harvest = 1,52,923.61 kg, effort = 6,234.36 fishing hours/year; at δ = 0.10, fish harvest = 1,47,494.14 kg, effort = 5,970.95 fishing hours/year and at δ = 0.09, fish harvest = 1,41,978.91 kg/year and effort = 5,707.79 fishing hours/year). But fish stock rises from 12,91,007.40 kg (δ = 0.11) to 13,00,101.70 kg. and finally to 13,09,187.00 kg as ä falls to 0.10 and 0.09. This result is in conformity with that obtained in the current state of economic biodiversity existing in Digha *Mohona* (Estuary) fishery. These are the values that are of particular interest to us. On comparing each level of discount rate over both cases, fish harvest in Case 1 and fishing effort in Case 2 becomes much more sharper with falling economic biodiversity. At δ = 0.11, we find that in the first case, 14,870.40 fishing hours/year is needed for 79,312.17 kg/year of fish harvest. In the context of the same discount rate, under Case 2, fishing effort of the level of 6,234.36 fishing hours/year leads to a catch level of At δ = 0.11, we find that in the first case, 14,870.40 fishing hours/year is needed for 79,312.17 kg/year of fish harvest. In the context of the same discount rate, under Case 2, fishing effort of the level of 6,234.36 fishing hours/year leads to a catch level of 1,52,923.61 kg/year. So we can see that when the fishery targets for more valued species to increase its profitability, a much larger fishing effort can plough in a relatively smaller catch leading steadily to a situation where no such economic incentives for fishing remains since price differential among species diminishes. This can be observed in each variation of the discount rate that is done under our sensitivity analysis.

Table 6 shows the effect that changes in the discount rate has on the optimal NPV of profit for the three alternative scenarios under our consideration. Also we compare the gains or losses associated with

1. the profit that is yielded from a much higher economically diverse fishery that

includes more highly valued fish species against the case of lesser economically diverse fishery with average biodiversity considerations taken into account.

2. the profit that is yielded when current average biodiversity considerations are included in the fishing process as against the case of a fishery where all species are equally valued and hence are non-diverse from the economic standpoint.

This has been further highlighted in Table 6 whereby the impact of a change in discount rate on NPV of profit under different biodiversity scenarios has been studied with regard to the base values.

First, let us look at the three situations at a particular discount rate. At each discount rate, NPV of profit when all species have the same economic value (Situation 3) is much higher than when we consider differentiated economic values of different species (Situations 1 and 2). Again, the decline in NPV of profit is sharper the larger is the number of species having different economic values (by comparing between Situations 1 and 3). For $\delta = 0.11$ (base case), we find that NPV of profit is highest in case of Situation 3 (₹ 22,47,745.50) followed by Situation 2 (₹17,33,954.10) and is the lowest for Situation 1 (₹9,74,557.84). As economic biodiversity decreases and we move from Situation 1 to 2 gives gain in NPV of profit of the amount ₹5,13,791.36/year to the fishery, which increases to ₹7,59,396.26/year when there is a move from Situation 2 to 3.

Again, at $\delta = 0.13$, NPV of profit is highest at ₹20,07,586.00/year under the third situation. It is ₹15,78,135.60 /year in case of second situation which is lower than the third and it is ₹9,43,252.23/year for the first situation which is the lowest. A move from situation 1 to 2 shows a gain in NPV of profit of ₹4,29,450.40/year. This gain increases when we compare between situations 2 and 3 (₹6,34,883.37/ year). At $\delta = 0.10$, the gain from moving from Situation 1 to 2 is ₹5,61,373.10/ year which further increases to ₹8, 31,035.15/year while moving from Situation 2 to 3. Also at $\delta = 0.09$, the gain in NPV of profit is ₹6,15, 943.60/year as we move from Situation 1 to 2 and later ₹9,10,619.46/year on moving from Situation 2 to 3.

The above analysis has been illustrated in Figures 1 and 2. So one can infer that, at any particular discount rate, NPV of profit $_{\text{situation 3}}$ > NPV of profit $_{\text{situation 2}}$ > NPV of profit $_{\text{situation 1}}$. Another important observation is that the gain in NPV of profit associated with decreasing levels of economic biodiversity is highest when we contrast between Situations 1 and 3 than between Situations 1 and 2. So,

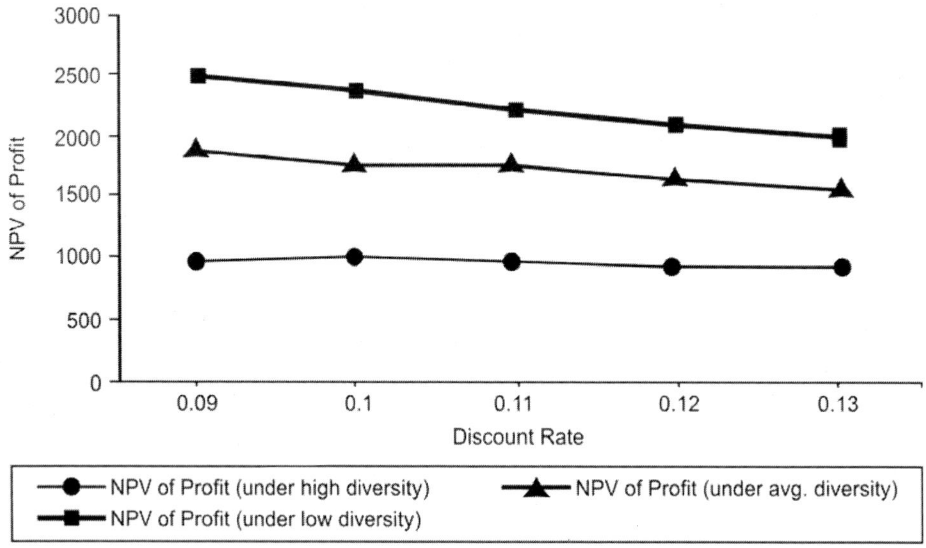

Fig. 1: Sensitivity Analysis of a Change in Discount Rate on NPV of Profit under Alternative Biodiversity Scenarios

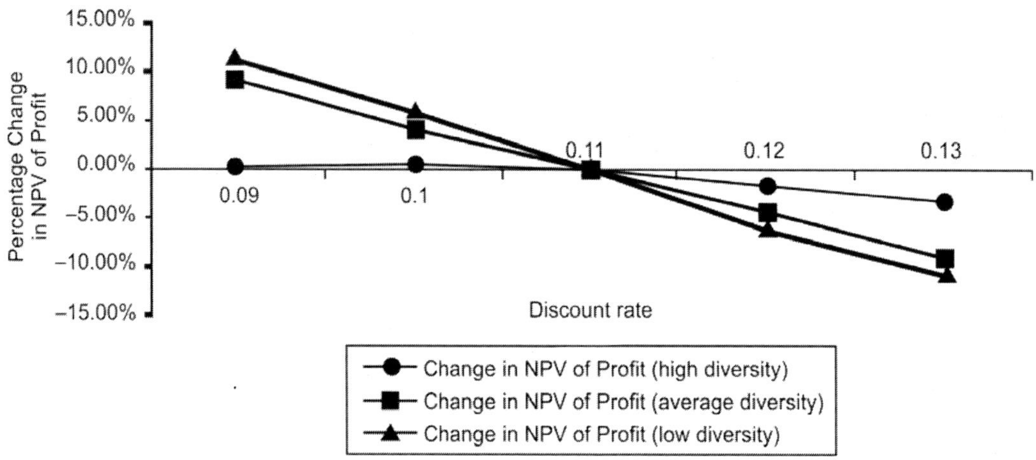

Fig. 2: Changes in NPV of Profit with Regard to its Reference Value Due to Perturbations in the Discount Rate

paradoxically, it can be seen that greater the targeting of the capture of the most expensive species and greater the loss in economic biodiversity the greater are the losses associated with the fishery. This occurs as demand in the markets triggers off greater exploitation of the expensive species and in this process large amounts of cheaper by-catches are discarded. So, the current trend towards the exploitation of only valuable fish species raises doubts about the profitability and hence sustainability of the fishery.

Table 7: Impact of Perturbations of the Discount Rate, δ (reference/base value: δ = 0.11) on Optimal Value of NPV of Profit under Three Alternative Scenarios: (1) High Economic Diversity, (2) Average Economic Diversity, and (3) Low Economic Diversity in the Fishery Model

Value of δ	Situation 1: NPV of Profit When a High Level of Economic Biodiversity in the Fishery is Present	Situation 2: NPV of Profit When Current Average Level of Economic Biodiversity in the Fishery is Present	Situation 3: NPV of Profit When there Does not Exist Any Economic Biodiversity in the Fishery	Gain in NPV of Profit at the Expense of Fall of Economic Fish Biodiversity from a High Level to an Average Level	Gain in NPV of Profit at the Expense of Fall of Economic Fish Biodiversity from an Average Level to a Low Level
	(1)	(2)	(3)	(4) = (1) – (2)	(5) = (2) – (3)
0.09	9,77,194.24	18,87,813.70	25,03,757.30	6,15,943.60	9,10,619.46
0.10	9,79,283.75	18,10,318.90	23,71,692.00	5,61,373.10	8,31,035.15
0.11	9,74,557.84	17,33,954.10	22,47,745.50	5,13,791.36	7,59,396.26
0.12	9,61,369.91	16,55,341.10	21,11,416.70	4,56,075.60	6,93,971.19
0.13	9,43,252.23	15,78,135.60	20,07,586.00	4,29,450.40	6,34,883.37

Table 8: Impact of a Change in Discount Rate, δ, on NPV of Profit under Different Biodiversity Scenarios with Regard to the Reference/Base Values

Change in Discount Rate	NPV of Discounted Profit in Situation 1 (₹/year)	Change with Regard to Reference/ Base Values for Situation 1	NPV of Discounted Profit in Situation 2 (₹/year)	Change with Regard to Reference/ Base Values for Situation 2	NPV of Discounted Profit in Situation 3 (₹/year)	Change with Regard to Reference/ Base Values for Situation 3
0.09	9,77,194.24	+ 0.27%	**18,87,813.70**	+ 8.87%	25,03,757.30	+ 11.38%
0.10	9,79,283.75	+ 0.48%	**18,10,318.90**	+ 4.40%	23,71,692.00	+ 5.51%
0.12	9,61,369.91	– 1.35%	**16,55,341.10**	– 4.53%	21,11,416.70	– 6.06%
0.13	9,43,252.23	– 3.21%	**15,78,135.60**	– 8.98%	20,07,586.00	– 10.68%

Now we would like to compare the NPV of profit between the different scenarios of economic biodiversity in the presence of perturbations in the discount rate. The presence of a large number of economically valuable species in the fishery depresses the NPV of profit. Increasing δ leads to increased fish catch and the economically valuable fishes are overfished leading to a fall in NPV of profit. As δ increases from 0.11 to 0.13, a decrease in NPV of profit takes place from ₹9,74,557.84/year to ₹9,43,252.23/year (Situation 1) from ₹17,33,954.10/year to ₹15,78,135.60/ year (Situation 2) and from ₹22,47,745.50/ year to ₹20,07,586.00/year (Situation 3). Similarly, as δ falls from 0.11 to 0.09, NPV of profit rises to ₹9,77,194.24/ year from ₹9,74,557.84/year in Situation 1; ₹18,87,813.70/year from ₹17,33,954.10/year in Situation 2 and ₹25,03,757.30/year from ₹22,47,745.50/ year in Situation 3. The fundamental equation of renewable resources equates the internal rate of return with the discount rate. So, as the discount rate increases, it implies more exploitation of fish stock (i.e. increase in fish catch) until the internal rate of return is again equal to the rate of discount. The impact of increase in discount rate leading to increase in fish harvest is shown in Table 8. Again, for a given fish price, increase in fish catch leads to an increase in revenue from fisheries. Again, there is a simultaneous increase in associated fishing effort leading to an increase in cost of fishery. The fall in the NPV of profit can be explained through a larger cost that offsets the higher revenue. The fall in the NPV of profit due to increase in discount rate is shown in Table 6. The utilization of the fishing effort changes with the interest rate. At low interest rates, the average fishing effort is lower than at higher interest rates. Thus assigning a smaller value to the future leads to an increase in the present effort to exploit the resource. Table 7 shows that change in NPV of profit with regard to reference/base values is sharpest for Situation 3 with respect to fall in δ (from 0.11 to 0.09) and lowest for Situation 1 for fall in δ (from 0.11 to 0.09). The change in NPV of profit with regard to reference/base values is more or less the same for Situations 2 and 3 and low for Situation 1 for increase in δ (from 0.11 to 0.13). This has been graphically illustrated in Figure 1.

One can hence conclude that the maximization of profit and economic biodiversity considerations are ultimately in conflict with each other in the context of sustenance of a fishery. This underlines the importance of economic scarcity and the role of market in a fishery.

Changes in the discount rate have been found to have effect on fish catch and

NPV of profit and hence on loss of economic biodiversity. The higher the discount rate or rate of interest on a project, the smaller the present value of a given payment in the future. It is important to consider the factors that lead to changes in the discount rate. These include the following: an excess demand for money, expansionary fiscal policies including income tax cuts and/or increases in government spending. Conversely, a decrease in government spending would lead to a reduction in interest rate and discount rate. In summary, policies that lead to a reduction in interest and discount rates will also lead to a loss of biodiversity. Such policies may include changes in government expenditure, income tax, money supply and improvements in financial markets.

Conclusion

Any fishery model needs at the aggregated level to incorporate important factors that affect fish harvest. One such component biodiversity occurs through the depletion of a number of fish species. Incorporation of biodiversity into a fisheries model is a difficult task. The main difficulty lies in choosing the relevant biodiversity measure to be used for our study. Simple biodiversity measures based on species number are widely used but even they have been criticized for ignoring the relative abundance of species. On the other hand, heterogeneity measures that combine species numbers and abundances have also been criticized for treating all species as equal. Following the work of Kasulo and Perrings (2001), we have used the economic biodiversity index which has been formulated on the basis of Simpson's biodiversity index.

Our work started with the standard Gordon-Schaefer model which has been modified to include the biodiversity variable. The parameters of the model are estimated using Schnute's (1977) method, as it reduces the bias in the estimates resulting from errors in the measurement of variables. Loss of biodiversity is linked to the development of the market in that it leads to overexploitation of valuable species, which results in a reduction in aggregate fish biomass.

We have also done sensitivity analysis by perturbating the discount rate and examined its impact on net present value of profit under alternative biodiversity scenarios. The economic impacts on the fishery in Digha that is brought about by an increase in the discount rate leads to reduction in the levels of fish stock and NPV of profit and to increase the levels of fish harvest and fishing effort. At low interest rates, the average fishing effort is lower than at higher interest rates. Also, we observe the existence of a negative relation between fish harvest and effort at each level of discount rate. This is associated with steadily declining NPV of profit as we move from higher discount rate to a lower discount rate. Thus, it has been found that biodiversity conservation and profit maximization are in conflict with each other. To resolve this conflict the government may impose landing tax where the tax rate is positively related to the price of the species. Apart from this a part of the tax collected can be used for benefit of the fishermen and this tax-transfer process can be governed locally through the *panchayats* (local government).

It is important to consider the factors that lead to changes in the discount rate. These include the following: an excess demand for money, expansionary fiscal policies including income tax cuts and/or increases in government spending. Conversely, a decrease in government spending would lead to a reduction in interest rate and discount rate. In summary, policies that lead to a reduction in interest and discount rates will also lead to a loss of biodiversity. Such policies may include changes in government expenditure, income tax, money supply and improvements in financial markets.

References

[1] Barbier, E.B., J.G. Burgess and G. Folke (1994). *Paradise Lost*, London: Earthscan Publications Limited.

[2] Boechlert, G.W. (1996). "Biodiversity and Sustainability of Marine Fisheries", *Oceanography*, 9(1), pp. 28-35.

[3] Das, T.K., R. Neogy and D. Chakraborty (1996). "Technology Choice under Risk in Marine Fishery", *Fishery Technology*, 32(2), pp. 116-120.

[4] Das, T.K., R. Neogy and D. Chakraborty (2000). "Sustainability of Marine Fishing: A Case Study of West Bengal", *Applied Economic Letters*, 7, pp. 707-710.

[5] Dhar, A. (2004). "Fishery Scenario and Marine Fishermen in West Bengal", in A. Roychowdhury and T.K. Das (ed.), *Economy of West Bengal: Some Contemporary Issues,* Allied Publisher.

[6] Central Marine Fisheries Research Institute (1984). *Annual Report.*

[7] Ganguly, T. (2004). "Unscientific Policies Lead to Decline of Marine Fish Production and Jobs", *The Week*.

[8] Glowka, L., F. Burhenne-Gulmin and H. Synge (1994). A Guide to the Convention on Biological Diversity, Gland and Cambridge: IUCN.

[9] Goda, T. and T. Matsuoka (1986). "Synthesis and Analysis of a Comprehensive Lake Model-With Evacuation of Ecosystems", *Ecological Modelling,* 31, pp. 11-32.

[10] Guha, I., R. Neogy, T.K. Das and D. Chakraborty (1994). *Report on the Economy of Marine Fishing in West Bengal, Digha-Coastal Region: A Socio-Economic Study of Marine Fishermen,* Department of Economics and School of Oceanographic Studies, Jadavpur University, Calcutta.

[11] Guha, I. and R. Neogy (1996). "A Socio-Economic Study of Marine Fishermen in West Bengal- A Micro-Study", *Conference Volume, XVI National Conference*, Bangiya Arthaniti Parishad, Department of Economics, Jadavpur University, February 17-18, 1996, pp. 151-164.

[12] Hanemann, W.M. (1988). "Economics and the Preservation of Biodiversity", in E.O. Wilson (ed.), *Biodiversity*, Washington D.C.: National Academy Press, pp. 193-199.

[13] Harper, J.L. and D.L. Hawksworth (1994). "Biodiversity: Measurement and Estimation: Preface", *Philosophical Transactions of the Royal Society of London Series B*, 345, pp. 5-12.

[14] Heywood, V. (eds.) (1995). *Global Biodiversity Assessment*, Cambridge: Cambridge University Press.

[15] Jana, S. (2004). *Bioeconomic Analysis of Marine Fish Production: A Case Study of West Bengal,* M.Phil Dissertation, Jadavpur University.

[16] Johnson, S.P. (1993). *The Earth Summit: The United Nations Conference on Environment and Development (UNCED),* London: Graham and Trotman.

[17] Kasulo,V. and C. Perrings (2001). "Fishing Down the Value Chain: Modeling the Impact of Biodiversity Loss in Fresh Water Fisheries – The Case of Malawi", *Mimeographed,* Environment Department, University of York, U.K.

[18] Lovejoy, T.E. (1980). "Changes in Biological Diversity", in G.O. Barney (ed.), *The Global 2000 Report to the President,* The Technical Report, Harmondsworth: Penguin Books, pp. 327-332.

[19] McAllister, D.E. (1991). "What is Biodiversity?", *Canadian Journal of Biodiversity*, 1, pp. 4-6.

[20] McNeely, J.A., K.R. Miller, W.V. Reid, R.A. Mittermeier and T.B. Werner (1990). *Conserving the World's Biodiversity*, Washington D.C.: IUCN, WRI, CI, WWF and World Bank.

[21] Monollos, D. and A. Lepretre (1999). "A Comparison of Species Diversity Estimators", *Researches on Population Ecology*, 41, p. 2.

[22] Norse, E.A. and R.E. McManus (1980). "Ecology and Living Resources Biological Diversity", in *Environmental Quality 1980: The Eleventh Annual Report of the Council on Environmental Quality,* Washington D.C.: Council on the Environmental Quality, pp. 31-80.

[23] OTA (United States Congress Office of Technology Assessment) (1987). *Technologies to Maintain Biological Diversity,* Washington D.C.: United States Government Printing Office.

[24] Pauly, D., V. Christensen, J. Dalsgaard, R. Froese and F. Torres Jr. (1998). "Fishing Down Marine Webs", *Science,* 279, pp. 860-863.

[25] Perrings, C. (2000). "The Biodiversity Convention and Biodiversity Loss in Sub-Saharan Africa", in C. Perrings (ed.), *The Economics of Biodiversity Conservation in Sub-Saharan Africa,* Chaltenham: Edward Elgar Publishing Limited, pp. 1-45.

[26] Rao, D.V. (2000). "The Bay of Bengal", in C. Sheppard (ed.) *Seas at the Millennium: An Environmental Evaluation*, Elsevier Science Ltd.

[27] Reid, W.V. and K.R. Miller (1989). *Keeping Options Alive: The Scientific Basis for Conserving Biodiversity,* Washington: World Research Institute.

[28] Schnute, J. (1977). "Improved Estimates from the Schaefer Production Model: Theoretical Considerations", *Journal of Fisheries Research Board of Canada,* 34(5), pp. 583-603.

[29] Sherman, K. (1990). "Productivity, Pertubations and Options for Biomass Yields in Large Marine Ecosystems", in K. Sherman, L.M. Alexander and B.D. Gold (ed.), *Large Marine Ecosystems: Patterns, Processes and Yields*, Washington, D.C.: American Association for the Advancement of Science, pp. 206-209.

[30] UNCED (United Nations Conference on Environment and Development) (1992). *Convention on Biological Diversity,* New York: UN.

[31] Turner, M.G. and R.H. Gardner (1991). *Quantitative Measures in Landscape Ecology,* Springer, New York.

Notes

1. For simplicity, in this chapter, we have not considered non-marketed species.
2. In the chapter we have formally distinguished between ecological and economic biodiversity. Roughly speaking, ecological fish biodiversity deals with species composition whereas economic fish biodiversity takes into account not only species composition but also the values of species in terms of their market prices. Actually, consequences of 'fishing down the food web' is captured in terms of 'ecological fish

biodiversity' whereas consequences of 'fishing down the vale chain' is captured in terms of 'economic fish biodiversity'. Thus, 'economic biodiversity conservation' implies conservation of highly valued species. For details, see Kasulo and Perrings (2001).

3. The coastal fisheries of West Bengal have seen both freshwater fishes and migratory marine species spawn during the monsoon. In the last three decades (1960-90), there have been catastrophic changes. Hilsa, an anadromous fish, which used to constitute about 70 per cent to 80 per cent of the total fish landings, is disappearing. Instead, marine catfish have become dominant here (Rao, 2000).

4. See Das, Neogy and Chakraborty (2000).

5. The term biological diversity has a long history of usage in a variety of contexts (OTA, 1987; Reid and Miller, 1989; McNeely et al., 1990; McAllister, 1991; Wilson, 1992; Johnson, 1993 and Sandlund et al., 1993). Harper and Hawksworth (1994) traces back its rise in the current sense to Lovejoy (1980) and Norse and McManus (1980) and mean essentially the number of species present in a community of organisms.

6. The contracted form 'biodiversity' was first coined in the first planning conference of the 'National Forum on Biodiversity' in 1986. Article 2 of the Convention on Biological Diversity (CBD) defined biodiversity as '*the variability among living organisms from all sources including inter alia, terrestrial, marine and other aquatic systems and the ecological complexes of which they are part; this includes diversity within species, between species and of ecosystems*' (UNEP, 1992). Furthermore, the Global Biodiversity Assessment (GBA) defines biodiversity as '*the total diversity and variability of living things and of systems of which they are a part. This covers the total range of variation in and variability among systems and organisms, at the various bioregional, landscape, ecosystem and habitat levels, at the various organismal levels down to species, populations and individuals, and at the level of the population and genes*' (Heywood, 1995). Ecosystem diversity is the highest level of diversity. It relates to the variety of habitats, biotic communities and ecological processes in the biosphere as well as the diversity within ecosystems (Pearce and Moran, 1994).

7. $H^* = -\sum_{i=1}^{s}(p_i)(\log p_i)$, where H^* is the Shannon index of species diversity, s is the number of species and p_i is the proportion of total sample belonging to ith species. The larger the value of H^*, the greater the diversity.

8. $D = \sum_{i=1}^{s} p_i^2$, where D is the Simpson's index, and p_i is the proportion of species i in the community. Diversity decreases with increasing D, which ranges from almost zero to one.

In some studies, for a measure of diversity, the complement of Simpson's index is used. It is given as:

$$1 - D = 1 - \sum_{i=1}^{s} p_i^2,$$

where 1 − D is the Simpson index of diversity. The Simpson's index of diversity ranges from zero for low diversity to almost 1.

9. A study comparing Shannon index and Simpson index has shown that the latter is the least biased between the two (Monillos and Leprêtre, 1999).
10. Annual Reports of the Digha Fish Traders' Association, Various issues.
11. Fishing effort has been calculated on the basis of a composite index constructed by us. It has been taken to be the weighted average of number of fishing hours involved in catching fish through fishing boats and trawling boats where the weights are the number of trips by fishing boats and trawling boats in an year.
12. The case of $D = 1$ gives us the single-species relationship. The case of $B = 1$ gives us the case of one valuable species in the fishery, i.e. all by-catches and discards are assigned zero value in the fishery. But it is always possible that $B = 1$ but $D \neq 1$.
13. The biodiversity measures that are introduced are adjusted to changing fishing effort since efficiency of capture varies. Efficiency varies usually by reducing mesh size or changing fishing grounds. This problem gets accentuated in case of multi-species multi-gear fisheries where the same unselective gear is operated in the fishery. This is exactly why we are using adjusted effort in the context of biodiversity loss.
14. Though the time period is quite short to conduct any regression analysis based on time series data our purpose in this chapter is to estimate the base values of the parameters instead of calibrating those values. So we have not considered any detailed economic analysis. Moreover, given the purpose of our chapter, we have deliberately conducted no time series test of the results.
15. See Choudhry et al. (2005) for details.
16. One can check that equation (12a) follows from the growth equation $\dot{X} = rX(1 - X/K - eW) - qEX$.
17. Here dmnl implies dimensionless.

Index

Contributors

Alagh, Y.K.

Yoginder K. Alagh is Chairman IRMA, Chancellor, Nagaland University and Vice Chairman of Sardar Patel Institute of Economic and Social Research. He was formerly Minister of Power and for Planning & Programme Implementation; Member, Planning Commission; and Vice-Chancellor, Jawaharlal Nehru University. Among several other distinguished positions, he has been Special Adviser to the Secretary General of the UN (RIO) Conference on Environment and Development, and been Senior Adviser and Consultant to several international organisations. He holds a Doctoral Degree in Economics from the University of Pennsylvania.

Banerjee, Sudeshna

Sudeshna Banerjee is Associate Professor, Department of History, Jadavpur University. She completed her PhD from the School of Oriental and African Studies, University of London. She has published articles in several national and international journals and in edited volumes. Her research interests include gender studies, urban studies, environmental studies, studies in science and society, notions of nationhood, cultural politics of globalization and cultural politics of sports. She serves on the international editorial board of the *South Asian History and Culture* published by Routledge.

Chattopadhyay Gupta, Anita

Anita Chattopadhyay Gupta is currently Reader and Head, Department of Economics at Muralidhar Girls' College, Kolkata. She did her Masters in Economics from Calcutta University, M.Phil in Economics from Jadavpur University and Ph.D. in Resource Economics from Calcutta University. She has worked as an associate investigator in Indo-Canadian Shastri Project in collaboration with Simon Fraser University, Vancouver. She is also a regular resource person in national and international training workshops held at State Institute of Panchayats and Rural Development, Kalyani and National Institute of Rural Development, Hyderabad.

Desai, Nitin

Nitin Desai was Under Secretary General from 1993 to 2003 dealing with economic and social affairs. Presently, he is Honorary Fellow of the London School of Economics and Political Science, UK, Distinguished Visiting Fellow at the Energy and Resources Institute

(TERI) and Honorary Professor at the Indian Council for Research in International Economic Relations (ICRIER). He is associated with the governing bodies of several NGOs and research institutions including the Institute of Economic Growth whose Governing Body he chairs. He is a trustee of Worldwide Fund for Nature (WWF) International. He writes a monthly column for the Business Standard, an Indian daily.

Forsyth, Tim

Tim Forsyth is Reader in Environment and Development at the Department of International Development, London School of Economics and Political Science. He has written on the politics of environmental science and policy processes, and on ways of achieveing more inclusive and deliberative forms of environmental governance in rapidly changing societies. He has worked mainly in South and Southeast Asia. He is the author of *Critical Political Ecology: The Politics of Environmental Science* (London: Routledge, 2003), and *Forest Guardians, Forest Destroyers: The Politics of Environmental Knowledge in Northern Thailand* (with Andrew Walker, Seattle: University of Washington Press, 2008).

Ghate, Rucha

Rucha Ghate is a researcher at SHODH: The Institute for Research and Development, Nagpur. She is also Coordinator of the Collaborative Research Center (India) of the International Forestry Resources and Institutions (IFRI), co-housed at Indiana University, Bloomington and University of Michigan. Her research interests are institutional economics, collective action, and forest management. She has co-edited a book entitled *Promise, trust and Evolution: Managing the Commons of South Asia*, published by OUP in 2008.

Gupta, Kausik

Kausik Gupta is Vice Chancellor, West Bengal State University, India. Prior to that, he was Professor of Economics and Director of Centre for Human Development and Human Rights, Rabindra Bharati University, Kolkata. He did his Masters in Economics from Calcutta University, PhD in Economics from Jadavpur University and Post-Doctoral Research at the University of York, UK, under the World Bank Aided Environmental Economics Overseas Fellowship Programme. He has published a large number of papers in various reputed international and national academic journals.

Kaechele, Karin

Karin Kaechele is currently on leave at Columbia University from her post as Deputy Coordinator of the Instituto Centro de Vida-ICV, a social environmental NGO that operates in Mato Grosso in southern Amazonia where she coordinates activities related to agriculture and environment. She is particularly interested in non-state market driven systems and initiatives related to commodity certification. She has served as a director of the Brazilian Society of Ecological Economics since 2006. She holds a master's degree in Environmental Science from São Paulo University (USP).

Ludwig, Grit

Grit Ludwig is working as a researcher in the Department Environmental and Planning Law at the Helmholtz Centre for Environmental Research in Leipzig, Germany, since 2008. She studied law at the University of Leipzig, Germany, and was awarded PhD in 2005. Earlier, she worked as a barrister (2000-2002) and also conducted development work in Mozambique in the forest sector (2005-2007), Her work is concerned with the law on biodiversity protection, legal issues on the use of bioenergy and international forest conservation.

Martinez-Alier, Joan

Joan Martinez-Alier is Professor of Economics and Economic History and researcher at ICTA at the Autonomous University of Barcelona. He is the author of *Ecological Economics: Energy, Environment and Society* (1990) and *The Environmentalism of the Poor: A Study of Ecological Conflicts and Valuation* (2002). He is a founding member and past-president of the International Society for Ecological Economics. He was a member (2000–08) of the European Environment Agency Scientific Committee.

May, Peter

Peter H. May, PhD, is Associate Professor in the Graduate Program in Development, Agriculture and Society at the Federal Rural University of Rio de Janeiro. He received the doctorate in Resource Economics at Cornell University in New York, USA. He also held staff positions at Ford Foundation, and served as a Forestry Officer at the FAO in Rome. A Past President of the International Society for Ecological Economics (ISEE), he is Founder and Past President of the Brazilian Society for Ecological Economics (ECOECO), and a former member of the Board of Directors of FSC-Brasil.

Mehra, Deepshikha

Deepshikha Mehra is Assistant Professor at Dept. of Humanities at Shri Ramdeobaba Kamla Nehru Engineering College, Nagpur. She has over eight years of research experience in issues related forest management such as role of local institutions, traditional knowledge, role of NTFP, forest-based development, and relocation of forest-dwellers. She has particular research interest in issues related to social capital as well as gender issues in forest management.

Nagar, Shailesh

Shailesh Nagar is Vice President at NR Management Consultants India Pvt Ltd, New Delhi. He has 14 years of experience spanning natural resource management, rural livelihoods and local governance aspects and has coordinated assignments related to research, project designing, implementation management and monitoring and evaluation. He is an alumnusof University of Cambridge, UK, and a Shell-Chevening scholar. He has published reports and papers on various Development related aspects. His current interest areas are climate change adaptation in general especially in forestry and agriculture sector, bio-energy and rural livelihoods.

Nagendra, Harini

Harini Nagendra is a DST Ramanujan Fellow at Ashoka Trust for Research in Ecology and the Environment, Bangalore, and the Asia Research Coordinator, Center for the Study of Institutions, Population, and Environmental Change at Indiana University. Her research examines the drivers and outcomes of ecological change in urban and forested landscapes in South Asia. Her recent co-edited volume *Reforesting Landscapes: From Pattern to Process* was published in 2010 by Springer.

Norgaard, Richard B.

Richard B. Norgaard is Professor of Energy and Resources at the University of California, Berkeley. Among the founders of the field of ecological economics, his recent research addresses how environmental problems challenge scientific understanding and the policy process, how ecologists and economists understand systems differently, and how globalization affects environmental governance. He served as President of the International Society for Ecological Economics (1998-2001), a visiting scholar at the World Bank and served on the Science Advisory Board of the U.S. Environmental Protection Agency.

Parikh, Kirit

Kirit Parikh is Chairman, Integrated Research and Action for Development (IRADe). He is Former Member, Planning Commission, Government of India, and was the Founder Director (Vice Chancellor) of Indira Gandhi Institute of Development Research (IGIDR), Mumbai. He was the Chairman of the Integrated Energy Policy Committee, Planning Commission. He was a Member of the Economic Advisory Council (EAC) of various Prime Ministers of India. A Fellow of the National Academy of Sciences, India, Dr. Parikh was honoured with Padma Bushan by the President of India in March 2009.

Primmer, Eeva

Eeva Primmer is a Research Coordinator of the Ecosystem Services Research programme of the Finnish Environment Institute where she has worked for over ten years. She holds a PhD in Agriculture and Forestry from the University of Helsinki. Dr Primmer's research focuses on forest biodiversity conservation policy and institutions, including formal policy processes and governance structures, organizational competencies and public-private organizational networks, attitudes and professional norms as well as rhetoric in policy. She is particularly interested in the integration of conservation and natural resource management as well as the formal and informal institutions that shape this integration in policy and in practice.

Sahu, Geetanjoy

Geetanjoy Sahu is Assistant Professor at the School of Habitat Studies of Tata Institute of Social Sciences (TISS), Mumbai. His research interests include environmental law and governance, analysis of judicial behavior on environmental litigation and politics of interaction between state and civil society over natural resource management. Currently, he is working on the impact of environmental judgments at the implementation level. Geetanjoy holds PhD in Political Science from the Institute for Social and Economic Change (ISEC), Bangalore.

Sankhayan, Prem Lall

Prof. Prem Lall Sankhayan is Professor-Emeritus with the Department of Ecology and NRM of Norwegian University of Life Sciences, Aas, Norway. He has worked in many parts of the world on issues relating to agricultural and environmental economics with the help of mathematical models. He has good number of publications in the reputed international journals.

Sharma, Rakesh Kumar

Rakesh Kumar Sharma is presently working with Himachal Institute of Public Administration (HIPA), Fairlawns, Shimla, India. Originally he is with the Higher Education Department (college cadre) of H. P. Government with more than twelve years of experience in teaching and research. He did his Ph.D. on bio-economic modelling of watershed resources. His current interest is to link ecological economics with environmental governance.

Shukla, Nimisha

Nimisha Shukla is Professor and Head department of Economics, Gujarat Vidyapeeth. Her Doctoral work is on Common property Land Resources in India. She has been supervising doctoral work in environmental economics, and is also conducting her researsh on Gandhian Economic Thought.

Singh, Ranveer

Ranveer Singh is Officer Incharge at Agro-Economic Research Centre, Shimla, India. He has worked as PI for many projects financed by agencies such as World Bank, ICIMOD, GTZ, USAID, Ministry of Agriculture, GOI and Govt. of Himachal Pradesh. He has authored two books and more than 50 research papers.

Sundararaman, N.

Narasimhan Sundararaman was founder Secretary of the Intergovernmental Panel on Climate Change (IPCC), where he served for 15 years, covering the tenure of 3 IPCC Assessments. A Master's in Space Physics and a Doctorate in Meteorology, both from from University of California, Los Angeles (UCLA), he had taught at California State University, Northridge and at UCLA.He has also worked with US Federal Aviation Administration and the World Meteorological Organization (WMO). He planned and arranged for scientific assessments of the ozone layer for the Vienna Convention and the Montreal Protocol.

The Editors

Jayanta Bandyopadhyay

Chaired the Scientific Committee of the 5th Biennial Conference of the INSEE. He provided valuable leadership in designing the programme of the conference and the contents of this book.

Born in Calcutta (India) in 1947, he obtained his doctorate in engineering in 1975 from the IIT Kanpur. His professional attention then turned to the complex interface between science and society, specially in the case of the Himalayas. He has been a senior professional staff at ICIMOD (Kathmandu). In 1991, he prepared the chapter on the world's mountains for Agenda-21. In 1993, he joined the International Academy of Environment in Geneva as Director of Research. In 1997, he was invited by the IIM Calcutta to be a member of the faculty.

He has been a coordinating lead author for the global report of the Millennium Ecosystem Assessment. He was the President of the Indian Society for Ecological Economics (2006-8) and is presently a Fellow of the India-China Institute in The New School, New York. He is an adviser to the Water Diplomacy Programme at Tufts University, USA. His research in the past 25 years has generated critical trans-disciplinary public interest knowledge on the environment and development. He has published more than 130 papers, books, articles, etc. His email id is: jayanta@iimcal.ac.in.

Kanchan Chopra

Formerly Director and Professor, Institute of Economic Growth, Delhi is currently Fellow of the Academy of Sciences for Developing Countries and Visiting Professor, TERI University, New Delhi.

A leading expert in issues relating to the environment and development in India, she received her Ph.D. degree from the Delhi School of Economics. She has authored and co-authored several books, the latest being "*Biodiversity, Land-use Change and Human Well-being: A Study of Aquaculture in the Indian Sundarbans*" (Oxford University Press 2009). In 2009, she edited "*Handbook of Environmental Economics in India*" published by Oxford University Press. She has been Member, Assessment Panel of the Millennium Ecosystem Assessment, from 2001–2005 and Member, Advisory and Management Committee, South Asian Network on Development and Environmental Economics in its early years.

Professor Kanchan Chopra was President of the Indian Society for Ecological Economics from 2010 to 2012 , of which she was a founder member in 1998. She was also President for the 64th conference of the Indian Society of Agricultural Economics in 2004. She can be contacted at kanchanc136@gmail.com.

Nilanjan Ghosh

Is an ecological economist by training, with interests in environmental and development economics, and commodity derivatives markets. Presently, he is the Chief Economist (Senior Vice President and Head of Research & Strategy) at Multi Commodity Exchange of India Limited. In this position, he is looking after various critical strategic and policy issues in relation to the development of markets.

His previous stints in his research and consulting career include institutions like Takshashila Academia of Economic Research (a sister concern of MCX (I) Limited), The Energy and Resources Institute (TERI), TERI University, among others. He was a Visiting Fellow at the School of Social Sciences, Växjö University (now Linnaeus University LNU) in December 2008.

Prof. Ghosh has been involved in various global environmental assessments, including the UNEP's flagship GEO-4 as lead author. He has conducted research and consultancy projects funded by illustrious donors like WWF, UNCTAD, UNEP, and many others. He has published four books (two authored and two co-edited including this volume), and a host of peer-reviewed journal papers and book chapters, apart from popular articles in newspapers and periodicals.

Presently, he is Vice President of the Indian Society for Ecological Economics (2012-14), and has previously served as the Society's Secretary (2010-12). Nilanjan obtained his doctorate from Indian Institute of Management Calcutta, and Masters' in Economics from Jadavpur University, Kolkata. He can be contacted at nilanjan.ghosh@gmail.com.